W9-CTO-204

Canada: The State of the Federation 1999/2000

Toward a New Mission Statement for Canadian Fiscal Federalism

Edited by

Harvey Lazar

Published for the School of Policy Studies, Queen's University
by McGill-Queen's University Press
Montreal & Kingston • London • Ithaca

Canadian Cataloguing in Publication Data

The National Library of Canada has catalogued this publication as follows:

Main entry under title:

Canada, the state of the federation

Annual.
1985-
Vols. for 1998/99-   have also a distinctive title.
ISSN 0827-0708
ISBN 0-88911-839-6 (bound : 1999/2000) ISBN 0-88911-843-4 (pbk. : 1999/2000)

1. Federal-provincial relations – Canada – Periodicals. 2. Federal government – Canada – Periodicals. I. Queen's University (Kingston, Ont.). Institute of Intergovernmental Relations.

JL27.F42   332.02'3'0971   C86-030713-1

The Institute of Intergovernmental Relations

The Institute is the only organization in Canada whose mandate is solely to promote research and communication on the challenges facing the federal system.

Current research interests include fiscal federalism, the social union, the reform of federal political institutions and the machinery of federal-provincial relations, Canadian federalism and the global economy, and comparative federalism.

The Institute pursues these objectives through research conducted by its own staff and other scholars through its publication program, seminars and conferences.

The Institute links academics and practitioners of federalism in federal and provincial governments and the private sector.

L'Institut des relations intergouvernementales

L'Institut est le seul organisme canadien à se consacrer exclusivement à la recherche et aux échanges sur les questions du fédéralisme.

Les priorités de recherche de l'Institut portent présentement sur le fédéralisme fiscal, l'union sociale, la modification éventuelle des institutions politiques fédérales, les nouveaux mécanismes de relations fédérales-provinciales, le fédéralisme canadien au regard de l'économie mondiale et le fédéralisme comparatif.

L'Institut réalise ses objectifs par le biais de recherches effectuées par son personnel et par des universitaires de l'Université Queen's et d'ailleurs, de même que par des conférences et des colloques.

L'Institut sert de lien entre les universitaires, les fonctionnaires fédéraux et provinciaux et le secteur privé.

CONTENTS

FOREWORD

This year's volume is dedicated to the memory of the Institute's first director, Ron Burns, who died last year. Mr. Burns was an outstanding expert and scholar on federal-provincial fiscal relations. Thus, it is fitting that this year's annual *State of the Federation* volume should focus on the state of Canadian fiscal federalism at the beginning of a new century.

One of the questions that initially motivated this volume related to the decentralization trend in our system of fiscal federalism that began in the late 1960s. The issue was whether this trend had run its course by the end of the 1980s and whether the policy changes of the 1990s had more to do with rebalancing than further decentralization. As the volume took shape, however, it became clear that there was a second and perhaps more fundamental issue raised by the various chapters. That is, there was a huge amount of uncertainty about the future of fiscal federalism in Canada at a time when we might have begun to expect a period of stability.

In the first sentence of a volume published in 1994, Keith Banting, Doug Brown and Tom Courchene wrote "Canadians are rapidly approaching a critical juncture in the evolution of their social programs and the system of fiscal federalism that underpins them." Since then, we have witnessed important reforms in the federal-provincial tax-collection agreements, the federal-provincial transfer system, the signing of the Social Union Framework Agreement, and a huge improvement in the fiscal situation of federal and provincial governments. These reforms responded in significant measure to the 1994 warning signals, while the strengthening of public finances has created the possibility of a more stable outlook.

Yet, a theme running through the chapters of this volume is the urgency of further reform. For example, there are well-documented concerns about the state of municipal finance, questions about the future financing of Aboriginal governments, doubts that the Canada Health and Social Transfer constitutes a stable political equilibrium, and proposals that structural decisions about fiscal federalism be decided outside the framework of the federal budgetary cycle.

These concerns are reflected in important parts of the political arena. The major opposition parties in the House of Commons are advocating further decentralization. The larger provincial governments have frequently issued similar demands. Some large municipal governments are also becoming increasingly outspoken about their desire for more fiscal autonomy.

From the federal government, the usual argument is that the federation is adequately decentralized and that what is needed is simply fine-tuning or re-balancing.

What may be lacking in this debate is a reconsideration of the basic purposes of Canadian fiscal federalism. In the early postwar decades, there was an informal mission statement for Canadian fiscal federalism. That statement was a reflection of the postwar consensus that aimed for high employment through counter-cyclical stabilization policy, social security against the contingencies of unemployment, old age and sickness or injury, and a system of last resort for those who were most disadvantaged. The tax-rental and tax-collection agreements and the system of intergovernmental and direct federal transfers were integral to that purpose. By the early 1980s, however, the postwar consensus had eroded. With its loss, fiscal federalism began to respond to the political needs of the moment, but without a new compass to guide it.

When taken together, the chapters in this volume suggest the need for a new mission statement for Canadian fiscal federalism. In a world where borders are becoming less important and intergovernmental collaboration more important, there is a need for the partners in the federation to be able to better trust one another. To secure trust, there is a need for individual governments to minimize the number of surprises they spring on other governments. But in the absence of some shared sense of purpose for Canadian fiscal federalism, this greater predictability in government behaviour may be difficult to achieve. There is therefore a need for a new public debate on these issues and this volume is intended to help animate it.

As in other years, we have included a chronology of major events in the federation. In this issue we have covered 18 months, from July 1998 to December 1999.

The production of this volume was made possible by the contributions of several people. Patti Candido and Mary Kennedy of the Institute of Intergovernmental Relations provided assistance and organizational expertise both in the conference that preceded this volume and in the preparation of the manuscript. Mary Wade and Charles-Henri Warren contributed translation assistance. The conference participants, the discussants and anonymous reviewers furnished the authors with valuable feedback on their work at important junctures in the process. Valerie Jarus, Mark Howes and Marilyn Banting managed the desk-top publishing, design and copy-editing assistance that helped turn a collection of pages into a book.

Finally, I would like to thank the federal Finance Department for its financial support for the 1999 Kingston symposium that was an important stepping stone in the preparation of this volume.

Harvey Lazar
August 2000

DEDICATION

It is entirely fitting that this volume of *Canada: The State of the Federation*, focused on current issues of fiscal federalism, should be dedicated to the memory of Ron Burns who passed away in Victoria, BC in June 1999.

Ron was the founding Director of the Institute of Intergovernmental Relations, leading the Institute from its inception in 1965 until his retirement in 1975. His interest in federalism and intergovernmental relations was wide-ranging, but his primary concern and expertise lay in the area of what was then called Dominion-Provincial financial arrangements.

He had unparalleled experience in the intricacies of these matters, as Director of financial negotiations in the federal Department of Finance, and as deputy minister of finance in both Manitoba and British Columbia. He had played a central role in the work of the Continuing Committee of Fiscal and Economic Matters, established in 1956 to provide support for the work of finance ministers. The committee was both an important step in what Don Smiley called "executive federalism," and an ongoing seminar on the shape of a rapidly changing federal system.

This was a period of major change in fiscal federalism — the end of the postwar "tax-rental agreements" and the adoption of "tax-sharing" and tax-collection agreements, establishment of the equalization program, increased tax abatements by which Ottawa provided increased room for provincial taxes, heightened debate over shared-cost programs, and the decision to permit Quebec to "opt-out" of some of these programs.

Underlying these debates were much larger questions about Canadian federalism: the Quiet Revolution in Quebec, and its desire to be *maitres chez nous*; increased provincial shares of revenues and expenditures and a concomitant growth in provincial bureaucratic capacity, self-confidence and assertiveness; and a shared desire to complete the construction of the Canadian welfare state.

As a civil servant, Ron Burns was at the centre of these discussions. He had also come to share the concern of Alec Corry, then Principal of Queen's, that these new developments were occurring in an ad hoc and piecemeal way — "tinkering and patching" as the first proposal for an Institute of Intergovernmental Relations at Queen's University put it. There was a need to stand back and analyze the future of federalism in a broader framework.

The proposal states, "The problems considered a generation ago by the Rowell-Sirois Commission are with us still in more bewildering profusion and complexity; the tensions in our federal system are greater than ever before." The Institute would become a kind of permanent Rowell-Sirois Commission.

Ron's experience and his ability to build networks both across the country and between practitioners and academics made him the ideal person to bring this vision to reality.

During his term, he set the Institute on the path that in many respects continues to drive its work today: a deep engagement with contemporary policy issues as they are played out in the federal and intergovernmental system; building bridges between the public service and academia; and a high standard of scholarship matched with a commitment to bring this scholarship to bear on public debate.

In his own work, he became increasingly interested in the machinery of intergovernmental relations. The system was shifting from the often paternalistic, Ottawa-led "cooperative federalism" of the postwar period toward a more equal partnership of governments which were at once autonomous and interdependent. His work helps us understand the shift, and in important respects helps lay the groundwork for current discussions of collaborative federalism exemplified in agreements such as the Social Union Framework Agreement of 1999.

That shift preoccupied me in my PhD thesis, later published as *Federal-Provincial Diplomacy*, in 1972. Its footnotes refer no less than nine times to the work of Ron Burns, and I still remember his painstaking and patient attempts to explain the complexities of fiscal federalism to a young graduate student.

The dimensions of fiscal federalism addressed in this volume are in some ways very different from the issues of Ron Burns' time; but in other respects they would be all too familiar to him; and he would be a vigorous participant in the debates.

Richard Simeon

RON M. BURNS (1910-1999)

CONTRIBUTORS

Frances Abele has been Director of the School of Public Administration at Carleton University since 1996. A political scientist, she teaches courses in the area of Canadian public policy and public management, and Aboriginal affairs.

Felina Arsenault graduated with an Honours BA in political science from Queen's University in the spring of 2000. She now lives in Jasper.

Richard M. Bird is Adjunct Professor and Co-Director of the International Tax Program at the Rotman School of Management, University of Toronto.

Robin Boadway is Sir Edward Peacock Professor of Economic Theory at Queen's University.

Edith Boucher is a senior policy analyst at the federal Department of Finance.

Estée Garfin graduated from Queen's University with an honours degree in Political Studies and is currently studying law at the University of Toronto.

Geoffrey E. Hale is Assistant Professor of Political Science at the University of Lethbridge.

Paul A.R. Hobson is Professor of Economics at Acadia University.

Harry Kitchen is Professor of Economics at Trent University.

Harvey Lazar is Director of the Institute of Intergovernmental Relations at Queen's University.

Jack M. Mintz is the Arthur Andersen Professor of Taxation at the Rotman School of Management, University of Toronto and President and CEO of the C.D. Howe Institute.

Ken Norrie is Dean of Arts and Professor of Economics at the University of Alberta.

Lars Osberg is McCulloch Professor of Economics at Dalhousie University and currently President of the Canadian Economics Association.

Michael J. Prince is Lansdowne Professor of Social Policy at the University of Victoria.

France St-Hilaire is Vice-President, Research at the Institute for Research on Public Policy (IRPP) in Montreal.

François Vaillancourt is a Fellow, C.R.D.E. and Professor of Economics at the Université de Montréal.

Arndt Vermaeten is an economist at the federal Department of Finance.

Ronald L. Watts is Principal Emeritus, Professor Emeritus of Political Studies, and Fellow of the Institute of Intergovernmental Relations, Queen's University.

L.S. Wilson is Professor of Economics and Fellow of the Institute for Public Economics at the University of Alberta.

I

Ideas, Theories and Concepts

1

In Search of a New Mission Statement for Canadian Fiscal Federalism

Harvey Lazar

Ce chapitre présente un survol du fédéralisme fiscal au Canada au cours des dernières décennies. La première section porte sur les tendances en matière de recettes, de dépenses et de transferts entre les gouvernements fédéral et provinciaux. On y conclut que la centralisation a atteint un sommet dans la deuxième moitié des années 1960. La tendance s'est renversée en faveur des provinces lors des deux décennies suivantes. Au cours des années 1990, il y a des mouvements tant de centralisation que de décentralisation, mais la situation actuelle demeure beaucoup plus décentralisée qu'il y a trente ans.

Lors des décennies suivant la Deuxième Guerre mondiale, le fédéralisme fiscal canadien poursuivait un ensemble d'objectifs relativement clairs. Toutefois, cet énoncé de mission a commencé à s'éroder au cours des années 1980. Le comportement des partenaires dans le système, y compris celui du gouvernement fédéral, a depuis varié en fonction des besoins et des circonstances, sans toutefois poursuivre d'objectif global clair. Ces variations font en sorte qu'il est difficile pour les différents niveaux de gouvernement de prévoir le comportement de leurs partenaires. Une compréhension commune des «règles du jeu» est nécessaire pour qu'une forme coopérative de fédéralisme soit mise en place. Sans cette compréhension, il devient trop difficile d'établir et de maintenir les relations de confiance sans lesquelles le fédéralisme coopératif ne saurait qu'être dysfonctionnel. D'où le besoin pour les gouvernements de s'entendre sur un nouvel «énoncé de mission» du fédéralisme fiscal canadien pouvant être mis en oeuvre parallèlement à l'entente-cadre sur l'union sociale de 1999.

Canada's system of fiscal federalism is complex and arcane. It is understood well by perhaps a few dozen people in government and an even smaller number in the academy and the think tanks.

The system is made up of several connected strands. They include the constitutional and political provisions for allocating revenues and expenditure responsibilities between orders of government, the intergovernmental transfers that are used as a way of offsetting imbalances between the revenues and expenditures of the various governments, and arrangements for harmonizing tax systems among governments. Each of these strands entails complexity.

Referring to the system in even this brief way helps to explain why fiscal federalism is a subject that few people know about or would want to know about if afforded the opportunity. Behind these words, however, are issues that do matter to Canadians — issues like fairness and opportunity for individuals, the survival of the distinctive peoples and nations that help to make up Canada, and indeed the very future of Canada as a country. So while the elements of fiscal federalism entail a vocabulary and set of arrangements that are highly specialized, the justification for this volume rests in the fundamental importance of these issues to the well-being of our country, its constituent units, and the citizenry at large.

The various chapters of this volume deal with these issues in detail. They focus on challenges and difficulties in relation to revenue assignment and revenue-sharing, issues of vertical and horizontal imbalance and the system of intergovernmental transfers. They deal not only with the federal-provincial dimensions of these issues but also with recent relevant trends affecting other orders of government, including Aboriginal governments, municipalities, school and hospital boards, and postsecondary institutions.

This introductory chapter draws on this rich analysis. It is in no way, however, a survey or summary of what the other authors have to say. Rather, it is an effort to stand back from the inherent complexity of fiscal federalism and provide a relatively straightforward overview of what is happening and why it is happening, with some assessment of implications.

Three themes underlie this chapter. One has to do with the uncertainty surrounding the direction of fiscal federalism. In the first quarter century after World War II, fiscal federalism was centralized. It subsequently underwent a large decentralization, a process that continued until the 1990s. In the 1990s, there were cross currents, but without a clear direction. Whether there is a further leg of decentralization ahead of us is unclear.

This uncertainty is linked to the second theme. Until the late 1970s or early 1980s, Canadian fiscal federalism had a "mission statement." Its sense of purpose mirrored the wider postwar consensus about the role that the state could play, through programs of redistribution and macroeconomic stabilization, in building a fair and compassionate society and a prosperous and stable economy. In turn, this consensus was predicated on the idea that there was a latent sense of Canadian political nationhood which could be mobilized in pursuit of these noble goals.

The golden age of consensus had eroded badly, however, by the early 1980s. And since then, fiscal federalism has also lacked a strong sense of purpose. It has continued to adapt and adjust in response to changing circumstances and pressures. But, with the important exception of the ongoing commitment to the concept of equalization, an overarching sense of purpose has been lacking, in many ways reflecting the broader uncertainty about the role of the state itself.

This leads to the third theme. The lack of a clear mission statement makes the behaviour of governments, especially the federal government, hard to predict. If federal and provincial governments were operating in watertight compartments, this might not matter much. But the forces of global and continental integration are increasing interdependence among economies and polities. For functional reasons, therefore, they are making intergovernmental collaboration a growing necessity for an ever-broadening range of issues, not only across international borders but also for governments within Canada.[1] For that collaboration to be effective, however, the various governments have to have some minimum level of trust for one another. The "rules of the game" must entail a measure of predictability about the behaviour of the partners. The absence of a mission statement for contemporary fiscal federalism erodes predictability, and therefore trust.[2]

The chapter begins by noting the criteria that are relevant to assessing fiscal federalism. It is then followed by a discussion of recent trends. Two questions are asked. Where has the system of fiscal federalism been headed in recent years? And where does it appear to be headed in the future? Finally, the trends are analyzed on a basis of our assessment criteria.

CRITERIA FOR ASSESSING TRENDS IN FISCAL FEDERALISM

As discussed by Robin Boadway in Chapter 2, it is conventional to assess systems of fiscal federalism for their impact on economic efficiency and equity. Assessing trends in fiscal federalism is about more than efficiency and equity, however. In a Canadian context, it is also about building the Canadian state and provincial states. And given the unique position of Quebec among Canadian provinces, it has also been about the building of a special Quebec state within Canada. Thus, it is important to consider the impact of fiscal federalism trends on the relative roles of the different orders of government and whether these trends are privileging some governments more than others. It is also relevant to assess whether these trends are leading to more independence or more interdependence among orders of government and whether the relationship between the orders of government is becoming more or less equal. In short, assessing trends in the fiscal arrangements is important not only for determining equity and efficiency effects but also because of their impact on the nature of the federalism practised in Canada.

Our system of fiscal federalism also influences the way in which our democratic institutions function. It raises considerations like the now familiar

concern about a "democratic deficit" and related issues of political accountability and transparency.

While the pages that follow immediately below are intended to provide an
overview of the main trends, ultimately what matters most is what these trends
imply for policy goals like equity and efficiency, for the nature of the federation and for democratic values.

TRENDS IN CANADIAN FISCAL FEDERALISM

Examining trends in fiscal federalism raises a question about the time period
that is of interest. We could focus on trends since 1867, the date of Confederation. This would allow for a broad historical sweep. Conversely, the focus of
our attention might be confined to the years since the re-election of the Chrétien
Liberals in 1997, allowing for a detailed analysis of the various initiatives
that federal and provincial governments have launched over the last three years.
For this chapter, neither of these extremes seemed appropriate. The world has
changed too much since 1867 to make the early years of Confederation relevant to this analysis. And it is too soon to have perspective about the events
since 1997. In any case, most of what follows covers two periods: first, the
period since the end of World War II; and, second, the decade of the 1990s.
Focusing on one of these periods risks the telling of a partial story only. But
by considering both, the analysis can provide more context and perspective to
the changing face of Canadian fiscal federalism.

CENTRALIZATION OR DECENTRALIZATION?

Much of the literature in fiscal federalism is about whether the tide is flowing
in favour of the federal government or the provinces and the factors that lie
behind those trends. Casual reporting of this issue often focuses on the power
struggle between orders of government. That there may indeed be struggles
between self-serving power structures is no doubt part of what makes this
question a subject of interest to political and policy analysts. Buried under-
neath this issue are, however, questions related to how individuals are affected
by the "Canadian state," including in this term the institutions of both the
federal and provincial governments. In this regard, perhaps the main issue is
whether the "sharing community" within Canada is the country as a whole or
its constituent units. To what extent is it the role of the provinces and their
residents to assure that opportunities and outcomes are distributed fairly and
reasonably and to what extent is this role the responsibility of Ottawa and all
Canadians?

The answers to these kinds of questions raise normative considerations about the merits of centralization and decentralization. And on this issue, there are several splits within the country. Two are touched on here. The first is in the political arena itself. Provincial spokesmen, sometimes from wealthier provinces and frequently from Quebec, talk about an arrogant, insensitive, and centralizing federal government. The Canadian Alliance (and the Reform Party before it), the Bloc Québécois, and to a lesser extent the Progressive Conservative Party tend to share that perspective. From the federal government side, there is a view that substantial decentralization has occurred over recent decades and what has been happening more recently is re-balancing or "fine-tuning" within a reasonably balanced federation. The less wealthy provinces sometimes share the federal government view. These governmental positions, on both sides, are often expressed in a context of bargaining for tactical advantage and therefore may not be the most reliable source for perspective on trends in fiscal federalism.

The academic community provides a second split. Here the dividing line appears to be between some but by no means all English-speaking analysts from outside Quebec, on the one hand, and mainly French-speaking Québécois, on the other. The mainly francophone group is often supported by English-speaking analysts who are generally "conservative" on economic and fiscal matters.[3] While political preferences may in fact also influence the views of these two broad groupings, their differences may have more to do with the different lens through which they observe the trends. In general, the Quebec view is filtered through the lens of how a "classical" federal system should operate. With respect to the view expressed often elsewhere in Canada, there may be a tendency to examine events without this kind of filter — to look at the data with less of a pre-disposition toward the classical model.[4]

Both academic perspectives capture important elements of Canada's economic and political reality. Accordingly, they have helped to shape the analysis below. In what follows, trends in the allocation of revenues and expenditures of the two senior orders of government, and the changing size and nature of transfers, are examined. Attention is also paid to the character of the intergovernmental relationship that is associated with distribution of taxing and spending actions of federal and provincial governments and with the intergovernmental transfer system.

World War II was an important watershed in the history of the Canadian federation. The war years saw a massive build-up in government activity dedicated to fighting and defeating the enemy. With defence and security matters the exclusive responsibility of the federal government, this wartime expansion of government inevitably took place at the federal level.

But the wartime expansion of government had implications that went well beyond the actions that were directly necessary for the prosecution of the war itself. For one thing, huge sums of money were needed which led to changes in the allocation of revenues between the two orders of government. The exigencies of the crisis precluded the kind of decentralization and tax competition that Canada had experienced in the inter-war years. In the event, a tax "rental" agreement was worked out between the federal and provincial governments. Under these arrangements, Ottawa alone would levy and collect personal and corporate income taxes and death duties in return for rent payments to the provinces. From the viewpoint of the way power is distributed within the Canadian federation, the war years were ones of very strong centralization.

Even before the war was over, political leaders and intellectuals in Canada and many other countries had begun to consider what kind of transformation might be necessary in order to make the postwar years safe and prosperous. For the liberal democracies of the Western world, there was enthusiasm for the creation of multilateral institutions to promote peace and security (notably the United Nations) and economic growth (the International Monetary Fund [IMF], the General Agreement on Tariffs and Trade [GATT], and the World Bank). The idea that fiscal and monetary policy could be used counter-cyclically to stabilize the economy and ensure high employment took root. The seeds of the modern welfare state were also planted.

The Cold War dominated the postwar era internationally. Defence spending thus remained a high priority for the country and the federal government, especially with the war in Korea. The IMF and GATT became the vehicles through which the international system of payments and trade were liberalized and it was the federal government that represented Canadian interests in those bodies. With regard to domestic policy, Keynesian counter-cyclical stabilization policy emerged as an accepted and viable role for the federal government. Ottawa also began to implement its vision of a modern welfare state. This had begun with unemployment insurance in 1940 and was followed by family allowances in 1945 and old age security in 1952.[5] With its responsibilities for defence and security, for liberalizing trade and payments, for economic stabilization, for tax harmonization, and for early developments in the postwar welfare state, the federal government remained the dominant actor in the Canadian federation even after the end of the war.

Constitutional responsibility for legislating and regulating in the areas of health care, education and social services were and remain areas of almost exclusive provincial legislative competence under the constitution. The Canadian constitution is also close to unique among federal countries in providing both orders of government with wide taxing authority in all of what are now the major sources of tax revenue (personal and corporate income tax, sales/value-added tax, payroll tax, etc.). Accordingly, it might have fallen to the provincial governments to lead the postwar reconstruction and the welfare state that were among the central achievements of the era. After World War II, however, the federal government was reluctant to give up all of the incremental revenues that it had begun collecting during the war years. Perhaps because

Ottawa had been responsible for fighting the war, it was natural for Canadians to look to the federal government for leadership in constructing the postwar peace. In the event, Ottawa was determined to build a more secure and fairer society than the one that Canadians had experienced in the 1930s. The federal government envisaged a social security system that would protect Canadians against the contingencies of unemployment, old age, and illness. This promised to be costly and was thus an incentive for the federal government to retain its strong revenue position. Ottawa also wanted to be able to implement a high employment policy. This required access to the large economic levers to effect macroeconomic stabilization and taxation was one of the key levers. Tax harmonization was also important to the federal government because it wished also to avoid a return to the system of checkerboard taxation that had been a hallmark of the 1930s, with all of the inefficiencies and inequities it entailed. In the event, Ottawa was able to negotiate agreements with most provincial governments to extend initially the tax-rental agreements. And, over time, the federal government secured provincial acceptance of a set of tax-collection agreements for personal income and corporate income taxes — allowing a harmonized tax system and a single tax-collection agency for signatory provinces. But Quebec declined to enter such an agreement for either personal or corporate income tax, and Ontario decided to collect its corporate income tax separately, as did Alberta at a later date.

Since the provinces had most of the authority for social programs, the federal government recognized that it could not act on its own. It could use its constitutional powers to design unemployment insurance programs and its "spending power" to deliver cheques to individuals.[6] But it lacked the constitutional power to design and deliver most social services. Accordingly, for key components of its vision, Ottawa could only act working with and through the provinces. The result included a series of federal-provincial shared-cost programs that included hospital care, medical services, postsecondary education, social assistance, and social services. The arrangements also included federal equalization transfers to the less wealthy provinces to enable them to provide reasonably comparable levels of services at reasonably comparable levels of taxation. Thus, power remained centred in Ottawa during the early postwar decades.

But during these same decades, events were also sowing the seeds of change in the workings of the Canadian federation, and especially the system of fiscal federalism. For one thing, as the scope and size of the Canadian welfare state grew to encompass more and more of these activities, the role and size of provincial governments began also to expand rapidly. The late 1950s and mid-1960s saw the introduction of public hospital insurance and medical insurance by the provinces under cost-sharing arrangements with the federal government.[7] At the same time, helped by fiscal incentives from Ottawa, provinces undertook a massive expansion of Canada's postsecondary education and social service systems. Provincial governments thus came to play a progressively larger role in the lives of Canadians. With these changes, they had a consequential requirement for additional sources of revenue. The result, however, was not a simple expansion of the provincial sector, but rather a provincial expansion in collaboration with the federal government as a cost-sharing partner. Motivated by economic efficiency and equity concerns, on the one hand, and nation-building, on the other, the federal government transferred large sums to the provinces to facilitate the construction of national programs for social purposes and postsecondary education.

The federal government's direct role in social policy also increased during these years. Through negotiation with the provinces, Ottawa secured their support for a constitutional amendment that allowed for the introduction of the Canada Pension Plan. The age of entitlement to benefits under this plan became 65 and entitlement to federal Old Age Security payments was also lowered to age 65 from age 70 at the same time. The coverage of Unemployment Insurance was also vastly broadened and the program made much more generous, especially with the major revisions to the *Unemployment Insurance Act* in 1971.

By the early 1970s, all of the basic building blocks of Canada's current welfare state were in place. The role of both orders of government had grown. But the provincial role had grown more because the largest program components, health care and education, were provincial responsibilities. And even as these provincial responsibilities were growing, there were three parallel developments that led inevitably to a declining program role for the federal government. The first was that the tension surrounding the Cold War had begun to ease. In relative terms, defence expenditures fell year after year. By the 1970s, well before the collapse of the Soviet Union, defence and security had shrunk dramatically as political and spending priorities. Second, counter-cyclical macroeconomic stabilization policy had come to be seen as ineffective. The combination of "stagflation" of the 1970s and the serious recession of the early 1980s led to the emergence of a new macroeconomic orthodoxy — one that placed much less weight on counter-cyclical macroeconomic policy and much more on getting the economic fundamentals right. With this shift in economic management, the case for Ottawa continuing to control a large enough share of the tax system to effect stabilization came to be diminished.[8] The third development was an accumulation of federal government deficits and rising debt-service costs that, over time, reduced its ability to undertake new spending initiatives and hence to shape and influence provincial spending patterns through the use of federal-provincial matching grants or other cost-sharing programs. The federal government even found it difficult to maintain its commitments for existing joint programs.

Centralization in the postwar Canadian federation probably may have peaked sometime in the 1970s or possibly the early 1980s, with the *Constitution Act, 1982*.[9] But from the perspective of spending and taxing only, and related policy initiatives, the peak in federal government power occurred in the second half of the 1960s.[10] In any case, the provincial tide has been rising for some time. Even with this relative shift in power from the federal to the provincial order of government, however, the distribution of effective authority between the two orders of government has remained nicely balanced. While there has been a shift toward the provinces, the federal government has by no means been emasculated as a political actor.

Figure 1 shows the changing relative role of the different orders of government. In 1945, of course, the distribution of spending reflects the federal government's role in financing the war effort. By the 1960s the implementation of the postwar welfare state was well under way. From 1961 to 1999 the overall size of the state was growing sharply (from around 30 to 45 percent of the gross domestic product). The strongest growth, by far, was experienced by provincial governments. In relative terms, provincial program spending almost doubled from 1961 to the early 1990s. At the same time, the federal share of total government program spending dropped by over 30 percent.

Figure 1: Program Spending of Federal, Provincial and Local Governments as a Percentage of Total Spending of all Governments (Excluding Spending on Intergovernmental Transfers)

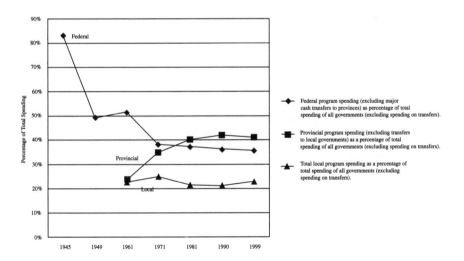

Source: Calculated from Statistics Canada, National Accounts, CANSIM Series and *National Accounts Income and Expenditure 1942-49.*

While Figure 1 provides a broad overview of the size of the two orders of government, the changed nature of program expenditures is equally striking. In 1955, for example, Ottawa spent more on defence than it did on transfers to individuals and other governments for social purposes. By the late 1990s, defence outlays had dropped to barely one-tenth of social spending. Close to 70 percent of federal program spending today is made up of transfers to individuals and provinces for social purposes. From a spending perspective, the contemporary federal state is overwhelmingly a *social* state.

The same trend is found on the provincial side. As already noted, beginning in the late 1950s and more strongly in the 1960s, health care, education, and social services became political priorities for Canadians. All three were labour intensive and hence costly. Provincial program spending thus rose dramatically. It was over 8 percent of the gross domestic product (GDP) in 1960 but was 18 percent in 1990. Despite recent cost cutting, provincial program spending remains at around 16 percent of GDP today.[11] At the new millennium, 75 percent of provincial spending is for social programs. Even more than Ottawa, the provincial state is thus about social programs.

Turning to the allocation of revenues, a similar story emerges. Figure 2 shows that in the early 1960s, Ottawa accounted for three-fifths of "own-source" revenues collected by governments. Provinces collected just under one-quarter of the total. By 1990, the two orders of government were raising equal shares of revenue as a result of rising provincial shares and declining federal shares.

Figure 2: Federal, Provincial and Local Government Own-Source Revenues as a Percentage of Total Revenues

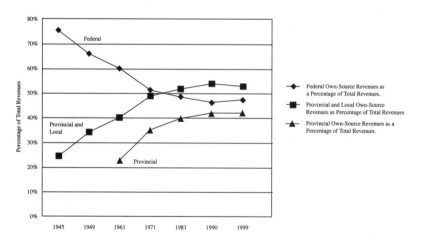

Source: Calculated from Statistics Canada, National Accounts, CANSIM Series and *National Accounts Income and Expenditure 1942-49.*

The data in Figures 1 and 2 are mainly a reflection of the expansion of the Canadian welfare state and the decline in military spending, as discussed above. The former are mainly the constitutional responsibility of provincial governments, whereas the latter are the responsibility of Ottawa.

As noted earlier, the growth of the provincial state was financed in part through the huge increase in its own-source provincial revenues. But it also reflected a growth in transfers from the federal government — payments Ottawa could afford to make in good measure because it had retained through negotiation much of the tax room it had occupied during the war. Other chapters of this volume go into the role of transfers in some detail. (See especially Chapters 6 and 7.) It is sufficient here to note that in the early years of the postwar welfare state, federal transfers were a major source of revenue to the provinces and that the transfers were all cash transfers. By the end of the century, however, transfers had become relatively less important as a source of provincial revenues. Moreover, almost one-third of federal transfers were in the form of "tax transfers," which for statistical purposes at least are recorded by Statistics Canada as "own-source" provincial revenues. The political controversy surrounding the issue of tax transfers is discussed in Chapter 4 of this volume. The main point to note here is that federal cash transfers to the provinces are now a relatively small share of provincial revenues, just over half of what they were in 1961 (although they remain very important in Atlantic Canada). This reflects more the huge growth in provincial "own-source" revenues than it does relative reductions in those federal transfers. Figure 3 shows these trends.

In summary, from the perspective of the broad trends in revenues and expenditures, the role of federal transfers to the provinces, and policy initiatives related to revenues, spending, and transfers, the peak in federal government power was reached during the 1960s. Since then, the provincial role has been increasing in relative importance, whether one is examining spending or revenues or the declining role of federal transfers to the provinces.

Moreover, when one digs deeper, this conclusion is reinforced. For example, the level of conditionality associated with federal transfer payments to the provinces has been lightened significantly over the last three decades. Today, the two largest transfers by far are the Canada Health and Social Transfer (CHST) and Equalization. The latter program has no conditions and the former, a bloc fund intended for provincial health, higher education, and social welfare programs, has only two sets of conditions. The first is that provinces impose no restrictions on eligibility for welfare for residents arriving from other provinces. The second is that provinces meet the five broad principles of the *Canada Health Act* in the design and delivery of their health services.[12] In recent years, all provinces have affirmed their support for the principles of the *Canada Health Act* (CHA) so it is arguable that these conditions themselves are not onerous for the provinces. It is true that some provinces have

Harvey Lazar

Figure 3: Major Cash and Tax Transfers as a Percentage of Provincial Revenues

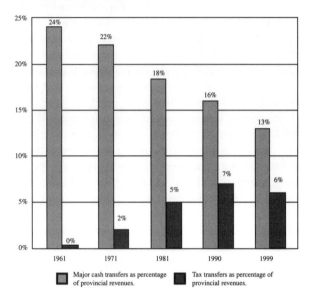

Source: Calculated from Statistics Canada, National Accounts, CANSIM Series and *National Accounts Income and Expenditure 1942-49.*

been strongly critical of the fact that it is the federal government alone that has formal responsibility for interpreting and enforcing the CHA.[13] But in an overall sense, it is clear that the conditionality in the transfer system has dropped significantly relative to the period of extensive cost-sharing during the 1960s and 1970s. During those years, the federal law determined which provincial expenses were eligible for cost-sharing and which were not. This not only necessitated additional record-keeping by the provinces, and some periodic hassles regarding the eligibility of expenses, it meant also that Ottawa might audit provincial books. There is none of this today.

A second example can be found in the area of personal and corporate income taxes. For reasons of economic efficiency, administrative efficiency and to avoid a "tax jungle," almost all provinces agreed to sign tax-sharing and then tax-collection agreements with Ottawa in the years after World War II. One result was a cost-effective personal and corporate income tax-collection system for the provinces. Another was that compliance costs of businesses that operated in more than one province were minimized.

These agreements did entail costs for the provinces, however. In the case of personal income tax, one cost was that the federal government required provinces to "piggyback" their income taxes on top of federal taxes, which narrowed the freedom of the provinces to design an incentive structure to meet local needs and political preferences. Provinces could raise and lower their tax rates but were not free to adjust the basic structure of the system. This has now changed. Chapter 9 documents the vastly increased autonomy of provincial governments in relation to personal income tax. Under new flexibility afforded by Ottawa, provincial governments are able to continue to secure the economies and efficiencies of a single tax-collection agency while obtaining much more room to design the incentive structure of their systems. This is an important growth of effective provincial power.

Finally, in the context of assessing the relative roles of the two orders of government on fiscal matters, it is very important to note that the federal government has not launched any new Canada-wide initiatives since the 1960s that are remotely similar in scale to the huge joint undertakings of that decade. Perhaps the most significant was the National Child Benefit (NCB) a few years ago. And it was arguably a replacement for earlier programs like Family Allowance and elements of provincial welfare. In sheer magnitude, the NCB is smaller than the big programs of the 1960s. Furthermore, the leadership in bringing it forward was shared between federal and provincial governments, whereas Ottawa drove the agenda of the 1960s.

The next question of interest here is whether the broad trend to decentralization persisted into the last decade. The answer is ambiguous. On the one hand, there was a further modest decentralization in spending. In this instance, both federal and provincial expenditures as a share of total government spending dropped slightly, with the share of municipalities rising. Second, some of the reduction in conditions on federal transfers, noted above, occurred in the 1990s. And much of the new flexibility in effective provincial power in respect of personal income tax has come about in the last year. On top of this, there is perhaps the beginning of a trend toward more fiscal autonomy for First Nations.

But federal and provincial shares of own-source revenues were more or less flat in the 1990s. And it was around ten years ago that Ottawa moved into the area of value-added tax, a revenue base that had, by convention, been largely the domain of the provinces. Moreover, in the last few years the federal government has begun exercising its spending power again in such diverse areas as child benefits, Millennium Scholarships and Canada Research Chairs.[14] There is also a view held by some that the Social Union Framework Agreement (SUFA) is effectively a centralizing document, cloaked in the guise of collaborative federalism.[15] While I read the SUFA differently, the "proof of the pudding will be in the eating," and this more sceptical perspective must be acknowledged.

Thus, the 1990s appear to have been a period of cross-currents rather than clear directions. The movement toward a relatively greater role for the provinces from a fiscal federalism perspective may thus have slowed or stalled over the last decade. But it has not been reversed. From a fiscal viewpoint, the Canadian federation remains much more decentralized than it was 30 years ago.

ASSESSING THE TRENDS

In the remainder of this chapter, the focus is on providing some perspective on these trends. Did the trend toward decentralization of the last several decades serve the public interest well? If so, how? If not, why not? Whatever the answer to these questions, what about the last decade? If some decentralization was appropriate, then is the slowing or stalling of decentralization over the last decade inappropriate? In seeking to shine some light on these questions, the assessment criteria introduced at the outset of this chapter, relating to policy, federalism, and democracy, will be our focal points.

POLICY GOALS

The early postwar decades were ones in which many of the advanced capitalist democracies built their modern welfare states. In Canada, as discussed above, although much of the constitutional power for promoting equity goals rested with the provinces, the federal government heavily influenced the construction of the systems of social security and last resort. Two main constitutional powers enabled Ottawa to play this role. One was the power to levy both direct and indirect taxes and thus to construct a progressive tax system. The second was the "spending power" which enabled the federal government to transfer money to provinces and to persons to achieve desired social goals.[16] The two powers were connected, in the sense that the revenues raised through the federal tax system provided the federal government with the financial wherewithal to exercise its spending power.

The transfer system, both direct and indirect, was used by Ottawa to promote equity and efficiency. While in the absence of a strong federal government, it is likely that some provinces would have developed the infrastructure of the welfare state on their own, it is unlikely that the result would have served Canada-wide equity or efficiency goals as well as the federal-provincial partnership did. The late 1950s and 1960s saw the establishment of a pan-Canadian system of universal publicly insured systems of hospital and medical services. Postsecondary education was expanded hugely. A last resort safety net ensured that the most disadvantaged would be able to survive with at least a modicum of dignity.[17] In all of these cases, federal-provincial cost-sharing was a key instrument. In addition, as noted earlier, country-wide systems of old age security, child benefits, and unemployment insurance were also introduced, in these instances through direct spending by Ottawa. This is not to deny the crucial role some provinces played in pioneering some programs, notably Saskatchewan in relation to both hospital insurance and medical care. Rather, it is simply to observe that federal initiative, and imaginative use of Ottawa's constitutional powers, accelerated the advancement of these goals.[18] At the same time, federal government leadership avoided a return to the tax jungles of the interwar years with all of the inefficiencies they entailed.

The importance of equity goals was also given concrete expression in the patriated constitution of 1982. Section 36 of the *Charter of Rights and Freedoms* committed both orders of government to "promoting equal opportunities for the well-being of Canadians"[19] and "furthering economic development to reduce disparity in opportunities." It also committed the Government of Canada to the "principle of making equalization payments to ensure that provincial governments have sufficient revenues to provide reasonably comparable levels of public services at reasonably comparable levels of taxation."[20] A basic instrument of fiscal federalism, the intergovernmental transfer, was thus given constitutional status to do its task.

By several criteria, regional differences in economic conditions were narrowed over the postwar decades, as reflected, for example, in provincial trends in GDP per capita. Part of this may have been attributed to the important role of intergovernmental transfers in the economy of the less wealthy provinces, including not only Equalization but also the transfers for health and especially higher education.[21] In those parts of the country, and most especially Atlantic Canada, transfers from Ottawa have been major components in provincial budgets, helping to promote the goals of reasonably comparable levels of services at reasonable comparable tax rates. One result, in particular, has been to improve education and skill levels relative to other regions of the country. The narrowing of the gap is shown in Figure 4.

The economics literature is, in general, supportive of the idea that decentralization of public services is a good idea for efficiency reasons. Chapter 2 in this volume by Robin Boadway speaks to both the benefits of decentralization, as well as its limitations. Thus, the general trend to decentralize spending, as outlined above, is consistent with this element of theory. However, there is a divide in the literature about whether it is as important to have decentralized revenue collection. For much of the postwar period, to the extent that there was a consensus, it was that there were advantages in centralized revenue collection and therefore some vertical imbalance was appropriate. There were thought to be efficiencies in a relatively centralized and harmonized system of revenue collection. These included administrative efficiencies in collection, efficiencies in compliance and the avoidance of spillovers associated with the differing fiscal capacities of the provinces. In this view, the vertical imbalance could be used by the federal government to support Canada-wide

Figure 4: *Average Annual Growth Rates by Province, 1961-1996*

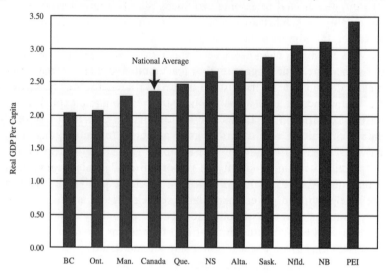

Source: Serge Coulombe, *Economic Growth and Provincial Disparity: A New View of an Old Problem* (Toronto: C.D. Howe Institute, 1999), Table 1.

equity goals. Chapter 3 by Ken Norrie and Sam Wilson develops this case further.

This relatively rosy picture of the policy impacts of fiscal federalism has become more blurred over the last decade and perhaps even a bit longer. For one thing, from at least some perspectives, it appears that Ottawa has reduced its commitment to equity. In Chapter 6, Paul Hobson and France St. Hilaire describe the replacement of Established Programs Financing and the Canada Assistance Plan (CAP) by the CHST bloc grant as the financial equivalent of terminating federal cost-sharing for provincial welfare (i.e., eliminating CAP). Given the political priority that health has these days, and to a lesser degree postsecondary education, relative to welfare, this characterization should not be dismissed lightly. Reinforcing this argument, Lars Osberg demonstrates in Chapter 8 that many of the gains that Canada was able to achieve in the 1970s and 1980s in dealing with poverty, and the way poverty was distributed across Canada, had eroded badly by the mid-1990s.

Moreover, the economics literature is more divided now than it once was about the merits of a central government collecting more revenue than it requires to finance its own programs and other orders of government collecting less. There is an increased concern that this leads the governments that are the recipients of intergovernmental transfers to spend more than would otherwise be the case. And there is a more general criticism that these transfers obscure accountability relationships. In this view, the government that spends should also be the government that levies the tax. This view heavily influences the proposals for tax re-assignments in Chapter 10 by Jack Mintz and Richard Bird.

The questioning of the efficiency aspects of federal transfers to the provinces overlaps two much broader concerns about the role that the Canadian state came to play during its postwar expansion. The first was the growth in public sector deficits and debt, including at the federal level. During the expansionary period of fiscal federalism, especially from the mid-1950s to the late 1960s, the fiscal base of the federal government was also growing rapidly. But starting in 1975, federal government spending exceeded federal revenues every year for more than 20 years. As the deficit problem grew, all government programs were subject to more scrutiny and question. This inevitably included the major federal transfers to the provinces, if only because they were among the largest programs in the federal budget.

The second development was the huge growth in economic linkages between Canada and the United States relative to the east-west links within Canada. Courchene has written eloquently about the growing interdependence of each of Canada's regional economies with its neighbours.[22] What is especially significant in this regard is that this process has been consciously accelerated by Canadian government policy, as reflected in the Canada-United States Free Trade Agreement and the North America Free Trade Agreement. The result is that the provincial economies are drawn into increasingly tight relationships with the US regional economies closest to them, from both a cooperative and competitive perspective. The economic self-interest of the wealthier provinces in seeing the federal government redistribute income to the less prosperous regions has thus been diminished.[23]

Under the twin pressures of deficit reduction and competitiveness, as noted above, Canada's system of fiscal federalism has not served Canada-wide equity goals as well in recent years as it did in earlier decades.[24] Public health insurance is under stress. Income-support programs have deteriorated. Tuition fees in postsecondary institutions have risen dramatically. These are all programs that were once heavily supported through federal transfers.

It might be thought that many economists would applaud the shift from cost-shared to bloc-funding and reduced transfers, at least from an efficiency perspective. But as noted above, the very idea of intergovernmental transfers has itself come under challenge by some analysts.[25] And therefore there is probably less consensus today about the efficiency benefits of fiscal federalism than there was when the system was less flexible. This does not deny the value of programs like Equalization in reducing differences in fiscal capacity and thus reducing the probability for economically inefficient migration of households or firms and in reducing horizontal externalities (as when a province with low investments in education can poach from others that invest more).

But in an era where the value of fiscal restraint has risen, the political weight attached to these particular efficiency arguments has weakened.

In summary with respect to policy matters, there is less consensus today than there was 20 or 30 years ago that the tools of fiscal federalism are effectively serving the goals of equity and efficiency. This is partly because the cash amounts being transferred have fallen substantially in relative terms. But it is also because the contextual setting has shifted. The twin concerns of fiscal restraint and provincial competitiveness are leaning against a return to the kind of fiscal federalism practised in the postwar decades.

IMPACT ON FEDERALISM

This in turn raises questions about the impact of fiscal federalism on the state of the federation itself. On the favourable side, Canadian fiscal federalism has been an important instrument for giving concrete expression to the idea that there is a social dimension to citizenship: that there are rights that accrue to Canadian citizens no matter where in Canada they may live. This is reflected in the various mechanisms for promoting mobility rights. In recent years, it has been reflected most profoundly in the apparently symbolic stature of Canada-wide medicare as a "right" of citizenship. If federations are polities that seek to bridge shared rule and self-rule, fiscal federalism has been an important tool for building the areas of commonality and for promoting the idea of Canada as a sharing society. The evidence for the success of these programs in building a sense of common purpose is reflected in the apparent determination of the citizenry today to preserve and repair the deterioration in the public health insurance system.

The federal government has played an essential leadership role in this process, providing much of the vision and important amounts of money. Provincial governments have also been vital to what has been achieved. In some cases, they have provided the ideas. And in most cases they are the government "on the ground," the jurisdiction responsible for designing and delivering the benefits and services. Working together, the two orders of government have accomplished much.

This does not mean, however, that these achievements came easily. From the viewpoint of provincial governments, each step along the way has involved serious concerns. In the 1950s and 1960s, the lack of clear rules around the use of the federal spending power in respect of intergovernmental transfers created tension. In subsequent decades, provinces continued to demand that they be fully involved in federal "spending power" decisions before they were taken. They also wanted transfers to be made less conditional and more stable. As discussed above, the transfer system is much less conditional today than it was 25 years ago. The 1999 SUFA agreement also included some new limits on unilateral federal use of its spending power. It provided as well for advance consultation provisions prior to renewal of or significant changes in social transfers to make federal funding more predictable for the provinces.

An "on again off again" tug of war around revenue-sharing has been a second source of conflict, with the provinces periodically arguing that the sharing of revenues between the federal and provincial governments has unduly favoured the federal government. On this latter point, the federal government has on two occasions ceded substantial tax room to the provinces, although the last time was 1977.[26] This tension remains today. Thus, in a report to premiers in 1998, provincial and territorial ministers of finance asserted that "there is a fiscal imbalance between the federal government and the provinces, even after the federal transfer system is taken into account" and that this imbalance "is likely to widen."

The third tension was related to the tax-collection agreements, the provincial argument being twofold. First, the federal government was not administering the agreements in a flexible enough way to accommodate provincial priorities. Second, provincial revenues were too vulnerable to changes in federal tax law. Whenever, in the case of personal income tax, Ottawa changed either the tax base or the federal tax rate, provincial revenues were automatically affected. Beginning in the 1970s, the federal government began allowing some kinds of provincial credits to be included in provincial personal income tax systems. Over the following quarter century, Ottawa became progressively more flexible, to the point where it agreed over the last few years that provinces would have autonomy, within the framework of the federal-provincial tax-collection agreements, to impose their tax on taxable income rather than on federal tax payable.[27] For their part, provinces that were in the tax-collection agreements undertook to adhere to the federal definition of taxable income. The result was to provide provinces with wide discretion in the design of their systems and somewhat more stability in forecasting revenues.[28] Provinces have since begun acting on this freedom. Whether this new arrangement fully meets provincial needs, however, remains to be seen.

Viewed over a period of decades, the above synopsis suggests that Canadian fiscal federalism does adapt to changing needs and circumstances. At any point in time, however, this kind of historical sweep is likely to be absent. In other words, the federal government's willingness to adjust invariably follows on a period of sustained provincial political pressure.

In the current context, the amount that Ottawa is transferring to the provinces under CHST, and more generally the reliability of Ottawa as a funding partner, are hot spots. For almost three decades, the federal government has been reducing the amounts it has committed to the provinces in support of jointly financed programs (although it bears noting that it has been a consistently reliable payer of Equalization). As one Parliament cannot bind another, there is no constitutional impropriety in the federal government changing its mind about how much money it transfers to the provinces for joint programs. It is also the case that the federal government requires flexibility to deal with the finances of the country as they shift. But politically, when Ottawa changes the financing of joint programs unilaterally, it undermines the confidence of the provinces in the federal government as a trustworthy partner and this is all the more so when the provincial governments believe that the federal action is lacking in basic fairness. Thus, federal-provincial relations reached a boiling point after Ottawa announced its planned cuts in transfer payments in conjunction with the introduction of the CHST. As is well known, this led to a united negotiating position among all provinces (Quebec included) and the signing of the Social Union Framework Agreement (Quebec excluded), as an effort to secure agreed rules around the uses of the federal spending power and stability in funding.

Two main points are being made here. The first is the simple one that the growth of Canada-wide programs has helped to build civic nationalism in Canada and that the tools of fiscal federalism were prominent in their accomplishment. This achievement has become a defining feature of the Canadian polity. The second is that while intergovernmental cooperation played an important role in the construction of this pan-Canadian nationalism, the process has also entailed periodic political conflict. The 1990s were particularly acrimonious in this regard and one of the legacies of that decade is too much mistrust between the two orders of government.

The above analysis excludes Quebec, which views pan-Canadian nationalism with considerable suspicion to the extent that it offers potential competition to deep-seated Quebec nationalism. Holding to a classical view of federalism, with its watertight compartments, consecutive Quebec governments have argued that the federal spending power makes a mockery of the division of powers embedded in the constitution. This view from Quebec can, of course, be criticized. It is not clear, for example, that the majority of the people of Quebec dislike the idea of a federal government playing some role in social policy, although they want cooperation, not bickering, between Ottawa and Quebec City. The attack on the spending power also suggests that only those parts of the constitution which Quebec governments like, such as the legislative division of powers, have legitimacy. In this regard, a case can be made that the federal spending power is a less centralizing provision than the constitutional powers of disallowance and reservation, both of which were assigned to Ottawa in 1867 although unused for over a half-century.

Furthermore, Ottawa has not been inflexible in its implementation relative to Quebec. The safety valve of opting-out was worked out between Quebec City and Ottawa on more than one occasion. For example, Quebec chose to stay out of the Canada Pension Plan and instead constructed its own earnings-related pension plan, the Quebec Pension Plan. It opted out of the Canada Student Loan Program and Youth Allowance programs. In 1960 the Quebec government became the first to receive a tax transfer from the federal government in the form of a special tax abatement. More recently, the federal government has relied on the Government of Quebec to collect the Goods and Services Tax (GST) in that province on Ottawa's behalf. So the system has been administered with some flexibility.

For those outside Quebec, the decentralization of the last two to three decades might be thought to be sufficient to relieve Quebec's concern about an arrogant and centralizing federal government. But, perspective is everything. From a Quebec perspective, the postwar expansion of the federal government was inappropriate to the extent that it encroached on the legislative powers assigned to the provinces. In this regard, the legislative powers of the federal government did not require Ottawa to hold on to as much tax room as it did, especially after the Cold War began to ease. Thus, in this view, the federal government remains too large and too intrusive in the affairs of provincial governments, or at least the Quebec government. Whether these "intrusions" have played a significant role in the growth of the secessionist movement in Quebec, or whether it would have developed on its own, is difficult to gauge.[29] To the extent that Quebec nationalism is a natural expression of the collective will of the Quebec people, it may be that Quebec nationalism would have grown regardless of federal use of the spending power. Moreover, in the counterfactual situation, where Ottawa would have hypothetically played a much smaller role in constructing a postwar safety net and thus a much smaller role in the lives of Québécois, this seeming indifference might have also led to feelings of alienation and support for secession. Whatever the answer to this question, the fact is that a strong state apparatus has been constructed in Quebec, one that forcefully and often effectively pursues the goal of protecting and advancing Quebec as a mainly French-speaking nation within Canada and North America.

In sum, looking broadly at the impacts on the federation, Canadian fiscal federalism has been instrumental in building a sense of political nationhood within Canada outside Quebec. The effects on bridge-building between Quebec and the rest of Canada are harder to evaluate. While fiscal federalism may not have played a decisive role in contributing to secessionist pressures from Quebec, as a minimum it has periodically served as a substantial irritant in Quebec-federal relations.

IMPACT ON DEMOCRACY

In the early decades of its development, there was little or no serious discussion about the implications of fiscal federalism for democracy. The 1960s were a decade of joint programming in such areas as hospital insurance, medical care, welfare, taxation, and higher education. Some of the most important political matters facing Canadians were being debated and discussed in the largely confidential confines of the federal-provincial conference and meeting. But it was not until the beginning of the 1970s that Donald Smiley coined the expression "executive federalism," a term that was not only descriptive but also normative.[30] And the concept of the "democratic deficit," developed initially to describe democratic shortcomings in the institutional structures and processes of the European Economic Community, only began to be used extensively in Canada after the secretive processes that resulted in the Meech Lake Constitutional Accord.

Since the collapse of Meech, governments have shown greater sensitivity to the criticism about inadequate transparency and the need to involve citizens more in the federal-provincial process. The differences between the Meech Lake process and the political process around the Charlottetown Accord and then the Calgary Declaration illustrate the growing awareness within governments about the democratic deficit. The 1999 Social Union Framework Agreement provides for a significant role for citizens and stakeholders in the making of social policy. It talks of the value of transparency and of the need for outcome measures through which governments can be held accountable for their actions.[31]

The democratic deficit is admittedly a vague notion. In our Westminster-style of government, power is concentrated in the executive and increasingly in the first ministers and finance ministers. The decision-making process in the Westminster system is also a relatively closed one. The democratic character of the system is based on the fact that those who hold high office have been elected in an open, fair, and genuinely competitive process. If the public is dissatisfied with the government's performance, the government can be removed at the next election. To the extent that this view of democracy is adequate, then it can be argued that the closed nature of the federal-provincial process is no different than the normal processes of Westminster-style government. The ministers representing both orders of government have been duly elected, they carry majority support within their legislatures and they are answerable in those legislatures and ultimately to the public in the next general election.

This latter view of Canadian democracy is too narrow a view for contemporary Canada, however, as the above innovations from both the constitutional and non-constitutional areas suggest.[32] Unfortunately, even with this greater openness to various forms of more deliberative and more direct democracy, the inherent complexity of fiscal federalism makes it difficult for the public to understand the issues that are at stake. And to the extent that the major decisions that affect the basic *structure* of fiscal federalism are taken within the context of the annual federal budgetary process, and the secrecy it entails, this problem of complexity is compounded. By the same token, if such structural issues were to be removed from the annual federal budgetary process, this would assist the deliberative dimension of democracy. It would leave more room for citizen and stakeholder involvement.[33]

LOOKING BACK

Looking back, it can be seen that Canada's system of fiscal federalism was highly centralized in the first quarter-century after World War II. Since then, it has undergone a very substantial decentralization. In the 1990s there was evidence of further decentralization but also some cross-currents. The cross-currents make it difficult to know whether the broad decentralizing trend has run its course or whether it still has a distance to cover.

In the postwar years leading up to the early 1980s, the report card for fiscal federalism was a relatively strong one. It advanced important policy objectives. It helped construct Canadian nationalism. There were periodic tensions in the federation but, on the whole, they proved manageable.

Underlying this period of success was a broad measure of consensus about the role of the state in the Canadian economy and society. The postwar objectives of fostering high employment and economic stability, helping to secure people against the contingencies of unemployment, sickness, and old age, and protecting the most vulnerable were the building blocks of those decades.

But by the early 1980s that consensus had begun to erode. The objectives of macroeconomic stabilization and high employment had been undermined by the stagflation of the 1970s. The weak productivity growth of that decade and weak government revenues had begun to raise questions about the affordability and sustainability of the social programs. And in the ongoing debate about the equity-efficiency trade-off, the balance began to shift toward the efficiency side of the equation.

The larger constitutional agenda that dominated the 1980s and early 1990s initially obscured the effect of these changes for the conduct of federal-provincial fiscal relations. With the politics surrounding the *Constitution Act, 1982* and the huge amounts of political energy expended on the failed Meech Lake and Charlottetown Accords, the more substantive issues of fiscal federalism were on the back burner.[34] The main changes in fiscal federalism in the 1980s were federal cuts in planned increases in transfers to the provinces as fiscal deficits began to acquire a larger place in the agenda of the country.[35] For the most part, however, this was a period of relative calm in Canadian fiscal federalism.[36]

Looking back, it seems that the re-fashioning of the Canadian state in the 1980s and 1990s — a re-fashioning that made it much slimmer and more market-oriented — left some unfinished business in its wake. During these years, the political landscape of the provinces began to tilt heavily to economic conservatism. That this had not yet run its course by the second half of the 1990s was reflected not only in the re-election of Ralph Klein's government in Alberta and Mike Harris' in Ontario, it was also seen in the political gains of the Saskatchewan Party in the 1999 Saskatchewan provincial election, the new fiscal orthodoxy of the Parti Québécois government, and in the election of Progressive Conservative governments in three Atlantic provinces. The fiscal retrenchment of the federal Liberal government elected in 1993, under Paul Martin's stewardship in the federal Finance Department, in some ways paralleled what was happening in the provincial level. Arguably, the smaller and less conditional federal transfers associated with the introduction of the CHST were a part of that overall trend. The signing of the Social Union Framework Agreement, with a new set of restrictions on the federal use of the federal spending power, was arguably similarly consistent in political direction. Even the more recent new federal flexibility around provincial personal income tax could be part of the same story.

Indeed, if the events described above were the full story, it might be possible to suggest that, over the 1990s, and contrary to what was suggested early in this chapter, a new mission statement had been written for Canadian fiscal federalism. That mission statement would have acknowledged a more modest role for fiscal federalism in an era when the state itself was attempting to do less. That statement would have emphasized the need for flexibility on the part of the federal government to accommodate the growing integration of provincial/regional economies with their US neighbours. It would have been a more conservative mission statement than the postwar statement in an era of increased economic conservatism. And it would have been a mission statement that was decentralizing in a world where Quebec nationalism and western Canadian assertiveness were powerful forces and the position of the Ontario government increasingly critical of the federal government. And if one were to look only at the cap on CAP, the CHST, new provincial freedoms under the federal-provincial tax-collection agreement, and the apparently reduced emphasis on equity considerations, it might be concluded that there was indeed such a new mission statement for fiscal federalism. To be sure, this statement would have acknowledged bumps in the road, including the destabilization of provincial finances and programming with the federal transfer cuts. But this arguably could have been portrayed as unfortunate but necessary pain in moving toward a more modest system of fiscal federalism.

The argument here, however, is that no such new mission statement has yet been written. There is in fact no overarching sense of purpose in contemporary fiscal federalism, in part because there is no new consensus on the role of government and no consensus on the nature of the federation. For example, Ottawa did not cut Equalization during the 1990s. It increased Equalization. As for the other major transfers, they were cut dramatically. At the time of the

CHST, the federal government dressed up its spending cuts with "noise" about the reduced conditions that the new transfer would require. This was portrayed as further evidence of flexible federalism. Thus, Finance Minister Martin declared, in his 1995 budget speech: "we believe that the restrictions attached by the federal governments to transfer payments in areas of clear provincial responsibility should be minimized."[37] The finance minister then talked about the removal of unnecessary strings attached to the Canada Assistance Plan. Yet, only moments later in that same speech, he asserted that there were national goals and principles that had to be preserved and he committed the federal government to maintaining the conditions of the *Canada Health Act*. The finance minister's speech did not provide a clear rationale for easing conditions around social assistance but not doing so for health. But few informed Canadians would have been confused by these decisions. There was strong public support for Ottawa to remain involved in public health insurance even though this is an area of provincial legislative competence and much less support for Ottawa doing so in the area of welfare. Ottawa's policy changes were a response to practical political choices. They did not derive from some larger set of principles regarding the nature of the Canadian federation.

In fact, the CHST was mainly about one thing — reducing the federal deficit. Ending cost-sharing for welfare was the price of that change. To be sure, there had been voices around Ottawa for some time, urging that the cost-sharing for provincial welfare should end and be replaced by a bloc grant.[38] But these voices were ignored until the fiscal crunch. In any case, by rolling the EPF and CAP into a single transfer, Ottawa hoped to be able to obscure the impacts of its financial actions on the individual programs.

Federal actions since then, including restoring some of the CHST cuts, either directly or indirectly through funding direct transfers to individuals, indicate that the federal behaviour surrounding CAP and CHST was grounded at least as much in pragmatic deficit considerations as some entirely new set of principles for fiscal federalism. And Ottawa's apparent determination to play a role in "saving" medicare during the debates of 1999 and 2000 adds to this view. Notwithstanding its modest financial contribution to the provinces for health care, it has been attempting to find a way of exercising leadership.[39] This has been reflected in its political challenge to the privatization initiatives in Alberta. It is seen also in its offer of further transfers to the provinces in exchange for a provincial plan to make medicare more effective and sustainable.

It is not the case that Ottawa has substituted direct transfers for intergovernmental transfers. As discussed in Chapter 4, since CHST, more money has been reinvested in intergovernmental transfers than direct transfers (notwithstanding the Millennium Scholarship Fund, the Canada Child Benefit, the Canada Research Chairs, and other direct initiatives). Nor has efficiency trumped equity as a goal. Rather, what we have is a series of "one off" federal decisions that reflect the details of the individual files and the exigencies of the moment. "Ad hocery," with the federal government moving back and forth between the postwar consensus and the more conservative mission statement referred to above, is what characterizes the current federal approach to fiscal federalism.[40] Thus, for an extended period after the cap on the CAP, Ottawa continued to transfer far more money to needy provinces on a per capita basis, relative to wealthier provinces, than it had done prior to the cap on CAP. This suggested that the federal government was heavily equity-oriented, an argument that was reinforced by the enrichment of Equalization in 1994, at a time when few federal programs were being enhanced. Now, the federal government is eliminating entirely the per capita differential in favour of the needier provinces as it moves swiftly to end the per capita differences among provinces in the CHST. Thus, outside Equalization, Ottawa has shifted, in roughly one decade, from having a needs-related component in its transfer programs (the Canada Assistance Plan), to a kind of super needs-related component (per capita preferences in CAP in favour of equalization-receiving provinces) to no needs-related component in CAP's replacement (with equal per capita transfers under CHST).

It could be argued that, to some extent, the enriched Canada Child Benefit is a substitute for the needs-related CAP. This would, however, miss the main point here, which is not to criticize any of these individual decisions. Rather, it is to illustrate the thesis that it is difficult to discern any overarching vision for the future of Canadian fiscal federalism from analyzing the recent actions of the federal government.

Nor have provincial governments been entirely consistent in their approach to fiscal federalism. For example, they came together in 1998 in presenting a joint position to the federal government, arguing that there was a vertical imbalance in public finances that needed redressing. They set out three broad options for removing the imbalance: a cash transfer option, an equalized tax point reallocation option and a tax field realignment option. Provinces differed in their preferences among those models.

In the context of proposing a Social Union Framework Agreement, the provincial governments developed a series of positions that included restraints on the exercise of the federal spending power and better stability in federal transfers to the provinces. The provincial negotiating position on SUFA also included proposals that would have enabled a province to opt out of a new Canada-wide initiative and receive full compensation from Ottawa. They pressed as well for a quite formal set of arrangements around dispute avoidance and resolution. In the event, provincial governments accepted weaker controls on the federal spending power, weak federal commitments for revenue stability, and a lesser provision on opting-out than they had proposed. The provisions around dispute avoidance and resolution were also well short of a provincial negotiating position. The incentive for the provincial premiers to go along with the compromise position was the lure of a large additional federal financial contribution to the CHST. In the event, the final SUFA deal was made in conjunction with enhanced federal transfers to provincial governments. These extra cash transfers thus corresponded to one of the options in the 1998 Finance Ministers' Report to Premiers. While it is always easy for those who are not engaged directly in the business of government to poke holes in what governments decide to do, there are few commentators who will dispute the notion that provincial governments backed away from a large part of their negotiating position in return for additional federal money. This may not have been an unwise decision by provincial governments. But it clearly does speak to the fact that provincial strategies have reflected heavily pragmatic considerations, much like Ottawa's.

LOOKING AHEAD

Over the last several years, federal and provincial governments have been experimenting with new forms of "collaborative federalism."[41] While collaborative federalism has some things in common with the "cooperative federalism" of earlier decades, it differs in important respects. One difference is that collaborative federalism envisages partnership and equality between orders of governments whereas cooperative federalism involves strong federal government leadership. And as a practical matter over the last few years, collaborative federalism has involved the federal government responding to provincial initiatives as much as provincial governments responding to federal initiatives. Several of the ideas now under federal-provincial negotiations or implementation emerged at least in part from the work programs of the annual Premiers' Conferences. Conditional transfers were a trademark of cooperative federalism. Bloc transfers are a hallmark of collaborative federalism. The era of cooperative federalism was one in which the federal government had substantial fiscal flexibility and could use its spending power to drive the federal-provincial agenda. The period of collaborative federalism began at a time when Ottawa was engaging in fiscal retrenchment. In some sense, the federal government was required to accept a more equal partnership by virtue of its inability to use money as an incentive to shape provincial behaviour.

Thus, a crucial issue for the future of Canadian fiscal federalism is whether the concept of collaborative federalism can survive a period of federal government fiscal prosperity. It was easy for the federal government to accept restraints on its spending power when it had little money to spend. But whether Ottawa is willing to accept the same constraints now that it is back in fiscal surplus is an open question. There are mixed signals from the federal government on this matter. Notwithstanding some real evidence to the contrary, the general picture in the period since SUFA was signed is of a federal government living within the rules of the restraints on its spending power, as

discussed in Chapter 4. There is also evidence that many federal public serv-
ants, especially in sectoral departments, are trying hard to make the
collaborative federalism of the Social Union Framework Agreement a meaningful reality. This is reflected in such diverse tables as those on disability,
labour markets, and children.

But provincial governments remain suspicious of federal *bona fides*. They
were clearly disappointed by the absence of large new funds for health care in
the 2000 budget. They suspect Ottawa is tempted to make greater use of direct
transfers than intergovernmental transfers. And they are alienated by the federal government's unwillingness to agree to a more substantive set of practical
arrangements for dispute resolution.

With the Chrétien Liberals in power, the possibility of a further tax transfer
to the provinces, or tax realignment, appears remote. In the event of a more
conservative party forming the next government, it is conceivable that Ottawa
might take a different stance. In that case, it would be reasonable to expect a
conscious effort to reduce vertical imbalances and perhaps greater commitments to preserve the stability of existing transfers. It would also be reasonable
to anticipate a re-drafted SUFA in which the restraints on the federal spending power become more stringent. This does not mean that such a government,
whether made up of the Canadian Alliance, the Progressive Conservatives or
some coalition would, or should, simply adopt stated provincial positions.
But a significant move in that direction would be consistent with the policy
positions the opposition parties have taken.

In the period immediately ahead, several important questions remain unan-
swered. The first is whether fiscal federalism will be characterized by the
paradigm of collaborative federalism, and an equal partnership among orders
of government, or whether it will revert to one in which the federal government attempts to play the role of senior government. A second is whether the
decision-making processes around fiscal federalism will become more transparent, with structural decisions taken outside the federal budget-making
process. A third has to do with the balance between equity and efficiency. And
a fourth has to do with whether fiscal federalism can be used constructively to
narrow the political gap between Quebec and the rest of Canada.

The answers to the first three of these questions may be intertwined and
determined by the readiness of the two orders of government to live by the
spirit of the Social Union Framework Agreement. This agreement proclaims
"mutual respect between orders of governments and a willingness to work
more closely together to meet the needs of Canadians." It provides for "joint
planning and collaboration." It has provisions for dispute resolution. So there
is already a federal-provincial plan to move in the direction of collaborative
federalism. SUFA also includes provisions for enhanced transparency in the
federal-provincial decision-making process and for a stronger public account-

ability regime. Since the social spending programs that are SUFA's focus are *also fiscal federalism programs*, the answer to the first two questions will depend in large measure on whether there is the political will among first ministers to breathe life into this agreement. The answer will also hinge on whether *major structural* decisions about the future of fiscal federalism are taken out of the political hot house of the annual federal budget-making process. If they remain there, the dice are loaded against the kind of equal partnership that SUFA contemplates and that, arguably, the current political context demands. Such a change would not require the federal minister of finance to surrender control of the federal fiscal framework to the provinces or other parts of the federal government. It would necessitate, however, that structural decisions relating to jointly financed programs or federal-provincial tax arrangements be worked out in a joint forum, not the federal budgetary process, which Ottawa must necessarily own. Under these conditions, the prospects for a reasonable balance between Canada-wide equity and efficiency goals are also enhanced because, in such a setting, there is a functional mechanism (i.e., SUFA) for promoting equity.

Whether fiscal federalism can help to bridge the Quebec-Rest of Canada divide is a separate issue. Perhaps perversely, the inherent complexity of fiscal federalism may be a bit of an advantage in this regard. This is because the technical nature of fiscal instruments makes them difficult to use for symbolic purposes. This does necessarily favour one side more than the other in the federalist-sovereignist struggle for Quebec. Thus, Ottawa seems to have received little credit from either the Government or people of Quebec for devolving labour market training to that province. And the PQ was unable to gain much support for an attack on Ottawa's decision to make CHST an equal per capita transfer. The issues appear to be too complex. To the extent that there is some truth in this analysis (and its truth will vary from item to item), it suggests that governments as different as those of Jean Chrétien and Lucien Bouchard should be able to do business with one another from time to time without putting at risk their longer term goals. That is, it should be possible for the federal and Quebec governments to work together on "meat and potato" fiscal-federalism issues related to taxation and spending. Whether this kind of collaboration will translate into a narrowing of the political chasm between the two sides is less clear, however. These larger differences between the federalist and sovereignist agendas will probably require changes in the political symbols and perhaps institutions of the country. But fiscal federalism may be a useful complementary instrument in this larger agenda, should there be governments in Ottawa and Quebec City that wish to tackle a political reconciliation agenda.

THE NEED FOR A NEW MISSION STATEMENT

The current era of global and continental integration is leading to growing functional interdependence among the peoples and governments of the world, whether the subject is financial markets, the environment, fighting organized crime, the migration of peoples or the spread of diseases. This interdependence applies as much to relationships within countries as between them.

In Canada, the functional need to manage this interdependence has arisen within a context where provincial governments were demanding respect for their position within the Canadian constitutional family and some academics were calling for more independence among governments as a way of assuring enhanced public accountability. In turn, these demands have led to changes in the structure of fiscal federalism which have served to strengthen *de facto* provincial independence on fiscal matters. Provinces rely less on federal cash transfers today than they did 30 years ago. The transfers they do receive have fewer conditions attached to them. Provinces are also less tightly tied into the federal income tax structure.

There are thus pressures for both interdependence and independence within the federation. While these two forces may appear to conflict with one another, in practice they need not always do so. On some issues, it may be sensible, even inevitable, that the two orders of government work closely together. On others, there may be little or no cost to governments working independently of one another and clear advantages to doing so. Even sorting these issues out, however, requires some kind of partnership and collaboration among governments.

Federal government documents and representatives have repeatedly declared their support for collaborative federalism. The 1997 Liberal *Red Book* stated: "Our philosophy of federalism is that the best way for the various orders of government to meet the needs of Canadians is to work together."[42] The federal minister of intergovernmental affairs enunciated the same viewpoint two years later stating: "Our federation is evolving toward greater cooperation and consensus-building, while respecting the constitutional jurisdiction of each order of government."[43] As already noted, SUFA, which Ottawa signed, enshrines this principle.

For collaboration to be effective, the behaviour of governments must have a substantial degree of predictability. If one order of government zigzags too much, the second order of government will find that first order too unpredictable and hence difficult to trust as a partner. In this regard, it is particularly important that the federal government be predictable because the intergovernmental impact of Ottawa's actions is much larger than that of individual provincial governments. And the analysis above suggests that the behaviour of governments is still not predictable enough to create and sustain the necessary trust relationships.

In the context of fiscal federalism, this suggests the need for a new mission statement. This is a tall order, but this chapter has already suggested some of the key elements. First, both orders of government should seek to reduce the number and size of the surprises they spring on the other. One way of doing this is to take seriously the joint planning provisions of SUFA. Joint planning should not, and will not, mean joint design and delivery of social programs. But it can and should mean jointly analyzing the challenges of the sectors, exchanging information that is relevant to those challenges, systematically documenting successes and failures and, where possible, setting objectives together. Individual governments would then be responsible for designing and delivering programs to meet those challenges and objectives. Among other things, this leaves lots of scope for asymmetry in the federation.

Second, the federal government should not attempt to deal with the big structural issues of fiscal federalism in the context of its annual budget cycle. If it does so, there is no real chance that provinces will be equal partners in the decision-making process. The big change to the transfer system in the 1970s was the decision to roll three large cost-shared programs (hospital insurance, medical insurance, and postsecondary education) into a single bloc transfer. This was worked out through a long negotiation between the two orders of government that was not dominated by the annual federal budgetary process. Whatever one thinks of the outcome, it was the product of both orders of government working together. This was different than the more or less unilateral processes that led to the cap on CAP and CHST and that have so poisoned intergovernmental relations since their implementation. Without this kind of shift in internal federal budgetary processes, joint planning at the sectoral level will be dysfunctional.

Third, there is a need to imbed the idea of mutual respect between the two orders of government. Not only is this necessary for functional reasons, it is also what the public wants, as evidenced in polling data.

Finally, the mission statement should confirm the importance of both equity and efficiency goals. Each is essential for a balanced public policy. It is important, however, to articulate what these commitments may mean in the year 2000. For example, the postwar federal-provincial tax rental and tax-collection agreements were linked to particular public purposes. These included a big role for federal fiscal policy in macroeconomic stabilization, achieving tax harmonization for purposes of economic efficiency; and Ottawa's perceived need to maintain a strong revenue position to help fund a more equitable postwar society. The first of these purposes is no longer present today. As for the second, it may remain but with growing north-south economic integration, it needs to be spelled out in a way that reflects current circumstances. In this regard, the recently reformed tax-collection agreements may be adequate for this purpose but this remains to be seen. Even the third goal merits re-examination to capture contemporary thinking about the shifting roles of security and opportunity in the Canadian social security system.

These four elements fall far short of a full statement of principles. And they in no way speak to the substance of policy content. If governments committed effectively to them, however, this would help to build the trust relations that are required to fashion a modern system of fiscal federalism which advances policy goals, supports democratic values, and respects the very idea of a federal state.

Notice that the statement does not imply that the current balance between orders of government is appropriate. Rather, what happens to centralization/decentralization will be an outcome of implementing a set of principles and agreed processes and not an end in itself. And sorting out the size of vertical imbalances will be at least in part a result of careful analysis about the efficiency and equity impacts of sustaining current imbalances relative to reducing them. That there is controversy about this issue will be seen in the different chapters in this volume.

Such a new mission statement would be constructed on top of the one element of fiscal federalism that is apparently not controversial, namely, the commitment to equalization. This commitment is not only imbedded in the constitution, the wealthier provinces as well as the federal government also support it politically. Governments of wealthier provinces often question whether an equalization component should be included in programs other than the formal Equalization program, but they are consistent in support of some substantial program to meet the equalization objectives set out in the constitution.

If Ottawa and the provinces are unable to agree on the role and purpose of fiscal federalism for the new century, the price will be large. Friction among governments within the federation will grow. National purpose will be eroded. Equity and efficiency goals will be undermined. The price of inaction could be huge.

The Social Union Framework Agreement provides that the governments involved will undertake a full review of the agreement and its implementation by the end of its third year. We are about halfway there in the middle of the year 2000. This is an important opportunity for beginning the task of renewing not only the governance structures and rules around the safety net but also the closely related system of fiscal federalism. This should be a priority item in the public policy agenda of the next few years.

NOTES

I would like to thank John McLean, Research Associate at the Institute of Intergovernmental Relations, Queen's University, for his extensive research assistance, especially in compiling the fiscal data.

1. For a fuller statement of this argument, see Harvey Lazar and Tom McIntosh, "How Canadians Connect: State, Economy, Citizenship and Society," *Canada: The State of the Federation, 1998/99: How Canadians Connect* (Kingston: Institute of Intergovernmental Relations, Queen's University, 1999), pp. 25-30.

2. The assertion that a clear mission statement is lacking requires a brief elaboration. First, the missing "mission statement" need not necessarily be a formal mission statement. Second, I am not asserting that governments do not, from time to time, make statements that appear to convey an overarching sense of purpose. At any point in time, there may be, for example, a federal government declaration that has coherence. As for provincial governments, they have in recent years issued some excellent papers on fiscal federalism. My argument is that over the last two decades there have been insufficient consistency and coherence in fiscal federalism to the point where neither order of government can have confidence about the limits within which the other order of government may act.

3. I would include in this group Paul Boothe, Tom Courchene, John Richards, and Bill Robson. Alain Noël has also made the case that there is no automatic link between more centralized approaches to governance and a social democratic perspective, on the one hand, and a more decentralized approach and fiscal/economic conservatism, on the other. See "Is Decentralization Conservative? Federalism and the Contemporary Debate on the Canadian Welfare State," in *Stretching the Federation: The Art of the State in Canada*, ed. Robert Young (Kingston: Institute of Intergovernmental Relations, Queen's University, 1999).

4. I am aware that the last two paragraphs oversimplify the differences among political and academic commentators.

5. Prior to the enactment of the *Old Age Security Act*, there was an income–tested state pension available under the 1927 *Old Age Pensions Act*. This provided for provincial administration of pensions, but with the then Dominion (i.e., federal) government paying one-half.

6. Section 94A of the *Constitution Act* was amended in 1964. The amendment allowed the Parliament of Canada to "make laws in relation to old age pensions and supplementary benefits" but with the qualification that no such federal law "shall affect the operation of any law present or future of a provincial legislature in relation to any such matter."

7. The Government of Saskatchewan introduced publicly insured hospital and medical services before the federal government acted.

8. The case by no means disappeared, however, given the role of tax harmonization in promoting economic and administrative efficiency and equity.

9. There are different dimensions to centralization/decentralization. I state that the peak "perhaps" was reached in 1982 because of the constitutional amendments then. I consciously leave this ambiguity since, from a fiscal federalism perspective, the peak was reached in the mid- to late 1960s.

10. I chose this date since, as noted in the main body of the text, the middle of the 1960s was the period when federal government initiatives led to several major

social programs. They included the federal-provincial agreements to provide public insurance for medical services, to create a single shared-cost program for needs-related provincial programs (the Canada Assistance Plan), to create the Canada and Quebec Pension Plans, and to expand Canada's postsecondary education systems. Once these initiatives were taken, it was inevitable that provincial program costs and revenue needs would grow rapidly.

11. If local governments are included, and under the Canadian constitution they are creatures of the provinces, combined provincial and local program spending increased from around 14 percent of GDP in 1960 to 24-25 percent of GDP by 1990. These figures are from Department of Finance, *Fiscal Reference Tables*, Table 30.

12. If provinces fail to meet the principles, the federal government may penalize the province by reducing its cash transfer. The principles include: universality, accessibility, comprehensiveness, portability, and public administration.

13. Section 6 of the SUFA appears to subject the "interpretation of the Canada Health Act principles" to the collaborative dispute avoidance and resolution provisions of that agreement but there is no public indication to date about how this is to be implemented.

14. Some of these actions were taken only after extensive negotiation with the provinces (as with child benefits). In other cases, negotiation with the provinces has been focused on how to jointly implement the federal initiative (such as scholarships).

15. *The Canadian Social Union Without Quebec: 8 Critical Analyses* (Montreal: Institute for Research on Public Policy, 2000).

16. The federal constitutional powers that were important in constructing the welfare state also included the authority to operate a system of unemployment insurance and the authority to make laws in relation to old age pensions and supplementary benefits (but with provincial powers in this area having paramountcy).

17. James Rice and Michael Prince, *Changing Politics of Canadian Social Policy* (Toronto: University of Toronto Press, 1999), pp. 54-80.

18. One example of what was achieved is illustrated by trends in the distribution of income in Canada relative to other countries. Over the last 20 to 30 years, labour market earnings have become more polarized and more unequal in virtually all advanced capitalist economies, including Canada. In general, the result has been that the distribution of disposable family income (i.e., after-tax, after-transfer family incomes) also became more widely dispersed. However, in Canada, thanks to an effective system of transfers and taxes, the distribution of Canadian family incomes managed to remain remarkably stable. This is one of the central messages in Chapter 8 by Lars Osberg.

19. *The Constitution Act*, sub-sections 36 (1) and 36 (2).

20. Ibid., sub-section 36 (2).

21. Serge Coulombe, *Economic Growth and Provincial Disparity* (Toronto: C.D. Howe Institute, 1999).

22. See Thomas J. Courchene with Colin R. Telmer, *From Heartland to North American Region State: The Social, Fiscal, and Federal Evolution of Ontario* (Toronto: Centre for Public Management, Faculty of Management, University of Toronto, 1998). In *Canada: The State of the Federation 1998/99: How Canadians Connect* (Kingston: Institute of Intergovernmental Relations, 1999) John F. Helliwell provides convincing evidence of the much greater density of economic linkages between the regions of Canada than between the Canadian regions and the United States. See Chapter 4. However, this does not deny that the growth rate in north-south linkages is much faster than the growth rate in east-west ties.

23. This assertion does not preclude the governments of wealthier provinces supporting Equalization payments for reasons other than economic self-interest.

24. The cap on CAP was intended to help protect the most vulnerable provinces during a period of fiscal restraint. The federal government decision to carry forward the legacy of this measure in the form of unequal per capita provincial CHST payments during the first few years of CHST can also be seen as a continuation of that policy. While this is evidence of federal concern to protect the most vulnerable regions, the ending of CAP as a distinctive policy has virtually ensured that the focus of provincial expenditure would shift to programs that do not involve the poorest of Canadians. More generally, the federal reductions in cash transfers, and in planned increases, associated with major transfers for health, education, and welfare over a period of years has weakened the equity goal.

25. See, for example, John Richards, "Reducing the Muddle in the Middle: Three Propositions for Running the Welfare State," in *Canada: The State of the Federation 1997: Non-Constitutional Renewal*, ed. Harvey Lazar (Kingston: Institute of Intergovernmental Relations, Queen's University, 1998).

26. The federal government offered to abate tax points to the provinces in the mid-1960s, in conjunction with the growth of shared-cost programs. Quebec took up the federal offer in 1965. The other provinces took up abatements for personal and corporate income tax in 1967.

27. In effect, this has enabled provinces to retain the efficiency benefits of having a central revenue collection agency while obtaining autonomy to design their own personal income tax systems.

28. When the federal government changes its personal income tax rates, this will no longer automatically impact on provincial income tax revenues. However, if the federal government adjusts the tax base, this will impact provincial revenues unless the province explicitly offsets the federal change by altering its tax rates or other elements of the tax structure that it is now free to shape, like credits.

29. While Quebec nationalists, both federalist and secessionist, often argue that Ottawa's incursions and provocations help to fuel support for an independent Quebec, it is difficult to know whether an entirely different federal strategy would have meant a weaker separatist movement. In this regard, it is noteworthy that the federal Royal Commission on Bilingualism and Biculturalism was appointed in 1963, well before many of the so-called federal provocations. A re-reading of that report, or of Quebec's Tremblay Report (Report of the Royal Commission

of Inquiry on Constitutional Problems, 1956), makes clear that Quebec nationalism was alive and well in the early postwar years.

30. Smiley uses this term and makes comments on the development of executive
     federalism in Donald Smiley, *Constitutional Adaptation and Canadian Federal-
     ism Since 1945* (Ottawa: Queen's Printer, 1970). For Donald Smiley's criticisms
     of executive federalism, see Donald Smiley, "An Outsider's Observations of
     Federal-Provincial Relations among Consenting Adults, " in *Confrontation and
     Collaboration: Intergovernmental Relations in Canada Today*, ed. Richard
     Simeon (Toronto: The Institute of Public Administration of Canada, 1979),
     pp. 103-13. For another criticism of cooperative federalism, see Albert Breton,
     "Supplementary Statement," in *Report of the Royal Commission on the Eco-
     nomic Union and Development Prospects for Canada*, Vol. 3 (Ottawa: Supply
     and Services Canada, 1985), pp. 486-526.

31. Mathew Mendelsohn and John McLean, "SUFA's Double Vision: Citizen En-
     gagement and Intergovernmental Collaboration," *Policy Options* (April
     2000):43-45.

32. For a survey of the various models of democracy, see David Held, *Models of
     Democracy* (Stanford: Stanford University Press, 1987).

33. This argument does not prevent the federal government from using the federal
     budget process for introducing the resolutions that would lead to the necessary
     legislation to enact major changes in fiscal federalism. But the substantive con-
     tent would have been discussed thoroughly with the provinces and debated
     publicly and in Parliament before the budget action.

34. They were on the back burner except in the sense that the Meech and
     Charlottetown Accords attempted to deal with issues like the federal spending
     power.

35. For a crisp chronology of federal cuts to planned transfers, see Thomas J.
     Courchene, *Redistributing Money and Power: A Guide to the Canada Health
     and Social Transfer*, Appendix A (Toronto: C.D. Howe Institute, 1995).

36. It is possible that these federal reductions in planned levels of transfers did not
     cause a major controversy with the provinces for at least three reasons. The
     federal transfers were still growing. Second, provinces were aware that fiscal
     restraint was becoming increasingly necessary. Third, the constitutional file was
     at the political forefront.

37. Budget Speech, 27 February 1995, p. 17.

38. This view essentially held that the federal CAP bureaucracy and the regulations
     it administered was impeding provincial innovation in welfare programs.

39. It is, of course, arguable that there is absolutely no link between the CHST and
     provincial health spending. Federal money flows into the consolidated revenue
     funds of provinces and then flows out based on provincial priorities. Even the
     1999 Health Accord between provincial governments and Ottawa is more about
     political symbolism than ensuring that federal "health dollars" are spent on health
     by provinces.

40. One example is that the federal government allowed large per capita discrepancies among provinces in the dollar amounts it was distributing for CAP. This per capita differential was rolled over and absorbed into CHST. The 1999 federal budget announced that CHST entitlements would be equal per capita beginning in 2001/2002. Thus, Ottawa has shifted from a transfer system that was partly needs-related (the CAP years), to one where need was arguably accentuated even more (the cap on CAP years because the least wealthy provinces were spared the CAP cuts) to one where need is not recognized (the equal per capita transfer in CHST that is coming).

41. For a fuller definition and discussion of collaborative federalism, see Harvey Lazar, "The Federal Role in a New Social Union," in *Canada: The State of the Federation 1997: Non-Constitutional Renewal*, ed. Harvey Lazar (Kingston: Institute of Intergovernmental Relations, Queen's University, 1998).

42. Liberal Party of Canada, *Securing our Future Together*, 1997, p 19.

43. Speech by Honourable Stéphane Dion, 22 April 1999.

2

Recent Developments in the Economics
of Federalism

Robin Boadway

Ce chapitre présente une revue de la littérature internationale récente sur le fédéralisme fiscal et des leçons qu'elle offre au cas canadien. On souligne, en premier lieu, les gains que la formation d'une fédération offre aux États membres, en particulier quant au marché commun interne et à la citoyenneté. De plus, on met en évidence l'attrait puissant qu'exerce la décentralisation des services publics aux juridictions internes pour des raisons d'efficacité. Une telle décentralisation peut, néanmoins, avoir des conséquences négatives en matière d'efficacité et d'équité dans une économie fédérale. Les effets négatifs sur l'efficacité proviennent du fait que la décentralisation crée des disparités fiscales et que la prise de décision de manière décentralisée peut mener à des chevauchements interjuridictionnels. Les effets négatifs sur l'équité proviennent eux aussi des disparités fiscales, mais aussi de l'importance des instruments politiques provinciaux en matière d'équité. Le rôle des ententes fiscales est d'éviter ces problèmes d'efficacité et d'inégalité qui accompagnent la décentralisation des responsabilités fiscales aux provinces, ce qui, par le fait même, facilite la décentralisation. Certaines caractéristiques des ententes fiscales pouvant mener à une fédération plus équitable et plus efficace sont évaluées, notamment la péréquation, l'utilisation conditionnelle du pouvoir de dépenser, l'harmonisation des politiques ainsi que les processus qui permettent d'obtenir une meilleure coopération.

INTRODUCTION

There is a growing interest among economists in issues of fiscal federalism. Much of the impetus comes from institutional changes faced by various governments around the world. Examples include the development of the European Union as an instrument for joint economic decision-making and the implications that has for the European nation-state; the requirement of the transitional economies to establish public sector institutions to replace state firms as providers of public services; and the need for rapidly developing countries to begin to provide public services that are traditionally provided by subnational governments. As well, the fiscal pressure faced by many governments in an increasingly competitive international environment has sparked a general interest in decentralization as a means of improving the effectiveness of public sector decision-making. Not surprisingly, the key features of the Canadian model have received much attention — our allocation of responsibilities, our evolving fiscal decentralization, and the main elements of our fiscal arrangements (equalization, tax harmonization, and the spending power).

Along with this interest has come an explosion of academic research on fiscal federalism, especially among Europeans, in a field that has traditionally been the preserve of the established federations. Modern instruments of economic analysis have been brought to bear on the issue of how governments do and should interact in multi-government settings. The models used mirror many of the models of economic analysis that have been developed in the postwar period. Simple game-theoretic models have been used to capture the outcomes of independent decision-making by governments in a federation. The principal-agent perspective and issues of commitment and time consistency have focused on the importance of the timing of decisions by various levels of government. The problems posed by public choice considerations and the opportunity for decentralized decision-making to overcome them have been studied. The preoccupation with constraints on economic policies resulting from the fact that policymakers have imperfect information about those whom the policies are intended to affect is of obvious relevance for decentralization: lower levels of government may be better informed about their citizens' wants, needs, and opportunities than are higher levels. The role of governments in shedding the risks faced by individuals by the provision of social insurance is of relevance for federalism insofar as risks might be more completely shared by higher levels of government. More generally, the level of government involved can affect the efficacy of delivering redistributive policies, which account for a substantial proportion of policies that governments undertake.

The literature on fiscal federalism is large and has led to many interesting and suggestive phenomena at the theoretical level which could serve to inform policy analysts. But it also has some shortcomings. Most of the work is theoretical, with very little empirical testing or substantiation. This reflects the natural difficulty of empirically testing models of government behaviour: policy changes are not frequent, they have potentially broad-ranging effects, and formulating the appropriate behavioural model to test is difficult if not impossible. The theoretical models, like many economic models, tend to be highly abstract, chosen so as to highlight particular phenomena of interest to the exclusion of others. There is a general tendency to ignore institutions and the complexities they impose, and also to ignore process. Models of political choice are beginning to be used; indeed, they are very much in fashion at the moment. But they are often fairly rudimentary: ranging from simple median voting models to rather more sophisticated political competition models to crude Leviathan models of government as predator. Nonetheless, they do capture some overriding influences that economists think to be important.

The purpose of this chapter is to provide an overview of the sorts of things that economists have been exploring in their study of the economics of federalism. The recent literature has not focused much on issues of Canadian concern. Nonetheless, some implications might be drawn. One does, however, come away from the economic literature with the firm feeling that no definitive prescriptions are possible. Anyone who suggests otherwise is probably reading more into the literature than is there. We proceed as follows. The following section provides a brief summary of the main message of the chapter, introducing some key concepts that will be explored in more detail in later sections. The next section provides two perspectives from which the economic consequences of federalism can be judged. One involves considering the gains that can be achieved by previously separate entities joining in a federation, while the other involves the opposite conceptual exercise of evaluating the gains from decentralization beginning from a unitary nation. Different lessons can be learned from adopting these two perspectives. The fourth and fifth sections consider in more detail the efficiency and equity effects of decentralizing fiscal responsibility in a federation, these being the two main criteria used by economists for evaluating any economic policies or institutions. Section six considers the consequences that these efficiency and equity effects have for the design of fiscal arrangements, including the size and structure of federal-provincial transfers and the various elements of policy harmonization. The final section then provides some comments on the implications that economic considerations might have for some of the current issues facing the Canadian federal fiscal system, especially with respect to the ongoing debate over decentralization. These comments are necessarily speculative and represent but one observer's judgement.

A SUMMARY OF THE MAIN MESSAGE

To put issues into perspective, it is worth briefly summarizing what have been the main preoccupations in the fiscal federalism literature. The analysis focuses largely on two issues. The first is that in an interdependent world in which governments act in the interest of their own residents, decisions taken by one government will inevitably impose spillover effects on residents of other jurisdictions. The second is that in a federation, there are both benefits and costs of decentralizing fiscal responsibilities to lower-level jurisdictions, and there is no unambiguous "optimal" degree of decentralization. Both the fact of fiscal externalities and the desire to achieve the benefits of decentralization have consequences for the role of the federal government as a coordinating institution. Resolving the role of the federal government turns out to be especially contentious when one recognizes that much of what is at stake revolves around the redistribution function that governments perform.

To be more specific, the main message of the literature is as follows. In nations with regionally diverse economies, there are sound economic arguments for decentralizing fiscal responsibilities to the provinces. This is especially true in the case of providing local public goods and public services that must be delivered to households and firms. At the same time, decentralizing the responsibility for raising revenue is not valuable in its own right, but mainly as a way of facilitating responsible fiscal decision-making at the provincial level. Put differently, the case for decentralizing expenditure responsibilities is much stronger than for decentralizing taxation.

The decentralization of fiscal responsibilities entails various spillover costs, what economists refer to as *fiscal externalities*. These fiscal externalities take three main forms. The first are the fiscal inefficiencies and inequities that arise from the fact that decentralization per se creates different fiscal capacities among provinces to provide public services at comparable tax rates. This implies that the net fiscal benefits (NFBs) that given residents obtain from their jurisdiction — the level of benefits received less the level of taxes paid — differs from what they would receive if they resided elsewhere in the federation. These NFB differentials create both fiscal incentives for firms and households to relocate (*fiscal inefficiency*) and horizontal inequities among those who stay put in the sense that otherwise like people are treated differently solely on the basis of their province of residence (*fiscal inequity*).

The second forms of fiscal externalities are the so-called *horizontal fiscal externalities*. These arise on the one hand from tax and expenditure competition, whereby one province's fiscal decisions serve partly to achieve its objectives at the expense of other provinces. For example, tax incentives serve to attract businesses from neighbouring jurisdictions or a reduction in welfare rates induces the poor to move elsewhere. On the other hand, a province may be able to export part of the burden of its fiscal policies to the residents of another jurisdiction. Horizontal fiscal externalities can on balance be positive or negative; that is, they can provide an incentive for provincial governments to set too high or too low a level of taxes and expenditures. Moreover, by interfering with the allocation of resources across the federation, they can be the source of inefficiencies in the internal economic union.

The third forms of fiscal externalities are *vertical fiscal externalities* whereby provincial governments can export part of their tax and expenditure burdens to the federal government. For example, increases in the rate of a tax will have as one of its effects a reduction in the tax base to which the tax applies. If the federal government occupies the same tax base, it will suffer a loss in revenues, which ought to be treated as part of the cost of the tax. Again, there will be an incentive for the provinces to adopt fiscal policies that may be non-optimal from a national point of view.

These disadvantages constitute the *limits to decentralization*. Although the limits are elastic, they do provide the rationale for provisions to offset the adverse consequences of decentralization, such as constitutional limitations on provincial policies or the ability of the federal government to enact policies to correct these fiscal externalities. Indeed, the fiscal arrangements, which encompass the financial relations between the federal and provincial governments, can be viewed as devices for facilitating the benefits of decentralization while reducing their costs. Greater decentralization puts more onus on the fiscal arrangements, and, perhaps paradoxically, more responsibility for managing the federation in the hands of the federal government.

The fiscal arrangements can include many components. In addition to the day-to-day financial relations between the federal and provincial governments and policy coordination agreements for various taxes and expenditure programs, there are the underlying constitutional and political constraints that govern the spheres of action of the various jurisdictions. These might include an overriding set of principles outlining some key functions of the various levels of government — a statement of citizen rights, the basic obligations or objectives of governments to pursue equity, the free flow of persons, capital, goods and services among jurisdictions, etc. Next, there might be a judicious division of legislative responsibilities between levels of government, including especially those for the delivery of important public services, transfers, and social insurance programs. Finally, there might be provisions that serve to resolve conflicts between governments or enable the federal government to facilitate the achievement of national objectives when provincial actions have national consequences. First and foremost might be a provision for the use of the spending power, which to an economist can be an effective instrument for achieving the benefits of decentralization without incurring the costs. But in many jurisdictions, more forceful means of federal oversight are contemplated, such as the ability to impose mandates on lower-level jurisdictions and the power to disallow their legislation. There is always the possibility to resolve interjurisdictional disputes and to achieve common national objectives by voluntary agreements among the provinces with or without the connivance of the federal government. But, while good in theory, voluntary agreements have proven to be elusive in practice because of the well-known problems of securing binding agreements among independent governments. The Canadian constitution is somewhat remarkable in the assignment of responsibilities, in its statements of obligations, and in the way it condones the essential elements of sensible fiscal arrangements.

In the end, there is a trade-off between the perceived benefits of decentralization and its costs, and with the extent of activism that the federal government should engage in to ensure that decentralization does not compromise national objectives. Where one comes down on that trade-off depends on a mixture of judgements and values. Most important is one's attitude toward the role and responsibilities of government in pursuing redistributive equity. Most of the arguments for national oversight rest in the end with the federal government's responsibility for redistributive equity. As well, arguments for decentralization depend in part on one's attitude toward the benevolence of government. Some observers see decentralization as a way of taming a rapacious government, intent on aggrandizing itself and its policy interventions at the expense of the private sector. Finally, arguments for decentralization will be informed by one's judgement about the way the economy works: How mobile are individuals and firms between jurisdictions? How elastic are tax bases? How important are externalities? How tight is the equity-efficiency trade-off? The fact is that there is no scientific answer to the question of the optimal degree of decentralization. Strength of conviction about decentralization undoubtedly reflects some underlying conviction about the role of government in the economy and the extent of benevolence that governments exhibit.

VIEWS OF THE ROLE OF A FEDERATION

Economists view the role of a federation through an economics prism, concentrating largely on the economic consequences of regions participating in a federation, and of the organization of public sector decision-making in a federation. There are two perspectives that one can adopt — the *bottom-up* and the *top-down* — and they emphasize somewhat different aspects of the economic consequences of federalism. The bottom-up approach focuses on the gains that regions obtain by joining a federation and succumbing to some common policy instruments. The latter begins conceptually with a centralized, or unitary, state and asks what is to be gained by decentralization. Lessons for actual federations can be learned from both these approaches.

THE BOTTOM-UP VIEW: THE GAINS FROM FEDERATING

Participating in a federation entails both breaking down borders and extending common citizenship to all members of the broader nation. This yields a number of potential gains.

Access to the Internal Economic Union. To the extent that a border is an economic barrier, the formation of a federation secures freer access to a larger market for goods, services, labour, and capital. As well, since a federation operates under a common currency, the benefits of monetary union are obtained, especially the reduction in uncertainty facing cross-border traders. This leads to gains from trade of the standard sorts.

Many of the benefits of the enlarged common market can be achieved without forming a federation. For example, countries can participate in free trade agreements (NAFTA) or economic unions (EU), and secure many of the advantages of enlarged markets. But, there are two aspects of federations that are difficult to replicate in economic unions of sovereign states. First, in a federation, all persons are citizens of the nation and enjoy the rights to reside and work where they choose. While economic unions might agree to the free mobility of labour among member states, it is undoubtedly the case that this falls short of the rights of citizenship that exist in a federation. We return to the implications of this below.

Second, federations have a consequential federal government with its own independent legislative authority, while economic unions do not. This implies that a level of government exists which can tend to issues of nationwide interest, without having to rely on the agreement of member states. This might be particularly important in a situation in which regions are joined together in an economic union or common market. The free flow of goods, services, labour, and capital is often thought to impose constraints on regions to engage in independent policies; indeed, this is a common argument with respect to the effects of globalization on policies of nations. Within a federation, this need not be a concern. There is a federal government role which is precisely to facilitate the ability of the regions to achieve their objectives in the face of pressure from neighbouring jurisdictions. Moreover, one of the acknowledged roles of the federal government in many federations is to enhance the efficiency of the internal common market by working against pressures that might exist for provinces to impose barriers of the free flow of products, labour, capital, and firms into and out of their jurisdictions.

Common Public Goods and Economies of Scale. Federations are able to provide federation-wide public goods and exploit economies of scale that might exist in the provision of public services or tax-transfer programs. Examples include defence arrangements, systems of justice, banking and monetary arrangements, management of the waterways, and environmental protection. Again, this is something that could potentially be accomplished by common assent by nation-states within an economic union. But it is clear that the unanimous agreement which would be needed to initiate and maintain suitable levels of national contribution to common public goods and to exploit economies of scale is very difficult to come by. A federal government is in a much better position to accomplish such a task.

Risk-Sharing against Regional Shocks. A traditional argument for federating, and one that has been prominent in the European literature, is that participation in a federation provides a form of insurance to regions against adverse macroeconomic shocks. Regions can use capital markets to self-insure to some extent. But, the ability to shed the risk of adverse shocks seems quite limited, perhaps because governments are not far-sighted enough to use debt reliably for such purposes.

There are various ways that federations can provide insurance to their regions against adverse shocks. The fact that regions are part of a common market implies that the adjustment to shocks might be smoother than it would be if they were more self-sufficient: workers who lose their jobs can move to neighbouring regions; capital can flow in relatively quickly, etc. Federal government tax-transfer programs implicitly provide insurance to regions. A common income tax system applies, which means that if incomes fall, so do tax liabilities; and, by the same token, transfers rise. Finally, the system of federal-provincial transfers will typically have a component that insures provinces against shortfalls in their revenues. In Canada, the Equalization program (and previously the Canada Assistance Plan) has that effect.

Citizenship/Equity/Sharing Benefits. Perhaps the most important, as well as the most controversial, consequence of joining a federation is that a region's citizens assume citizenship in a broader nation. What citizenship entails is a matter of judgement. One view of the economic content of citizenship is that at a minimum it carries with it the right to horizontally equitable treatment, that is, the right to be treated equally with others of like circumstances regardless of the province of residence. This is a right that is virtually taken for granted in unitary states, where the central government agenda dominates. It is somewhat more difficult to accomplish in a federation, but serves as one of the prevalent aims of federalism, one that is enshrined in the Canadian constitution.

The importance of the principle of horizontal equity derives from the fact that much of what governments do is redistributive in nature, as we shall repeatedly stress in what follows. Moreover, in a federation, this also applies to provincial levels of government. Extending the principle of equal treatment of equals to a federal setting is not a trivial undertaking, especially in a decentralized federation. It is not a value that will be shared by all, especially in a federation where provinces have systematically differing levels of per capita income and perhaps different community make-ups. Applying the principle of horizontal equity means that not all participating communities will gain: some will persistently be net contributors and some will be net recipients. Moreover, one of the key lessons from the Canadian experience is that decentralization, to which we turn next, makes it more difficult to satisfy the principle of equal treatment of equals.

THE TOP-DOWN VIEW: THE GAINS FROM DECENTRALIZING

The bottom-up view is useful for reminding us of what might be expected from being a member of a federation. The most pressing federalism policies of the day, however, come from adopting the top-down perspective. The issue here is what economic responsibilities to decentralize to lower levels of government. It is in the nature of their discipline that economists favour decentralization of economic decision-making. The analogue with the private sector is compelling. It is an article of faith that decentralization of decisions in the private sector to the lowest level of agents (households and firms) is efficiency-enhancing. Incentives are better, lower-level agents are better informed, and property rights are exercised more responsibly. There has been a tendency to transplant similar arguments to the public sector, and the arguments are almost as compelling, at least from an efficiency perspective. A summary of the economic arguments for decentralization follows.[1]

Catering to Local Preferences and Needs. The classic argument for decentralization is that different communities have different demands for types and levels of public goods and services.[2] These may simply come from personal preferences of the residents themselves, or they may come from more objective factors such as geographical differences (terrain, population density, etc.), demographic differences (age structure of the population), or relative price/ cost differences. The presumption is that central provision will be uniform, so that efficiency could be improved if local communities were allowed to provide their own local public goods and services.

The famous model of Tiebout went one step further and argued that the make-up of communities themselves was endogenous, and that decentralized decision-making would facilitate the formation of optimal mixes of communities.[3] There would be a natural tendency for persons with similar preferences to congregate together, and this would induce local governments acting competitively to provide efficient levels of public goods and services for their residents. While there is a grain of truth in the Tiebout view of federal economies, the literal acceptance of the Tiebout hypothesis has been largely discredited. For one thing, mobility among communities or provinces is nowhere near the magnitude required to generate optimal communities, with the possible exception of intra-city mobility. As well, the Tiebout model was too simplistic and one-dimensional. It turned out to be fairly simply to formulate Tiebout-type models in which either equilibrium did not exist (households would always want to move elsewhere) or if they did, they would be inefficient. Indeed, the existence of zoning laws is evidence that in the context of cities, unfettered mobility of households and firms is not likely to result in acceptable outcomes.

Nonetheless, the main message of the Tiebout model is a powerful one. In the face of heterogeneous communities, decentralized decisionmakers constrained by the need to cater to potentially mobile households and firms will strive to provide the best mix of public goods and services for their residents that they can. Against this must be set three considerations. First, its message is really meant only to apply to public goods and services that serve community residents. Many public programs have benefits that are further flung than that, which implies that spillover effects will occur which will limit the efficiency of decentralized decision-making, an issue we return to below.

Second, catering to local preferences can conflict with the efficiency of the internal economic union. Different communities may have different preferences concerning environmental degradation, product safety, cultural protection, labour standards, and so on. These might lead to policies that interfere with the free flow of products and factors across borders.

Third, profound issues arise with respect to the redistributive dimension of local programs. Different communities may have different preferences for redistribution, not only relative to each other but also relative to the national government. An unavoidable conflict arises as to which level's preferences will prevail. The resolution of this conflict necessarily involves a compromise, perhaps the most important of the many compromises that constitute an interdependent federal system of government. The extent to which federal versus provincial preferences for redistribution prevails depends on how decentralized the federal system is. Roughly speaking, the more decentralization, the more scope there is for federal and provincial redistribution policies to be in conflict. As we shall see, this possibility for conflict over redistribution is a key determinant of the desired extent of decentralization, and is also an important consideration in designing fiscal arrangements for an already decentralized system.

Information Asymmetries. There are some spheres of policy-making in which lower-level jurisdictions may be better informed and therefore better able to provide public services effectively. We have already mentioned the advantage they may have in knowing the preferences and needs of local residents to determine the optimal amounts of public goods and services to provide. As prominent in the literature have been the information issues associated with administering public programs and delivering public services. Such programs are typically delivered by agencies on the ground (public, private, or nonprofit). These agencies are not subject to the profit motive so have to be monitored by the public sector. This gives rise to standard "agency problems" of management and control.[4]

One such problem, analogous to the *adverse selection* in insurance contexts, is that agencies serving different populations may have systematically different costs of delivery.[5] If the bureaucracy does not know these costs precisely, it is not clear how much funding is required to run the agency. For example, what are the costs of running a school in a high-income neighbourhood relative to a deprived one? If that is not known, the result is that resources might be wasted. It is argued that lower-level governments may be better able to monitor the true costs of providing such public services.

Another problem is analogous to *moral hazard.*[6] It may be difficult to monitor the effort that providers of public services are putting out, and it may be difficult to ensure that they are targeting the services to the intended population. Programs like unemployment insurance, disability benefits or welfare are intended for particular groups, and may be contingent on those groups satisfying some conditions (searching for work, taking training, etc.). Again, in the absence of careful monitoring, this is likely to lead to significant waste. Lower-level governments may have an advantage at such monitoring.

Finally, decentralization may itself reduce the administrative costs of delivering services by cutting down the number of layers of bureaucracy. This constitutes a further argument for decentralization.

These information-based arguments are relatively powerful ones in a world where administrative costs are an important part of the costs of delivering some programs. They apply with much more force to public services that are delivered to persons or firms than to large-scale transfer programs or to tax collection, for which there may be significant economies of scale. Indeed, many of the arguments for decentralization have that feature. It is therefore not surprising that in many federations the delivery of public services is much more decentralized than the system of taxes and transfers.

To anticipate a line of argument to be taken up later, these arguments for decentralization are based on efficiency considerations. Many of the important public services that provinces provide have an important equity dimension — examples of health, education, and welfare come immediately to mind. The federal government may therefore have an interest in how well and at what level the services are delivered. If decentralization were unaccompanied by other measures, independent-acting provincial governments might well design their programs in ways that do not satisfy national norms of equity. One role of the fiscal arrangements is to address this issue.

Innovation and Cost-Effectiveness in Public Programs. Decentralization may lead to improvements in program design and program delivery because of the opportunities and constraints faced by lower-level decisionmakers. Because there are many provinces, perhaps in competition with one another, there are more opportunities for innovations in program design and delivery to occur. And, once improvements do occur, other jurisdictions can imitate them.

The existence of neighbouring jurisdictions can itself have a salutary effect on service delivery. Yardsticks for delivery costs will become available which will serve to discipline a given jurisdiction. And such mobility as there is will induce lower-level jurisdictions to deliver their services in a cost-effective way. Of course, such competition may have its downside as well, an issue to which we return in the next section.

Political Economy Arguments. Public choice economists are prone to use market analogies to judge public sector outcomes. They see political competition induced by decentralization to be a force for greater efficiency.[7] The arguments are not always fully articulated in an economic model and they are sometimes difficult to substantiate, but they have some intuitive plausibility. A common notion of political competition is based on the Tiebout-type presumption that households and firms, especially desirable ones, are mobile across jurisdictions. This constrains competing governments from excessively high tax rates or public service levels. Of course, this argument can cut both ways. Given that it might be the better-off households that are the most mobile, competitively reduced levels of public programs may make it more difficult to achieve redistribution objectives. This is why decentralization is often identified with those who wish to constrain government's ability to redistribute.

An extreme form of this argument is based on the notion that governments are essentially self-serving Leviathans intent on aggrandizing themselves at the public's expense. In the well-known version of Brennan and Buchanan, governments maximize their size.[8] Decentralization can serve to tame the Leviathan by constraining the ability of the government from extracting resources from an unwitting electorate.[9] This argument, too, relies on interjurisdictional mobility as the source of the constraint: firms and households can exercise their exit option.

Political economy arguments also come in other forms. A common argument is that lower-level governments are more "accountable" because they are "closer to the electorate." Political accountability might be enhanced by decentralization because it is possible to identify given public programs with given levels of government, and given tax dollars with given expenditures. But, the accountability argument is a not a clear-cut one. There is no compelling evidence that lower levels of government are more accountable to their electorates. In fact, given that the glare of media publicity is typically directed at the central government, one could argue just the opposite. Moreover, one could also argue that the lines of responsibility get blurred rather than clarified as one decentralizes responsibilities.

A final political economy consideration concerns the effect of decentralization on anti-social political behaviour — rent-seeking, influence peddling or outright corruption. It is argued that decentralization reduces the possibilities for such behaviour, perhaps by reducing the size of the rewards for engaging in it.[10]

Decentralization as an Antidote to Time Inconsistency. In the economics literature, a major source of inefficient government decision-making arises because
of the so-called *time-inconsistency problem*, which typically leads to excessive government taxation and spending. Unlike with many public choice
explanations for excessive government, this one applies even if governments
are fully benevolent. It arises essentially because of the inability of governments to be able to abide by long-term commitments. If a government
announces a policy that has long-run effects, it will presumably want to take
account of all the long-run consequences of it, especially the effect it has on
the long-run decisions of its residents. However, once time has passed, and
firms or households have committed themselves to long-run decisions and
cannot undo them, the government will have an incentive to renege on its
previously announced policy. For example, taxes on capital will discourage
investment and governments would prefer not to implement them at high levels.
However, once investment is in place, it is to some extent irreversible. The
government has an incentive to levy high tax rates on it. This kind of argument has been used to explain high tax rates on capital and wealth, as well as
the tendency of governments to accumulate debt and run down the funds of
public pensions, and to bail out declining or inefficient industries. Decentralization and the resultant political competition it induces can serve as an antidote
to these tendencies.

EFFICIENCY EFFECTS OF DECENTRALIZATION

The arguments for decentralization are compelling from the point of view of
enhancing the ability of provincial jurisdictions to meet the needs and desires
of their constituents as effectively as possible. But decentralization has its
adverse consequences. As the literature continually emphasizes, the benefits
of decentralization can only be acquired by inducing some *potential* sacrifices in efficiency and equity. Whether those sacrifices are realized depends
critically on the complementary measures that accompany decentralization.
This section and the next one outline the various consequences that decentralization by itself might have for efficiency and equity in the federal economy,
respectively. This will provide the foundations for considering how the fiscal
arrangements might be structured to facilitate the achievement of the benefits
of decentralization while avoiding adverse effects on efficiency and equity.

There are broadly speaking three main sources of inefficiency: *fiscal inefficiency* arising from the financial consequences of decentralization, *horizontal
fiscal externalities* arising from the interaction between provinces, and *vertical fiscal externalities* arising from the interaction between the federal
government and the provinces. We consider each in turn.

FISCAL INEFFICIENCY

In a federation consisting of heterogeneous regions or provinces, fiscal decentralization is likely to lead to fiscal disparities. Different provinces will have different capacities to finance the provision of public services. And different provinces will have different needs to provide public services because of different demographic compositions of the population, different illness rates, and so on. As has been long-recognized, a consequence of this is likely to be that otherwise identical persons residing in two different provinces will receive different *net fiscal benefits* — roughly speaking the value of public services provided to them less the tax price they pay — from their provincial government.[11] A simple example commonly found in the literature supposes that provinces all tax the incomes of their residents at the same proportional tax rate and use the proceeds to provide public services of equal per capita value. In this case, the NFB differential between any two provinces is just the difference in per capita tax revenues, here the tax rate times the difference in average incomes. As Dan Usher has put it, the pool of provincial income is like a common property resource that residents of a province have access to for financing public services.[12] The problem is a unique consequence of decentralization because in a unitary nation the presumption is that all residents of the country have access to the national income pool for tax purposes.

The consequence of NFB differentials is that they provide a fiscal incentive for households and firms to locate in provinces with higher NFBs. Resources may not therefore be allocated according to their most productive uses. The problem can be circumvented if the NFB differences can be neutralized by the fiscal arrangements. As we shall see, this is one of the arguments for equalization grants, though not the most compelling one.

Differences in NFBs can come from various sources. Differences in residents' per capita incomes across provinces are an important one. Differences in source-based tax capacity — that is, business revenues that are taxed at source regardless of ownership, such as resource rents and corporate income — are a source of NFB differentials which can be particularly unequally distributed. On the expenditure side, differences in need are important for determining provincial requirements to finance important public services like education, health, and welfare. Similarly, there will be differences in need for making transfer payments to the less well-off members of society. The relevance of these sources of NFBs depends, of course, on the sorts of responsibilities decentralized to the provinces. Some important types of expenditures that would otherwise lead to differences in need may not be decentralized, such as unemployment insurance. The same might be said for the tax system. In some federations, major sources of resource rents may not be available to the provinces as a source of revenues. Indeed, in some federations there is relatively little tax decentralization to match expenditures (e.g., Australia, South Africa). In these cases, almost all NFB differentials arise from expenditure needs.

In attributing fiscal inefficiency to decentralization, a number of caveats must be kept in mind.

Benefit Taxation. NFB differentials only arise to the extent that persons of a given type do not get benefits commensurate with the taxes they have paid. If all provincial public expenditures were financed by benefit taxation, there would be no NFBs and no fiscal inefficiency from decentralization. But most observers presume that provincial government budgets, like their federal counterparts, are redistributive in nature. That being said, there may be some programs that are financed roughly according to the benefit principle. For example, funded social insurance programs, like workers' compensation might be of that sort. Or, activities financed by user fees or licences, such as fishing, driving an automobile, etc. are close to the benefit principle. No corrective action would be required on account of these.

Costs versus Needs. Differences in provincial expenditure requirements to serve persons with different needs are a legitimate source of inefficiency. Differences in the costs of providing public services are not. It may well be inequitable that some persons face higher prices for public services as a result of costs of provision being higher in their province of residence. But if it costs more to provide public services in a region, efficiency in the allocation of resources would require that that not be neutralized.

Capitalization Effects. NFB differentials may to some extent be reflected in local property values. If so, their effects on relocation will be offset. Regions with higher NFBs would have correspondingly higher land costs, so there would be no fiscal incentive to move. In effect, for this to happen, all future NFBs must be capitalized into land values implying that their entire benefit went to the landowners sometime in the past. It is unlikely that full capitalization occurs. That would require perfect foresight concerning future government policies, which is hard to imagine. Moreover, it should do no harm to correct for NFB differentials since to the extent that the capitalization hypothesis does apply, the correction will simply be absorbed into further capitalization.

Empirical Significance. Quite apart from the capitalization effect possibly rendering NFB differentials ineffective, the empirical significance of fiscally induced relocation may be limited. Migration may simply be very unresponsive to differences in NFBs. Empirical studies have tended to indicate that the effect is limited, though they have usually concentrated on labour migration.[13] It is conceivable that relocation of entrepreneurs, firms, and skilled persons might be more responsive to NFBs than the average worker. As with the capitalization hypothesis, the finding of limited fiscally induced migration turns out not to be a devastating blow to the case for undoing NFB differentials. As we shall see in the next section, to the extent that efficiency arguments do not apply, equity ones do. It is one of the relatively few instances in economic policy that efficiency and equity arguments are self-reinforcing.

Equalizing NFBs versus Equalizing Incomes. It is worth cautioning at this point about a source of considerable confusion in the literature on the relevance of NFB differentials, a confusion that has been perpetrated, especially in the literature on equalization. The argument for equalizing NFB differentials, whether on efficiency or equity grounds, is not based on vertical equity considerations. That is the job of the interpersonal redistribution system. Equalization is intended solely to facilitate the process of decentralization by ensuring that all provincial governments have the capacity to deliver required public services at comparable tax rates. The implication is that the success of equalization should not be judged according to how well it redistributes from the better-off to the less well-off.[14] This is obviously most relevant when equity arguments are at stake, as in the next section.

HORIZONTAL FISCAL EXTERNALITIES

A federation is, among other things, an economic union in which markets are not constrained by borders. This means that the actions of provinces will have effects that go beyond their jurisdictions, and will have effects on the residents of neighbouring provinces. Since a provincial government is answerable only to its own constituents, these spillover effects will not be taken into account in provincial decision-making leading to inefficient resource allocations across provinces and inefficient levels of taxes and public services within each jurisdiction. These effects are referred to as horizontal fiscal externalities, the analogy standard market externalities being apparent.

There is an enormous literature on the consequences of horizontal fiscal externalities arising from the main provincial policy instruments and applying in all three major markets: capital, labour, and product.[15] We can summarize only the main themes in the literature.

Tax Externalities. Tax externalities arise because tax bases are mobile across borders. Taxes levied in one province can spill over into others in a variety of ways, and this can have positive or negative effects on other provinces. Economists find it useful to summarize the effects of tax externalities using the concept of the *marginal cost of public funds* (MCPF).[16] The MCPF is a measure of the cost to the economy of extracting a marginal dollar of tax revenues. The idea is that an additional dollar of resources transferred by taxation from the private to the public sector has a true cost of more than a dollar. The true cost includes not only the dollar's worth of resources transferred, but also the increment in the deadweight loss due to the tax distortion. The latter arises because a tax levied on, say, consumption drives a wedge between the consumer and producer prices of consumer goods preventing the economy from operating efficiently. At the margin, additional consumption forgone has a value to consumers in excess of the productive resources saved. Thus, excess value is the marginal deadweight loss associated with a reduction in consumption induced by higher taxes.[17] This marginal deadweight loss can increase dramatically as the tax rate rises. For our purposes, it is useful to write the marginal cost of raising an increment of tax revenues as follows MCPF = $-\Delta W/\Delta R$, where ΔW is the change in welfare and R is the change in tax revenues from a given tax rate change.

Positive tax externalities arise from *tax competition* effects. An increase in the tax rate on a tax base that is mobile across provinces causes the province to overestimate the true MCPF. In the above expression for the MCPF, the term ΔR (positive for an increase in taxes) is underestimated since part of the tax base flees to other jurisdictions yielding an increase in their revenues. This tends to make the tax rate too low from an efficiency point of view. The tax competition effect is obviously more important the more mobile the tax base in question. Thus, capital and capital income taxes are more prone to tax competition than taxes on labour income, which is far less mobile. The latter includes both payroll taxes and general consumption taxes, both of which are essentially taxes on the supply of labour. Specific excise taxes also have relatively mild tax competition effects. In this case, the mobility of the base involves cross-border shopping. The least mobile tax bases are those whose location is fixed, such as real property or natural resources, although capital used in conjunction with these fixed factors will itself be mobile.

One important type of positive tax externality occurs in the context of specific projects when provinces engage in *strategic tax competition* or *beggar-thy-neighbour policies* to attract businesses. This involves the use of tax incentives or subsidies to individual firms. The trouble with beggar-thy-neighbour policies is that all provinces are likely to treat similar types of firms as being desirable, and therefore are likely to provide competing tax incentives for them. In the end, no one province will succeed in providing a more favourable tax environment, so the allocation of firms across provinces is not likely to be affected much. Instead, the firms receive favourable tax treatment no matter where they reside, which is a self-defeating outcome from the provinces' point of view.

Negative tax externalities arise from *tax exporting*, whereby part of the burden of a tax is borne by non-residents. This can occur when taxes are imposed on incomes generated in a province that accrue to non-residents. Thus, business income taxes, taxes on natural resources and withholding taxes on capital income may partly be exported. As well, taxes levied on products that are purchased by non-residents can be exported. In terms of the formula, the magnitude of ΔW and therefore the MCPF are underestimated, so there is an incentive to set tax rates too high. However, tax exporting can be severely limited by adjustments in relative prices. An attempt to tax non-residents on their capital income earned in a province will be at least partly offset by the capital fleeing. Similarly, an attempt to capture tax revenue from the sale of products to non-residents will be frustrated by a reduction in demand. In a small open economy that is a price-taker on outside markets, tax exporting cannot occur. It may well be that the provinces are in such a position.[18]

The existence of horizontal fiscal externalities is undoubtedly a fact of life, although their magnitude may be disputed. Options for the federation to deal with them are limited. They have implications for the assignment of taxes. It is widely accepted that, on efficiency grounds, taxes on mobile bases should be assigned primarily to the federal government and those on less mobile ones assigned to the provinces. Thus, taxes on capital income, capital, and businesses would be mainly federal, while provinces (and their municipalities) could access taxes on consumption, labour income, natural resources, and real property. Of course, assignment based on efficiency may well conflict with that based on equity or administrative considerations.

Some of the consequences of tax externalities can in principle be addressed by cooperation among the provinces. Tax bases and tax rates could be harmonized by agreement, as could codes of conduct to preclude beggar-thy-neighbour policies. But binding cooperative agreements are difficult to achieve, and are rarely effective in practice. They require not only unanimous agreement, but also a dispute settlement mechanism that binds future legislative decisions, something that seems to be difficult to achieve in a decentralized setting.

Alternatively, fiscal arrangements between the federal government and the provinces could address some effects of tax competition. Tax competition will be less, the smaller the tax room occupied by the provinces. This is an argument for a vertical fiscal gap. The federal government may be instrumental in encouraging the provinces to harmonize their taxes on mobile tax bases, possibly by arrangements akin to the Tax Collection Agreements. Some authors[19] have suggested that the federal government could use matching grants based on provincial tax effort to induce provinces to internalize the tax externalities, though they have not been used. They would involve grants to the provinces which are some proportion of revenues that the provinces themselves raise, with the purpose being to offset the disincentive that provinces have to levy taxes on bases that are mobile (e.g., capital taxes, inheritance taxes, cigarette taxes). Ideally, the proportions would have to vary by type of tax. But, since the sizes of the externalities arising from tax competition are difficult to ascertain, such corrective grants are impractical. The grant formula may, however, contain elements that offset tax externalities. For example, the Canadian Equalization system effectively sanitizes tax competition effects for the have-not provinces by compensating them for any losses in their tax bases.[20] But, that probably goes too far, for tax-base losses from any source are sanitized, not just those from tax competition. The result is that the MCPF perceived by the have-not provinces could be effectively unity.

Expenditure Externalities. The effects of provincial expenditure programs may spill over into other provinces as well. Expenditures on roads may benefit travelers from neighbouring provinces, higher education and health facilities may be used by non-residents, education and training may be provided to workers who change provinces of residence, transfers to low-income persons may attract them from other provinces, and so on. These interjurisdictional spillovers result in the classic argument for matching grants in a federation as a way of inducing provinces to take account of the benefits they impose on other jurisdictions. It is an argument that is undoubtedly overstated, given the relative unimportance of these spillover effects and the fact that they cannot be measured in any case. Matching grants have gone out of fashion.

A more important type of expenditure externality involves the strategic use of beggar-thy-neighbour policies. Provinces may attempt to attract businesses using infrastructure investments or outright subsidies. Procurement and local hiring policies may discriminate against non-residents. Residency restrictions may be put on access to provincial public services such as welfare, education, and health care. Such measures will distort the internal economic union if they are effective. But if all provinces engage in them, they are likely to be self-defeating and ineffective. Preventing them involves the same considerations as in the case of tax incentives. It is hard to see how such measures can be effective without the participation of the federal government.

Regulation Externalities. Virtually identical arguments apply in the case where provinces impose regulations that affect non-residents. Regulations can apply on all three major markets. Capital market regulations may restrict the free flow of capital among jurisdictions, for example, by favouring locally owned capital. Similarly, labour market regulation may preclude non-residents from taking employment in a province. Different curricula across provincial educational and training programs may make it difficult to pursue further education in another province. Different environmental or health and safety regulations may impose different costs on businesses across provinces. Regulation to foster local customs, culture, and language will typically favour residents. In all these cases, there is inefficiency induced in the internal economic union by the relevant regulation. While some of the regulations may reflect legitimate social policy objectives, others constitute outright protection. Avoiding it therefore involves not only appropriate forms of cooperative agreement with or without the connivance of the federal government, but also some judgement as to which sorts of discriminatory regulation are justified by social arguments.

VERTICAL FISCAL EXTERNALITIES

The third source of inefficiency arising from decentralized decision-making in a federation is one that has been prominent in the literature only recently. It involves externalities between upper and lower levels of government. The idea is that budgetary actions taken by, say, the provincial government affects not only its budget but also that of the federal government. Consider changes in a province's tax rate on a base that is co-occupied by the federal government, such as labour income. While this will raise more revenue,[21] it will also cause the tax base to shrink. Since the federal government occupies the same tax base, it will find its revenues shrinking as well. The province neglects to take account of this, implying that the MCPF it perceives is less than the true MCPF. To see this, recall the expression MCPF = $-\Delta W/\Delta R$. The province overestimates the full change in revenue ΔR from a tax change since it neglects the fall in revenue to the federal government. This same effect applies even if the provinces and the federal government do not occupy precisely the same tax bases. All major tax bases overlap to some extent, so changes in, say, provincial payroll taxes are likely to affect not only federal payroll tax bases, but also federal income and consumption tax bases.

This tendency to underestimate the MCPF because of vertical fiscal externalities has a number of implications. It gives the provinces an incentive to raise too much revenue since it underestimates the cost of doing so. It especially encourages the provinces to levy excessive taxes on bases that bear a high federal tax rate. On the other hand, to the extent that tax bases are mobile among jurisdictions, the vertical fiscal externality offsets the tax competition effect that tends to make provinces overestimate their MCPF. As with the MCPF itself, there is some uncertainty about the magnitude of the vertical fiscal externality, though given the size of federal tax rates in Canada and the fact that the provinces occupy the major tax bases, the expectation is that it can be reasonably large. There is certainly strong evidence that vertical tax interaction effects exist. Besley and Rosen found for the United States that increases in the federal excise tax on both cigarettes and alcohol caused states to increase their excise taxes significantly, indicating *prima facie* evidence of a vertical fiscal interaction.[22] Hayashi and Boadway studied the interaction between the federal and provincial governments in the setting of business income taxes.[23] They also found that changes in the federal tax rate significantly affected provincial rates, but the sign was negative in this case. Of course, unlike with cigarettes and alcohol, capital is highly mobile across provincial borders so that vertical and horizontal externalities both apply. Evidence that vertical interaction effects exist.

In principle, the same kind of vertical externality also applies in the opposite direction: changes in the federal tax rate will cause a loss in revenues to the provinces because their bases shrink. But there is good reason to believe that this will not induce the federal government to behave inefficiently. It is sensible to suppose that the federal government acts as a first-mover or leader with respect to the provinces' policies.[24] If so, it will anticipate the effects of its tax policies on provincial behaviour in setting its tax rates. (The provinces acting as followers take federal tax rates as given.) The federal government will therefore choose its tax rates to minimize the consequences of vertical fiscal externalities of the provinces. In very simple settings, this can involve the federal government levying only lump-sum taxes and turning over the responsibility for redistribution to the provinces.[25] But more generally, little can be done to avoid vertical fiscal externalities. As long as the federal government is imposing taxes, such externalities will exist. Perhaps sophisticated formulas for grants can be designed that penalize provincial tax effort by enough to offset vertical externalities. But as of now that approach is probably impractical as well as being politically difficult to achieve.

These vertical externalities can in principle also arise on the expenditure side, though less directly.[26] For example, an increase in labour training at the provincial level can increase the income tax base and generate tax revenue for the federal government. This form of externality would provide an incentive for provinces to provide too little of the expenditure relative to the efficient level. As with interjurisdictional spillovers, this could potentially be corrected using matching grants.

The literature has also dwelled on the possibility of the provinces' being first-movers in the policy interaction with the federal government. In this case, a province's policies are conditioned by how it expects the federal government will subsequently react. This, it turns out, leads to some rather unexpected results, results that arise because of the ability of the provinces to exploit the future behaviour of the federal government. One result is an application of the so-called Samaritan's Dilemma.[27] Suppose the federal government operates an equalization system that transfers to provinces according to some measure of their residents' well-being — average income, tax capacity, etc. To the extent that provincial policies can influence such measures at some cost, they will have an incentive not to make themselves better off, anticipating the transfers that the federal government will make to them. The real-world relevance of the Samaritan's Dilemma is obvious. Another result is in a sense the opposite, and is an application of what is known as the Rotten Kid Theorem. If provincial governments enact some expenditure programs that have benefits nationwide, left to their own devices they will tend to provide too low a level of the programs since they are costly to provide. But if the federal government tends to equalize after-tax incomes, provinces will have an incentive to contribute efficiently to such programs because the marginal cost of an increased contribution will, to some extent, be covered by the expected transfer.[28]

OTHER SOURCES OF INEFFICIENCY IN FEDERATIONS

There are other reasons why resources may be allocated inefficiently in a federation, and these are just coming to be studied by fiscal federalism scholars. The process of regional development might itself be characterized by externalities that render market solutions inefficient. This is something that geographers have long studied, but it has been slow to penetrate fiscal federalism theory, which tends to be based on conventional economic modeling. One argument is that there are economies of agglomeration, which enhance the efficiency of labour and capital markets as they become more concentrated. Information exchange is improved and there is more opportunity for matching skills to jobs the larger are regional labour markets. These agglomeration benefits are unlikely to be taken account of by those persons or firms choosing their locations. The result is that resources may not be allocated efficiently across regions. In fact, there might be multiple possible optima, depending on which locations grow to be large. In practice, history determines which regions will grow and which will not.

Not only will the allocation of resources be inefficient in this context, but also government policies may themselves be detrimental to an efficient agglomeration of regions or urban areas. For example, equalizing grants may serve to perpetuate a dispersed population, resulting in a version of the so-called dependency hypothesis, albeit one that is based on different reasoning than in the fiscal federalism literature. Although this is a possible problem, there is simply not the knowledge available to know how to deal with it.

Related to the agglomeration issue is the burgeoning field of endogenous growth theory, which also has regional implications. Endogenous growth theory posits that the growth of a given economy is determined partly by factors that are both endogenous to the economy in question but external to the decision-makers in the economy. Thus, human capital investment and R&D contribute to productivity growth, but those undertaking them do not appropriate the rewards from these activities, so that too little is undertaken. For example, persons with high skills pass some of the knowledge and techniques associated with the skills on to other workers in the same local labour market. An implication is that the in-migration of highly skilled workers will provide external benefits to existing workers, benefits that are not accounted for when location is decided. The result is that resources could be inefficiently allocated within a federation, and regional growth rates are not as high as they could be.

Again, the literature has not developed to the extent that policy prescriptions can be proposed on the basis of the models. But the possibility of these agglomeration and regional interaction effects being important cautions one not to be too doctrinaire in adopting policies for a federation.

EQUITY EFFECTS OF DECENTRALIZATION

The more important, or at least controversial, consequences of decentralization are its implications for equity. They are controversial because as we have emphasized, much of what governments do revolves around equity, which itself is a value-laden concept. Fortunately, we do not really have to take a stand on the larger question of how redistributive government policy should be. Much of the literature on fiscal federalism applies whatever judgement is made in that regard. Federations are decentralized largely for efficiency reasons. The literature is more concerned with how a decentralized federation can deliver whatever degree of redistributive equity governments desire. The main conflict is probably between the federal and provincial governments, which may take rather different views about redistribution.

The one substantive judgement that must be made involves the principle of *horizontal equity* — the principle that the fiscal system should treat those in equal circumstances equally. In the context of a federation, horizontal equity would suggest that persons should be treated comparably no matter where they reside. In a decentralized federation where provinces exercise their responsibilities independently, horizontal equity cannot be satisfied as long as different governments want to behave differently. To force them to treat all households of a given kind identically across jurisdictions would involve essentially abrogating their independence and would contradict the principal purpose of a federal system of government. Thus, inevitably horizontal equity must be compromised. We take the view that a reasonable way to compromise horizontal equity is to ensure that all provinces have the resources to implement policies that are horizontally equitable, though they may not choose to do so. This seems a reasonable compromise between the social value of horizontal equity and the spirit of federalism.

The ways in which decentralization impinges upon equity is parallel to the efficiency case.

FISCAL EQUITY

Fiscal equity is simply the version of horizontal equity outlined above: the potential of all provinces to treat identical persons identically. Accepting horizontal equity in a federation is equivalent to assuming that all persons count equally in the nation's "social welfare function," something that citizenship could be viewed as conferring on all members of society. In what follows, we shall accept fiscal equity as a social objective. Others may well disagree.

Fiscal decentralization leads to fiscal inequity simply because it gives rise to different abilities of provinces to provide public services for their residents at given tax rates. Thus, in the absence of corrective action, NFB differentials are likely to occur. Just as NFB differentials led to fiscal inefficiency, so they lead to fiscal inequity. But there is one important difference. NFB differentials cause fiscal inefficiency only to the extent that they induce migration. They cause fiscal inequity only to the extent that migration does not occur. If there were costless migration, otherwise equal persons could not end up being unequally well-off; they could migrate so that they are equally well-off in all jurisdictions. Thus, the principles of efficiency and equity are not in conflict, as is usually the case. Instead they are self-reinforcing.

We have already discussed the sources of NFB differentials when considering their consequences for fiscal inefficiency. The same sources apply here. As well, the same remedy for fiscal inequity applies — undo the NFB differentials through a system of equalizing transfers. As discussed in the next section, equalization transfers is a major component of a system of fiscal arrangements that respect the principle of fiscal equity.

One way to view fiscal inequity is through the fictitious device of the unitary state. In a unitary state, governments are presumed to provide common public services to all citizens and to finance them with a common tax schedule. This ensures the equal treatment of equals. If the unitary state then becomes federated and fiscal responsibilities decentralized, fiscal inequity would fail (unless migration were perfect). Provinces with more tax capacity and less need would be able to provide a given level of public services at lower tax rates than those with less tax capacity and more need. If a system of equalization transfers were implemented to offset the NFB differentials, all provinces would have sufficient resources such that they could implement the unitary state outcome if they so choose. Of course, they may choose not to, but in any case we shall say that fiscal equity prevails.

HORIZONTAL FISCAL INTERACTION

Just as horizontal interaction gives rise to fiscal externalities (tax and expenditure competition, tax exporting, beggar-thy-neighbour policies), so too it gives rise to adverse consequences for equity. At a general level, mobility of households and firms can cause provinces to compete away some redistribution: less redistribution attracts higher income persons and repels lower income ones.

How important this is in practice is an open question. If mobility is restricted, it may not be quantitatively important. As well, to the extent that equalization compensates for losses in tax base, provinces should not be too concerned with redistribution-induced migration. There is some evidence that provinces respond to competitive incentives in choosing their redistribution policies. In the Canadian case, inheritance taxes were quickly competed away when they were turned over to the provinces. And, provincial welfare programs responded when the federal government imposed a cap on transfers to the high-income provinces.[29]

VERTICAL FISCAL INTERACTION

Vertical fiscal externalities have similar consequences for redistribution as they do for efficiency. Part of the deadweight loss of provinces raising taxes to finance transfers to lower income persons is effectively borne by the federal government. That is, an increase in taxes by a province shrinks both its own tax base and that of the federal government, so the cost of that shrinkage in terms of lost revenues is partly borne by the federal government. As a consequence, there is an incentive on this account for provincial tax rates and the expenditures they finance, including transfers to the poor, to be too high, an incentive first noted by Johnson.[30] This is an interesting innovation in the literature since it casts doubt on the standard argument that decentralization is unambiguously bad for redistribution. But, as in the case of efficiency, vertical and horizontal fiscal externalities have contradictory effects.

It is not at all obvious what the policy implications are. The harmonization of the rate structure in the income tax system, as in the Canadian case, is a way of ensuring that national standards of redistributive equity apply, albeit ones that are chosen by the federal government. But in the absence of that it is not clear how policies could be designed that avoid the effect of fiscal externalities, both horizontal and vertical, on provincial redistribution policies.

TOO MUCH OR TOO LITTLE REDISTRIBUTION?

We are apparently left with the finding that it is not clear *a priori* whether decentralization will provide an incentive for too much or too little redistribution. Vertical externalities reduce the perceived costs of redistribution to the provinces; horizontal externalities increase the costs. In principle, either one could dominate. The more mobile people are across jurisdictions, the more important will be the tax competition effects, which tend to inhibit redistribution. Vertical externalities are more important the more elastic the tax bases within the province and the higher the federal tax rates on co-occupied tax bases.

An implication of this analysis is that the case against decentralizing redistribution functions to the province is much weaker than has traditionally been assumed.[31] Provided the provinces have comparable fiscal capacities, there is no strong argument against relying on them to undertake redistribution. Indeed, as we have seen, they may well be relatively more efficient than the federal government at implementing redistribution through the provision of public services, leaving the federal government to pursue vertical equity through the tax-transfer system.

THE FISCAL ARRANGEMENTS

The fiscal arrangements, encompassing the fiscal relationship between the federal government and the provinces, are a critical element of a decentralized federation. The preceding sections have stressed the benefits of decentralization, but also the fact that decentralization by itself can cause various inefficiencies and inequities in the internal economic union. The fiscal arrangements can facilitate decentralization by offsetting some of these inefficiencies and inequities, a task that becomes increasingly important the more decentralization there is. The fiscal arrangements include both the system of fiscal transfers between the federal government and the provinces as well as policy coordination or harmonization measures. The existence of federal-provincial transfers presumes a mismatch between revenue-raising and expenditure responsibilities at the two main levels of government, or a *vertical fiscal imbalance* (also called a fiscal gap). We begin with a brief discussion of that before turning to the components of the fiscal arrangements.

VERTICAL FISCAL IMBALANCE (VFI)

A feature of almost all federations is that the federal level of government raises more revenue than it needs and transfers the excess to the provinces.[32] But the extent of VFI varies widely across countries, being very large in Australia and Germany, but much smaller in Canada and the United States. There is no established theory to serve as a guide to choosing the right level of VFI. Only recently has fiscal federalism even attempted to analyze the optimal degree of VFI.[33] In general terms, there seems to be two main reasons for a VFI.

The first argument for a VFI is that the case for decentralizing expenditures to the provinces is much greater than that for decentralizing taxes. Provinces might be more efficient at delivering public services to individuals and firms. Major public services in areas like health, education, and welfare constitute a substantial component of public sector budgets, and in many federations are highly decentralized. On the other hand, there are strong arguments for not decentralizing taxes to as great an extent. Taxes can readily be administered at the centre, where a common tax system can apply with the benefits of a single collection agency. Distortions in the internal economic union due to a fragmented tax system can be avoided by centralized collection, and a uniform standard of redistribution can be applied. Some of the benefits of a single tax system can be achieved by tax harmonization agreements, but those too can be more readily maintained if the federal government maintains a dominant share of the tax room. The exact size of the VFI based on these arguments remains a matter of judgement. Too much VFI is argued to reduce the accountability of the provinces since they are not responsible for raising the revenues that they are spending.

The second argument for a VFI is that the federal government needs to make transfers to the provinces in order to fulfil its responsibility for achieving efficiency and equity in the internal economic union. To assess this argument, we turn to the role of federal-provincial transfers in a decentralized federation.

FEDERAL-PROVINCIAL TRANSFERS

Federal-provincial transfers exist not only to "close the fiscal gap," but have important objectives in their own right. Three main forms of transfers, each with its own role, can be distinguished — equalization, matching, and conditional. Consider each in turn.

Equalization. There is a worldwide interest in equalization, and an enormous literature to draw on, much of it emanating from Canada.[34] But the issues are general and apply in all federations. Equalization transfers exist primarily to offset the NFB differentials that occur in a decentralized federation and cause fiscal inequity and/or fiscal inefficiency. As we have seen, these differentials can arise due to differences in tax capacity at the provincial level as well as differences in the need for public expenditures. The design of an equalization system to deal with these things faces both measurement problems and incentive problems. Measuring tax capacity and need is not straightforward, especially in a heterogeneous federation where provinces adopt different policies. If provincial tax bases are reasonably uniform, the representative tax system approach works well. But as provincial tax bases become more diverse, which is more likely to happen the more decentralized is the federation, the definition of standard tax bases becomes further removed from tax bases actually used. And need is even more difficult to measure, especially for public service. For transfers, the representative tax system approach could in principle be used, with need being incorporated into the standard base for the transfers. As provinces become more diverse, for example, because of greater degrees of decentralization, the representative tax or expenditure approach becomes less accurate, and cruder approximations might be used. These might take the form of simple macro indicators, such as per capita income.

The extent of equalization should in principle be 100 percent, though in practice it rarely is. The payments may only apply to those provinces with below-average NFBs per capita. Or some elements of tax capacity might be less than fully equalized, such as natural resource revenues. This may be because they are too costly for the federal government to equalize, or because provinces are deemed to have independent property rights to the resources.[35] Some authors have even argued that the federal government need not get involved with equalization at all. The have provinces would voluntarily make equalization payments to the have-nots as a way of internalizing the fiscal inefficiencies from NFB differentials.[36] But this argument, which is an analogue of the famous Coase theorem, really applies only in very special circumstances, including where individuals in each jurisdiction are all identical.

Incentive effects are also an important consideration in designing an equalization system. Ideally, equalization payments should depend on some objective indicator of the ability to provide public services at given tax rates, but it is practically impossible to design suitable indicators which abstract completely from provincial behaviour. In the representative tax-system approach, there may be incentives for provinces to change either their tax rates or their tax bases in order to exploit the equalization system. The former case can arise if one province makes up a significant portion of a given tax base. Much more relevant is the fact that the representative tax approach roughly equalizes on the basis of provincial tax bases. If provinces can influence the size of their tax bases, they will be discouraged from increasing them because of the loss in equalization they will suffer. This can be a potent deterrent to resource development, and another reason for not equalizing resource rents fully. It can also cause provinces to misperceive the MCPF of raising revenues from various sources. Recall that the MCPF exceeds one essentially because tax bases shrink when taxes are increased. If the tax-revenue consequences of the shrink in a tax base are undone by equalization payments, provinces will have an incentive to over-tax. This may help explain why provinces levy sizable taxes on capital income despite the fact that these are presumably mobile tax bases.

Finally, a secondary function of equalization is to serve as a device by which risk-sharing can take place among provinces. If provinces are subject to idiosyncratic shocks, an equalization system that transfers to them when their incomes fall and vice versa will act as an insurance device. This has been the focus of some recent literature, which has also emphasized the incentive problems with this form of insurance.[37]

Matching Grants. Matching grants are the traditional device for the federal government to use to correct for interjurisdictional spillovers. They were quite important in the development of social programs in Canada as well as in some shared-cost projects in transportation and agriculture, but have now gone out of fashion. The basic argument for matching grants is quite seductive. If provincial programs cause spillover benefits to other provinces, they will have no incentive to take account of those benefits when deciding levels of public expenditure. The spillover benefits can, however, be internalized by a properly chosen matching grant formula, where the rate of matching reflects the share of spillover benefits in the total benefits of the project. Similar arguments could apply to the correction of misperceived MCPFs due to tax competition, but matching grants based on revenue sources or tax effort have not been common.[38] Implementation of the optimal matching grant system is problematic, since by definition external benefits are difficult to measure. Most matching grant programs use formulas of the order of one dollar of grant for every dollar of provincial expenditures, which is far in excess of any reasonable estimate of the size of spillovers. Presumably the matching rate was intended to fulfil other purposes. In the case of major social programs, one objective was to bribe the provinces into establishing such programs. The matching formula might also serve as a rough measure of need. Greater provincial expenditures on welfare, for example, reflect greater provincial need. Matching grants could therefore be considered a form of equalization in a system where need was not otherwise included in the formula. Alternatively, the matching grant for welfare could be viewed as compensating for the fact that transfers were not treated symmetrically with taxes in the equalization formula, a point emphasized long ago by the Breau Committee report.[39]

The trouble with matching grants used for these purposes was that they introduced adverse incentive effects into the transfer system. The availability of "50-cent dollars" could potentially cause rational governments, which had already established the shared-cost programs, to expand the size of them significantly. It has been alleged that the increase in welfare rates in various periods in the 1970s and 1980s was partly attributable to the matching grant formula.[40]

Conditional Grants. An important reason why matching grants have gone out of fashion is that it has been recognized that many of their alleged objectives could be achieved by conditional bloc (non-matching) grants. By avoiding the matching aspect, adverse incentive effects would be avoided. The size of the grants by jurisdiction could be designed to reflect need as well as whatever spillover benefits there were thought to be.

But conditional grants can have a much broader purpose. They can be the vehicles by which provincial spending programs can be induced to conform to norms of national efficiency and equity. Conditions such as the rights of non-resident citizens to have access to provincial public services, principles of accessibility, need, and comprehensiveness can all be attached to the use of conditional grant funds. Such conditions can be designed so that decentralized decision-making does not result in the violation of efficiency in the internal economic union, or that equity standards are not compromised. The conditions can be made biting by reducing the size of the grant in the event of non-compliance. Conditional grants of this sort should be seen as complements to equalization and not substitutes. Equalization addresses the particular issues of fiscal inefficiency and fiscal inequity, while conditional grants deal with the other potential violations of national efficiency and equity outlined above.

The use of conditional bloc grants is an exercise of the federal spending power, and its use has been controversial in Canada. The problem is that the federal spending power appears to contradict the independent exercise of provincial legislative authority. It is not at all clear how to avoid this. If the federal government is seen as the custodian of national equity and efficiency, it is hard to imagine a policy instrument other than the spending power that it might use to achieve its objectives. The spending power is widely used in federations around the world, typically much more intrusively than in Canada.[41] Compared to other potential policy instruments such as disallowing provincial legislation or imposing mandates on the provinces, it is relatively non-intrusive.

POLICY COORDINATION AND HARMONIZATION

The fiscal arrangements may involve more than financial transfers; they may also involve agreements to harmonize policies. Harmonization serves various purposes: securing efficiency in the internal economic union, implementing common standards of equity, and simplifying the administration of fiscal programs for governments and citizens alike.

The need for harmonization differs by policy area. A high priority is in the area of taxation. The costs of collection and compliance and the transparency of tax laws can be reduced by a tax system that has features of the base in common, and even has a single tax-collecting authority. In addition, if taxpayers are involved with more than one province, some form of coordination is essential to avoid double taxation. The transfer system might also be simplified by harmonization, especially if it too is administered alongside taxes. Harmonization of public services is perhaps less urgent on administrative grounds, since there tends to be relatively little jurisdictional overlap for users. Of course, there may be issues of national efficiency and equity that could be addressed by interprovincial harmonization in the event that the spending power is not used. Finally, harmonization of regulations is also desirable, especially where taxpayers operate in different provinces.

The manner in which harmonization can be accomplished is controversial. Some observers argue that much of it can be achieved by horizontal agreement among the provinces, with or without the participation of the federal government.[42] As we have mentioned, achieving horizontal agreement among governments has proven to be difficult. The need for unanimous agreement makes substantive agreements very hard to negotiate as the threat of veto can be used to obtain one's preferred components. It also restricts the scope of agreements to those in which all provinces stand to gain. Thus, horizontal agreement over interprovincial equalization, dividing up a given amount of federal transfers, or many policies involving national equity objectives would be infeasible. The participation of the federal government would not seem to make a difference. If agreement could be secured, enforcement would then be an issue. Dispute settlement mechanisms could be constructed, but their ultimate effectiveness would always run up against the sovereignty of parliaments.

These considerations make the use of the federal government as facilitator attractive. The federal government has the power of the purse, which allows it to enforce or induce harmonization in a way that not only respects democratic decision-making but also avoids the use of the courts. In the case of harmonizing spending programs, this involves the use of the spending power. This need not be done in a heavy-handed manner; the conditions attached to its use could be made only as intrusive as necessary for the purpose, and the provinces could be consulted on an ongoing basis. But in the end, the need to report to the national electorate is the real check. To harmonize taxes, provincial participation seems to require a quid pro quo such as a single tax-collecting authority and some provincial input into tax policy issues, as well as enough federal dominance in the tax field so that the federal government can assume a leadership role in defining the broad parameters of the tax. This has implications for the degree of vertical fiscal imbalance and for the tax mixes used by the federal government and the provinces.

CANADIAN FISCAL FEDERALISM ISSUES

After this long discourse on the principles of fiscal federalism, we conclude with a brief discussion of its implications for the Canadian practice. Given the judgements that must be made along the way about the role of governments, the weight that ought to be given to redistributive equity, the merits of decentralization, and the responsibilities of the federal government, conclusions are bound to be subjective. Moreover, the conclusions we draw are bound to be controversial given that they contradict much of what is being advocated by policy research institutes and the national media, and question the direction in which most recent governments have taken the federation.

THE CONSTITUTIONAL AND ECONOMIC SETTING

Canadian constitutional prescriptions as well as political and institutional practice are aligned remarkably well with economic arguments. The constitution assigns to the provinces responsibility for delivering important public services in areas of health, education, and welfare, as well as providing them access to all the major broad-based taxes for financing. As a result, a high degree of fiscal decentralization is achieved, significantly greater than comparable federations (e.g., Australia). At the same time, the constitution recognizes as matters of principle the responsibilities the federal government has for national equity issues. Section 36(1) explicitly recognizes the joint responsibility of the federal government and the provinces for providing essential public services to all Canadians, for fostering equality of opportunity, and for reducing economic disparities. These are various dimensions of redistributive equity, and significantly, ones whose fulfillment involves policy instruments that are the exclusive legislative responsibility of the provinces. Section 36(2) recognizes the federal responsibility for addressing fiscal inequities and inefficiencies by prescribing an equalization system that would eliminate NFB differentials. Perhaps surprisingly, the only main national economic objective left out is that of securing the efficiency of the internal economic union. But that seems to be the one objective that is non-controversial.

The constitution also provides the federal government the policy instruments in the form of broad taxing and spending powers to achieve national equity and efficiency objectives. The spending power enables the federal government to engage in active tax-transfer policies and to maintain a vertical fiscal imbalance necessary to enable it to use the instrument of federal-provincial transfers to full advantage and to facilitate a harmonized tax system. Most important and controversial, it enables the federal government to use conditional grants as a vehicle for fulfilling its joint responsibility with the provinces for redistributive equity (section 36(1)) and for pursuing an efficient internal common market.

HOW MUCH DECENTRALIZATION?

Fiscal decentralization has been the operative policy in the 1990s' world of fiscal discipline and government retrenchment. In practice, this has meant a reduction in federal transfers and a corresponding increase in provincial reliance on own-source revenues, since the provinces have already assumed responsibility for major public services in health, education, and welfare. The combination of reduced federal transfers and increased provincial occupancy of the major tax bases has potentially serious effects on the ability of the federal government to fulfil its responsibilities for achieving national equity and efficiency goals.

To appreciate this argument, it must be understood that the spending power is virtually the only policy instrument available for the federal government to pursue the equity responsibilities set out in section 36, and to pursue efficiency in the internal economic union, which almost all observers agree is a useful goal. Moreover, on economic grounds, the spending power is in principle an ideal policy instrument for the task. It is a relatively non-obtrusive way of combining provincial responsibility for delivering major public services with the legitimate interest the federal government has in the equity and efficiency consequences of decentralized delivery. In other words, it is a powerful policy instrument for the management of the decentralization.

The gradual process of the provinces assuming more responsibility for raising their own revenue undermines the use of the spending power. Although greater reliance by the provinces to rely on own-source revenues might lead to greater accountability, it also results in more resistance to the federal spending power. The ability of the federal government to induce national standards into the provision of important public services is considerably lessened if the federal share of funding is relatively small. Moreover, greater provincial self-sufficiency itself exacerbates NFB differentials across provinces, making it more difficult to achieve fiscal equity and efficiency both economically and politically.

This is not to say that the use of the spending power has been perfect in the past and could not be improved. It is clear that part of the reason for its demise can be attributed to the sometimes insensitive and secretive way that it has been exercised. There could obviously be more openness and more consultation with the provinces in its use, an issue we return to below. The alternatives to the spending power are impalatable. One is simply to abrogate the federal responsibility for national equity and efficiency issues where they involve provincial programs. There are those who would argue that the provinces could be relied on to come to an agreement among themselves, or even jointly with the federal government, to devise their programs in ways that abide by national standards. There is virtually no evidence that meaningful agreements would be forthcoming. National equity objectives would simply not be achieved, which may well suit the agenda of opponents to the spending power. The other alternative of giving the federal government more direct powers to achieve national objectives, such as exercising its disallowance powers, are simply not on. The only practical way for the federal government to achieve national objectives is through the spending power.

Reducing the vertical fiscal gap has a further adverse effect on the efficiency and equity of the economic union. By requiring the provinces to raise more of their own revenues, their occupancy of tax room increases, possibly in ways that threaten the integrity of tax harmonization. The Canadian tax-collection agreements have been a model of tax harmonization for federations elsewhere, and with good reason. They combine the benefits of a common base and single tax-collecting authority with provincial power over their own tax rates. Not surprisingly, as the provinces have come to occupy more and more of the income tax room, they have insisted on more and more discretion in tax policy. This has led to gradual erosion of the integrity of the agreements to the point where their survival is in jeopardy. A full discussion of the consequences of this for tax policy in the federation is beyond the scope of this paper.[43] Suffice it to say that decentralization of revenue-raising responsibility cannot but put strains on tax harmonization.

PROCESS CONSIDERATIONS

Our argument leads inexorably to the views that decentralization should leave a sufficient vertical fiscal gap to enable the federal government to pursue its legitimate objective of equity and efficiency in the internal economic union, and that the spending power should be nurtured as the only feasible policy instrument available for the federal government to achieve its objectives. This implies that some work must be done to avoid the strains that the past use of the spending power has caused for the federation. The exercise of the spending power in recent decades has been characterized by excessive secrecy, inadequate notice to the provinces of major changes that affect their budgetary plans, a lack of public transparency and consultation, and an apparent absence of a long-term perspective in managing the fiscal arrangements. A good part of the problem may stem from the fact that major changes in the fiscal arrangements typically take place as part of the federal budget process, which is necessarily shrouded in secrecy and which often has short-to-medium-term fiscal objectives in mind.

Other federations have institutions for managing the federation in a much more open and consultative way. Advisory bodies exist with more or less influence on the fiscal arrangements in federations like Australia, India, South Africa, and the United States. Arm's length advisory bodies can adopt a suitably wide perspective, can serve as a vehicle for full consultation with the provinces, and can provide a forum for much more open discussion and debate, leading to a more informed management of the fiscal affairs of the federation. Such a body has performed an extremely valuable function in Australia, and has succeeded in bringing the states into a meaningful dialogue with the federal government over fiscal issues of mutual concern, despite the fact that the fiscal stature of Australian states is much less than Canadian provinces. It is worth considering whether more rationale and far-sighted decision-making can be brought to the Canadian case by such an institution. The institution of the social union agreement is a useful step in that direction, and is discussed elsewhere in this volume. It remains to be seen if it will serve as a useful device for furthering goals of national importance in a way that involves the provinces and the federal government in a true partnership, or whether it will further stultify the federal government's legitimate role in achieving national equity and efficiency objectives.

NOTES

This chapter is based on work that is being supported by the Social Sciences and Humanities Research Council of Canada. I am grateful for helpful comments on an earlier draft by Paul Hobson, Harvey Lazar, and two anonymous referees.

1. Further discussion of the consequences of decentralization may be found in Robin Boadway, "The Folly of Decentralizing the Canadian Federation," *Dalhousie Review* 75 (1996):313-49.

2. Wallace E. Oates, *Fiscal Federalism* (New York: Harcourt Brace Jovanovich, 1972).

3. Charles M. Tiebout, "A Pure Theory of Local Expenditures," *Journal of Political Economy* 64 (1956):416-24.

4. The notion of agency problems is well known to economists, but perhaps less well known to non-economists. It refers to the fact that managers of organizations or programs are unable to manage efficiently because they cannot perfectly observe relevant characteristics of those under their control. These include the costs of delivering programs, the effort or productivity of those in the organization, the need for the service by the target population, and so on.

5. Adverse selection arises when those being insured fall into different risk categories, but the insurer cannot observe to which category a particular person belongs. This prevents insurance being provided on actuarially fair terms to the least risky persons because more risky ones will want to purchase it. This prevents markets from providing insurance efficiently, and may even cause the market to break down.

6. Moral hazard in the insurance context occurs when those being insured can take actions that affect the chances of a claim being filed, or its size. Again, insurance cannot be operated efficiently in this context. An analogous phenomenon occurs when employees' efforts are hidden so that their contributions (rather than the contribution of some extraneous force) to the output of the enterprise cannot be determined.

7. See the discussion and further references in Albert Breton, "Designing More Competitive and Efficient Governments," in *Defining the Role of Government: Economic Perspectives of the State*, ed. Robin Boadway *et al.* (Kingston: School of Policy Studies, and McGill-Queen's University Press, 1994), pp. 55-98.

8. Geoffrey Brennan and James M. Buchanan, *The Power to Tax: Analytical Foundations of a Fiscal Constitution* (New York: Cambridge University Press, 1990).

9. An elegant demonstration of this may be found in Jeremy S.S. Edwards and Michael J. Keen, "Tax Competition and Leviathan," *European Economic Review* 40 (1996):113-34.

10. An analysis of this may be found in Motohiro Sato, "Essays in Fiscal Federalism and Decentralization," PhD Thesis, Department of Economics, Queen's University, 1998.

11. The classical reference is James M. Buchanan, "Fiscal Grants and Resource Allocation," *Journal of Political Economy* 60 (1952):208-17, elaborated in James M. Buchanan and Charles J. Goetz, "Efficiency Limits of Fiscal Mobility: An Assessment of the Tiebout Model," *Journal of Public Economics* 1 (1972):25-43. A formalization of the argument for a decentralized federation may be found in Robin Boadway and Frank R. Flatters, "Efficiency and Equalization Payments in a Federal System of Government: A Synthesis and Extension of Recent

Results," *Canadian Journal of Economics* 15 (1982):613-33, and its consequences for equalization in Boadway and Flatters, *Equalization in a Federal State* (Ottawa: Economic Council of Canada, 1982).

12. Dan Usher, *The Uneasy Case for Equalization Payments* (Vancouver: The Fraser Institute, 1995).

13. See, for example, Stanley L. Winer and Denis Gauthier, *Internal Migration and Fiscal Structure: An Econometric Study of the Determinants of Interprovincial Migration in Canada* (Ottawa: Economic Council of Canada, 1982); and Kathleen M. Day, "Interprovincial Migration and Local Public Goods," *Canadian Journal of Economics* 25 (1992):123-44. William G. Watson, in "An Estimate of the Welfare Gain from Fiscal Equalization, "*Canadian Journal of Economics* 19 (1986):298-308, has argued argued that the estimated migration levels translate into relatively limited welfare consequences.

14. This tendency to evaluate equalization in terms of its effect on interpersonal redistribution may be found in Usher, *The Uneasy Case for Equalization Payments* and Paul Boothe and Derek Hermanutz, *Simply Sharing: An Interprovincial Equalization Scheme for Canada* (Toronto: C.D. Howe Institute, 1999).

15. See the recent surveys in works by Ben Lockwood, "Tax Competition and Tax Co-Ordination under Destination and Origin Principles: A Synthesis," unpublished paper, University of Warwick; and J.D. Wilson, "Theories of Tax Competition," *National Tax Journal* 52 (1999):269-304.

16. This is the approach taken in the survey of fiscal externalities by Bev Dahlby, "Fiscal Externalities and the Design of Intergovernmental Grants," *International Tax and Public Finance* 3 (1996):397-411.

17. This is an efficiency approach to the MCPF. Equity considerations can also be incorporated, as discussed in Bev Dahlby, "Progressive Taxation and the Social Marginal Cost of Public Funds," *Journal of Public Economics* 67 (1998):105-22.

18. Of course, in the short run, when capital has been installed, it will be possible to tax it without the capital fleeing. But such a policy is not sustainable in the long run, because capital owners will not want to install capital equipment if they expect that it will be taxed once in place. This is the problem of time consistency which was referred to earlier.

19. For example, Dahlby, "Fiscal Externalities."

20. For an analysis of this, see Michael Smart, "Taxation and Deadweight Loss in a System of Intergovernmental Transfers," *Canadian Journal of Economics* 31 (1998):189-206.

21. Unless the tax rate is on the wrong side of the Laffer curve, which is a distinct possibility in a federal setting as Michael Keen and Christos Kotsogiannis show in their paper, "Federalism and Tax Competition," unpublished paper, University of Essex, 1995.

22. Timothy J. Besley and Harvey S. Rosen, "Vertical Externalities in Tax Setting: Evidence from Gasoline and Cigarettes," *Journal of Public Economics* 70 (1998):383-98.

23. Masayoshi Hayashi and Robin Boadway, "An Empirical Analysis of Intergovernmental Tax Interaction: The Case of Business Income Tax in Canada," unpublished paper, Department of Economics, Queen's University, 1999.

24. There is some evidence that the federal government is in fact first-mover with respect to the provinces. Hayashi and Boadway, "An Empirical Analysis of Intergovernmental Tax Interaction," found that to be the case for business income taxes levied by the two governments.

25. See the analyses in Robin Boadway and Michael Keen, "Efficiency and the Optimal Direction of Federal-State Transfers," *International Tax and Public Finance* 3 (1996):137-55; and Robin Boadway, Maurice Marchand and Marianne Vigneault, "The Consequences of Overlapping Tax Bases for Redistribution and Public Spending in a Federation," *Journal of Public Economics* 68 (1998):453-78.

26. See Dahlby, "Fiscal Externalities and the Design of Intergovernmental Grants."

27. The Samaritan's Dilemma refers to a situation in which a potential recipient of assistance from a donor (the "Samaritan") exploits the situation by choosing a course of action that impoverishes himself in (correct) anticipation that the Samaritan will provide remedial support.

28. See the analysis in A.J. Caplan, R.C. Cornes and E.C.D. Silva, "Pure Public Goods and Income Redistribution in a Federation with Decentralized Leadership and Imperfect Mobility," unpublished paper, 1998. Models also exist in which households move first, followed by federal and provincial governments. If the households anticipate the equalizing policies that the governments will implement in the future, the allocation of labour will be inefficient. Mitsui and Sato construct a simple example in which households prefer to live in the largest community, which leads to concentrations of population that are too high, Kyoshi Mitsui and Motohiro Sato, "Ex Ante Free Mobility, Ex Post Immobility, and Time-Consistent Policy in a Federal System," *Journal of Public Economics* (forthcoming).

29. For some recent evidence, see Michael Baker, A. Abigail Payne and Michael Smart, "An Empirical Study of Matching Grants: The 'Cap' on CAP," *Journal of Public Economics* 70 (1999):269-88.

30. See W.R. Johnson, "Income Redistribution in a Federal System," *American Economic Review* 78 (1988):570-73.

31. The classic approach to fiscal federalism in Richard A. Musgrave, *The Theory of Public Finance* (New York: McGraw-Hill, 1959); and later in Oates, *Fiscal Federalism* argued strongly that redistribution should be the responsibility of the federal government.

32. The exceptions are China and Russia where, for historical reasons, tax collection is highly localized and revenues are passed up to the centre.

33. See Boadway and Keen, "Efficiency and the Optimal Direction of Federal-State Transfers."

34. For a summary of the issues in Canada, see Robin Boadway and Paul A.R. Hobson, *Intergovernmental Fiscal Relations in Canada* (Toronto: Canadian Tax

Foundation, 1993); and Boadway and Hobson eds., *Equalization: Its Contribution to Canada's Economic and Fiscal Progress* (Kingston: John Deutsch Institute for the Study of Economic Policy, Queen's University, 1998). A contrary view may be found in Usher, *The Uneasy Case for Equalization Payments*.

35. The case for partial equalization on these grounds was put by Boadway and Flatters, *Equalization in a Federal State*, and proposed by the Economic Council of Canada, *Financing Confederation: Today and Tomorrow* (Ottawa: Supply and Services Canada, 1982).

36. G.M. Myers, "Optimality, Free Mobility and Regional Authority in a Federation," *Journal of Public Economics* 43 (1990):107-21.

37. See especially T. Persson and G. Tabellini, "Federal Fiscal Constitutions: Risk Sharing and Redistribution," *Journal of Political Economy* 104 (1996):979-1009; and "Federal Fiscal Constitutions: Risk Sharing and Moral Hazard," *Econometrica* 64 (1996):623-46; and A. Alesina and R. Perotti, "Economic Risk and Political Risk in Fiscal Unions," *Economic Journal* 108 (1998):989-1008. These authors have also emphasized some of the political economy aspects of decentralization.

38. See Dahlby, "Fiscal Externalities and the Design of Intergovernmental Grants," for an analysis of the theoretical case for this.

39. Canada, *Fiscal Federalism in Canada: Report of the Parliamentary Task Force on Federal-Provincial Fiscal Arrangements* (Ottawa: Supply and Services Canada, 1981).

40. Some recent evidence of this may be found in Baker *et al.*, "An Empirical Study of Matching Grants."

41. See Ronald Watts, *The Spending Power in Federal Systems: A Comparative Study* (Kingston: Institute of Intergovernmental Relations, Queen's University, 1999) for a wide-ranging survey of the use of the spending power in other federations. There is very little economics literature on the spending power. Economists tend to take its use for granted.

42. A prominent recent exposition of this view is found in Thomas Courchene, *ACCESS: A Convention on the Canadian Economic and Social Systems*, Working Paper prepared for the Ministry of Intergovernmental Affairs, Government of Ontario.

43. See Robin Boadway and Harry M. Kitchen, *Canadian Tax Policy* 3d ed. (Toronto: Canadian Tax Foundation, 1999) for further discussion of tax policy issues in a federation.

3

On Re-Balancing Canadian Fiscal Federalism

Kenneth Norrie and L.S. Wilson

Les ministres provinciaux des finances soutiennent que le fédéralisme canadien est marqué par un déséquilibre fiscal vertical, puisque les provinces ont des besoins financiers plus élevés que leur capacité de prélever des recettes, alors que le gouvernement fédéral se retrouve dans la situation inverse. Cependant, sauf quelques exceptions mineures, les deux niveaux de gouvernements ont accès aux mêmes sources de financement. Il n'est donc plus possible de parler d'une situation traditionnelle de déséquilibre vertical, c'est-à-dire d'une situation où l'un des niveaux de gouvernement a d'importantes responsabilités financières tout en ayant un pouvoir de taxation limité par la Constitution. On se demande, dans ce chapitre, s'il est possible de parler de déséquilibre vertical sans qu'il y ait de limites constitutionnelles au pouvoir de taxation. Selon une première hypothèse, il en coûterait moins cher au gouvernement fédéral qu'aux gouvernements provinciaux et territoriaux de prélever des recettes par la taxation. Selon une autre hypothèse, les provinces et territoires pourraient prélever des recettes de manière aussi efficace que le gouvernement fédéral, mais ne peuvent le faire puisque ce dernier occupe déjà l'espace fiscal. Enfin, il existe des raisons politiques et distributives justifiant les transferts fédéraux aux provinces et aux territoires.

INTRODUCTION

Canadian fiscal federalism is once again under the microscope. Provincial and territorial ministers of finance issued a report last year on the state of Canadian fiscal federalism. The basic premise of this document is that there is a fundamental vertical fiscal imbalance in Canadian federalism in that, "the distribution of revenue sources between orders of government ... is out of line with the distribution of spending responsibilities."[1] Provinces have spending needs greater than their revenue-raising capacities, while the federal government is in the opposite position. This fiscal imbalance has existed throughout the postwar period, in their view, but it became particularly acute in the years of federal fiscal restraint in the 1990s as cash transfers to the provinces were cut significantly more than other federal program spending. Further, it will get worse in the future since provincial expenditure responsibilities in the areas of health, education, and social assistance in particular are widely expected to grow significantly, outstripping the natural growth in their revenue.

The ministers recognize that the federal government provides fiscal transfers to offset this fiscal imbalance, but they argue that there are three basic objections to such payments. First, the amounts are inadequate. Second, provinces have been subject to sudden and arbitrary changes in the amounts of the transfers, making budgeting difficult. Third, Ottawa has often attached conditions to what should, in principle, be unconditional transfers, thereby distorting provincial spending priorities. This final problem is most acute in the case of health spending, although it extends to social assistance as well.

The report concludes that there is a pressing need for fiscal re-balancing. Expenditure responsibilities for the major areas of health, education, and social assistance are properly assigned to the provinces in their view, so the only recourse is to transfer some revenue capacity to them. The transfer can take any of three forms: increased cash transfers, equalized tax point reallocations or tax field realignment. The report discusses briefly the pros and cons of each option, but makes no recommendations on a preferred option.

The concept of a vertical fiscal gap is familiar in the fiscal federalism literature. All federal systems must assign expenditure responsibilities and tax powers across levels of government. In principle, these assignments are done separately, expenditure function by expenditure function, and revenue source by revenue source. The question in each case is where, on efficiency and equity grounds, the responsibility is best lodged. Not surprisingly, the accepted view is that it is unlikely to be optimal to match revenues and expenditures perfectly. Almost certainly, some governments will find themselves with significant expenditure obligations, yet be formally excluded from exploiting one or more of the major tax sources. Conversely, other orders of government will be able to raise revenue in excess of their assigned expenditure obligations.

If taxes and expenditures do not match perfectly, a vertical fiscal gap exists and intergovernmental fiscal transfers are called for. The jurisdiction with the "surplus" fiscal capacity taxes in excess of its expenditure obligations and makes transfers to those who face formal (e.g., constitutional) constraints on their revenue-raising ability.[2] Most often, the gap is such that transfers flow from national to subnational orders of government. The arguments for assigning tax powers to higher levels of government seem strong while expenditure responsibilities often seem better assigned to lower levels of government.[3] Transfers for fiscal gap reasons are appropriately purely unconditional in design.

The assignment of taxation authority between federal and provincial governments in Canada is unique, however, in that, with minor exceptions, both levels of government have full access to all current major revenue sources. Thus, the traditional reason for expecting a vertical fiscal gap — one order of government with significant expenditure responsibilities but constitutionally shut out of one or more major tax-revenue sources — does not apply. On the surface at least, it would seem that provinces can spend what they wish on social and other programs as long as they are willing to bear the political and other costs of funding them with their own taxation efforts. They simply have to weigh the perceived benefits of additional expenditures against the perceived costs of financing them. Thus it is tempting to view the finance ministers' position as an attempt to avoid politically unpopular taxes.

The belief in the need for fundamental fiscal re-balancing in the Canadian federation is too deeply ingrained to dismiss this easily, however. It is important to ask whether a vertical fiscal gap is possible *even if* there are no important constitutional constraints on taxation. We shall address that question in the remainder of this chapter. We begin in the next section by setting out very briefly the traditional concept of a vertical fiscal gap. We then move on to consider how vertical fiscal gaps might exist in the absence of constitutional constraints. One possibility is that, whatever the constitutional situation, the economic cost to the federal government of raising revenue through taxation is actually lower than it is for provinces and territories. Thus it is efficient for Ottawa to tax in excess of its expenditure obligations and transfer cash unconditionally to the other orders of government. We examine this argument in the third section.

This first possibility clearly calls for unconditional cash transfers. The finance ministers' document considers cash transfers, as noted above, but it also calls for tax point transfers from the federal government to provinces and territories. Essentially it suggests that Ottawa should reduce its taxation efforts in the main revenue categories so that provinces and territories can take up the room. The argument seems to be that provinces and territories could exploit this tax room as efficiently as the federal government does, but that they are prevented from doing so by Ottawa's prior occupancy. We examine this possibility in the fourth section. Section five looks at two other possibilities and the final section provides some brief concluding comments.

THE TRADITIONAL CONCEPT OF A VERTICAL FISCAL GAP

We shall not attempt a broad review of the considerations for the optimal assignment of tax and expenditure powers across levels of government. Excellent reviews are available in Boadway and Hobson and Boadway, Roberts and Shah.[4] When all arguments are considered, however, the conventional wisdom places relatively more taxation powers at the national or central order of government and relatively more expenditure responsibilities at the regional or provincial order. This conclusion implies that the fiscal gap, in a system with the optimal allocation of powers, is such that national governments must transfer funds to subnational governments.

Much government expenditure is on private or local public goods such as education, local services such as roads and health care. The standard argument is that there are few spillovers from these types of expenditures to the nation as a whole, and that the regional/provincial level can be more responsive to local needs and preferences. Thus, a large portion of expenditure responsibility should be assigned to that order of government. The efficiency gains from tailoring the services to the preferences of the local populations will outweigh the efficiency losses from having some spillover of benefits into neighbouring jurisdictions. Where the reverse is true, as in defence expenditures, for example, the responsibility is best assigned to the federal government. The presumption, however, is that the former types of expenditure outweigh the latter by a considerable margin in a regionally diverse nation such as Canada.[5]

Taxation, on the other hand, as described in detail in the next section, is perceived as having large spillovers, with the implication that central control is desirable. Many of the main tax bases — labour income, taxes on capital such as corporation and taxes on interest earnings — are quite mobile. This feature invites tax competition among provinces and the inefficient allocation of resources or the tax burden. Factor inputs, for example, may locate inefficiently so as to minimize the tax burden. Tax competition among provinces may result in a level of overall government expenditure that we might view as too small: the "race for the bottom" as it has been called.

This, then, is the standard depiction of a vertical fiscal gap in a federation. For efficiency reasons, the bulk of expenditure responsibilities are assigned constitutionally to provincial, territorial and local governments. Likewise for efficiency reasons, the main taxation power is vested in the central government. Society is best served if the central government is the main taxing authority, transferring some of the revenue unconditionally to subnational governments to cover their expenditure responsibilities.

This standard story presumes that the assignments of taxation and expenditure authority are done formally. In this instance, a vertical fiscal gap exists because subnational governments are excluded from one or more important revenue sources. But this is not the case in Canada, as already mentioned. With a couple of minor exceptions, provincial and territorial governments have access to the same tax bases as the federal government. The standard story does not hold, in other words. The question though is whether provinces and territories are constrained in their access to the main revenue sources *in fact,* if not in principle. We address this question in the next section.

Before doing so, however, it is important to note that there are other reasons to argue that the central government should retain a significant share of the tax base. Management of the macro economy and thus fiscal policy is usually thought best done at the national level,[6] and this task requires the federal government to have sufficient control over taxes to pursue these policies. The tax system is also a main policy tool for redistribution among persons. Thus, if equity is seen as a policy that should be pursued, nationally this tool must be available to the federal government. These considerations apply whether the federal government spends the revenues itself or transfers the funds to other governments; it is the share of the tax base that is at issue.

There is yet another important reason why the federal government will tax in excess of its own program expenditure needs, one that provincial and territorial governments in Canada embrace, it should be noted. Horizontal equity is important across provinces. The general idea that citizens of equal ability need to be treated equally by government in its entirety implies that citizens should have approximately equal access to government services at similar tax rates wherever they live. This is a basic idea of the equalization system. Equalization would be possible with a "net" system, where "have" provinces transferred funds directly to "have-not" ones.[7] In Canada, however, it is not done this way. Rather the federal government raises the potential revenues of the have-nots up to some level, currently the "five-province average." This commitment requires that the federal government have revenues in excess of its expenditure needs, that is, that there be a fiscal gap in favour of the federal government.

In closing this section, we should note that there is a contrary view of transfer payments in the fiscal federalism literature. Essentially, this group argues against separating taxation and expenditure decisions.[8] Governments at all levels should face some tax responsibility in order to make them accountable to their constituents for efficient management and expenditures. This condition is normally seen as satisfied if governments have to raise their own funds at the margin for any extra expenditures. The Canadian equalization system, for example, is carefully designed so that recipient provinces receive transfers based not on what their actual revenues are but rather on what they would get if they were to apply the average rate of taxation to the average base. This leaves provincial governments free to make their own tax decisions, without any impact on the amount of equalization they receive, and leaves them responsible to their citizens for prudent expenditure and taxation decisions.

While the literature is fairly clear on the optimal assignment of taxes and expenditure powers across levels of government, the Canadian situation only partly conforms to this wisdom. In particular, as discussed above, both levels of government have virtually full access to all major tax bases. In this situation it is less clear why a fiscal gap might exist, and it is this question we turn to now.

A CASE FOR CASH TRANSFERS

The case for cash transfers rests on the premise that it is socially efficient for the federal government to raise revenues in excess of its program expenditure needs, and transfer the surplus to provinces and territories. There are at least two reasons why this situation might hold.

ELASTICITY PERCEPTIONS

Assume initially that there are no fiscal transfers in the federation. Each order of government sets its own program-spending priorities and finances them by exploiting its own tax-revenue sources. There is a marginal benefit to government program spending, denoted as MB_f for the federal government and MB_p for a provincial government. These terms can be thought of as representing the value that residents in a given province place on one more dollar of federal and provincial government program spending respectively.

There is a cost to raising an extra dollar of government revenue, known as the marginal cost of public funds and denoted as $MCPF_f$ for the federal government and $MCPF_p$ for a provincial government. Briefly, the marginal cost of public funds can be thought of as a measure of the social cost of the government collecting one more dollar of revenue. It includes the private opportunity cost of the income transferred to the government plus the costs of any distortions in the economy that taxes bring about. An example of such a distortion would be the value of the output foregone if higher income taxes caused workers to work fewer hours. The MCPF typically will vary among tax bases, although governments acting optimally will equalize the marginal social cost across different sources. If it is less costly to get revenue by taxing base A than by taxing base B then taxes would be lowered on B and raised on A. Thus, we can think of the MCPF as the social cost of raising one dollar of taxes from the least-cost revenue source open to the government.

Governments acting optimally will expand spending to the point where the marginal benefit from the last dollar of program spending equals the marginal cost of raising that last dollar. Thus in equilibrium, $MB_f = MCPF_f$ for the federal government and $MB_p = MCPF_p$ for each provincial government. Assume now that $MCPF_f < MCPF_p$; that is, that for some reason the cost to the federal government of financing the final dollar of program spending is less than it is for the provinces. From a citizen's perspective, the implication is that $MB_f < MB_p$. The marginal benefit to taxpayers of the last unit of federal government program spending is less than the marginal benefit of the last unit of program spending by their provincial government.

Here then is the case for fiscal transfers. Residents would clearly be better off if the federal government were to reduce its program spending by one dollar, and transfer the dollar to the provincial government to allow it to increase its program spending by that amount. The loss from lower federal program spending is more than made up for by the gain from higher provincial program spending. Increasing provincial program spending and reducing federal program spending will narrow the gap between MB_f and MB_p. Transfers should continue as long as there is such a gap, however. The optimal level of transfer is that amount sufficient to ensure that $MCPF_f = MB_f = MCPF_p = MB_p$. A vertical fiscal gap can be said to exist in this case if the value of cash transfers falls short of this optimal amount.

The key to either result is the assumption that $MCPF_f < MCPF_p$; that is, that the cost to the federal government of raising a dollar of revenue from its existing revenue sources is less than that for the provinces from their existing sources. In the absence of transfers, and assuming all governments push program spending to the point where the marginal benefits equal marginal costs, the federal government will overspend relative to the provincial government. The obvious question then is why this condition might hold.

Provincial perceptions of the social costs of raising extra revenues depend on the elasticity of the bases they tax. Because of the possibility of interprovincial migration of these bases, there can be significant differences between the elasticities of the bases an individual province faces and the elasticities the federal government would face were it to tax across all provinces. This will be true of all bases — labour, capital, and consumption — except land. We might think capital to be particularly mobile.[9] Any individual provincial government is thus very different than either a coalition of all provincial governments, acting in unison, or the federal government, perhaps acting on behalf of the provinces.

To the extent that provincial governments perceive that their tax base is quite elastic because of this possibility of migration to other provinces, they will "under-tax"[10] and "under-spend," compared to what they would do if they faced the same base elasticities as the federal government. The marginal cost of raising the revenue is higher, due to the potential tax distortions, so they will spend less. In this sense then, even though both federal and provincial governments have full access to the same tax sources, it cannot be said that individual provinces face the same bases as does the federal government. Hence the case for unconditional cash transfers.

One might argue that the provinces could collude to raise taxes, thereby by-passing the need to rely on Ottawa's compliance. If all agreed to raise their rates in unison the problems of migration of the bases between provinces would be minimized, although, as in response to a federal tax increase, bases may still be induced to migrate internationally. In this sense then, if they are able to reach a collusive agreement, the provinces can be said to face the same tax bases as does the federal government. The marginal cost of raising public funds would be the same, and there would be no case for a transfer of revenue capacity from the federal government.

In principle this collusion might seem straight-forward. There are, however, obvious reasons why it may not work so well. These mainly parallel the reasons we normally believe other forms of oligopoly will be unstable. First, it may be difficult for the provinces to agree on an optimal overall tax rate. Even in collusion, each will face different bases and have different needs and social preferences so each would prefer to agree on a different, standardized, tax rate. There may, however, be a number of uniform tax rates that would represent an improvement across all provinces even if the one chosen would not necessarily be the optimal one from the point of view of any individual province. In addition, provinces may all be able to improve their positions, not by agreeing on a uniform overall rate, but by being able to agree on a uniform increase from their current rates, which may all differ from each other. Thus, all may currently have different rates and all can improve their welfare by agreeing to a uniform increase, leaving them all continuing to have different rates.

A more difficult problem is the standard problem of any oligopoly — that it pays individual provinces to cheat or break ranks. As with other oligopolies, any individual player can do better by going its own way, assuming others continue to play by the rules of the oligopoly. In this case then, any province would be better off lowering its tax rates if it has the expectation that the other provinces will not follow. A general question is how exactly a province might behave in this situation. Will they expect that their own behaviour will have no impact on what the others do? Will they expect some sort of implicit collusion such that if it raises its rates, the others will follow? Casual empiricism suggests provinces compete to have low tax rates, implying they do not believe others will follow their lead and thus that they do not implicitly collude.

One way of colluding in a "binding" fashion is to get the federal government to levy the taxes on the part of the provinces. In this case, once agreement is reached between the federal government and the provinces, "cheating" could be much more difficult and, depending on the arrangements, less important.

There are various possible ways in which the revenues collected by the federal government could be distributed. One possibility is that the federal government would be the equivalent of a collection agency for the provinces, as indeed it already is for personal income taxes for all but Quebec, transferring to each province all revenues collected from the bases within that province. Here, then, provinces would continue to levy their own taxes, collected through the current arrangements, but in addition the federal government itself could levy taxes with the promise that the revenues from these would be passed on to the provincial governments. These federal government levied taxes would have the feature that individual provinces would not be able to alter the rates that applied to bases within their own jurisdictions. Assuming, however, that the provinces continued to have enough tax revenues under their direct control, they would be able to counteract the agreed-upon overall rates by changing their provincial tax rates, in other words to "cheat" on the collusive arrangement just as if the federal government were not involved. This arrangement, then, would be equivalent to transferring tax points to the provinces.

Alternatives where the federal transfers of taxes collected on behalf of the provinces were less directly related to the base within the particular province would reduce the incentives for individual provinces to break the collusive arrangement. Arrangements to transfer taxes collected as lump sums or fixed per capita amounts would break the link between base size and provincial transfer revenues (or per capita revenues). In the case of per capita transfers, for example, changes in the provincial tax rates will affect the provincial base, and direct provincial revenues, perhaps including equalization payments, but this will not affect their federal government transfers from the agreement. In the previous case, where the amounts of federal transfers that provinces receive are dependent on their bases, changes in provincial tax rates will affect both own revenues and transfers as the impact of tax changes on the base will feed through both sources.

Provinces still have the incentive to alter their rates, and thus change their bases, because of the impact on their own revenues, but if this makes up a smaller portion of their overall revenues this will be less important. In this sense, then, arrangements where federal revenues collected on behalf of the provinces are distributed in some way unrelated to the provincial tax base provide less incentive for the provinces to "cheat on," or counteract, the agreement than would arrangements where transfers depended on the base. These sorts of arrangements are thus likely to be more stable and provinces might prefer them.

This introduces another factor which may make it more difficult for the provinces to agree than would be the case in the simple collusion case as a collusive arrangement to raise taxes does not require the provinces to also decide on the distribution of revenues. At the same time, having the federal government involved does provide an arbiter with some authority. If, as we argue, the provinces need the federal government in order to provide stability in collusion, this gives the federal government at least some power to impose distributional arrangements.

Finally, it is clear that the need to have the federal government involved to impose discipline on collusion, combined with the fact that distribution of tax revenues in ways other than according to base is desirable, means that this argument for federal involvement is inextricably entwined with the arguments around redistribution of revenues across provinces. Some provinces may like a system where the federal government taxes and redistributes on a per capita basis because they stand to be significant gainers, for example, while others may be enthusiastic because it allows provinces to raise revenues without competition over the bases. These two arguments therefore reinforce one another.

FISCAL EXTERNALITIES

The literature on fiscal externalities in federal systems suggests that provincial fiscal decisions will not be optimal.[11] The type of collusion, whether with or without the federal government's help, discussed in the previous section will correct for some, but not all, of these externalities.

There are externalities from both the taxation and expenditure decisions of both levels of government and these externalities can be both horizontal, in the case of provincial governments, and vertical. Provincial government taxation decisions, through causing migration of the bases, can have impacts on revenues in other provincial jurisdictions. If Newfoundland raises its income tax rate, causing people to migrate to other provinces where they pay taxes, then Newfoundland causes a horizontal fiscal externality. If some of the impact of this Newfoundland tax increase is to reduce hours of work or investment in training or otherwise lower the overall income tax base then this will cause a vertical externality in that federal tax revenues will decrease.

There are parallel externalities in expenditures. Some provincial expenditure will have impacts on residents of other provinces. Flood control expenditures in Alberta, for example, may also benefit residents of Saskatchewan. This is the classic and best-known argument for interprovincial transfers in federal systems. There can also be horizontal expenditure externalities that work through provincial government fiscal variables. An example of this would be where expenditure on education in Alberta raises the productivity of someone who ends up paying higher income taxes in Saskatchewan. Finally, expenditure on education by the Alberta government, by raising workers' productivity will also raise federal tax revenues. This is an example of a vertical fiscal expenditure externality.

All of these types of externalities suggest that provincial (and federal) governments will not make optimal tax and expenditure decisions because they do not take the full implications of their decisions into account. Collusion among provinces so that they raise their taxes in concert, thus facing the same elasticities as would the federal government, will correct for horizontal fiscal externalities but not vertical ones. If the provinces raise their rates together then bases will not migrate between provinces and thus horizontal fiscal externalities will be eliminated. There may still be an impact on the overall size of the base nationally, however, and thus the vertical — between the provinces and the federal government — externalities will remain. In general, in taxation, the two externalities will oppose one another in effect such that we cannot say whether provincial tax rates will be too high or too low for overall economic efficiency. Correction for only the horizontal externalities, then, seems likely to ensure that provincial taxes are too high as only the vertical fiscal externality effects on federal revenues will remain. This, then, will provide a further argument for having the federal government play an important role in the collusion process. If the federal government taxes and transfers to the provinces then the full fiscal impact, both vertical and horizontal, of the tax can be taken into account and taxation would be closer to optimal in this sense.

SUMMARY

In summary, provincial governments realize that the tax bases they face are more elastic than those same bases are when taxed by the federal government because of the possibility of migration between provinces. If provincial governments believe they are acting independently, then they will feel that the social cost of raising revenues is higher than it would be if they could act in concert or get the federal government to act on their collective behalf. Collusion is difficult among provinces for the same reasons that we think other forms of oligopoly are unstable, in particular that it pays any individual "player" to cheat on the collective group. For this reason a system where the federal government plays an important role will be or should be attractive to the provinces.

Involving the federal government means that the allocation of these federal revenues to the provinces is an issue in a way that it would not be if the provinces taxed for themselves, directly. Depending on the method of allocation of revenues, some provinces will have an additional interest in enforcing collusion through the federal government.

There are reasons to believe that taxation decisions will not be made optimally by either level of government because of horizontal and vertical fiscal externalities. Collusion between provinces to act in concert will correct for horizontal externalities. Using the federal government to enforce collusion, on the assumption that provinces would otherwise cheat on the collusive arrangements, will be only partially successful as the provinces could still partially off-set the federal share of taxes collected on their behalf by lowering their own rates. On the other hand, the direct involvement of the federal government in the arrangements may allow for some accommodation for the vertical fiscal externalities existing between the federal and provincial decisions.

A CASE FOR TAX POINT TRANSFERS

In the preceding section, the appropriate response to a vertical fiscal gap was unconditional cash transfers. The finance ministers considered this solution, but they also called for tax point transfers. Ottawa would lower its taxation rates on the main revenue sources, allowing provinces and territories to take up the room. Implicit in this position is the assumption that there is no difference in the marginal cost of public funds facing national and subnational governments. The federal government dominates taxation because of prior occupancy, and not because of any natural efficiency advantage. The obvious question is how prior occupancy can provide such an advantage.

Suppose first that the marginal cost of public funds does not differ significantly between national and subnational jurisdictions. Suppose further that there is some maximum combined federal and provincial tax rate that is acceptable, say, because we believe rates cannot go beyond a certain amount higher than those in the United States. Put differently, suppose the marginal cost of public funds for the combined government sector rises steeply beyond current taxation levels. Suppose, finally, that the marginal benefit of provincial and territorial program spending is greater than that for Ottawa. Provinces and territories must tax more if they are to spend more, and if they are to tax more then Ottawa must tax less.

In principle this is a bilateral bargaining situation where there is a fixed amount that must be divided some way. One might argue that the provinces are at a disadvantage in this bilateral bargaining. First, to force reallocation of this fixed amount, the provinces would have to raise taxes hoping to force the federal government to lower theirs. Which level of government would win out in this confrontation presumably depends on public opinion. Because the federal government already "occupies" this tax room, the provinces will be seen as the ones raising taxes. "Prior occupancy" is thus important.

Second, as noted above, this is only a bilateral bargaining situation if the provinces act in concert. A single province raising its rates will not be able to force the federal government into reducing its tax rates on the base nationally — the province will stand out in public opinion as the government raising taxes to unacceptable levels.

The notion of prior occupancy certainly figures prominently in the general history of federal-provincial fiscal relations in the postwar period.[12] The federal government assumed full control over personal income tax, corporate income tax, and succession duties during World War II, renting these revenue sources from the provinces. This tax rental system continued after the war, albeit on a voluntary basis. Provinces that wished could opt out of the arrangement and levy their own taxes, in which case they received an abatement of a specified percentage of the federal taxes. In effect, Ottawa lowered its taxes on individuals and businesses in the opting-out provinces, giving the provincial government room to levy its own taxes.

The opting-out option with abatement from federal taxes continued in 1957 when tax-sharing replaced tax rentals. Tax-sharing gave way in 1962 to the tax-collection agreements that underlie the present system. All provinces received a standard abatement of personal and corporate income tax points, and were free to set their own tax rates as a percent of the basic federal tax. The standard abatements rose in a series of adjustments, the last coming in 1977 under the established programs financing arrangements when they reached 44 points for personal income tax and ten points for corporate income tax.

This general transfer of revenue capacity from the federal to the provincial governments is evident in Figure 1. As late as 1966 the federal government accounted for nearly two-thirds of total own-source revenue, while the provinces accounted for one-third. The federal share fell quickly thereafter, when the federal abatements were increasing, reaching just above 50 percent by the late 1970s. It flattens out thereafter, when there were no further changes in abatements. There have been some fluctuations in the shares since then, largely because of variations in provincial government resource revenues, but essentially the trend is constant.

This pattern appears to be consistent with the prior occupancy thesis, wherein provinces can only increase their tax efforts when the federal government reduces its effort. The situation is not that straightforward, however. Provinces responded differently to the freedom in the 1962 tax-collection agreements to set their own rates as a percentage of basic federal tax. Apparently, some provinces had more room than others between the ceiling rates and the room occupied by the prior federal effort. This outcome is not inconsistent with the

Figure 1: Federal and Provincial Shares of Own-Source Revenue, 1966-1996

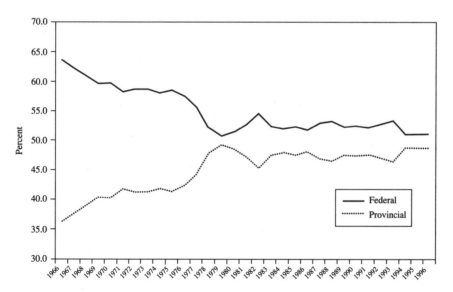

Source: Authors' Compilation.

prior occupancy thesis, but it requires that the marginal benefits of public spending or the marginal costs of public funds vary among provinces in a particular fashion.

Certainly, the tax efforts of provincial governments have varied considerably in the postwar period. The solid line in Figure 2 shows the average of own-source revenue as a percent of gross domestic product (GDP) for all provinces for the period 1961-95. The trend is clearly upward, rising from 6.4 percent of GDP at the start of the period to 18.2 percent by the mid-1990s. There is considerable variation among the provinces, however. The bottom line in Figure 2 shows the lowest values for own-source revenue as a percent of GDP, while the top line shows the highest values. Even in 1961 the spread between the lowest (4.9 percent of GDP) and the highest (8.5 percent of GDP) values was 3.6 percentage points. The spread fell slightly to 1970, and then rose more or less continuously to the late 1970s when it reached nearly ten percentage points. It has remained roughly constant since then, albeit with some fluctuations. Removing Alberta, with its swollen energy revenues, from the data narrows the spread in the 1970s and early 1980s only a little.

Figure 3 shows the coefficient of variation of own-source revenues as a percentage of GDP for all provinces for the period 1961-95. This value fell markedly in the 1960s, rose again just as dramatically in the 1970s, fell from

Figure 2: Highest, Lowest, and Average of Own-Source Revenue as a Percent of GDP, All Provinces, 1961-1995

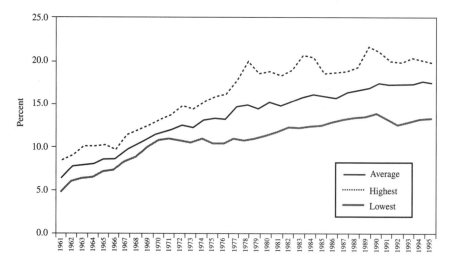

Source: Authors' Compilation.

Figure 3: Own-Source Revenue as a Percent of GDP, Coefficient of Variation, All Provinces, 1961-1995

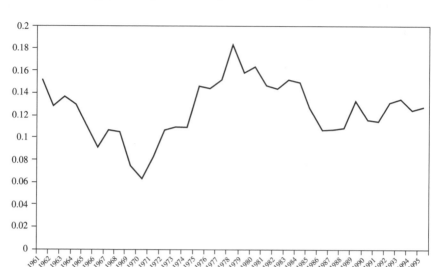

Source: Authors' Compilation.

the late 1970s to the mid-1980s, and has remained virtually constant since. Again, removing Alberta from the data moderates the trends only slightly.

Figures 2 and 3 indicate two facts about provincial taxation efforts. First, despite the equalization program, there is considerable variation at any moment in time among the provinces in the ratios of own-source revenues to GDP. Second, there is considerable change over time in this variation of tax effort among provinces. It is not easy to reconcile these facts with the prior occupancy thesis, which implies that provinces only have the tax room between some upper overall limit on taxation and the first-in share of the federal government.

OTHER CONSIDERATIONS

Thus far, we have examined situations where the case for fiscal realignment rests on potential real differences between the federal and provincial governments with respect to the cost of raising public funds or on the fact of prior occupancy of the key tax fields. It is always possible, of course, that the real motives lie elsewhere. We look briefly at two such explanations in this section.

POLITICAL CONSIDERATIONS

One possibility is that the provincial/territorial case for fiscal transfers is purely politically motivated. They may believe that the tax-expenditure decisions of government in total are not well understood by the public, and thus that getting the other level to do the taxing, while they do the spending, will be politically popular. In this case, the social cost of taxation as the provinces perceive it includes a "blame" factor. Thus even though $MCPF_p$ may not in fact be higher than $MCPF_f$, the provinces act as if it were. This argument can explain a call for unconditional fiscal transfers, but presumably not for tax point transfers or tax field realignment.

A variant of this point is that the *changing* of rates is politically costly even if the actual level of rates is not. If governments believe that leaving rates as they are will keep taxes from being an issue, and that taxpayers are only reminded of how unpopular taxes are if rates are changed, in particular raised, then there is some bias to keep rates as they are. In the last few years, when the federal government has been in surplus, then, an overall political cost-minimizing strategy might be for the federal government to pass some of this surplus onto the provinces, as opposed to having the federal government lower, and the provinces raise, taxes. This would require some myopia on the part of voter/taxpayers, but it is possible.

Another possibility is that the marginal political cost of raising funds differs from what we have called the MCPF. Hettich and Winer suggest that governments do not behave as we have described, equating marginal benefits of expenditure to the marginal cost of public funds, but rather choose taxes and expenditures so as to equate the marginal political cost of funds (MPC) to the marginal political benefits (MPB) of expenditure where these are measured as voting possibilities.[13] The government maximizes its expected vote where the probability of any individual voting for the government depends on functions of expenditure and taxation. The marginal cost of public funds and marginal benefit of expenditure to individuals is quite closely related to these MPC and MPB concepts, but, for example, some beneficiaries may not be voters so these concepts will not be the same. In addition, once a voter is committed to the government, extra benefits, in the form of reduced taxes or increased expenditures, will have no impact on voting behaviour and thus will have no political benefit. The two levels of government may differ in their calculations of the MPC and MPB of extra expenditure, and governments might see this as a reason for transfers.

DISTRIBUTIONAL CONSIDERATIONS

A further political reason for some provinces to favour fiscal transfers would be the implicit redistribution inherent in the arrangements. Most straightforwardly, those provinces in which average income was less than the national average might expect they would be better off with a system in which the federal government taxed and transferred to the provincial governments. This would, of course, depend on the tax and transfer arrangements. Taxes can be expected in our system to be roughly proportional to income. Thus, if transfers were "progressive," say on a per capita basis, the average person in provinces with average incomes less than the national average would benefit. Given that the majority of provinces have average incomes below the national average, any system that gives roughly equal weight to each province, or to each provincial premier in First Ministers' Meetings, might pressure the federal government to tax and transfer.

A more sophisticated argument for federal involvement in financing provincial provision of goods is in articles by both Bos and Wilson.[14] They argue that decisions on the public provision of private goods, which are essentially decisions on redistribution, will depend on the ratio of the median to the mean income in a jurisdiction. There are reasons to believe that this ratio will be lower nationally than in individual provinces[15] — there is more diversity across the nation as a whole than in individual provinces. Thus, the federal government, if it somehow responds to the median federal voter, will be more likely to tax and spend to supply goods to voters than would any provincial government. In this theory, in this case where the federal government must work through the provincial governments, it will be necessary for the federal government to constrain the provincial governments to ensure the transfers are actually made. Thus the concern of the federal government in the recent negotiations that the provinces might use the transfers for tax cuts rather than to increase expenditures on medical care.

CONCLUSION

Provincial governments in Canada have persistently argued that there is a fiscal gap such that it is easier for the federal government to raise sufficient revenue to meet its needs than for the provinces to meet theirs. This has been used to press for more federal-provincial transfers of either cash or tax points. At the same time, Canada is unique in that the lower level of government, the provinces, have virtually the same access to the tax bases as does the higher level. The question arises, therefore, of whether this fiscal gap really exists and, if so, of the policies that might best be used to correct for it.

While much of the motivation of the provinces for claiming this fiscal gap might be political, there are good reasons to believe that, despite having access to the same tax bases, the provinces are at a disadvantage in using them. In particular, the fact that many, or all, of the tax bases are more mobile interprovincially than internationally makes it more socially costly for the provinces to raise revenue than for the federal government to do so. Provinces could solve this by cooperating to set rates but this has the usual problems of collusion. One way to enforce collusion is to enter into an arrangement to have the federal government tax and transfer funds to the provinces. This is an argument, as well, in support of the federal government transferring cash rather than tax points.

There are other arguments for leaving the federal government with a large share of the tax base, such that transfers are necessary. If the federal government is to properly pursue a macro-stabilization policy it needs control over a significant portion of revenues. Coordination of tax policies to ensure that factors of production and other goods and services are allocated efficiently can most easily be done if the national government plays an important role in these policies. Third, the goals of personal income distribution and horizontal equity in the country as a whole require a permanent role for the federal government. In particular, equalization of provincial revenue capacities, if this is to be done from federal revenues, requires a federal surplus of revenues over own expenditures. Transferring, however this is done, too much tax room to the provinces endangers the federal government's ability to do this as, not only do federal government revenues fall, but provincial revenues, and thus the amounts needing equalization rise.

There is some evidence that provincial governments have been steadily increasing their share of overall tax revenues. At the same time, their share of overall expenditure responsibilities has also been increasing so this cannot be said to necessarily mean that the fiscal gap has been narrowing. There is also evidence that many provinces have not "hit a wall" in terms of their ability to raise revenues. It seems rather that they are politically restrained in some way. This conclusion follows from the wide range of provincial own-source revenue to GDP ratios observed across the provinces.

NOTES

1. Provincial/Territorial Ministers of Finance, *Report to Premiers* (Ottawa: Supply and Services Canada, 1998), p. 13.

2. The clearest example of a vertical fiscal gap is the situation brought about by the fiscal arrangements introduced with the *Constitution Act, 1867.* Customs and excise duties were the major source of government revenue at the time. Provinces were prohibited from levying them, so as not to interfere with interprovincial trade. But provinces still had significant expenditure responsibilities, even though they had no access to the sole significant revenue source. Thus, Ottawa provided statutory subsidies to the original four provinces, and to new ones as they entered the union.

3. This is not necessarily the case, however. One might argue that the fiscal gap ran in the other direction in Canada in the energy-crisis years of the 1970s and

early 1980s when some provincial government coffers were swollen by natural resource royalties denied to the federal government.

4.   Robin Boadway and Paul Hobson, *Intergovernmental Fiscal Relations in Canada* (Toronto: Canadian Tax Foundation, 1993); and Robin Boadway, Sandra Roberts and Anwar Shah, *The Reform of Fiscal Systems in Developing and Emerging Market Economies: A Federalism Perspective*, Policy Research Working Paper Series No. 1259 (New York: World Bank).

5.   This argument ignores the possibility that the federal government could tailor its policies regionally or, conversely, that provincial and territorial governments could collude to offer national ones. See Albert Breton and Anthony Scott, *The Economic Constitution of Federal States* (Toronto: University of Toronto Press, 1978), for a model where these possibilities are considered by including comparative transactions costs.

6.   Ignoring the possibility of provincial governments colluding in this task. See the previous note.

7.   See Paul Boothe and D. Hermanutz, *Simply Sharing: An Interprovincial Equalization Scheme for Canada* (Toronto: C.D. Howe Institute, 1999), for a discussion of such a scheme.

8.   See Boadway, Roberts and Shah, *The Reform of Fiscal Systems*, p. 20.

9.   There are a large number of studies showing the mobility of labour. See Stanley Winer and Denis Gauthier, *Internal Migration and Fiscal Structure* (Ottawa: Economic Council of Canada, 1982); K.E. Mills, M.B. Percy and L.S. Wilson, "The Influence of Fiscal Incentives on Interregional Migration: Canada 1961-78," *The Canadian Journal of Regional Science* 6, 2(1983):207-29; and R. Paul Shaw, "Fiscal versus Traditional Market Variables in Canadian Migration," *Journal of Political Economy* 96, 3 (1984):648-66. See Bev Dahlby, "Distorting Taxation and the Design of Intergovernmental Grants," Edmonton: Department of Economics, University of Alberta, unpublished paper, re: consumption and cross-provincial boundary shopping. There is, of course, elasticity in the bases even nationally — international capital flows, emigration, some cross-border shopping.

10.   While provinces are under-taxing compared to what they would wish to do if they could somehow control migration of their bases, they are not necessarily under-taxing compared to an efficient outcome. We will explain below that there are two types of externalities from provincial tax decisions and these may work in opposite directions. Thus, while it is likely that the level of provincial taxes will not be optimal we cannot say whether they will be too high or too low compared with the efficient level.

11.   See William R. Johnson, "Income Redistribution in a Federal System," *American Economic Review* 78, 3 (1988):570-73; and Bev Dahlby and L.S. Wilson, "Fiscal Capacity, Tax Effort and Optimal Equalization Grants," *Canadian Journal of Economics* 27 (1994):657-72, and "Tax Assignment and Fiscal Externalities in a Federal State," in *Reforming Fiscal Federalism for Global Competition: A Canada-Australia Comparison*, ed. Paul Boothe (Edmonton: University of Alberta Press), pp. 87-107.

12. For a general history of federal-provincial fiscal relations, see Boadway and Hobson, *Intergovernmental Fiscal Relations in Canada;* or Peter M. Leslie, Kenneth Norrie and Irene K. Ip, *A Partnership in Trouble: Renegotiating Fiscal Federalism* (Toronto: C.D. Howe Institute, 1993).

13. Walter Hettich and Stanley Winer, *Democratic Choice and Taxation: A Theoretical and Empirical Analysis* (Cambridge: Cambridge University Press, 1999), pp. 44-46.

14. Dieter Bos, "A Voting Paradox of Fiscal Federalism," *Journal of Public Economics* 11 (1979):369-82; and L.S. Wilson, "The Socialization of Medical Insurance in Canada," *Canadian Journal of Economics* 18, 2 (1985):355-76.

15. See Wilson, "The Socialization of Medical Insurance in Canada," p. 373.

4

The Social Union Framework Agreement and the Future of Fiscal Federalism

Harvey Lazar

Ce chapitre étudie les effets possibles de l'entente-cadre sur l'union sociale de 1999. On y soutient que cette entente pourrait devenir une innovation importante en termes d'élaboration des politiques sociales dans la fédération. Comme les ententes fédérales-provinciales sur les politiques sociales majeures constituent un élément essentiel du fédéralisme fiscal, il est de mise d'étudier les interactions possibles entre l'entente sur l'union sociale et les instruments et processus du fédéralisme fiscal.

L'analyse ici présentée conclut que l'ECUS prévoit un rôle continu tant pour les transferts fédéraux aux provinces que pour les transferts fédéraux directs. On y soutient aussi que la simple existence de l'entente sert sans doute à diminuer la probabilité d'un transfert de points d'impôt d'Ottawa aux provinces. L'entente témoigne aussi d'une plus grande préoccupation, de la part d'Ottawa, face aux déséquilibres horizontaux plutôt que verticaux. Les clauses sur la planification concertée jouent cependant le rôle d'un contrepoids. Si elles sont proprement mises en oeuvre, elles pourraient réduire les coûts externes associées à une fédération décentralisée et ainsi ouvrir la porte à une plus grande décentralisation. Nul ne peut toutefois prédire comment ces forces contradictoires s'équilibreront.

En ce qui a trait à la pratique du fédéralisme fiscal, il y a une tension entre le rôle central qu'ont traditionnellement joué les ministres des finances provinciaux et fédéraux dans le développement du fédéralisme fiscal et le rôle accru que l'ECUS assigne aux ministres responsables des affaires sociales dans la planification des programmes sociaux. Si les décisions fondamentales en matière de transferts sociaux sont prises dans l'environnement extrêmement politisé de la planification du budget fédéral, il sera difficile de mettre en oeuvre les principes sous-jacents de l'ECUS. Il faudra que les ministres des finances se montrent ouverts à la participation des ministres responsables des affaires sociales pour que l'ECUS fonctionne.

Federal and provincial finance ministers and their officials have been the principal architects of Canadian fiscal federalism in the decades since World War II. They are the ones who have shaped the way in which taxation revenues are shared and harmonized. They have also played the lead role in devising the system of intergovernmental transfers that has served to reduce vertical and horizontal fiscal imbalances among provinces. The federal Finance ministry in particular has been especially influential in determining the size of these transfers and the design of the Canada-wide social programs associated with them.

Among other things, this chapter investigates the possible impacts on Canadian fiscal federalism of the 1999 agreement to establish A Framework to Improve the Social Union for Canadians.[1] The SUFA (Social Union Framework Agreement) was negotiated mainly through intergovernmental and social ministries, not finance ministries.[2] It is argued here that the Framework Agreement could turn out to be a major innovation in the workings of the federation, heralding a new era of collaboration, mutual respect among orders of government and a more coherent and systematic approach to social policy-making. It could accordingly mean a different set of dynamics in our system of fiscal federalism. Alternatively, it could be ignored by its signatories and relegated to a footnote in the country's history. The energy and spirit with which government leaders implement the agreement's provisions during its initial three-year term will help to determine which of these directions will be followed.

An analysis of SUFA is important for this volume because of the large overlap and interaction between the Framework Agreement and Canadian fiscal federalism. Fiscal federalism, through its use of the federal spending power, has played a large role in promoting interprovincial equity and in facilitating the creation and maintenance of Canada-wide social programs. SUFA is in part about joint intergovernmental planning of social programs and the uses of and limitations on the federal spending power. Thus, there is an apparently tight link between these two sets of policies.

This chapter is by no means restricted, however, to the effects of SUFA on fiscal federalism. The agreement is also analyzed from a broader perspective, in part because such an assessment has merit in its own right but also because it helps to create a context for the discussion of possible implications for fiscal federalism. The objects of this chapter are thus three-fold. The first is to describe the architecture of SUFA. The focus here is on its broad scope: what it contains and what is excluded. Second, taking account of the analysis in the first section, the accord is then examined for its potential effects on the design and implementation of *social policy*, on the institutions and processes of *democratic government* and on the workings of the *federal principle*. The last section then focuses on what SUFA may mean for the future of fiscal federalism in Canada.

PART 1: ARCHITECTURE OF THE FRAMEWORK AGREEMENT

Section 1of the Framework Agreement sets out a series of *principles* which signatory governments agree to abide by in the design, implementation, and evaluation of social policy. In general, the principles are very broad. Among other things, they commit governments to "treat all Canadians with fairness and equity," "promote equality of opportunity for all Canadians," "ensure access for all Canadians, wherever they live or move in Canada, to essential social programs and services of reasonably comparable quality," "promote the full and active participation of all Canadians in Canada's social and economic life" and "ensure adequate, affordable, stable and sustainable funding for social programs." Intertwined with these principles is a rather more specific commitment, namely, respect for "the principles of medicare: comprehensiveness, universality, portability, public administration and accessibility." Appropriately, the principles involve a balancing act. For example, principles that appear to support benefit entitlements, such as "provide appropriate assistance to Canadians in need" and "ensure access for all Canadians ... to essential social programs and services of reasonably comparable quality" are balanced by the principle related to affordability cited above.

There is more than one way of analyzing SUFA. One way is to examine to what extent the remaining six sections (sections 2-7) of the agreement are concerned with *process* and to what extent with *substance*. On this basis, at least at first blush, five of the sections appear to deal mainly or exclusively with process. These include section 3 on "Informing Canadians — Public Accountability and Transparency," section 4 on "Working in Partnership for Canadians," section 6 on "Dispute Avoidance and Resolution," and section 7 on "Review of the Social Union Agreement." Section 5 on "The Federal Spending Power – Improving Social Programs for Canadians" is also about process. Only section 2 on "Mobility within Canada" is mainly about substance.

But, of course, this distinction between process and substance implies a clear separation of purpose that in some cases may be more apparent than real. The section on the spending power effectively re-affirms the legitimacy of this instrument in the eyes of signatory governments and also sets out some limitations on its use. These spending-power provisions do not, in themselves, constitute changes in the substance of social policy. Arguably, however, they are of substantive significance in the context of how federal and provincial governments wish to manage the federation and will also in due course bear on the future of Canadian social policy. Similarly, over time, the requirement to better inform Canadians about the outcomes of current programs may be expected to help shape their future evolution. It may also be expected that citizens and social activists will point to the principles laid out in section 1 as a basis for demanding improved social policies and programs. Other examples can be provided. So it is indeed possible that SUFA will have an important substantive impact on social policy. Indeed, some officials who were involved in the negotiation of SUFA believe that, in the eyes of the public, SUFA's ultimate success or failure will be judged by its results in terms of social policies and programs.[3]

In the years immediately preceeding the social union agreement, commentators from the research community recognized that one of the fundamental issues that needed resolution in the social union debate was how best to balance three sets of vital public interests: the quality and effectiveness of social policy; protecting and advancing the institutions and processes of democracy; and respect for Canada's federal character.[4] Looking at SUFA through this perspective, it can be seen that the section 1 principles touch mainly on the goals and purposes of social policy. This is evident from re-reading the several principles cited above (relating to equality, medicare, assistance to those in need, affordability, etc). Secondarily, that section implicitly acknowledges the risk of a democratic deficit in the social union. And it seeks to attenuate this possibility by committing governments to "work in partnership with individuals, families, communities, voluntary organizations, business and labour, and ensure appropriate opportunities for Canadians to have meaningful input into social policies and programs." All the section 1 commitments to the various policy and democratic principles noted above are to be carried out by governments "within their respective constitutional jurisdictions and powers." In this way only does section 1 allude to Canada's federal character.[5]

As noted above, section 2 is about mobility. It includes some quite precise undertakings by governments to remove existing barriers to mobility and to avoid creating new ones. In part, these are re-statements of old commitments found in either the *Canadian Charter of Rights and Freedoms* (section 6) or chapter 7 of the Agreement on Internal Trade. But the language of the section also extends these commitments, as will be discussed further below. It is the only section of the agreement that focuses on *policy*, as such. In this regard, the accord's architecture is quite different than the Agreement on Internal Trade, which contains substantive policy chapters on such issues as government procurement, energy, transportation, and indeed labour mobility.

Section 3 is concerned heavily with the *democratic* processes, committing governments to ensure "effective mechanisms for Canadians to participate in developing social policies and reviewing outcomes." It also provides for "appropriate mechanisms for citizens to appeal unfair administrative practices and bring complaints about access and service" and requires governments to "report publicly on citizen's appeals and complaints." Perhaps most importantly, it requires each signatory government to "monitor and measure outcomes of its social programs and report regularly to its constituents on the performance of these programs." It thus proposes to make available to the public the kind of information that could enable citizens to engage one another, and their governments, in serious dialogue about policy choices.

The remaining sections are about how federal-provincial relations are to be conducted in relation to social policy. Section 4 commits governments to "undertake joint planning [sic] to share information on social trends, problems and priorities and to work together to identify priorities for collaborative action...[to] collaborate on implementation of joint priorities when this would result in more effective and efficient service to Canadians." It also requires governments to "give one another advance notice prior to implementation of a major change in a social policy or program which will likely substantially affect another government" and to "offer to consult prior to implementing new social policies and programs that are likely to substantially affect other governments or the social union more generally." That section also provides the equivalent of a most-favourite-nation clause to the effect that "for any new Canada-wide initiative, arrangements made with one province/territory will be made available to all provinces/territories in a manner consistent with their diverse circumstances."

The provincial governments were the driving force behind the negotiations that led up to the Framework Agreement for reasons that were straightforward. They had been badly shaken by the large cuts in federal transfers associated with the introduction of the Canada Health and Social Transfer (CHST). They wanted a new set of "rules" that would enable them to plan their programs and financial affairs within a more stable policy and fiscal framework. To achieve this, they negotiated for an agreement that would give them more influence over the federal government's use of its spending power, greater stability in intergovernmental transfers (i.e., rules regarding the federal government's freedom to reduce transfers) and an agreed mechanism for settling disputes.[6] Thus, in section 5, the federal government makes three basic commitments relating to its use of that power. The first is to "consult with provincial and territorial governments at least one year prior to renewal of or significant changes in existing social transfers to provinces/territories ... and build due notice provisions into any new social transfers to provincial/territorial governments." The second is a new decision rule regarding new Canada-wide initiatives supported by financial transfers from Ottawa to provinces/territories. This will be discussed further below. Suffice it here to say that such new initiatives require the support of a majority of provinces, although without any requirement that those six provinces represent some minimum share of the Canadian population.[7] And while there is no formal "opting-out" rule in this area, the detailed provisions offer a *de facto* opting-out provision that makes available to provinces at least as much flexibility as does current practice (as will be discussed further in the next section). The third commitment is that before the federal government introduces new Canada-wide social programs funded through direct transfers to individuals or organizations, "it will, prior to implementation, give at least three months' notice and offer to consult" other governments. Importantly, there is no "opting-out" clause, *de jure* or *de facto*, in relation to direct transfers.

Section 6 is also focused on federal-provincial relations, in this case dispute avoidance and resolution, another area where the provinces pressed for new arrangements. The section suggests that governments may be able to avoid disputes through the information-sharing, joint planning, collaboration, and advance notice and consultation provisions referred to above. It emphasizes joint fact-finding, including the use of third parties to fact-find, mediate or advise on dispute resolution. Although there is no requirement that any government accept the findings of a third party, that is, the sovereignty of all governments remains intact, governments did commit to "report publicly on an annual basis on the nature of the intergovernmental disputes and their resolution." So the affirmation of their sovereignty does not mean that they will be able to avoid public scrutiny of their behaviour. Section 7 provides that governments will jointly review the Framework Agreement after three years and make appropriate adjustments.[8]

In essence then, sections 4-7 are the framework for a "code of conduct" about how the two orders of government are to relate to one another in relation to social policy and the social union. From one perspective, these sections reflect the recognition of the two orders of government that they are necessarily and inevitably becoming more interdependent. But constitutional powers remain as they have been all along. Thus, from a second perspective, they also establish rules about the obligations of governments to one another to the extent that they act independently. In brief, signatory governments have given voluntary undertakings to be more sensitive to other governments as they conduct their business.

In the press coverage prior to and following the 4 February 1999 agreement, much attention was given to the political dynamics that had surrounded the negotiating process. In particular, journalistic coverage focused on the interplay between three factors: first, the fiscal negotiations surrounding the size of the increase in the federal government's CHST payment to the provinces; second, the objective of ensuring that the incremental CHST payments would be used by the provinces for health-care purposes only; and finally, the actual content of SUFA. A common media interpretation of the results was that provincial governments accepted weak controls on the federal spending power in exchange for incremental CHST dollars. This view was stated most colourfully by Gordon Gibson who observed, just before the agreement was signed, that " the premiers look for all the world like a bunch of squeegee kids, circling the prime-ministerial limousine and offering to clean the windshield for another 100 million loonies. They wait for the great man to smile or snarl."[9] Writing afterwards, Andrew Coyne observes that most media commentators saw the agreement as a "great big pile of fudge."[10] From the French-language Quebec media, with few exceptions, there was a sense that the agreement did not go far enough to satisfy Quebec's demands.[11]

While some of these views have some validity, they reflect a very partial analysis of the intergovernmental dynamics. For one thing, the provincial negotiating position became public (through a leak), and thus it was relatively easy to determine the distance between their negotiating position and the final agreement. The federal negotiating position was not as widely known. Thus, the concessions made by the federal government received less coverage. In any case, these kinds of criticisms have focused mainly on alleged deficiencies of SUFA rather than analyzing it for what it is. The next part of the chapter seeks to fill this gap by examining the implications of the agreement for social policy, democracy, and federalism.

PART 2: IMPACT ON SOCIAL POLICY, DEMOCRACY AND FEDERALISM

SOCIAL POLICY IMPLICATIONS

What needs to be evaluated here has as much or more to do with process than with social policy substance. Thus, it should not come as a surprise that the direct and immediate effects of the social union accord on *social policy* are modest. They are not, however, inconsequential. Provincial governments endorsed the five principles of the *Canada Health Act*. This suggests the possibility that provincial privatization initiatives have become less likely and that the use of facility fees has been rendered more remote. Provincial governments had indicated support for the five principles in the past but sometimes in conjunction with additional principles that provinces considered significant.[12] On this occasion, the endorsement of provincial signatories was unqualified.

The most substantive policy references in the agreement are section 2. In it, reflecting mainly Ottawa's desire to reinforce and broaden mobility, governments commit that no new barriers to freedom of movement will be created as a result of new social policy initiatives. They promise to "eliminate within three years, any residency-based policies or practices which constrain access to post-secondary education, training, health and social services and social assistance unless they can be demonstrated to be [both] reasonable and consistent with the principles of the social union framework."[13] While this qualification may turn out to be a loophole, it is noteworthy that the onus is on governments to demonstrate that their exceptional practice meets these two conditions. There is also a commitment to ensure that full compliance with the mobility provisions of the Agreement on Internal Trade has been achieved by 1 July 2001 including requirements for mutual recognition of occupational qualifications and the elimination of residency requirements for access to employment opportunities. Sector ministers are called upon to submit annual reports to the Ministerial Council identifying residency-based barriers and action plans to end them.

The explicit extension of the mobility provisions to postsecondary education is new. Whether it has implications for provinces that wish to charge higher tuition fees to out-of-province postsecondary students than for in-province students is not obvious. A similar question arises in relation to geographic restrictions on the use of provincial loans, scholarships, and fellowships. In both cases, however, SUFA appears to provide a mechanism through which these kinds of questions can be tackled and potentially resolved. Indeed, it is understood that the removal of out-of-province limitations on student loans is now being examined as one possible outcome of current deliberations inside governments.[14]

As for the explicit reference to "training" in the mobility section, it is similar to provisions found in the nine federal-provincial bilateral agreements that Ottawa has signed with provincial governments on the devolution of training to the provinces. What is new here is that, in the event of dispute, there are modestly more elaborate dispute settlement mechanisms in SUFA than in the bilateral agreements.[15]

At first glance, it may appear that the mobility commitments relating to health and social services and social assistance are only a re-hashing of provisions found in the *Canada Health Act* (CHA) and the CHST. Under these provisions, mobility rights are protected by those legislative provisions that enable the federal government to penalize financially any province that violates them. That is, the enforcement mechanism is based exclusively on federal law. In fact, however, there are several differences from what had existed previously. First, many provincial health and social services are beyond the reach of the CHA and CHST. For instance, home care, pharmacare, and some social services are not clearly covered by those federal statutes. And some of those particular service areas are growing rapidly. SUFA now covers them. Second, the mobility provisions will also apply to federal activities. They may have implications, for example, for federal programs that affect Aboriginal people when they move off-reserve. Third, with the new Framework Agreement, enforcement may not be as heavily dependent on the *de jure* federal unilateralism associated with CHST and the CHA. It seems logical that where there are disputes, provinces will seek to ensure that they are resolved through SUFA's dispute settlement arrangements. In this regard, it is especially noteworthy that the section 6 dispute avoidance and resolution provisions declare that the "commitments on mobility, intergovernmental transfers and interpretation of the Canada Health Act principles, and as appropriate, on any new joint initiative" are covered.

Potentially very significant in the accord are the provisions that could, over time, add coherence to social policy. The commitments to "undertake joint planning to share information on social trends, problems and priorities and to work together to identify priorities for collaborative action " (section 4) have the prospect of improving policy in three ways. The first is by providing a mechanism for minimizing the number of situations where federal and provincial policies work at cross-purposes, thwarting, and undercutting one another. Second, they should reduce situations of duplication and waste between orders of government, to the extent that these may exist. Third, if both orders of government acquire the habit of sharing information, reviewing trends, and assessing priorities together, the knowledge brought to bear on policy choices will be broadened and enriched.

These commitments to joint planning and collaboration go well beyond past practice. There has never been ongoing federal-provincial information-sharing or joint planning in the social area, although there have been periodic attempts that have not been sustained. At present, there are joint activities on many issues, including early childhood development, health, skills and learning, disability, homelessness, youth, older workers, and Aboriginal affairs. While this list understates the scope of intergovernmental discussions in the social area, in and of itself the length of the list is not unusual. It is true that there is more federal-provincial momentum on social policy now than there was during much of the 1990s, mainly because the 1990s were dominated by fiscal restraint. But the current range of issues under review by sectoral tables would not appear unusual to anyone associated with social policy tables of the 1960s and 1970s. What sectoral tables have lacked in the past, however, was an ongoing systematic attention to their sectors. Federal and provincial labour market ministers, for example, have not regularly reviewed the labour market outlook for the coming year and set priorities in the light of that outlook. Labour market and social service ministers have not systematically examined the interaction between federal Employment Insurance and provincial Social Assistance. Health ministers have not systematically analyzed epidemiological trends and their implications for health policy. SUFA commits governments to change this and, as a result, joint planning has the potential to improve significantly the quality of social policy. Whether in fact these undertakings by governments are implemented seriously is, of course, the issue.[16] In this regard, a vigilant citizenry has an important role to play.[17]

In summary, the Framework Agreement is not mainly about the content of policy. It does offer, however, some new benefits to Canadians, mainly related to mobility. It also strengthens existing commitments related to mobility and public health care. Much more importantly, there is the prospect that joint planning will generate more coherence, better value for money, and a more intelligent way to establish priorities. Only time will tell, however, whether SUFA in fact delivers on this potential.

IMPLICATIONS FOR DEMOCRACY

In the discussion above, SUFA's heavy emphasis on joint planning and collaboration was noted. And section 5 sets out the federal-provincial decision rules for the use of the federal spending power. Moreover, the preamble to the agreement refers to the fact that it is based on mutual respect between various orders of government and "a willingness to work more closely together to meet the needs of Canadians." So if SUFA is successfully implemented, executive federalism will also be strengthened.[18] And other things being equal, stronger executive federalism could mean more decision-making behind closed doors. When deals are struck, it will be difficult for the public to change them, as the deals will reflect whatever fine balance was struck in the intergovernmental negotiation that led up to them. SUFA thus raises the issue of democratic deficit.

The negotiators of the accord were aware of these dangers. Their effort to address them is reflected in section 3 on "Informing Canadians — Public Accountability and Transparency." Specifically, it commits governments to three kinds of undertakings that might help the workings of the democratic process. The first is a regular flow of information from each government to its constituents reporting on the outcomes of social programs. Over time, it anticipates that different governments will use comparable indicators to measure progress so that this flow of information to the public will enable those who are interested to compare results in their jurisdiction to results in other jurisdictions. Second, the agreement contemplates effective mechanisms for Canadians to participate in developing priorities and reviewing outcomes. Third, there are obligations to individual citizens which would enable them to appeal administrative decisions that they consider unfair and this appeal mechanism is strengthened by requirements that governments make publicly available eligibility criteria and service commitments for social programs. This last commitment should be relatively easy for governments to honour. The same is not true of the first two.

On the surface, the first of these undertakings is precise and straightforward. Implementing some system of monitoring and "output" measurement is indeed a relatively simple exercise given political will. But the agreement mentions measuring "outcomes," not "outputs," and measuring outcomes in a meaningful way is a huge and difficult challenge. It is, for example, one thing to measure the number of medical and surgical procedures a hospital carries out in a year and the cost per unit procedure. It is another thing to determine the health outcomes of those expenditures and to determine whether the health benefits of those outputs exceed the benefits of an equal sum spent on public health. In short, constructing meaningful outcome measures may be a slow task. In some cases, output measures may have to serve initially as very weak substitutes for outcome measures. From the perspective of improving the democratic process, however, understanding outcomes is basic to being able to understand policy choices. Therefore, this is an area that will require intense effort in the coming years if this accountability technique is to be truly meaningful.

The second undertaking in section 3 — "ensure effective mechanisms for Canadians to participate in developing social priorities and reviewing outcomes" — is both ambiguous and difficult to achieve. The challenge of "citizen engagement" is one that governments everywhere struggle with and, to date, the results everywhere are disappointing. *In part*, this aspect of accountability is linked to the role of legislators and legislatures. Citizens vote for representatives and one way that citizens might be able to influence the decision-making process is by influencing the people who represent them in legislatures. However, the role of Parliament and of provincial legislatures is not discussed in SUFA, leaving one to assume that legislatures, as such, will have at best their usual relatively small role with respect to executive federalism. And unless new mechanisms are invented, the same may be equally true for interest groups and individual citizens who wish to interact directly with ministers and officials who are in decision-making positions. In any case, there is at present no evidence that signatory governments have a blueprint up their sleeves for improving democratic processes in relation to the social union.

One way to better involve legislatures would be for each of the signatory governments to establish a legislative committee on the social union in its jurisdiction. That committee might hold regular hearings reviewing compliance with SUFA undertakings. It could call witnesses on the development of performance indicators and on the relationship between the indicators and outcomes. It could also review government reports on appeal procedures and assess the workings of the dispute-settlement mechanisms. If membership had some continuity, and there was adequate professional staff, legislators might carve out for themselves a recognized if modest role on SUFA, notwithstanding the well-known executive dominance of Westminster-type systems. Even more audaciously, such committees might periodically hold joint meetings with one or more comparable committees from other jurisdictions, perhaps focusing on items that are not jurisdiction-specific, such as performance indicators. Such committees might also serve as mechanisms through which interest groups and individuals were able to have their voices heard on matters of policy and administration.

One proposal that has been talked about for some time is the idea that one or more third parties be selected to review the outcomes of social programs — the idea of an independent social audit. This merits further consideration. One

possibility, of course, is that governments/legislatures will individually appoint an arm's length body to conduct this function, a kind of auditor-general/
ombudsman for social programs in their jurisdictions. A related question is
whether all governments that are signatories to the agreement should jointly
appoint a third party to monitor the overall workings of the social union and,
in particular, whether the commitments of governments, one to the other, are
being respected. An intergovernmental auditor would be a bold innovation
and could potentially serve as an important force for governments to live up
to their commitments.

Even if measures along these lines are implemented, more will be needed.
It would be useful, for example, to have an independent research organization
assessing trends in social outcomes and differences across the country in relation to those outcomes. After all, the processes of the social union must, at the
end of the day, be evaluated not only for how they affect Canadian democracy
and federalism. They must also be assessed on whether they serve to strengthen
the very idea of "social union," which presumably must take account of whether
social outcomes are converging or diverging from region to region across
Canada.[19] With suitable adjustments, the Caledon Institute and Canadian Policy
Research Networks might fill play a role in carrying out this function.

These are among the issues that governments and citizens need to address.
They are also the kinds of issues that are easy to ignore. The social union
accord has bowed curtly in their direction. Governments and citizens need to
do more. Indeed, the more successful the social union turns out to be from an
executive federalism perspective, the greater the risks that it will increase the
size of the democratic deficit and the greater the need to put real flesh on the
bare bones of section 3.

IMPLICATIONS FOR FEDERALISM

In the weeks leading up to the signing of SUFA, all ten provinces as well as
the two territories[20] presented a common negotiating position to the federal
government. The federal government countered. In the end, both sides made
some concessions. Although only those who were directly involved in the
negotiations know the exact details of the "give and take" that occurred, it
appears that the federal government modified its position on such issues as
public accountability and dispute settlement while the provincial/territorial
side adjusted their position on the extent of their influence over the federal
spending power. It was for the last reason, in particular, that the Government
of Quebec chose not to sign. In press commentary after these events, Premier
Bouchard was quoted as saying that the social union accord was a centralizing document. Ironically, in the Bouchard perspective, he alone (a sovereignist)
had defended the federal system whereas the other premiers had failed to do
so.[21]

What in fact does this agreement mean for Canadian federalism? Is it a centralizing document? Is it best viewed through the lens of which order of government "won" and which "lost"?

We begin with Quebec's objections. In an article written a few months before the signing of the social union accord, the Quebec minister responsible for Canadian intergovernmental affairs declared: "For Quebec, only a true opting out clause with full fiscal compensation can concretely assure respect for Quebec's responsibility in relation to social matters."[22] But in the final weeks and days of bargaining leading up to the final deal, as noted above, a formal opting-out provision was lost by the provinces. While the equivalent of an opting-out provision remains in relation to Canada-wide programs funded partly by federal transfers to the provinces, there is no provision for opting out in relation to direct transfers to individuals or organizations. In the event, Quebec chose not to sign the agreement, pointing mainly to the inadequate opting-out provisions.

Turning first to the issue of opting out in relation to new jointly financed Canada-wide initiatives, SUFA provides that such initiatives may be launched by the federal government, exercising its spending power, when it has the support of at least six (that is to say, a majority of) provinces. Once the majority support rule has been satisfied, a province that had initially withheld its support would nonetheless be able to design and deliver its own program and receive federal compensation provided it decides to offer its residents a program that *meets the agreed objectives* of the Canada-wide initiative. In this sense, SUFA is somewhat similar to the opting-out provisions of the Meech Lake and Charlottetown Accords. Under Meech Lake, for example, an opting-out province was to receive reasonable compensation if it carried on a program or initiative that was *compatible with the national objectives*. And in two ways SUFA goes further than Meech Lake and Charlottetown in terms of accommodating provinces. It provides that a "provincial/territorial government which, because of its existing programming, does not require the total transfer to fulfill the agreed objectives would be able to reinvest any funds not required for those objectives in the same or a related priority area" (section 5). Second, the opting-out provision of the Meech Lake and Charlottetown Accords was limited to "shared-cost" programs whereas the SUFA provisions include jointly-financed programs that are not based on cost-sharing.[23] Thus, although the expression "opting out" is not used in SUFA there is *de facto* opting out that is modestly more flexible than what was contemplated in the Meech Lake and Charlottetown Accords. In fact, since six provinces are required to launch such an initiative, some federal officials think of these provisions as a kind of "opting in."[24]

Robson and Schwanen express concern that SUFA "says nothing about the conditions under which provinces might opt out if their own priorities ... are at odds with those of other provinces."[25] If there were a consensus to start a new Canada-wide program on, say, early childhood development, and one province wanted to give priority to retraining of older displaced workers instead of to early childhood, that province would not qualify for its federal share of funds. If this is what is meant by a province being "at odds" with the priorities of other governments, then this concern is probably quite fair. But previous federal-provincial negotiations to secure intergovernmental agreement on opting out also excluded provision for this kind of large difference in priorities. For example, as noted above, the Meech Lake Accord would have required the Government of Canada to "provide reasonable compensation to the government of a province that chooses not to participate in a national shared cost program ... [only] if the province carries on a program or initiative that is compatible with the national objectives."[26] The Charlottetown Accord provisions were the same. Moreover, the hypothetical example above, based on the wide difference between early childhood programs and older worker retraining, is quite unrealistic. The differences in priorities among provinces are virtually never that wide and all governments will normally be active in both areas. In other words, it is probable that there will be relatively few (if any) situations where the concerns expressed by Robson and Schwanen will have practical consequences. Thus, Claude Ryan's conclusion that, in practice, "this new system will closely resemble what we have known until now" is probably not far off the mark.[27] I would re-state, however, to the extent that SUFA differs, it leans toward accommodating provinces.[28]

It must be acknowledged, however, that there is one "wild card" in this conclusion. Since only six provinces are required for Ottawa to launch a new Canada-wide program, in theory the six could be made up of the six smallest provinces that together contain only 15 percent of the Canadian population. Since all six of those provinces are equalization-receiving provinces, they might have a self-interest in the implicit redistribution in their favour that would flow from a new national program that distributed funds on a needs basis or even an equal per capita basis. For this reason, Robson and Schwanen speculate that this element "may turn out to promote centralization rather than the flexibility that ought to be the hallmark of a federation."[29] This could indeed put the federation under strain. There is an alternative view that may be equally plausible however, namely, that no federal government would risk launching a new Canada-wide initiative against the opposition of the four largest provinces. In this perspective, this relatively easy formal threshold could have the effect of thwarting rather than facilitating new programs. Larger provinces could take the line that Ottawa should act on new Canada-wide initiatives if it so wishes since it is free to do so without their support. They could plausibly deny that their opposition to new programs is an obstacle to Canada-wide action even though in practice their opposition might deprive Ottawa of the political legitimacy it requires to act. In this alternative speculation, the majority-province rule could turn out to be anything but centralizing. In this regard, it is noteworthy that the majority-rule provision originated with provincial governments, not Ottawa.[30]

As for the issue of opting out in relation to direct transfers, this is what has Quebec most concerned. Under SUFA, there is no explicit or implicit provision for provincial opting out, as Quebec was able to negotiate many years ago in relation to the Canada Student Loan Program. Since that loan program was first put in place, Ottawa has transferred federal money to Quebec City and the provincial government has made loans to Quebec's postsecondary students. Neither the students nor their tax-paying parents have been made aware that a share of the funds comes from Ottawa. The social union accord does not explicitly anticipate a similar opting-out arrangement in relation to a new program. At the same time, SUFA does not prevent a federal government from agreeing to such an opting-out arrangement in relation to some future direct transfer program. In other words, SUFA does not tie Ottawa's hands in this regard. But SUFA certainly does signal that Ottawa will not agree to such arrangements lightly.

The position of the current Parti Québécois Government of Quebec is, at least in principle, broadly similar to that which both federalist and sovereignist governments in Quebec have held for several decades. In essence, it is that while the federal spending may be constitutionally valid, it lacks political legitimacy.[31] By enabling the federal government to spend in areas of the constitution that are within the exclusive legislative competence of the provinces, the spending power undermines the federal character of Canada. It destroys the federal pact that is the bedrock of Canada as a political nation. Opting out enables Quebec to retain exclusive authority within the legislative areas reserved for the provinces.

Underlying the official Quebec position is the classical view of federalism espoused by K.C. Wheare. In that view, the federal principle entails "the method of dividing powers so that the general and regional governments are each, within a sphere, co-ordinate and independent."[32] For Wheare, a federal state is one in which each order of government is sovereign within its own sphere of constitutional competence and neither order of government is unduly dependent on the other.

Few modern federal states function in this classical way. Watts has shown that in most federations there is a wide array of concurrent powers.[33] Also, in all federal states that were the subject of a second study by Watts, there was the equivalent of Canada's federal spending power.[34] Whereas a "classical" federation is characterized by *independence* and an *absence of hierarchy* (co-ordinate) between orders of government,[35] contemporary federations are characterized by *interdependence* with varying degrees of *hierarchy* between orders of government, with the central government often the more powerful.

In this regard, the Canadian federation has less interdependence and less hierarchy than most federations, for at least four reasons. First, there are only a few concurrent legislative powers in the Canadian constitution (relating to agriculture, immigration, and old age pensions). Second, both orders of government have taxing powers in relation to what are today the main revenue bases of modern states. Third, some of the federal government's general powers (such as the power to disallow and to reserve provincial legislation) have fallen into disuse. Fourth, to the extent that the federal government makes use of its spending power to transfer funds to provincial governments, there is a low level of conditionality attached to those transfers compared to similar transfers in other federations. Owing in particular to the last three of these reasons, there is relatively little hierarchy in the Canadian federal system (compared, say, to the American, Australian or German federations) [36] although there are certainly some areas that have significant hierarchical attributes.[37] And the extensive revenue-raising powers of the provinces make them somewhat independent of Ottawa, at least in respect of government finance.[38]

But there is also considerable interdependence among Canadian governments and it is growing. Apart from the interdependence recognized in SUFA, other recent illustrations include the Agreement on Internal Trade, the Canada-Wide Agreement on Environmental Harmonization, and the National Child Benefit. Older intergovernmental arrangements that have been amended recently include the Canada Pension Plan and bilateral agreements relating to the labour market.[39] Moreover, as domestic policy becomes increasingly subject to international disciplines, including in areas that are wholly or partly within provincial legislative competence, the need for cooperation between the two orders of government can only be expected to grow. The negotiation of the Kyoto climate change agreements is a recent illustration; and the implementation effort associated with that international agreement requires even more extensive federal-provincial collaboration.

The reasons prompting provincial governments to seek a social union accord were discussed above. Having been burned by the large cuts in cash transfers associated with the introduction of the CHST, they pressed for some formal understandings regarding the federal government's use of its spending power, in relation both to Ottawa's freedom to launch new programs and its discretion to reduce spending on existing ones. They also looked for rules to help settle federal-provincial disputes, believing that they would be better served by a regime in which disputes are settled through rules rather than raw power. Provincial reasoning on this latter point is analogous to the position that the federal government often takes in relation to international economic matters. On international trade, for example, Ottawa has long believed it is better served by a regime that is rules-based, like the World Trade Organization, than it would be by a series of bilateral agreements, where Canada's trade interests might be vulnerable to decisions by much more powerful governments, especially that of the United States.

As for the federal government's interests in SUFA, it had a particular desire to strengthen the mobility rights of Canadians and more generally promote the idea that Canadian citizenship carries with it "equal opportunities to participate fully in the social and economic opportunities of the country."[40] The federal government also attached substantial importance to the accountability provisions, perhaps in part because it hoped that, eventually, extensive public reporting would lead to cross-provincial comparisons and support a growing commonality of programs based on best practice.[41] Also, federal initiatives could be undermined by provincial government actions in the absence of good cooperation. Prior to the National Child Benefit, for instance, Ottawa was concerned that any increase in the federal refundable tax credit for relatively low-income families with children would flow to provincial coffers, not poor families with children.[42] The federal government may have also attached some weight to having its spending power recognized in a federal-provincial agreement. The value that Ottawa attached to this, however, is uncertain and possibly not very high given that the constitutional validity of the power had not been challenged and that, as just noted, it enjoyed political legitimacy in most of Canada.[43]

Thus, it is being argued here that whatever the short-term political dynamics that gave rise to SUFA, it is not now most constructively viewed in terms of who "won" and "lost." Provinces can be said to have "lost" to the extent that they had to modify some of their original negotiating position, including on the opting-out clause.[44] But it could also be argued that the provinces "won" to the extent that Ottawa agreed to put into an intergovernmental agreement a set of decision rules that gives the provinces a formal if modest role in the exercise of that power that they had not previously had. It could also be argued that provinces won to the extent that the federal government agreed to dispute-settlement mechanisms. As for the accountability provisions, they represent a nice balance between federal and provincial negotiating positions.

In any case, the Framework Agreement is consistent with the idea of a modern federal system that recognizes both the interdependence and independence of both orders of government. Most provinces and the federal government are comfortable with this concept. In the absence of a wide and explicit opting-out provision, however, it is not consistent with the classical federalism preferred by Quebec governments.

The lack of a Quebec signature on SUFA is also consistent with recent trends in Quebec's approach to federal-provincial relations. Quebec signs intergovernmental agreements when it is convinced that those agreements advance or protect Quebec's autonomy, improves its finances or fit with its broad economic strategy.[45] Otherwise, it declines to do so fearing that what the federal government calls "collaboration" is a poorly disguised attack on Quebec's areas of exclusive sovereignty. The number of cases where Quebec has not signed recently (although observing in some cases it concurs with the stated objectives of the agreement) has now become quite significant. They include the Canada-Wide Agreement on Environmental Harmonization, the National Child Benefit, and, of course, SUFA. In this regard, it is noteworthy that the leader of the opposition in Quebec has stated that he too would not have signed SUFA as negotiated, although he also declared that he could have negotiated a better deal for Quebec.

There are some commentators who interpret Quebec's unwillingness to sign SUFA as indicating that it will not receive its "share" of federal funds the next time there is a new federal-provincial jointly financed Canada-wide initiative. Andrew Coyne is among the most hard-line, writing: "If Quebec opts out of some future shared-cost program, it should not get one dollar of federal funds."[46] Robson and Schwanen are more cautious on this same point. They observe: "In practical terms, every new initiative under the agreement will present a fresh dilemma: Quebec will either get transfer money without having had to agree to broad terms on engagement vis-à-vis Canadians in other provinces, or the federal government will deny Quebec money that the other provinces are receiving."[47]

In the short run, these views are probably off the mark. In particular, it is most unlikely that Ottawa will pay much attention to Coyne. Rather, it can be expected that the federal government and the other provinces will avoid social initiatives that they know to be inconsistent with Quebec's policy directions. And because there will not be inconsistency between the new initiatives under SUFA and what Quebec is doing, Ottawa will likely transfer the same amount of funds to the Quebec authorities as Quebec would have received had it signed SUFA. This will be rationalized on the grounds that the Quebec government's actions are consistent with the objectives of the new Canada-wide initiative. While this approach may buy some time for Ottawa, it is not a happy resolution of the dilemma noted by Robson and Schwanen. And over time, it may not be sustainable.

In a carefully crafted piece for the journal *Inroads,* Claude Ryan concludes that the only resolution to this problem is to allow Quebec "the right to withdraw unconditionally from all Canada-wide programs within provincial jurisdiction.... accompanied by financial compensation."[48] This solution will not be acceptable to a Chrétien government. But with different governments in Ottawa and Quebec City, some form of explicit opting-out arrangement may sooner or later be required as a way of better managing if not fully resolving the dilemma.[49]

In this regard, it is important to distinguish between substance and symbolism. With regard to intergovernmental transfers, it was suggested above that there are *de facto* opting-out provisions in SUFA that are, if anything, more accommodating to provincial needs and circumstances than what previous Quebec governments had agreed to in the Meech Lake and Charlottetown

Accords. Moreover, the recent trend in the area of federal-provincial transfers is toward lightly conditioned federal bloc transfers, not cost-sharing. To the extent that this trend continues, from a substantive perspective, formal opting-out arrangements in SUFA would not add to Quebec's flexibility, at least as compared to the flexibility it has experienced in the decades since World War II.

But substance is not everything. Symbolism also matters. The fact is that the vision of the federal system found in SUFA does not correspond to the traditional Quebec position. Even if SUFA exceeds what Meech Lake and Charlottetown offered in terms of opting out, which the above analysis demonstrates, it only does so implicitly, whereas those two accords would have done so explicitly.

Similarly, without a SUFA, the issue of direct transfers would not have arisen for Quebec as a matter of principle. New direct transfer programs would have been dealt with on a case-by-case basis, as in the past. It is true that SUFA provides the provinces with a commitment from Ottawa to "give at least three months' notice and offer to consult" before acting. This should make provinces less vulnerable to unanticipated federal initiatives, especially when this provision is read in conjunction with other sections of SUFA, such as those related to joint planning. So, in substance provincial governments are better off in relation to direct transfers. But again the symbolism looks different. From a Quebec perspective, on a case-by-case basis, it was possible to opt out of some previous direct transfer programs whereas SUFA does not deal explicitly with this possibility.

All of this suggests that some modifications on the issue of opting may be needed if SUFA is to be signed by a future Quebec government. Four features of such an opting-out provision might be part of some new middle ground. I use the expression "new middle ground" recognizing that, for the federal government, SUFA entailed some movement on its part in relation to the spending power and, in that sense, for Ottawa, SUFA is the "middle ground." The first is the provision in section 3 of SUFA that each government agrees to "publicly recognize and explain the respective roles and contributions of governments." Thus, in a new direct or jointly funded program, an opting province would publicly acknowledge the federal financial contribution. The second is a requirement that the opting-out province use the funds in one of two ways. The funds would have to be used in a way that is broadly compatible with the purposes of the new program. Alternatively, if the province's existing programming had already enabled it to achieve the Canada-wide program objectives, it would be able to use the funds in the same or a related priority area. This would be less than the unconditional withdrawal called for by Ryan but, as a practical matter, not too far from it. Moreover, if Quebec was truly offended by the purposes of a new national initiative, and had signed SUFA, it could register its objection publicly and forcefully. In a setting where there is the kind of joint planning that is called for by SUFA, it would be an unwise federal government that would launch a new program that was so far removed from Quebec's objectives (recall we are writing about areas of exclusive provincial jurisdiction) that Quebec would be unable to opt out and reasonably provide its own program under one of the two carve-outs noted above.[50] Third, to reduce the possibility of Ottawa agreeing with six small provinces on Canada-wide priorities, a rule under which seven provinces representing at least half the population would be better as a measure of national consensus. Fourth, and given the above analysis, perhaps most important, the opting-out arrangements would be explicit, for the symbolic reasons noted, and not inferred.

The first three of these features need not, in substance, make a big difference relative to what is now in SUFA. Smaller provinces might dislike the 50 percent of the population rule and so they would have to judge whether the disadvantages of giving up that provision were outweighed by the prospects of a Quebec signature. As for Ottawa, while opting out of direct programs is something that the federal government might prefer not to contemplate, it has in fact agreed to this in the past in specific cases and is likely to do so in the future.

So the big difference comes in the symbolic recognition that opting out would in some cases be possible under SUFA and that it is consistent with the traditions of post-World War II federalism practice in Canada. From a federal government perspective, a broad opting-out "right" might be seen as a strong incentive for Quebec to opt out of many social programs that are Canada-wide, including the kinds of programs that Quebec has not opted out of in the past. But symbolic recognition would not necessarily have to be drafted as an indisputable right. Rather, it could be drafted as a possibility that would be open for discussion and negotiation on a case-by-case basis.[51] While the Quebec government would no doubt prefer opting out as a "right," *explicit* recognition of opting out as a possibility might be enough to bring it to the negotiating table. In any case, this possibility should be considered when SUFA is up for review in the next couple of years.

In the meantime, the *de facto* asymmetry of the federation grows. Given the real differences between Quebec and other provinces, this may be inevitable and even desirable, up to a point. But much of the essence of the Canadian reality is about social sharing. And if Quebec remains outside the Framework Agreement that oversees that sharing process, the long-term consequences for the future of the federation are troubling. This suggests the federal government and other provinces should be willing to pay a price to persuade a future Quebec government to sign the SUFA. Moreover, as argued elsewhere, the federal government may have its hands more than full in the coming decades in managing the interface between Canadian governments and the growth of international governance associated with a world that continues to integrate across borders.[52] This would also suggest that it play a lighter role in social areas that are within the exclusive legislative competence of the provinces.

PART 3: IMPLICATIONS FOR FISCAL FEDERALISM

It was observed at the outset of this chapter that the impact of SUFA would depend on the extent to which governments chose to adhere to principles and processes. This leads to the pedestrian conclusion that if governments largely ignore SUFA, then its implications for fiscal federalism will be equally modest. Its impact on the processes and content of fiscal federalism will be not much different than they would have been had there been no agreement.

What if governments slowly but systematically implement their commitments? In that case, one can posit a number of possible implications. These are speculations rather than forecasts.

The first flows from the fact that, in important respects, fiscal federalism is about integrating the benefits of decentralized design and delivery of government services while preserving the benefits of a larger market, both for reasons of economic efficiency and to widen the population base for risk-sharing and redistribution. Unfortunately, as Boadway notes elsewhere in this volume, there is no optimal level of centralization/decentralization.[53] What can be said, however, is that the greater the degree of decentralization, the greater the risk of externalities that flow from decentralized programs (such as government-induced incentives for labour or capital to move in an economically inefficient manner from one province to another). In this regard, the section 4 provisions for joint planning and collaboration and reciprocal notice and consultation can reasonably be interpreted as providing for the kind of ongoing communication among governments that would minimize such externalities. While current arrangements among governments do enable some of these issues to be dealt with reasonably, SUFA has the potential to serve as a much more effective vehicle for systematically managing them.

A second and possibly related impact is that the joint planning provisions and the role envisaged for the Ministerial Council have the potential to lead to a strengthening of "line" social departments at both the federal and provincial levels, in relation to finance ministries. As suggested above and has been argued elsewhere, especially at the federal level,[54] the Finance Department has played the dominant role in shaping joint federal-provincial social programs. While the federal Finance ministry has always been a crucial player in such activities, through much of the 1990s it was the dominant actor on the federal stage. The experience of the 1990s can be contrasted with earlier periods, when line social departments also played a significant role. When the Established Programs Financing (EPF) was being negotiated during the 1970s, for example, finance and health ministries worked jointly on this program and officials from both federal departments met jointly with provincial counter-parts.[55] Furthermore, the EPF decisions were not taken mainly in the political hothouse of the federal budgetary process. Rather, they were seen as struc-tural policy matters, not cyclical budgetary ones, and worked out over a period that was not governed principally by the federal budgetary cycle. When issues are settled in the context of budget preparation, finance ministries inevitably control the terms of the debate and structural factors tend to get less consid-eration than fiscal considerations. Decision-making around EPF can be contrasted, for example, with the way in which the cap on CAP (Canada As-sistance Plan) and the decision to create the CHST were decided. In these latter cases, the federal Finance ministry overwhelmingly controlled the pro-cesses of decision-making and the policy content associated with those measures. A second impact of the Framework Agreement may therefore be to help restore a more balanced equilibrium between line social ministries and their Finance colleagues in the development of social policy.

In this regard, it was suggested earlier in this chapter that the use of legis-lative committees to review progress on implementing SUFA, and the use of third-party social auditors, could be important in ensuring that the vision rep-resented by SUFA is realized. One impact of improving the transparency implied by such steps would be to reinforce the public responsibility of line social ministries and thus to potentially give them relatively more clout in social policy-making.

Third, while SUFA provides some new formal limitations on the unilateral exercise of the federal spending power by Ottawa, it is equally the case that all provinces except Quebec have again confirmed its political legitimacy. Moreover, SUFA itself specifies a process for helping to ensure that it is used appropriately. So if anything, the legitimacy of the spending power may have been strengthened a little. This observation is not inconsistent with the argu-ment above that, over time, the opting-out provision will need to be re-visited.

Fourth, with the federal spending power still available, the actual role of the federal government in paying for social programs is unlikely to change drastically. The spending power is a principal instrument through which the federal government is able to remain active in the social area and social ex-penses are by far the largest claim on the public purse. Consequently, the federal government's needs for revenues are similarly unlikely to drop drasti-cally (although they are likely to fall modestly relative to provincial revenue needs). As noted in the chapter by Norrie and Wilson in this volume, provin-cial governments have been calling for a transfer of revenue from federal to provincial coffers on the grounds that there is a growing vertical fiscal imbal-ance between orders of government. The purpose here is not to comment on that claim but rather to make the simpler point that, with a continued role for the federal spending power, there is unlikely to be any incentive for a major transfer of tax room from federal to provincial governments. Those who worry about the inefficiencies of a further large decentralization in revenue collection may draw at least some solace from the spending power decisions.[56] This conclusion does not, however, deny that some cash reallocation in favour of the provinces may be in order.

On a related matter, to the extent that SUFA itself can be viewed as an instrument for strengthening what Courchene calls Social Canada,[57] and leads Ottawa to focus on social initiatives, whether through intergovernmental or direct transfers, this will by definition entail the transfer of money from wealthier to less prosperous provinces. In this sense, SUFA can be seen as an instrument for narrowing horizontal fiscal imbalances. This orientation, however, bumps up against claims from the wealthier provinces that Ottawa should focus more on vertical fiscal imbalances and transfer more tax room to the provinces. To the extent that such new initiatives are more about promoting common rights of citizenship than explicitly about reducing disparities in living standards across provinces (and therefore more likely to result in equal per capita transfers than needs-related transfers) this conflict will be muted but not eliminated.[58]

Fifth, it is a nice question as to whether the decision rules surrounding the spending power will create an incentive for Ottawa to prefer direct spending relative to intergovernmental transfers. The section 5 rules surrounding programs financed in part through intergovernmental transfers appear to constrain the federal government more than do the rules in respect of direct transfers. Thus, one possible outcome is that the accord will create a bias toward direct transfers. Such an outcome would be attractive to those who call for a strong federal government and who want to strengthen the direct relationship between Ottawa and the citizenry.

While this incentive appears real, it can also be exaggerated. In my discussions with officials from both orders of government who were involved in SUFA negotiations, they emphasized that the provisions of section 5 should not be read on their own but in connection with the spirit and letter of the whole agreement. The spirit is captured in the preamble that refers to the agreement as one "based upon a mutual respect between orders of government and a willingness to work more closely together to meet the needs of Canadians." And the letter includes a section on "Joint Planning and Collaboration." So the apparently less constraining rules on direct transfers may not be much different in practice than the limits on new "Canada-wide initiatives supported by transfers to provinces." It also bears noting that if the counterfactual to SUFA is the *status quo ante*, then the new rules that require the federal government to give three months advance notice and consult on direct transfers are more constraining than was the situation prior to SUFA. This is simply because there were no rules previously, just federal practices that varied from situation to situation and program to program. Thus, under the new rules, Ottawa would have been compelled to give notice of the Millenium Scholarship Fund. Instead, the decision was announced as a *fait accompli* even though the federal government was open to negotiation about the modalities of the implementation. Formal notice and consultation under the terms of the Framework Agreement more or less assure provinces that a new federal proposal will attract public attention; and if provincial views are dismissed out of hand, Ottawa will be seen to be making light of the accord. At the same time, it must be acknowledged that "advance consultation" rules do not guarantee provinces a particular outcome.

In the short run, certainly for the life of the Liberal government now in office in Ottawa, direct spending might be preferred to new intergovernmental transfers. The political reasons for this would presumably include the government's belief that some strengthening of its direct link to individual citizens is important. Recent evidence includes the Millennium Scholarship Fund, the federal government's increasing transfers for the National Child Benefit and its proposal to make Employment Insurance benefits for parental leave more accessible. The federal government may also attach some weight to the idea that political accountability for spending is greater when the government that taxes spends directly rather than acting through another level of government. But once again, even under the Chrétien government, this tendency can be exaggerated. The Equalization program was one of the very few in Ottawa that was not cut during the first mandate of the federal Liberals. And Ottawa poured substantial money back into CHST in the 1999 budget. So while the Chrétien government may lean toward direct transfers, recent experience suggests it will not rely exclusively on this approach.

Moreover, provincial governments may lean the other way. They will not want new heavily conditioned transfers from the federal government. But SUFA does not contemplate heavily conditioned transfers. Rather, it contemplates both orders of government agreeing on Canada-wide objectives, the federal government transferring some funds to the provinces to assist them in pursuing the objectives, provinces then designing and delivering their own programs to achieve the objectives and public accountability for the results. So the new transfers will not be unconditional. But the conditions would be general and provinces would have played a large role in shaping them. In many situations, provinces will prefer this kind of intergovernmental transfer to a direct transfer.

Given the apparent leanings of both orders of government, a plausible outcome is that both direct and intergovernmental will be with us for a long time. And the choice of instrument will depend not only on the kinds of broad arguments set out above but also on the specifics of the individual files in question.

Finally, if SUFA is to have a policy impact, and not only an effect on the processes of government, then it will necessarily have to be reviewed periodically from the viewpoint of whether it is facilitating convergence or divergence of social outcomes. While the Framework Agreement does not require this measurement, section 3 does anticipate all governments monitoring and measuring outcomes and reporting regularly to constituents. Almost certainly, this will over time provide a factual basis for determining whether social outcomes are diverging or converging. Other thing being equal, therefore, this will, as a minimum, create an incentive for governments to pay some attention to the redistribution role of fiscal federalism.

In terms of fiscal federalism, the accord is also significant for what it does not say. In particular, it does not provide provincial governments with guarantees of revenue stability in their transfers from Ottawa.[59] It is true that section 5 does require the Government of Canada to consult with provincial/territorial governments "at least one year prior to renewal or significant changes in existing social transfers to provinces/territories ... and build due notice provisions into any new social transfers to provincial/territorial governments." While this is a positive step, it is worth noting that, in late 1993, federal Finance Minister Martin forewarned his provincial counterparts that he would have to cut intergovernmental transfers — the notice that led ultimately to the CHST. But the provincial governments were genuinely stunned by the size of the reductions announced in the 1995 budget, reductions that did not actually kick in until 1996. And what is disappointing in the Framework Agreement is that it does nothing to prevent another disproportionately large federal cut to provincial transfers at some future date. Although it is understandable that the federal government would want to preserve the right to reduce provincial transfers during periods of fiscal stress, it is arguably inconsistent with the spirit of the accord that there are no rules that govern provincial vulnerability to disproportionately harsh federal cuts.

CONCLUSIONS

SUFA implies modest changes in the content and conduct of Canadian fiscal federalism. On the content side, SUFA contemplates an ongoing role for both intergovernmental and direct transfers. Both are, of course, fundamental instruments of fiscal federalism. Second, the mere existence of SUFA probably serves as a force against the transfer of tax room from the federal to provincial governments. Third, it also implies perhaps a greater concern for issues of horizontal fiscal imbalance than vertical fiscal imbalance.

Conversely, the joint planning provisions of SUFA create a vehicle for reducing the externalities associated with a decentralized federation, which in turn might imply more scope for further decentralization. How these contradictory forces balance out is, of course, part of what remains unknown.

As for the conduct of fiscal federalism, the analysis above suggested the possibility that line social departments will play a larger role than they have in the past in designing the principal features of new social transfer programs. This is crucial to the future of SUFA. If basic political decisions about large social transfer programs continue to be decided in the political hot house of the federal budgetary cycle, the principles that underlie SUFA will almost certainly be impossible to sustain. If SUFA is to work, therefore, finance ministries will have to leave adequate room for the social ministries to do their job.

NOTES

1. The Government of Quebec did not sign the agreement. While the main purposes of this chapter do not include an analysis of Quebec's decision not to sign the Framework Agreement, this issue is touched on below.

2. Each government was represented by the minister appointed by his or her first minister. At the federal level, the minister selected was the Justice minister, presumably appointed because of the personal qualities she brought to the task and not because of her portfolio. Several provinces, including Ontario and Quebec, were represented by their intergovernmental ministers. In the final week of negotiation, the file was shifted to first ministers, who finalized the arrangements. The key point to note here is that finance ministers did not manage this file.

3. Author's interviews with government officials.

4. Margaret Biggs, *Building Blocks for Canada's Social Union*, Working Paper No. F-02 (Ottawa: Canadian Policy Research Networks, 1996); Keith Banting, "The Past Speaks to the Future: Lessons from the Post-War Social Union," in *Canada: The State of the Federation 1997: Non-Constitutional Renewal*, ed. Harvey Lazar (Kingston: Institute of Intergovernmental Relations, Queen's University, 1998); Harvey Lazar, "The Federal Role in a New Social Union: Ottawa at a Crossroads," in *Canada: The State of the Federation, 1997*, ed. Lazar; Harvey Lazar, "The Social Union: Taking the Time to Do it Right," *Policy Options* (November 1998).

5. The Framework Agreement is a political and administrative agreement. Whether its commitments are on process or substance, there is no change in the constitutional powers of either federal or provincial governments. Similarly, nothing in the agreement "abrogates or derogates from any Aboriginal treaty or other rights of Aboriginal peoples including self-government" (section 1).

6. Lazar, "Taking the Time to Do it Right," pp. 43-46.

7. It is noteworthy that the agreement refers to the agreement of a "majority of provincial governments," not "majority of signatory provincial governments." In effect, the agreement of six provinces is apparently required, not five of the nine signatory provinces.

8. The section also provides that the public must have "significant opportunities" for input.

9. *The Globe and Mail*, 19 January 1999, p. A21.

10. *The National Post*, 8 February 1999.

11. See, for example, *Le Devoir*, 13 February 1999, article by Andr Burelle; *Le Soleil*, 16 March 1999, article by Michel David. See also Alain Noël, "Canada, love it or don't leave it," *Policy Options* (forthcoming).

12. For example, the January 1997 report of the Conference of Provincial/Territorial Ministers of Health, *A Renewed Vision for Canada's Health System.* This explicitly endorses the five principles but does so in a context that raises many other matters.

13. Note: The author has added the word in parentheses.

14. Based on author's interviews.

15. At the time this was written (December 1999), the federal government and the Ontario government had still not signed a bilateral agreement.

16. If joint planning becomes effective, this will create an additional significant mechanism for discussing financial relations between the two orders of government. In turn, this could have an impact on the relative roles of finance ministries and line social ministries in the making of social policy and in the workings of fiscal federalism. This is discussed further in part 4.

17. The argument in this paragraph speaks to the issue of information-sharing and -planning. I recognize that in some sectors there are at times frequent meetings of ministers or their officials. Frequent meetings are often, however, the result of the need to deal with a crisis. A good recent example is the federal-provincial health ministers dealing with the tainted blood crisis through 1997 and 1998.

18. SUFA also calls for "clarification of roles and responsibilities" and thus it contemplates governments acting independently of one another where there is no particular public interest in or need for collaboration. To this extent, SUFA contemplates competition among governments as well as collaboration.

19. See the chapter in this volume by Lars Osberg.

20. During the negotiation period, Nunavut had not yet been officially established.

21. For a complete statement of Quebec's position just prior to the SUFA signing, see "Declaration by Prime Minister of Quebec, 27 January 1999, at <www.premier.gouv.qc.ca/discours/a990127.htm>

22. Joseph Facal, "Pourquoi le Québec a Adhéré au Consensus des Provinces sur L'Union Social," *Policy Options* (November 1998):12-13. (Author's translation.)

23. While it might be argued that there is nothing to be "opted out from" in the case of bloc transfers, there can in principle be conditions attached to the bloc transfer (as with CHST).

24. Author's interviews.

25. William B.P. Robson and Daniel Schwanen, "The Social Union Agreement: Too Flawed to Last," C.D. Howe Institute Backgrounder, 8 February 1999, p. 3.

26. Section 106A. (1), the 1987 Constitutional Accord. The word in brackets is my addition to the authoritative text.

27. Claude Ryan, "Quebec and the Social Union," *Inroads* 8(1999):34. I assume that Ryan was alluding to what had been promised at Meech and Charlottetown. In fact, Quebec did not opt out of the major shared-cost programs of earlier years like the *Hospital Insurance and Diagnostic Services Act*, the *Medical Care Act* and the Canada Assistance Plan. The most important "opting out," using this

term in a loose sense, was Quebec's decision not to have Québécois participate in the Canada Pension Plan and instead set up the Quebec Pension Plan. This was a direct transfer program, not a jointly funded one.

28. David Cameron has taken a very similar view to the one expressed here. See "The Social-Union Agreement: A Backward Step for Quebec," unpublished paper, 8 February 1999. Claude Ryan has taken the opposite view in "Quebec and the Social Union," pp. 35-36. Ryan ignores the points noted in this chapter. He instead focuses on three alleged deficiencies of SUFA relative to Meech Lake. The first is that other provisions of the Meech Lake Accord, "most notably a constitutional provision explicitly recognizing the distinct character of Quebec society," would have gone a long way toward meeting the demands of Quebec. The second is that SUFA is an administrative agreement that initially at least lasts for only three years, whereas Meech Lake would have meant constitutional entrenchment. While these are accurate statements by Ryan, it is unclear to me why they would have afforded Quebec more freedom to opt out than does SUFA. Ryan sees a connection that is not, on the face of it, obvious. On Ryan's third point, it is simply unclear why Ryan believes that the Meech Lake words are more open to "supple interpretation" than the words of SUFA, especially when SUFA contemplates provinces that have satisfied a Canada-wide objective using federal transfers for other purposes in a "related priority area."

29. Robson and Schwanen, "The Social Union Agreement: Too Flawed to Last," p. 3.

30. Author's interview with provincial official. The explanation for this provincial position is that when the interprovincial consensus was being forged, an equality of provinces perspective helped secure the support of some smaller provinces.

31. See, for example, the "Declaration by Premier Lucien Bouchard," 27 January 1999, which may be found at http://www.premier.gouv.qc.ca/discours/a990127.htm

32. K.C. Wheare, *Federal Government*, 4th ed. (London: Oxford University Press, 1963), p. 10. Note that the term "co-ordinate," as used by Wheare, is in some sense the opposite of "subordinate." It implies equality among orders of government.

33. Ronald Watts, *Comparing Federal Systems in the 1990s* (Kingston: Institute of Intergovernmental Relations, Queen's University, 1996).

34. Ronald Watts, *The Spending Power in Federal States: A Comparative Study* (Kingston: Institute of Intergovernmental Relations, 1999).

35. K.C. Wheare, *Federal Government*, p. 10.

36. The Swiss situation is different not only because it is a confederation with residual powers resting with the cantons but because of its extensive use of plebiscites to amend the constitution.

37. The *de jure* federal responsibility for interpreting and enforcing the provisions of the *Canada Health Act* is one example.

38. This statement is obviously highly qualified in respect of those provinces most dependent on federal equalization payments, that is, the four Atlantic provinces.

39. For a more detailed discussion of these items, see Harvey Lazar, "The Federal Role in a New Social Union: Ottawa at a Crossroads," in *Canada: The State of the Federation 1997*, ed. Lazar.

40. See, for example, the speech by the federal minister of intergovernmental affairs, "Social Union: Canadians Helping Canadians," 10 December 1998, at http://www.pco-bcp.gc.ca/ala/ro/doc/spchdec 1098.htm. The quotation is from federal Justice Minister Anne McLellan, "Modernizing Canada's Social Union: A New Partnership Among Governments and Citizens," *Policy Options* (November 1998):6.

41. Ottawa may have also thought that extensive reporting would put pressure on governments to spend money in a more cost-effective fashion, a view that could have carried considerable weight given that governments were still feeling the effects of heavy expenditure reductions. Since more social programs are designed and delivered by the provinces than by the federal government, the burden of these provisions falls more heavily on provinces than on Ottawa.

42. This might have happened to the extent that provinces reduced their social assistance rates for children, dollar for dollar with the increase in the federal benefit.

43. For a contrary view, see Noël, "Canada, love it or leave it."

44. For a commentary on the provincial negotiating position, see Lazar, "The Canadian Social Union: Taking the Time to Get it Right."

45. Examples include the Agreement on Internal Trade, the bilateral federal-Quebec labour market agreement, the February 1999 Health Accord and the March 1999 Employment Assistance for Persons with Disabilities cost-sharing agreement.

46. *The National Post*, 15 February 1999.

47. Robson and Schwanen, "The Social Union Agreement: Too Flawed to Last," p. 5.

48. Ryan, "Quebec and the Social Union," p. 40.

49. For the views of the Quebec Liberal Party see article by Jean J. Charest, Leader of the Quebec Liberal Party, in *Le Soleil*, 15 February 1999.

50. Had SUFA been in effect several years ago, with Quebec a signatory, I would speculate that the federal government would have found it politically impracticable to launch the Millennium Scholarship Program as a unilateral federal initiative.

51. Such a proposal could borrow heavily from the existing language of SUFA. For example, it could provide that "in respect of any new intergovernmental transfer to promote an agreed Canada-wide objective, a province may seek to opt out with financial compensation if the new initiative interferes with its freedom to select the program mix and design that meets the objective." In substance, this would represent little or no change from what SUFA now effectively says. And it should result in relatively few cases of opting out if the overall SUFA provisions are respected as there would be little from which to opt out. For direct transfers, the SUFA might provide that "in relation to direct transfers, a province may seek financial compensation to replace the federal transfer where that province can show that its effort to reach objectives similar to the program

objectives are being unduly thwarted or made inefficient by the federal program." In practice, this is likely to be what happens under SUFA in any case. If Ottawa launches a new direct program, the Government of Quebec will press for the funds saying that it knows better how to spend those funds wisely in Quebec than does the federal government. In some cases, the federal government may agree and in others it may not.

52. Harvey Lazar and Tom McIntosh, eds., *Canada: The State of the Federation 1998/99: How Canadians Connect* (Kingston: Institute of Intergovernmental Relations, Queen's University, 1999).

53. See Boadway, "Recent Developments in the Economics of Federalism," in this volume.

54. See Edward Greenspon and Anthony Wilson-Smith, *Double Vision: The Inside Story of the Liberals in Power* (Toronto: Doubleday Canada, 1996); and Donald Savoie, *Governing from the Centre: The Concentration of Power in Canadian Politics* (Toronto: University of Toronto Press, 1999).

55. The author participated directly in these processes as a federal Finance official.

56. See chapter 2 in this volume.

57. Thomas J. Courchene, *Social Canada in the Millennium: Reform Imperatives and Restructuring Principles* (Toronto: C.D. Howe Institute, 1994).

58. It is recognized that programs that provide for common social entitlements for all citizens may not result in equal per capita distribution across provinces where there are objective differences among provinces. A province with a larger share of seniors than the national average will, for example, attract a larger than average per capita amount of old age payments than do other provinces on average. The general point, however, is that needs-related programs will normally lead to more interprovincial redistribution than those that are not explicitly needs-related.

59. Harvey Lazar, "Taking the Time to Do it Right."

II

The Federal-Provincial Transfer System

5

Changes to Federal Transfers to Provinces and Territories in 1999

Edith Boucher and Arndt Vermaeten

Le gouvernement fédéral fournit une assistance financière directe aux provinces et territoires via trois principaux programmes: le Transfert canadien en matière de santé et de services sociaux (TCSPS), la péréquation et la formule de financement des territoires (FFT). Le TCSPS procure une aide financière dans les domaines de la santé, de l'éducation post-secondaire et de l'assistance sociale. Grâce au programme de péréquation, les provinces moins prospères reçoivent une assistance financière qui leur permet d'offrir des services comparables à ceux offerts dans les autres provinces tout en imposant des taux d'imposition comparables. Finalement, la FFT définit les termes du support financier aux trois territoires. En 1999, ces trois programmes ont subi des modifications importantes. Ce chapitre décrit ces programmes de même que les changements qui leur ont été apportés. Les mesures annoncées dans le budget 2000 ne sont pas discutées parce que le chapitre a été complété avant le dépôt du budget.

The federal government, pursuant to its national responsibilities for equality of opportunity among all Canadians, transfers funds to other orders of government primarily through three major programs — the Canada Health and Social Transfer (CHST), Equalization, and Territorial Formula Financing (TFF). Including the value of tax transfers, the CHST support for health, postsecondary education, and social services and social assistance amounts to approximately $29 billion. The federal government also transfers over $9.5 billion a year to lower-income provinces under Equalization, which enables them to provide public services that are reasonably comparable to those provided in other provinces. Transfers to the three territorial governments amount to approximately $1.4 billion per year. In 1999, significant changes were made to all three of these programs.[1] This chapter describes the programs and outlines the recent changes. It does not discuss measures introduced in the 2000 budget because the budget was tabled after the completion of the chapter.

CANADA HEALTH AND SOCIAL TRANSFER: THE CHST

ORIGINS OF THE CHST

The federal government has had a long history of partnership with the provinces in health, higher education, and social services. Over the years though, the nature and structure of the federal-provincial relationship has undergone substantial change. During the 1980s, federal support for provinces was provided under two programs: the Canada Assistance Plan (CAP), a cost-shared program that helped fund provincial social assistance and social service programs, and Established Programs Financing (EPF), a block-fund transfer providing assistance to provinces for health care and postsecondary education. By the early 1990s, financial pressures led both the federal and provincial governments to re-examine the design and funding of social programs.

In its 1994 budget, the federal government laid out its objectives for reviewing, with provincial governments, Canada's social security system and reforming the system of transfers that supported it. It moved to establish fiscal parameters and a predictable funding environment for reform to ensure that the system was financially sustainable and "more effective and responsive to the needs of people."[2] In line with the deficit reduction exercise, the 1994 budget indicated that social security transfers would "be no higher after reform in 1996-97 than 1993-94 levels."[3] The budget also made clear that "if social security reform fails to achieve these savings by 1996-97, alternative measures to take effect in 1996-97 will be implemented to ensure the savings are realized."[4]

The 1995 budget announced the creation of the CHST "to create a system that is both better suited to contemporary needs and financially sustainable."[5] The CHST was a block-fund transfer replacing two existing programs — EPF and CAP. It came into effect in fiscal year 1996-97 and marked a further step in the evolution from specified-purpose transfers to a single transfer conditional on very broad principles. The new transfer was also smaller than EPF and CAP and thereby contributed to federal expenditure restraint.

Although provinces are "able to spend these transferred resources on priorities of their own choosing,"[6] the transfer was not totally unconditional. Provisions were included "to invite all provincial governments to work together on developing, through mutual consent, a set of shared principles and objectives that could underlie the new transfer."[7] Provinces must comply with the principles of medicare as set out in the *Canada Health Act* and they must not impose residency requirements for social assistance programs.

Established as a block fund, the CHST gave provinces[8] greater flexibility to design and administer social programs and to allocate funds among social programs according to their priorities. The CHST reduced rigidities associated with cost-sharing under the Canada Assistance Plan by extending the flexibility that already existed under Established Programs Financing to allocate funds between health and postsecondary education as deemed appropriate by the provinces and territories to social assistance programs. There are neither specific limitations on how provinces may choose to spend CHST funds or notional allocations among the three sectors that the CHST supports.

The funding formula for the CHST follows the model of EPF. Provincial entitlements are calculated on a per capita basis and include both a cash and a tax component. This structure reflects decisions by federal and provincial governments that led to the creation of EPF in 1977. At that time, the provinces and the federal government agreed to redesign the delivery of federal support by making the entitlements equal per capita and by converting part of the federal support from cash transfers to tax transfers. The tax transfer was put into effect when the federal government reduced its personal income tax rates by 13.5 percent and its corporate rate by 1 percent and provinces simultaneously raised their tax rates by corresponding amounts. The federal government then provided cash support to top up each provincial government to its total entitlement.

The determination of EPF entitlements as the sum of the value of tax points and cash served to ensure that all provinces would have the same overall federal support, per capita, to provide health care and postsecondary education regardless of differences in provincial income and growth rates. Provinces with higher personal income or with persistently faster growth rates would also have higher revenues or faster growing revenues from the transferred tax points. Basing the transfer on entitlements meant that richer provinces would receive more of their support from the tax points than from cash transfers. As the value of tax points relative to other provinces increased, the cash transfer decreased. Thus, the value of these tax points had an important impact on the interprovincial distribution of the cash component of the transfer.

Initially, the CHST had essentially the same basic design as EPF. Total CHST entitlements were established, and then the value of the transferred tax points were subtracted from this number to determine the total size of the federal cash payment. The entitlement was fixed, and the cash payment varied inversely with the value of tax points.

In the 1995 budget, the level of CHST entitlements was set at $26.9 billion for 1996-97, about $2.8 billion less than the combined EPF and CAP in 1995-96. Of this, the value of the tax points was estimated at the time to be about $12 billion. Entitlements for 1997-98 were originally set at $25.1 billion (of which tax points were expected to be about $13 billion).[9] The 1996 budget set out a new five-year funding arrangement for the CHST, maintaining the national entitlement level for 1998-99 and 1999-2000 at $25.1 billion.[10] After that, growth in entitlements was to equal the rate of growth of gross domestic product (GDP) less 2 percent for 2000-01, GDP less 1.5 percent for 2001-02, and GDP less 1 percent for 2002-03.

As entitlements were set to decline initially and then to grow at a rate below GDP, the tax component of CHST, which should grow more or less in line with GDP, was expected to become a larger share of total entitlements and the cash component was expected to decline. This situation had already occurred under EPF due to the restrictions on the growth of EPF entitlements implemented in the early 1990s. In the 1990 budget, EPF entitlements were frozen on a per capita basis for two years — 1990-91 and 1991-92.[11] The 1991 budget extended the freeze for three more years through 1994-95 and announced that EPF entitlements would grow at a rate corresponding to the growth in GNP minus 3 percent after 1994-95.[12] Between 1992-93 and 1995-96, tax points generally grew at a faster rate than total entitlements. As a result, the EPF cash transfer went down from $11.0 to $10.6 billion over this period.

In the 1996 budget, the government established an $11-billion cash floor to "ensure that cash remains a large component of the CHST."[13] The total cash contribution to CAP and EPF was $18.5 billion in 1995-96 — the last year these two programs were in operation. It was expected to drop to $15 billion in 1996-97, to $12.5 billion in 1997-98, to $11.8 billion in 1998-99, and to close to the $11-billion floor in 1999-2000. The cash component was then expected to begin growing again as the GDP-based formula allowed entitlements to rise.

By 1997-98, the federal government's fiscal position had improved substantially. At the same time, strong economic growth increased the value of the provinces' tax points faster than expected and reduced the federal cash contribution below the levels previously forecast. In 1998, the government passed legislation increasing the CHST cash floor by $1.5 billion to $12.5 billion beginning retroactively in 1997-98. The floor was operative immediately. Federal cash contributions were thus no longer determined residually as the difference between entitlements and tax transfers. From this point, federal cash contributions were determined by the floor, and total entitlements varied with the value of tax points.

CHANGES INTRODUCED IN THE 1999 FEDERAL BUDGET

By 1998, the years of federal and provincial expenditure restraint had created a much healthier fiscal climate in Canada.[14] However, the restraint had engendered growing concern by Canadians about the adequacy of resources for the health-care system. The 1999 federal budget sought to respond to these concerns and specifically to provincial requests for additional federal funds through the CHST to deliver basic health care.

The federal government announced in the budget that it would increase CHST cash funding by $11.5 billion over the five years from 1999-2000 through 2003-04. Support effectively increased the floor by $2 billion to $14.5 billion in 1999-2000 and 2000-01, and by $2.5 billion to $15 billion in each of the following three years. Including the value of tax points, the level of CHST entitlements was expected to reach $30 billion by 2001-02, which would just exceed the level of EPF/CAP entitlements in 1995-96. Figure 1 shows cash, tax points and total entitlements both under EPF/CAP and under CHST from 1993-94 through 2003-04.[15]

Prior to the 1999 budget, at a first ministers' meeting in February, all provincial premiers and territorial leaders undertook to spend any incremental CHST funds on health services in accordance with health priorities within their respective jurisdictions. This commitment was confirmed in an exchange of letters with the prime minister. Of the $11.5-billion incremental CHST cash, $3.5 billion was paid into a third-party trust and made immediately available to provinces to draw upon according to their priorities over the three years from 1999-2000 to 2001-02. The use of a trust fund allowed the federal government to record the expenditure in fiscal year 1998-99 when its fiscal position was in surplus, while giving provinces flexibility to draw funds when they needed them.

The 1999 budget laid out a notional draw-down schedule under which provinces were shown to draw down the trust by $2 billion in 1999-2000, $1 billion in 2000-01, and $500 million in 2001-02 consistent with the figures shown in Figure 1. However, under the terms of the trust, provinces could draw their share of the funds more quickly or slowly. The remaining $8 billion of the $11.5-billion increment was provided by increasing the legislated cash from

Figure 1: CHST: 1993-94 to 2003-04

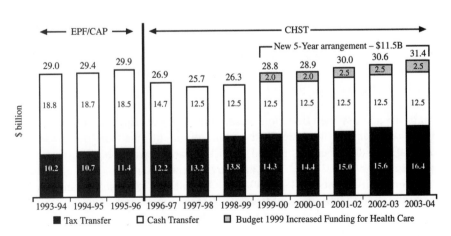

$12.5 billion in 1999-2000 to $13.5 billion in 2000-01, to $14.5 billion in 2001-02 and to $15 billion in 2002-03 and 2003-04.

CHST ALLOCATION

EPF entitlements for each province were calculated on an equal per capita basis while CAP was a cost-shared program under which the federal government paid 50 percent of eligible provincial social assistance and social services costs.

Prior to 1990-91, CAP covered 50 percent of eligible costs for all provinces. In 1990-91, the federal government limited the annual growth in CAP payments to 5 percent for higher-income provinces not eligible for equalization — Ontario, Alberta, and British Columbia.[16] The so-called "cap on CAP" was part of a broader expenditure restraint plan. The seven equalization-receiving provinces continued to benefit from the open-ended, cost-sharing arrangements.

Although this was originally intended to be a two-year temporary measure, CAP payments to the three affected provinces continued to be subject to the "cap on CAP" until 1994-95.[17] In 1995-96, CAP payments were frozen at 1994-95 levels for all provinces.[18] As a result of the "cap on CAP" and the freeze, the share of federal CAP transfers to the three higher income provinces fell substantially relative to the transfers to other provinces and this differential treatment of provinces became a growing source of strain on federal-provincial relations.

When the CHST came into effect in 1996-97, provinces received the same share of CHST as their previous combined share of EPF and CAP transfers.[19] As a result, the uneven per capita allocation caused by the "cap on CAP" was carried over into the CHST. (In 1998-99, for example, per capita CHST entitlements ranged from $800 in Alberta[20] to $939 in Quebec.) After consultations with the provinces, the federal government announced in its 1996 budget that these per capita disparities would be reduced by 10 percent a year, over five years from 1998-99 to 2002-03.[21] This would reduce the disparities by half at the end of the five-year track. Figure 2 shows the per capita distribution of CHST entitlements in 1998-99.

Increasing the resources for CHST in the 1999 budget provided an opportunity to address the allocation issue while still ensuring that all provinces benefited from the increase. Rather than eliminating half the disparities by 2002-03, the 1999 budget ensured that all disparities would be eliminated one year earlier by 2001-02.[22] This measure meant that provinces with below-average entitlements in 1998-99, such as Alberta, Saskatchewan, British Columbia, and Ontario, would receive larger incremental amounts over the period while their entitlements were catching up with the average. As Figure 2 shows, by 2001-02 all provinces will receive identical CHST entitlements

Figure 2: Provincial CHST Entitlements

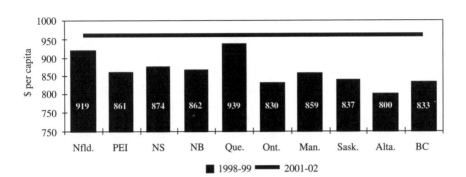

estimated at $960 per capita. After 2001-02, all per capita entitlements will grow by identical amounts.[23]

Although entitlements will become equal per capita by 2001-02, the differential value of tax points among provinces means that the federal cash contribution, per capita, will continue to vary as it did under EPF. Provinces with higher income will generate more of their entitlement from their tax points while the equalization-receiving provinces will need more federal cash, per capita, to bring their entitlements to the national average.

Some observers have argued that since tax points now belong to provinces, only the cash component of federal transfers to provinces is actually relevant. However, the CHST calculations incorporate the value of tax points transferred to provinces at the inception of EPF to ensure that each province receives the same value of resources through the program for the provision of health care, postsecondary education, and social assistance. If the CHST cash component were allocated on an equal per capita basis, the total per capita entitlements would be higher for provinces with higher income than for those with lower income because of the higher value of tax points in higher income provinces.

PROVINCIAL REACTION

The measures announced in the 1999 budget provided a significant increase in federal funding for health care. However, all provinces continued to argue for further increases in funding. Provinces have also argued for a transfer of federal tax room to meet their spending needs. Some provinces, particularly those receiving above-average CHST entitlements, were critical of the federal government's decision to eliminate the disparities in per capita entitlements.

Provinces' concerns are reflected in the consensus reached at the Annual Premiers' Conference held in August 1999 and in a common position paper released by provincial premiers in December 1999.[24] Provinces are calling for the restoration of the CHST cash component to its 1994-95 level of $18.7 billion by 2000-01 and then the implementation of an escalator to the CHST cash portion. Provinces are also asking for the elimination of the ceiling of the Equalization program. "This would parallel, to a degree, recent federal action to reverse constraints affecting more affluent provinces under the CHST, namely the removal of the "cap" on Canada Assistance Plan payments."[25] In a letter to the prime minister dated 3 February 2000, premiers and territorial leaders reiterated their consensus and promised to use any additional funding provided through the CHST for health care and social programs according to their respective priorities.[26]

EQUALIZATION

Equalization is the second largest transfer to provinces. Because all parts of the country are not equally prosperous, provincial governments, even if they exercise comparable tax effort, cannot all generate the same revenues with which to finance public services. The purpose of the Equalization program is to provide transfers to less prosperous provinces to enable them to provide public services reasonably comparable to those provided by more prosperous provinces at comparable rates of taxation. Equalization is unique among transfers to the provinces in that its purpose is entrenched in the Canadian constitution.[27]

Currently, seven provinces qualify for equalization payments: Newfoundland, Prince Edward Island, Nova Scotia, New Brunswick, Quebec, Manitoba, and Saskatchewan. All provinces except Ontario have qualified at some time in the past, and Saskatchewan has occasionally not qualified. Equalization payments are unconditional, and receiving provinces are therefore free to spend these payments according to their own priorities.

Since the inception of the program in 1957, and with the exception of a two-year renewal in 1992, Equalization legislation has been renewed on a five-year cycle.

DESCRIPTION OF RENEWAL PROCESS

Prior to the expiry of Equalization legislation, and before the introduction of new legislation for the next five-year term, the program is subjected to an extensive "renewal process," in close consultation with all provinces, during which modifications to the program are considered. While both federal and provincial officials continually monitor the program's operation, the renewal process involves a focused and comprehensive review to identify possible technical changes and improvements to the program's design and structure.

The renewal process that preceded the enactment in March 1999 of Equalization legislation for the current five-year period took place over a period of more than two years and involved numerous meetings of federal and provincial officials. Issues were discussed at several meetings of federal and provincial finance ministers. The technical review of the Equalization program is done largely by officials at meetings of the Equalization Subcommittee and special working groups.

HOW EQUALIZATION WORKS

Equalization payments are calculated according to a formula set out in federal legislation (and accompanying regulations). Comparisons are made of the relative capacities of provinces to raise revenues from taxes and from other (non-tax) revenue sources. This is done each year by estimating the potential per capita revenues that each province could derive from a representative tax system (RTS). The results are then compared to a standard consisting of the estimated average per capita RTS revenues of Ontario, British Columbia, Quebec, Saskatchewan, and Manitoba.[28] Provinces with revenue-raising capacities below this standard receive Equalization transfers to bring them up to the standard.

The revenue-raising capacity of provinces is calculated separately for more than 30 revenue sources available to provincial and local governments. In order to objectively compare the capacity of provinces to raise revenues from each source, this capacity has to be estimated in a standardized way for all provinces. Note that what is of interest is not what revenues provinces *do* (in fact) raise, but what revenues provinces *could* (potentially) raise from a typical tax system. Both the actual tax rates and actual tax bases upon which provinces levy taxes vary significantly from one province to another. But for the purpose of calculating Equalization entitlements, standardized tax bases are defined, and what is measured is what each province could raise in revenues if it applied the national-average tax rate on these standardized tax bases.

Uniform or standardized tax bases are the key element of the RTS. A standardized tax base for a revenue source is a measure of what is typically taxed by provinces in deriving revenues from that source. The standardized base for corporate income taxes, for example, is the amount of profit earned by corporations in a province; for alcohol revenues, it is the number of litres of alcoholic beverages sold in a province; and for tobacco taxes, it is the number of cigarettes sold in a province. The base may either be an average of the actual statutory bases on which provinces levy the tax or some proxy that can be expected to have a distribution among provinces similar to that of the true base. Standardized bases are meant to incorporate the common elements of the tax systems of provinces.

A province's fiscal capacity with respect to a revenue source is calculated by multiplying the standardized base for the province by the national-average tax rate. The national-average tax rate for a revenue source is the sum of the (actual) revenues collected by all ten provinces from the revenue source divided by the total standardized tax base of the ten provinces for the source.

In determining Equalization entitlements, the total per capita revenue-raising capacity of each province is calculated by summing its per capita fiscal capacities for all revenue sources. If a province's estimated total per capita revenue-raising capacity is higher than the standard, it is ineligible for Equalization. If a province's total per capita revenue-raising capacity is lower than the standard, it receives transfers equal to its per capita shortfall multiplied by its population. Total Equalization payments for 1999-2000 are currently estimated to be $9.5 billion.[29]

Figure 3: The Equalization Formula, 1999-2000

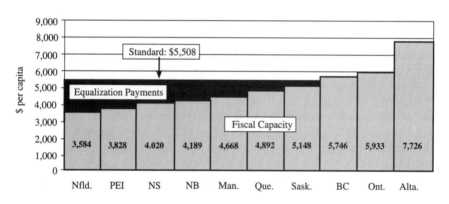

Source: October 1999 Equalization estimate for 1999-2000.

OVERVIEW OF CHANGES

The changes made to the Equalization program for the 1999-00 to 2003-04 fiscal arrangements period are significant but not fundamental. The basic mechanics of the system remain the same, and the five-province standard first adopted in 1982 remains in place. The ceiling and floor provisions of the program were modified, and a substantial number of revenue sources and bases were redefined. Several administrative changes were also introduced.

CHANGES TO PROGRAM PARAMETERS

Ceiling. Ceiling provisions set an upper limit on the growth rate of Equalization entitlements and are meant to protect the federal government from rapid
and unaffordable increases in payments. As mentioned earlier, provinces have
requested the elimination of the Equalization ceiling in addition to additional
CHST funding in their recent provincial consensus.

The previous ceiling (prior to the 1999 changes and beginning in 1994-95)
limited the growth rate of total entitlements to the growth rate of gross national product (GNP) from a 1992 base year.[30] This ceiling did not apply during
the five-year period from 1994-95 to 1998-99. For 1998-99, the ceiling was
approximately $10.4 billion, about $800 million higher than entitlements for
that year.[31]

In response to concerns expressed by the Auditor General, the initial level
of the ceiling for the new fiscal arrangements period was set at a fixed dollar
amount rather than at the level of entitlements for a base year. Setting the
initial ceiling at the level of entitlements for a base year created uncertainties
because the ultimate level of entitlements for the base year is not known until
30 months after the end of that year when the final entitlement calculations
are made. This means that the level of the ceiling is unknown during an initial
portion of the fiscal arrangements period.[32]

The new ceiling was set at $10 billion for fiscal year 1999-2000. For the
four fiscal years after 1999-2000, the ceiling increases from $10 billion in
proportion to cumulative GDP growth. If total entitlements in any fiscal year
exceed the ceiling for that year, entitlements are scaled back for all receiving
provinces on an equal per capita basis until total entitlements are reduced to
the ceiling level.

Floor. Floor provisions limit year-over-year reductions in Equalization entitlements for individual provinces. They are meant to protect provinces from
large annual declines in entitlements.

The old floor provisions (for 1994-95 to 1998-99) were more generous for
some provinces than others. Year-over-year reductions in entitlements were
limited to 15 percent of total entitlements for provinces with own-source revenue-raising capacity above 75 percent of the national average, to 10 percent
for provinces with revenue-raising capacity of 70-75 percent of the average,
and to 5 percent for provinces with revenue-raising capacity below 70 percent
of the average. These floor provisions came into effect for Saskatchewan in
1994-95 and in 1996-97, but did not affect entitlements for any other province
or any other year during the 1994-95 to 1998-99 period.

The new floor provisions for 1999-2000 to 2003-04 provide the same protection for all provinces, regardless of their fiscal capacity. Per capita declines
in entitlements are limited to a maximum of 1.6 percent of the per capita five-
province standard (or about $90).[33]

ADMINISTRATIVE CHANGES

Thirty-Month Closing. Previously, equalization calculations were finalized (or closed) 24 months after the end of the fiscal year to which they pertain.[34] CHST calculations, on the other hand, were left open for 30 months after the end of a fiscal year. As a result, population data used to calculate Equalization and CHST entitlements differed between the two programs. To make the programs consistent, the closing of equalization calculations has been extended to 30 months after the end of the fiscal year.

Transition from Old to New Revenue Source and Base Definitions. The new tax base and revenue-source definitions will be phased in over a five-year transition period. The main reason for this phase-in is to ensure that undue weight is not placed on new data sources early in the new fiscal arrangements period. Some of the data sources referred to in the new base definitions have only recently been developed, or are still under development, as part of Statistics Canada's Project to Improve Provincial Economic Statistics (PIPES). The reliability and accuracy of these sources will not be fully understood until later on in the fiscal arrangements period.

The phase-in is also meant to prevent abrupt impacts on the distribution of entitlements from the change in definitions.

CHANGES TO TAX BASE AND REVENUE-SOURCE DEFINITIONS

The new revenue-source and base definitions are expected to result in an increase in entitlements of about $50 million for 1999-2000, rising to an estimated $200 to $300 million by 2003-04 when the definitions are fully phased in. The most significant changes are as follows:

Sales Tax. The sales tax base was redefined to take into account both the value-added sales tax systems of Quebec, New Brunswick, Nova Scotia, and Newfoundland, and the traditional sales tax systems used in other provinces.[35]

The old base did not do this adequately. It included or excluded various categories of expenditures (such as expenditures at retail outlets, expenditures on capital equipment, expenditures on residential construction materials) on the basis of whether or not those items were typically taxed by provinces. Whether an item was "typically" taxed was determined by a majority rule. Expenditures were included in the base if they were taxed under the sales tax systems of provinces representing a majority of the population. Thus, for example, expenditures on school supplies were fully included in the base, even though consumption of school supplies was exempt from tax in some provinces.

With this majority rule, the old equalization base for sales taxes closely resembled Ontario's statutory sales tax base. This base used to be reasonably representative of the statutory bases of other provinces because provincial sales tax systems were similar to Ontario's. But with the adoption of value-added tax systems by some provinces, the old base no longer adequately reflected the statutory base upon which value-added taxes are levied.

The new sales tax base is an "average" rather than a "majority" base. It includes a weighted average of expenditures on a commodity-by-commodity basis. The weight given to expenditures on any particular commodity is proportional to the extent to which that commodity is taxed, on average, across all provinces. The base thus reflects the average taxing practices of all provinces and takes into account both value-added and traditional sales tax systems.

The new base is highly representative and constitutes a significant improvement over the old base. It makes use of data, including input-output data, that have only recently become available as a result of PIPES.

Gaming. With the introduction and rapid rise of video lottery, slot machine, and casino gambling, the gaming field has undergone a significant change over the past several years.[36] Due to this change, the old revenue-source and base definitions used to equalize provincial gaming revenues — definitions which had originally been put in place when provincial gaming revenues consisted mainly of ticket lottery revenues — were no longer adequate.

Provincial gaming revenues consist of the remitted profits of provincially-owned gaming corporations. Under the old definitions, all provincial gaming revenues were equalized as part of one revenue source (called "Lottery Revenues"). This included revenues derived by provinces from ticket lottery operations, as well as revenues derived from video lottery, casino, and other gaming operations. The base for this revenue source though was the gross dollar value of lottery tickets sold in each province.

The old revenue-source and base definitions resulted in a mismatch between revenues subject to Equalization and the base. All gaming revenues — including both revenues derived from traditional ticket lotteries and revenues derived from other games of chance — were equalized on a ticket lottery base, a base that did not in any way reflect differences in fiscal capacity among provinces with respect to non-ticket lottery gaming. The revenue-raising capacity of provinces with low sales of lottery tickets but with a high capacity to raise revenues from video lotteries and casino gaming was thus underestimated, while the revenue-raising capacity of provinces with high sales of lottery tickets but with low revenue-raising capacity for video lotteries and casino gaming was overestimated.[37]

One way of addressing this problem would have been to simply add the dollar value of sales of non-traditional gaming products to the lottery ticket sales included in the old base to create a more inclusive consumption base. This would, however, have been problematic due to the fact that tax effort for non-traditional gaming varies significantly among provinces. Some provinces have extensive casino and video lottery gaming operations while others do not have any. The level of consumption of these types of games in a province is therefore more a reflection of the availability of the games (and thus the fiscal choices of the province) than of the underlying fiscal capacity. There is, for example, no video lottery consumption in Ontario because the province does not permit this type of gaming. But this does not mean — as a pure consumption base would indicate — that Ontario has zero fiscal capacity in the video lottery field. Measurement of fiscal capacity must be independent of the *actual* tax effort exerted by provinces and should reflect what provinces *could* raise in revenues *if* they exerted the same (national average) level of tax effort.[38]

The solution implemented for the new fiscal arrangements period was to split the old lottery revenue source into two separate revenue sources and to adopt a multi-variable base for each of these sources. One revenue source consists exclusively of the revenues derived by provinces from ticket lotteries, while the other includes revenues derived from all other games of chance.[39] The bases for these two revenue sources each consist of three weighted components: a consumption component, a disposable income component, and a population component. The consumption component is given a high weight in the ticket lottery base (80 percent versus 10 percent for disposable income and 10 percent for population) and a low weight (20 percent versus 40 percent for disposable income and 40 percent for population) in the base for other games of chance. The consumption component of the ticket lottery base consists of the dollar value of sales net of prize payouts for ticket lotteries, and the consumption component of the base for other games of chance consists of the dollar value of sales net of prize payouts for non-ticket lottery games.[40]

The consumption component was given a low weight in the other games of chance base because tax effort for other games of chance (including video lottery gaming, casino gaming, provincially operated electronic bingo, slot machines, etc.) differs significantly from province to province. Disposable income and population (which together have a weighting of 80 percent) were chosen as the main indicators of fiscal capacity for non-traditional gaming because the propensity of individuals to engage in gaming activities is positively, though not proportionally, related to disposable income. Empirical evidence indicates that as disposable income increases, the percentage increase in average gaming expenditures for an income group is approximately one-half of the percentage increase in income. The inclusion of both a disposable income and a population component in the base, and the equal (40 percent) weighting of the two, is designed to reflect this fact. The two components together constitute a proxy measure of gaming fiscal capacity. They function in the base to indicate that a province whose residents have a per capita disposable income that is, for example, 5 percent lower than that of residents of the five standard provinces, has a fiscal capacity that is 2.5 percent lower. This proxy measure is a good indicator of fiscal capacity for non-traditional gaming because it is correlated with fiscal capacity in a reliable way and because it is independent of provinces' tax effort.

In addition to the main disposable income and population components, a small consumption component was also included in the base for other games of chance. It takes into account the possibility that there is some substitution among ticket lotteries and other types of games.[41] Also, a consumption component may contain some additional relevant information on fiscal capacity not captured by the disposable income and population components alone.

The consumption component was given a high weight in the ticket lottery base because tax effort for ticket lotteries is very similar across provinces. Lottery tickets are available in all provinces, and the lottery corporations of all provinces attempt to maximize sales and profits. Sales (consumption) of lottery tickets are therefore a good indicator of the relative fiscal capacities of provinces.

A pure consumption base could have been used for ticket lotteries, but a small proxy element (consisting of disposable income and population components) was also included in the base to address a potential incentive problem. With a pure consumption base, receiving provinces which reduce tax effort for lottery tickets could trigger an increase in their Equalization approximately equal to the reduction in own-source gaming revenues resulting from the reduced tax effort. A pure consumption base might therefore cause equalization-receiving provinces to reduce their tax effort relative to non-receiving provinces. This undermines the consumption base since its usefulness as an indicator of relative fiscal capacity for ticket lotteries in the first place is premised on the fact that all provinces exert equal tax effort. More generally, the Equalization program is not supposed to influence provincial fiscal choices, but a pure consumption base would run the risk of doing so.

Resource Revenues. Some of the most interesting discussions during the renewal process concerned the treatment of natural resource revenues.

Provinces generate most of their natural resource revenues through taxes on the value (or in some cases the volume) of resources produced. In most cases, costs of production (i.e., costs of resource extraction) are not deducted from the statutory tax base, even though a resource that costs less to produce represents greater fiscal capacity to a province than one that costs more. This is because producers with lower costs are better able to pay taxes than ones with higher costs. Provincial tax *rates* on production bases take into account differential production costs, with higher rates levied on resources with lower extraction costs. Some provinces are able to levy significantly higher tax rates on resource production than others because resources in different locations often have very different costs of extraction.

Indeed, it could be argued that the true source of fiscal capacity for natural resources is the net profit (after extraction costs) or, more specifically, the economic rent, generated by those resources. Although the statutory base upon which provinces levy natural resource taxes is production volume or production value with no province *directly* taxing economic rent,[42] both economic theory (efficient taxation theory) and observation of actual provincial taxing practices indicate that it is really economic rent that is being (*indirectly*) taxed.[43]

These observations suggest that economic rent should be used as the Equalization base for resource revenues. Equalization bases are supposed to reflect the relative fiscal capacities of provinces, and if these fiscal capacities are ultimately determined by economic rent, then economic rent is the correct base for resource revenues.[44]

This conflicts, however, at least to some extent, with the representative tax-system approach (RTS) generally used to select Equalization bases. Under the RTS approach, Equalization bases should reflect the actual taxing practices of provinces — and the actual statutory bases taxed by provinces are not economic rent bases. Furthermore, good economic rent data are not available at the provincial level for most resource types.

Changes to specific natural resource bases were made with these general considerations in mind. All resource bases were significantly improved, with an attempt being made to balance different conceptual viewpoints. In several instances, use is made of new data that have become available from Statistics Canada's PIPES project.

Mining. There were previously four mining revenue sources — potash, coal, asbestos, and other minerals. For the new fiscal arrangements period, these four have been combined into a single revenue source. In addition, the old mining bases (of which two were volume of production bases and two were value of production bases) have been replaced by a single pre-tax net profit base.[45]

The new revenue-source and base definitions improve on the old definitions in several ways. First, the new base is an improved indicator of underlying fiscal capacity since the net mining profits, which constitute the new base, approximate economic rent. Second, the new base better reflects the actual taxing practices of provinces. Mining is the one resource sector for which provinces, in fact, directly tax profits rather than volume or value of production.

Finally, the new base eliminates the need to use the "generic" tax-back provision of the Equalization formula. This is an ad hoc provision in the formula meant to deal with an incentive problem which arises when one equalization-receiving province has a very high proportion of the total tax base for a given revenue source[46] — a rare situation that occurs only with natural resource bases. In particular, it has occurred with potash and with asbestos, for which production is highly concentrated in, respectively, Saskatchewan and Quebec. With the new mining base, invocation of the formula's tax-back provision is no longer necessary because the new base is a combined base for all mining — including coal, asbestos, potash, and other minerals — and is thus much more evenly distributed across provinces than were the old separate bases. There is no exceedingly high concentration of the new base in any one province and therefore no need to use the provision.

Forestry. The old forestry revenue source was split into two separate sources — forestry revenue from private lands and forestry revenue from provincial Crown lands — and the old *volume* of production base was replaced with two *value* of production bases.

Value of production is a better indicator of fiscal capacity than volume of production. The volume of forestry production in two provinces may be the same, but the value of that production will differ significantly if, for example, the tree species harvested in one province differ from those harvested in the other. Since higher value production can be taxed at higher tax rates than lower value production, a province with higher value production has more fiscal capacity than one with a lower value production. The old base incorrectly assigned the same fiscal capacity to two provinces with the same volume of production and thus overestimated the fiscal capacity of provinces with lower per unit value of production relative to those with higher per unit value of production.

Separate revenue sources were created for forestry revenues derived from provincial Crown lands and forestry revenues derived from private lands because of differences in fiscal capacity. Production on Crown lands can generally be taxed at higher rates. With the old revenue-source and base definitions, the fiscal capacity of provinces with a high proportion of production on private lands was being systematically overestimated relative to the fiscal capacity of provinces with a low proportion of production on private lands.

Although the new value of production bases represent a significant improvement over the old volume of production base, it can be argued that the new bases are still not ideal because they do not take into account differences in production costs. Unfortunately, good economic rent data by province are currently not available for the forestry sector. However, work toward developing an economic rent base for forestry will continue in the next renewal round.

Oil. Two new revenue sources — light/medium third-tier oil revenue and heavy third-tier oil revenue — were added to the existing oil revenue sources, and some of the old revenue sources were redefined. Two new value of production bases which correspond to the new revenue sources were added to the existing value of production bases.

The reason for adding the two new oil revenue sources is that production costs vary significantly for different types of oil deposits and for different vintages of oil pools. In general, recovery costs are higher for more recently discovered oil pools. Oil production from these pools is less profitable and therefore cannot be taxed at the same rate by provincial governments as oil production from older pools.

Oil from the newest pools (in the case of Alberta, pools discovered after 1 October 1992) is called "third-tier" oil. Revenue derived from this oil was previously included among new-oil and heavy-oil revenues. The new classification system will lead to an improvement in the measurement of the provinces' relative fiscal capacities — particularly for Saskatchewan and Alberta. The proportion of third-tier oil in total oil production is higher for Saskatchewan than Alberta, and the old revenue-source definitions, which failed to distinguish the less highly taxed third-tier oil from other types of oil, therefore resulted in Saskatchewan's fiscal capacity being overestimated relative to Alberta.

Natural Gas. The domestic and exported natural gas revenue sources have been combined into a single revenue source, and the old volume of production bases have been replaced with a single value of production base.

The two revenue sources were combined because domestic and exported gas are taxed at the same rate by provinces. A value of production base has been adopted in place of the old volume of production base because value of production is a better indicator of fiscal capacity. (See the discussion of the forestry base earlier.)

Because it does not take into account differences in the cost of production, value of production is still not an ideal base. Work toward developing an economic rent base for natural gas revenues will be undertaken during the next renewal round.

Payroll Taxes. The payroll tax revenue source was redefined to exclude payroll taxes paid by provincial and local governments. These revenues do not add to the fiscal capacity of the consolidated provincial-local government sector, and their inclusion in revenues subject to Equalization therefore constituted double counting.

The base, which previously consisted of all wages and salaries earned in a province, was modified to exclude wages and salaries paid by provincial and local governments (consistent with the changes to revenues subject to Equalization). To make it more representative of actual provincial taxing practices, the base was also modified to exclude a weighted average of the wages and salaries below the tax exemption cut-offs of the various provincial payroll tax systems.

Miscellaneous Revenues (User Fees). The miscellaneous revenue source includes various tax and non-tax revenues which are not included in any of the Equalization program's other revenue sources. A large portion of miscellaneous revenues (approximately 80 percent) consists of user fees. The remainder consists of various minor taxes and non-tax revenues.

All user fees collected by the provincial general government sector, the local government sector, and the school-board sector — as those sectors are defined by Statistics Canada — were previously equalized. User fees collected by the university and college sector and by the health and social services sector were not equalized.

Henceforth, only 50 percent of the user fees previously equalized will continue to be equalized.[47] At the same time, revenue coverage for the miscellaneous revenue source will be expanded to include certain non-tax revenue (including fines and penalties) collected by local governments and were previously excluded from equalization.

The reason for reducing the percentage of user fees subject to equalization is that these revenues, which are benefit charges, do not create fiscal disparities. In fact, it can be argued that theoretically, user fees should not be equalized at all.[48] However, no longer equalizing user fees would have constituted an abrupt change with substantial impacts on entitlements. Furthermore, the theoretical argument against equalizing user fees assumes that none of the user fees levied by provincial and local governments exceed the costs of the goods or services on which those fees are charged.[49] But this may — as indicated, for example, by a recent Supreme Court decision on provincial probate fees[50] — not be the case. For these reasons, rather than not equalizing user fees at all, it was decided that the percentage of user fees subject to Equalization should be reduced to 50 percent.

Other. Changes were made to a number of other revenue-source and base definitions as well. These include:

- *Capital Taxes.* For reasons identical to those discussed in the previous section, the percentage of debt-guarantee fees subject to Equalization was reduced by 50 percent.[51]

- *Property Taxes.* Although participants in the renewal process agreed that the current property tax base is unsatisfactory, only minor changes, consisting of the updating of some parameters, were made.

- *Medical and Hospital Insurance Premiums.* Base parameters were updated and new components were added to the base to reflect changes in provincial premium structures.

- *Gasoline Taxes.* Changes were made in the data sources and methodology used to calculate the gasoline tax base for Ontario.

- *Race Track Taxes.* Wagers are now included in the base on the basis of where (in which province) those wagers are made rather than on where the races on which they are made are run.[52]

FUTURE CHALLENGES

Property Tax. The treatment of property taxes has always posed a problem for the Equalization system.[53] The current base is not a representative base which reflects the statutory bases upon which provincial and local governments levy property taxes. This is partly due to the fact that, although they are generally based on some measure of property value, statutory property tax bases differ significantly from province to province.

More importantly, it is questionable whether property value constitutes the correct Equalization base for property taxes, because it is not clear to what extent the capacity of provincial and local governments to raise property taxes is actually a function of property values. It could be argued that property values serve mainly to determine how property taxes are *distributed* among citizens in a jurisdiction rather than to determine the overall capacity of a government to raise revenues from property taxes.

During this most recent renewal process, concerns with the property tax base continued to be raised. The current multi-variable base is too complex and lacks clear theoretical justification. There are also statistical and design problems with specific components of the base and with the way components are combined in the base.

No clear alternative to the current base emerged during the consultation process. The decision was therefore made to keep the existing property tax base (with some updated parameters) for the time being and to continue research to improve this base.

Representative Tax System versus Macro Approach. A second research priority is to examine macro-indicator approaches to Equalization.

There are two major approaches to measuring fiscal capacity recognized in the literature.[54] One of these is the representative tax system approach and the other is the macro-indicator approach. The RTS approach measures the per capita revenues that can be raised by a typical tax system. This is done separately for each revenue source. With the macro-indicator approach, fiscal capacity is determined by a single indicator (e.g., GDP) used as an overall measure of fiscal capacity for all revenue sources.

Although the RTS approach has much to recommend and has generally served the Canadian Equalization program well, it also has certain shortcomings. A number of conceptual criticisms of the RTS have been raised in the literature. For example, it fails to take into account interrelationships among the various tax bases, and it does not measure what is ultimately available to be taxed — income.[55] The RTS approach has also frequently been criticized — most recently in the Parliamentary debates and hearings on the 1999 Equalization legislation — for being too complex. Finally, significant controversy arose among participants in the recent Equalization renewal on the measurement of fiscal capacity for some important revenue sources, which raises concern. Differences of opinion on the property tax base, in particular, often appeared to be fundamental. The RTS framework does not provide any clear means of resolving questions of how fiscal capacity should be measured for certain revenue sources, and this may make difficult any future progress in improving the Equalization program within an RTS framework.

Interaction with Aboriginal Issues. Many of the services generally funded by provincial governments (education, health services, social services) are, in the case of First Nations, funded by the federal government. Also, self-government agreements, comprehensive land-claim agreements, and other recent developments (such as the opening of casinos run by First Nations) are increasingly resulting in a sharing of tax room between provincial and Aboriginal governments. Both of these issues have implications for Equalization.

Some initial discussions of the interaction of Equalization with the financing of public services for Aboriginals took place during this last renewal round, but no changes to the Equalization program were immediately implemented. It was, however, decided that detailed research on this topic would be undertaken and given high priority for the next renewal round.

TERRITORIAL FORMULA FINANCING (TFF)

CONTEXT

The federal government provides funds to the three northern territorial governments — the Yukon, the Northwest Territories and Nunavut — through a formula-based grant. Territorial Formula Financing was established in 1985-86 and is generally reviewed and renewed every five years. In 1999, besides the regular review, the federal and territorial governments also had to redesign the financial arrangements to accommodate the division of the Northwest Territories to create Nunavut.

The Territorial Formula Financing agreements provide annual unconditional transfers to enable the territorial governments to provide a range of public services comparable to those offered by provincial governments. As the name indicates, the size of the grants to the territories is determined by a formula. This formula provides for annual increments and adjustments to a base level of support depending on such things as population, fiscal developments in the territories and the level of public services provided by provincial governments. TFF payments take into account the high costs of providing public services in the north, due to its vast land mass and scattered population, as well as the less-developed state of the territorial economies.

The financing formula is defined in agreements between the federal finance minister and territorial governments, rather than by legislation as is the case with the other major transfers.

Although territorial governments have the authority to raise their own revenues by taxation and the sale of goods and services, TFF provides between 65 and 90 percent of territorial revenues. As an unconditional transfer, it provides the territories with autonomy to design and manage their own public services and allows them to be accountable directly to their citizens. The agreements also include financial incentives to promote economic development and to encourage greater territorial self-sufficiency. In 1999-2000, the federal government will transfer about $1.4 billion: $550 million to the Northwest Territories, $540 million to Nunavut, and $320 million to the Yukon.

HOW ARE TFF PAYMENTS CALCULATED?

Like Equalization, Territorial Formula Financing is based on a gap-filling principle. Territorial expenditure needs are measured by the gross expenditure Base, which, subject to a ceiling, is indexed to grow in line with provincial spending to reflect the public services provided by governments in other parts of the country. It is also adjusted for territorial population growth relative to that of Canada as a whole.

Revenue-raising ability is measured by estimating the revenue that a territory would have at its disposal if it exercised a tax effort similar to that in other parts of the country (adjusted to recognize the special circumstances of the north).

Federal transfer payments fill the gap between the calculated expenditure needs and the revenues estimated to be available to territorial governments.

NEW FUNDING ARRANGEMENTS

The federal and territorial governments conducted their review and restructuring of the financing arrangements to accommodate Nunavut over the course of 1997 and 1998. New funding arrangements were finalized for all three territories and took effect 1 April 1999. The main changes from the previous agreements were:

- The development of two separate expenditure bases to reflect the division of the Northwest Territories and the creation of Nunavut. This includes the provision of incremental funding of about $95 million, starting in 1999-2000, to meet the costs of running two governments instead of one while maintaining the current level of services.

- Simplification of the revenue formula in the agreements with the Northwest Territories and Nunavut. Only major revenues are calculated annually while minor revenue sources will be treated as fixed for the duration of the agreement.

In addition, there were administrative changes to the estimate and payment processes to bring them in line with the other transfer programs. There will now be two estimates and adjustments to payments per year instead of one.

Finally, the length of time that a payment remains open for adjustment due to data revisions has been reduced to three years from five (with the exception of population).

CONCLUSION

The CHST measures introduced in the 1999 budget, and the renewal of Equalization and Territorial Formula Financing, constitute incremental adjustments rather than fundamental changes to the transfer programs. Taken together though, the changes in 1999 were substantial. Over the period from 1999-2000 to 2003-04, the federal government will provide an extra $11.5 billion for health care through an increase in the CHST cash component. The CHST allocation formula will ensure equal per capita entitlements for all provinces as of 2001-02. The structural changes to the Equalization program improve the measurement of provincial fiscal capacity and the calculation of appropriate levels of support. The new TFF agreements reflect the division of the Northwest Territories and the creation of Nunavut. A total of $95 million will be provided to recognize the incremental costs of running two governments instead of one and maintain the provision of the current level of services. All three major programs are now on a common predictable five-year renewal cycle and are designed to operate in their current form from 1999-2000 through 2003-04. It will continue to be essential to keep these programs under review as the fiscal circumstances underlying federal-provincial and territorial relations continue to evolve.

NOTES

The authors work for the federal Department of Finance. The views expressed in this paper are those of the authors and do not necessarily represent official federal government views.

1. CHST and Equalization are both governed by the *Federal-Provincial Fiscal Arrangements Act*. The terms of Territorial Formula Financing are set out in separate agreements with each of the three territories.

2. *Budget Plan*, February 1994, p. 38.

3. Ibid.

4. Ibid., p. 39.

5. *Budget Plan*, 27 February 1995, p. 51.

6. Ibid., p. 53.

7. Ibid.

8. Territories, as well as provinces, are eligible for CHST. However, for simplicity, the term "provinces" is used to refer to both provinces and territories here unless otherwise indicated.

9. Ibid.

10. *Budget Plan*, 1996, p.57.

11. *The Budget*, 20 February 1990, p. 78.

12. *The Budget*, 26 February 1991, p. 66.

13. *Budget Plan*, 1996, p. 57.

14. *The Budget Plan 1999*, 16 February 1999, p. 83 and *Federal Financial Support for the Provinces and Territories*, published with the 1999 budget.

15. Levels are re-estimated in February and October and posted on the Finance Website, http://www.fin.gc.ca, under Publications and Federal Transfers to Provinces and Territories.

16. *The Budget*, 20 February 1990, p. 76.

17. *The Budget*, 26 February 1991, p. 66.

18. *The Budget Plan*, February 1994, p. 39.

19. *Budget Plan*, 27 February 1995, p. 54.

20. Alberta had responded to the cap on CAP by reforming its social assistance programs with the result that by 1996-97, the federal contribution under CAP remained close to 50 percent of eligible spending.

21. *Budget Plan*, 6 March 1996, pp. 58-59.

22. *The Budget Plan 1999*, 16 February 1999, pp. 89-90.

23. Ibid.

24. Fortieth Annual Premiers' Conference, Press Releases, "A Balanced Approach for Better Competitiveness" and "Priority Health Sector Issues," Québec City, 10-11 August 1999. Also, Common Position of Provincial and Territorial Finance Ministers, "Improving the Competitiveness and Standard of Living of Canadians," Ministère des finances du Québec, December 1999.

25. Common Position of Provincial and Territorial Finance Ministers, p. 9.

26. Premiers and Territorial Leaders, "Letter to the Prime Minister of Canada," Meeting of Premiers and Territorial Leaders, Québec City, 3 February 2000.

27. "Parliament and the Government of Canada are committed to the principles of making Equalization payments to ensure that provincial governments have sufficient revenues to provide reasonably comparable levels of public services at reasonably comparable levels of taxation" (subsection 36(2) of the *Constitution Act*).

28. This standard has been in use since 1982-83. It is a population-weighted average of the per capita fiscal capacity of each of the five "middle-rich" provinces.

29. This figure is from the second official entitlements estimate for 1999-2000 made in October 1999 (rounded from $9,501 million).

30. The base level for the ceiling was set at the amount of Equalization provinces would have received for 1992-93 had entitlements been calculated using the formula introduced in 1994-95. The ceiling for the five fiscal years beginning with 1994-95 was then set at the base level plus a percentage equal to the cumulative percentage growth in GNP from 1992 to the calendar years ending in those fiscal years.

31. The ceiling estimate is based on GNP figures for 1998 from the 1999-Q2 National Accounts. Equalization entitlements for 1998-99 were estimated at $9,614 million in October 1999.

32. This is true unless the base year that is chosen precedes the first year of the new fiscal arrangements period by at least three years. In that case, entitlements for the base year will have been finalized by the end of the first fiscal year of the new fiscal arrangements period.

33. As in the previous fiscal arrangements period, the ceiling would apply to total Equalization entitlements after any floor adjustments had been made. In the unlikely event that both the ceiling and floor provisions apply in the same year, the floor provision will be less than 1.6 percent of the per capita standard.

34. Except for some calculations which rely on local government data.

35. Alberta has no sales tax.

36. Whereas only a few years ago, virtually all provincial gaming revenues were derived from ticket lotteries, today only about 35 percent are derived from this source.

37. Also, with the old revenue-source and base definitions, an equalization-receiving province could both increase its own-source revenues from gambling by expanding non-ticket lottery gaming and at the same time trigger an increase in the Equalization transfers it received.

38. Note that if there were a high degree of substitution by gaming patrons among different types of gaming, an expanded consumption base might still be appropriate for Equalization purposes, despite the large differences in tax effort among provinces in the non-traditional gaming area. This is so, because for ticket lotteries, tax effort is similar for all provinces. Consequently, if there were a high degree of substitution between ticket lottery gaming and other types of gaming, low consumption of non-traditional gaming products in a province (because of restricted availability) would translate into correspondingly higher consumption of ticket lottery products (which are equally available in all provinces). An expanded consumption base could therefore fully capture the demand for gaming products in a province, regardless of the availability of non-traditional gaming, and would thus adequately reflect provinces' relative fiscal capacities. However, substitution among different gaming types is actually very low. There have been only very small decreases in the rate of growth of lottery ticket sales in provinces that have implemented video and casino gaming relative to provinces that have not implemented video lottery and casino gaming.

39. More precisely, it includes revenues derived from all non-ticket lottery gaming other than race track taxes. Race track taxes continue to be equalized as a separate revenue source, as was the case prior to the renewal.

40. Sales net of prize payouts, rather than gross sales, are used as the consumption measure because the percentage of gross wagers returned to players in the form of prizes varies significantly among different games. This variation occurs both among major gaming types and within major gaming types (e.g., among different ticket lottery games). In a gross wagers base, games with high prize payouts would be given too large a weight and games with low prize payouts would be given too low a weight, so that provinces' relative fiscal capacities would not be measured accurately.

41. As stated earlier (see note 38 above), there is, in fact, only limited substitution between ticket lottery games and other games of chance. But to the extent that there is substitution, higher fiscal capacity in non-traditional gaming that is associated with lower consumption of lottery tickets will, at least partially, be captured by the consumption component.

42. Exceptions are Crown lease sales and mining taxes. Crown lease auctions capture in a fairly direct way the economic rents that resource properties are expected (at the time of the auction) to generate. Most mining taxes are taxes on profits.

43. For example, in the forestry sector, we observe provinces setting higher stumpage fees for species that are more profitable than for species that are less profitable. We observe provinces adjusting tax rates to reflect changes in prices and input costs (both of which affect the amount of economic rent available to be taxed). And in provincial documents, we see references to such concepts as "responsible sharing of profits" with the private sector.

44. The actual statutory bases taxed by provinces (volume or value of production) are inferior indicators of fiscal capacity because those bases cannot be taxed at the same rates by all provinces. Two provinces can have production bases of equal size, but one province may be able to levy a much higher tax rate on its base because there is more underlying economic rent available to be taxed. The relative volume or value of production of a natural resource in two provinces may thus be a misleading indicator of the relative capacities of the governments of those provinces to raise revenues from the resource.

45. Mining profits will be determined using provincial input-output data from Statistics Canada. As a result of PIPES, these data are now of higher quality, and are available on a more timely basis than in the past.

46. The problem arises if such a province raises its rate of tax on such a base. The resulting increase in its own-source revenues is completely (or almost completely) offset by a corresponding decrease in Equalization. In the absence of some alleviating mechanism, the Equalization program thus creates incentives that could inappropriately distort provincial tax policy. The generic tax-back provision stipulates that if a province has 70 percent or more of a total tax base for a revenue source, the revenues subject to Equalization for that source are scaled back by 30 percent. This substantially reduces the decrease in Equalization that would result from an increase in tax rates and thus the effect of Equalization on the province's taxing decisions.

47. Note that like all other redefinitions of revenue sources and bases, this change will be phased in, so that in 1999-2000, 90 percent of user fees will be equalized, in 2000-01, 80 percent will be equalized, and so on.

48. See, for example, Robin Boadway, "The Economics of Equalization: An Overview," in *Equalization: Its Contribution to Canada's Economic and Fiscal Progress*, ed. Robin Boadway and Paul Hobson (Kingston: John Deutsch Institute for the Study of Economic Social Policy, Queen's University, 1998), p. 78.

49. To the extent that user fees exceed the cost of the goods or services provided by government, these user fees are taxes, not benefit charges, and they create fiscal disparities.

50. Eurig Estate (Re) — 22 October 1998.

51. Debt guarantee fees are a type of user fee. Whereas all other user fees are included in the miscellaneous revenue source for Equalization purposes, debt guarantee fees are included in the capital tax revenue source.

52. The new base is an improvement over the old base because race track taxes are levied on the amount *wagered in a province* (regardless of where the races on which wagers are placed are run). The province where a bet is placed can differ from the province in which a race is run for simulcast races. Simulcast racing has become increasingly common over the past several years.

53. Boadway, "Economics of Equalization," p. 77.

54. See Stephen Barro, *State Fiscal Capacity: An Assessment of Measurement Methods* (Washington, DC: SMB Economic Research Inc., prepared for the US Department of Housing and Urban Development, April 1984).

55. See, for example, Richard Bird and Enid Slack, "Equalization: The Representative Tax System Revisited," *Canadian Tax Journal* 38, 4 (1990):913-27; and especially Barro, *State Fiscal Capacity*.

6

The Evolution of Federal-Provincial Fiscal Arrangements: Putting Humpty Together Again

Paul A.R. Hobson
France St-Hilaire

Les années de restrictions budgétaires fédérales se sont traduites par des changements radicaux dans les programmes de transferts aux provinces. D'abord avec le plafond imposé aux dépenses engagées dans le cadre du Régime d'assistance publique du Canada (RAPC), ensuite avec la fusion du RAPC et du financement des programmes établis (FPE) dans le nouveau Transfert canadien en matière de santé et de programmes sociaux (TCSPS) donnant lieu à des coupures massives des transferts en espèces aux provinces, et, plus récemment, avec la restauration partielle et conditionnelle de ce financement uniquement pour les soins de santé, la décennie 1990 aura été une période des plus tendues pour les relations fédérales-provinciales. Tant le principe que la politique de péréquation ont été remis en cause. Le budget fédéral de 1999 signale-t-il un désir de rétablir un certain équilibre?

Ce chapitre examine l'évolution, les modalités et la distribution du TCSPS jusqu'au budget de 1999. Les auteurs considèrent le nouveau programme de transfert dans toutes ses dimensions et plus particulièrement en tant qu'un des éléments constituants de l'union sociale canadienne.

INTRODUCTION

The signing of the Framework Agreement on the Social Union in February 1999 and the measures related to fiscal transfers announced a few weeks later as part of the federal budget have been interpreted by many as a turning point in the evolution of federal-provincial relations in the area of social policy.[1] However, looking back at the events of the last five years, it can be argued that the real turning point occurred much earlier, in 1994, with the release of the Axworthy Green Paper[2] which set the stage for a major re-engineering of social policy in Canada. While the fiscal crisis of the mid-1990s did provide the real impetus for change, much of the rationale and basic elements underlying the most significant reforms to the social policy infrastructure in the past six years can be traced back to this document. These changes have had a profound impact on the federal government's role in social policy and have fundamentally altered the federal-provincial fiscal framework upon which the Canadian social union has rested for decades.

Although the Green Paper dealt significantly with issues of social policy delivery at the provincial level, the implications for Canadian fiscal federalism were treated almost as an afterthought. Yet, the principal reform options set out in the paper carried with them the potential for large reductions in transfers to the provinces under Established Program Financing (EPF) and the Canada Assistance Plan (CAP) and paved the way for the introduction of new federal social programs. In the event, it was the Canada Health and Social Transfer (CHST) that was to be the vehicle for implementing massive cuts in cash transfers to the provinces, while at the same time doing away with the last major federal-provincial cost-sharing program.

The social union talks, at the outset, were a province-led initiative in reaction to the years of unprecedented cuts and unilateral changes in federal fiscal transfers and other social programs, much of which followed the release of the Green Paper. The negotiations were aimed at establishing the ground rules of a new intergovernmental partnership in the area of social policy. The provinces were also eager to discuss provisions for adequate funding of social programs and changes to fiscal arrangements within the context of these negotiations. However, the federal government opted to hold parallel talks on these issues. This approach seemed somewhat incongruous, since, from the time when they were first established, federal-provincial fiscal arrangements have had a determining effect on the design, the evolution, and the allocation of resources to social programs. But then again, perhaps not.

One of the conclusions of this chapter is that rather than an instrument of social policy, the CHST, as it has evolved, is little more than a mechanism for distributing federal revenues back to provincial governments. It appears that fiscal federalism is no longer the preferred instrument for maintaining a federal role in the areas of health care, postsecondary education, and social assistance. Recent federal budgets reflect a new policy stance whereby Ottawa wishes to establish a distinct federal presence in these areas by implementing new and highly visible initiatives such as the Millennium Scholarship Fund and the National Child Benefit and by reverting to conditional and earmarked transfers for health care. In our view, this approach is inconsistent with the respective role that each level of government has come to play in these areas of social policy and it creates significant gaps in our social safety net. It also redefines the principle of fiscal equity upon which national social programs had initially been established. In the process, the promotion of equal opportunity for all Canadians has been replaced by a new objective — that of fiscal equality. Using "equal per capita" as the new benchmark for fiscal arrangements certainly provides greater simplicity and transparency, but it does not necessarily make for good social policy. In sum, the CHST fails on several grounds to epitomize the set of fiscal arrangements required to make the transition to a new social union framework, especially one as loosely defined as the February 1999 agreement.

The chapter begins by providing some historical perspective from which the CHST must be assessed. We review the evolution of the various elements of federal-provincial fiscal arrangements over the postwar period, including the gradual return of tax room to the provinces, the advent of Equalization, the transition to block-funding under EPF in lieu of cost-sharing in health and postsecondary education, and cost-sharing for welfare programs under CAP. In particular, we highlight the equalization elements in these latter programs — pertaining to provinces' fiscal capacities in the case of EPF and to expenditure need in the case of CAP. We then track the CHST from birth through its formative years, both in design and in its role as the vehicle for instituting massive cuts in cash transfers made to the provinces for social programs. This is followed by a critical assessment of the CHST as an instrument of social policy, arguing that changes to fiscal arrangements in the 1990s have fundamentally altered the scale, the function, and the allocation of federal social transfers to the provinces.

Next, we provide our own assessment of the fiscal state of the social union in the shadow of the Green Paper and in light of subsequent actions by the federal government. Finally, we conclude by making the point that the proper design of funding arrangements requires recognition that these are instruments of social policy, not merely mechanisms for distributing federal money. This should not be misconstrued as simply a desire to put Humpty together again. In coming years, pressures to reform and adjust our social programs will continue unabated as a result of changes in need brought about by new realities. The implications for health care of an aging population and rapid medical advances, the changing face of poverty, and unemployment are only some of the challenges that loom on the horizon. Appropriately designed fiscal arrangements are more important than ever.

SOME BACKGROUND

THE PRE-1990S SOCIAL CONTRACT

Over the past decade, the system of intergovernmental transfers has come under much criticism for being unnecessarily complex and obscure. More importantly, it has come to be viewed in certain regions of the country as unfair and inequitable, so much so that simplicity and equality have become paramount on the agenda for reform of fiscal federalism,[3] often to the detriment of other considerations. Our purpose in retracing the evolution of the federal-provincial fiscal arrangements over time is not to reminisce about the good old days or rehash past injustices, but to remind ourselves of the reasons these were put in place, the objectives they served, and to understand how we have arrived at our current situation and what this implies for the future.

The social programs that Canadians have come to regard as part of their fabric and identity were for the most part established after the Second World War. At that time, the federal government, having acquired effective control of the entire income tax field as a result of the Wartime Tax Collection Agreement with the provinces, was able to retain sufficient control to implement its "national agenda" for social welfare. In practical terms, this meant that the provinces had to accept Ottawa's control over the major tax fields even though the constitution also gave them access to these. By establishing a variety of cost-sharing programs in the fields of health, postsecondary education (PSE), and welfare, the federal government was then able to assume a key role in social policy, even though these programs were in areas of provincial jurisdiction.

Thus, over the next three decades, both orders of government set out to promote the growth of social services demanded by the public, to ensure universal access to a given minimum level of services to all Canadians and reduce interprovincial disparities in the levels of public services provided. This period of cooperative federalism was to produce well-established national health care, university, and welfare systems; tax-collection agreements facilitating tax harmonization; the equalization program; and revenue stabilization arrangements.

THE DIVISION OF TAX ROOM

Ultimately, the whole history of federal-provincial fiscal arrangements revolves around the division of income tax room between the federal government and the provinces.[4] The process was one of evolution, with the postwar tax rental agreements giving way to the 1957 Tax Sharing Agreements (whereby the provinces received a fixed percentage of income tax revenues collected in their jurisdictions) and finally the 1962 Tax Collection Agreements that underlie the present system. Under the tax-collection agreements, the federal government yielded income tax room to the provinces by lowering its rate schedule and allowing the provinces to increase their rates to fill the gap as they wished, provided they accepted the federal definition of the base and rate structure by applying a single rate to the basic federal tax.

Subsequently, the federal government also began providing further tax room to the provinces in lieu of specific-purpose transfers, a trend that culminated in 1977 with the move to block-funding for programs in the areas of health and PSE through EPF. The federal government's objective at the time was to sever the cost-sharing link to provincial expenditures and to have the provinces eventually assume entire responsibility for these programs, which by then were considered "established."

EQUALIZATION

Coupled with the tax-sharing and tax-collection agreements, the Equalization program was put in place to ensure that provinces with below average fiscal capacities were able to provide comparable levels of public services at comparable levels of taxation. When it was first introduced in 1957, Equalization was designed to raise the fiscal capacities of the "have-not" provinces to a level equivalent to that of the top two provinces. Income tax points transferred to the provinces at that time were therefore "fully equalized." Under the 1962 arrangements, the number of revenue bases eligible for equalization was increased and a new national average standard was adopted. While revenue-neutral at the time, this posed a problem of how to accomplish any further devolution of income tax room without widening fiscal disparities across provinces, since transferred tax points would be equalized only up to the national average.

The inclusion of resource revenues among the bases eligible for equalization proved to be particularly problematic. The energy shocks of the late 1970s and early 1980s created a situation whereby the federal government was being forced to equalize provincial revenues without reference to expenditure needs and with only limited access itself to the one revenue source that was creating the problem. Finally, in 1982, this problem was addressed by adopting a "representative" standard which excluded Alberta and the four Atlantic provinces — the five-province standard still in effect today. The key point, for purposes of this chapter, is that Equalization serves the role of raising per capita revenues in recipient provinces up to the standard (a level slightly below the national average); that is, it reduces, but does not eliminate, fiscal disparities.

ESTABLISHED PROGRAMS FINANCING

The introduction of EPF in 1977 permitted a major devolution of income tax room to the provinces in place of direct cost-sharing arrangements for health care and postsecondary education.[5] In its original design, approximately one-half of the total EPF entitlement took the form of a transfer of tax points, equivalent in value to half the amount of federal transfers in the previous year, with the other half provided as an equal per-capita cash transfer. Thereafter, the value of the tax points would have grown in accordance with the tax base; the cash transfer was to grow in accordance with the gross domestic product (GDP). Since the (equalized) value of the tax points differed between the recipient provinces under Equalization and the non-recipient provinces, total EPF grants were not equal per capita; only the cash component was. This remained the case until 1982, when the EPF arrangements were modified so that total entitlements (cash plus the value of the tax points) would be on an equal per capita basis. From that point on, each province's per-capita cash transfer under EPF was to be calculated as the difference between its equal per-capita entitlement and the per capita value of the EPF tax points.

The decision to combine the cash component with the value of the EPF tax points had important implications which still characterize current transfer arrangements under the CHST. Most significantly, the method of calculating the cash transfer by residual, in effect, adds a "super equalization" component to the transfer by raising the per-capita value of EPF tax points in *all* provinces to a top-province standard. This, indeed, was the genius of the 1982 version of EPF — it accomplished a "fully equalized" transfer of tax room to the provinces. In other words, it accomplished a transfer of tax room without opening up wider gaps in fiscal capacities between the "have" and "have-not" provinces.

This process is illustrated in Figure 1. The value of the EPF tax points is calculated on the basis of 13.5 percentage points of federal personal income tax revenues and one percentage point of federal corporate income tax revenues. In addition, EPF tax points are subject to equalization under the Equalization program — this is the "associated equalization" in the figure. Thus, all recipient provinces under Equalization show the same equalized value of tax points per capita. Per-capita cash entitlements are then calculated as a residual.[6] The allocation of EPF cash across provinces can be decomposed into two components. First, EPF cash has the effect of raising the (equalized) value of the tax points to an Ontario standard — the "super equalization" mentioned earlier (as indicated by the dotted line). This applies equally to those provinces that are recipients under the Equalization program and to those, Alberta and British Columbia in this case, that are non-recipients. Second, cash transfers beyond that level are equal per capita across provinces.[7]

Total per-capita entitlement was designed to grow in line with per-capita gross nationa product (GNP). Subsequent federal budgets, however, restrained this growth formula significantly, culminating in a five-year freeze imposed in 1990-91. The total value of the EPF transfer therefore failed to grow in step with the economy, let alone in step with growth in income tax revenues. Put differently, had the federal government simply ceded tax room to the provinces in 1977 equivalent to the total value of the EPF transfer (twice the number of EPF tax points), the value of the associated tax points would have grown in step with income tax revenues. Thus, there has been an erosion of the effective transfer of tax points made in 1977.

Figure 1: EPF Entitlements Per Capita by Province, 1992-1993

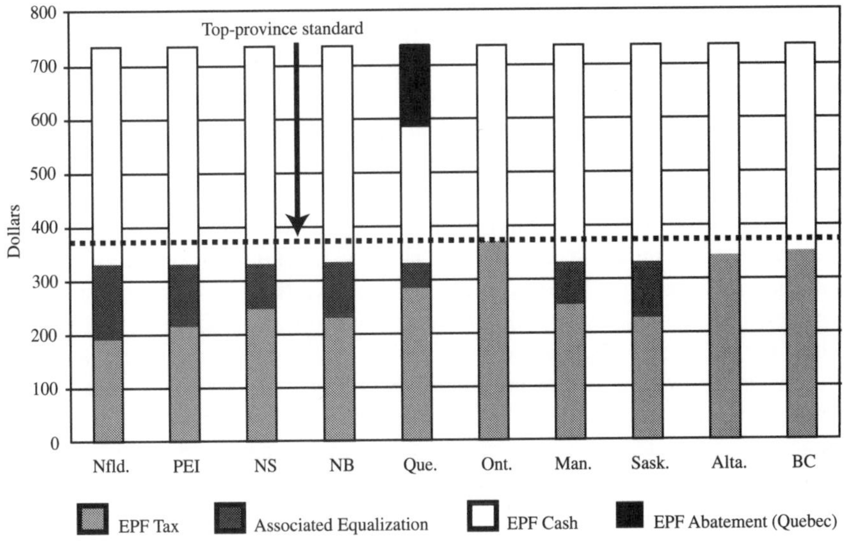

Source: Created from data provided by the Federal-Provincial Fiscal Relations Division, Finance Canada.

The design of EPF also gave rise to certain incongruities that remain as part of the current set of arrangements. For instance, notwithstanding its nature as a block grant for health and PSE (which in effect simply becomes part of provincial general revenues), the federal government continued to separate the total EPF transfer into a notional transfer for health and a notional transfer for PSE based on 1975-76 shares in total transfers (67.9 percent for health and 32.1 percent for PSE). It also adopted the practice of reporting EPF transfers to the provinces as the combined value of the cash transfer and the value of the EPF tax points, as though the tax transfer were a yearly event.[8] In fact the tax transfer occurred once, in 1977, when the federal government lowered its rate schedule to make room for the provinces to increase theirs (i.e., it was the tax points that were transferred). Thereafter, the associated revenues have been collected directly by the provinces while federal tax rates (and provincial rates, for that matter) have evolved quite independently. The point is that even though the structure of EPF has made it necessary to keep track of the value of the tax points in order to calculate the value of cash transfer payments, they do not constitute a transfer — they are simply part of the provinces' own-source revenues.

THE CANADA ASSISTANCE PLAN

The intent of the CAP, established in 1966, was for the two orders of government to share the costs of provision of income support to needy individuals who had exhausted all other avenues available to them — it was the program of last resort for the unemployable. CAP was designed as a matching grant program under which the federal government picked up 50 percent of eligible, provincial social assistance expenditures.

For Ottawa, CAP became increasingly problematic for two reasons: first, wealthier provinces which could afford more generous welfare programs were seen to benefit unduly from this cost-sharing formula and second, CAP did not lend itself to expenditure control measures on the part of the federal government. Moreover, welfare did not remain a program of last resort. Over the latter part of the 1980s and the early 1990s, social assistance became one of the fastest growing areas of provincial spending with obvious repercussions on federal transfers under CAP. Over time the employable unemployed have come to represent a significant share of the welfare caseload (by a margin of

Figure 2: *Welfare Recipients as a Proportion of Population by Province, 1982-1997*

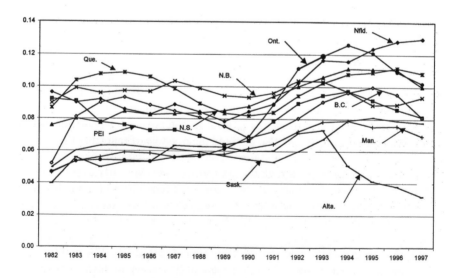

Source: Authors' calculations. Constructed from recipients data found in National Council on Welfare, *Another Look at Welfare Reform* (Ottawa: Minister of Public Works and Government Services Canada, 1997), p. 2, and population data provided by the Federal-Provincial Fiscal Relations Division, Finance Canada.

three to one according to estimates by the National Council of Welfare)[9] both as result of economic restructuring and the cumulative effects of changes implemented by the federal government to the Unemployment Insurance program. Thus, the national social assistance rate has increased from 5.5 percent in the 1970s, to 7 percent in the 1980s, and to 9.5 percent in the 1990s.[10] And while poorer regions continue to have consistently high welfare dependency ratios, all regions have become increasingly susceptible to the welfare impact of economic downturns, even wealthier provinces like Ontario and British Columbia (see Figure 2). Indeed, CAP payments, in addition to providing support to poorer regions, had also come to play important insurance (economic risk-sharing) and stabilization roles in the provinces.[11]

The 1990 federal budget fundamentally changed the nature of these arrangements. In addition to imposing a freeze on EPF entitlements, the budget measures included a 5 percent annual growth ceiling on CAP payments (the cap on CAP) to the three non-recipient provinces under Equalization (Ontario, Alberta, and British Columbia). The ceiling was initially put in place for two years, but it was extended for a further three years in the 1991 federal budget. The timing of this measure, just at the onset of a severe recession that hit Ontario the hardest, generated significant inequities in the transfer system that persist to this day. Cost-sharing of social assistance expenditures in Ontario, for example, fell to roughly 25 percent compared to 50 percent in the Atlantic provinces.

THE TRANSITION TO BLOCK-FUNDING: IN SEARCH OF A NEW FEDERAL-PROVINCIAL BALANCE

THE CANADA HEALTH AND SOCIAL TRANSFER

The effect of the cap on CAP was to create a two-tier system whereby seven provinces continued to benefit from cost-sharing arrangements for social assistance while for the three others CAP became more a block-funding arrangement. In its 1995 budget, Ottawa declared that the time had come "to complete the gradual evolution away from cost-sharing to block funding of programs in areas of provincial responsibility."[12] The announcement that EPF and CAP were to be combined and replaced by a single block fund meant the end of the last major federal-provincial matching grant program. The new transfer arrangements were to significantly alter both the scale and the distribution of federal resources across provinces and, in our view, have dramatically changed the federal government's role in the social union.

First introduced as the Canada Social Transfer (CST), the new transfer was presented as advantageous for all parties involved. At the time, it was argued that compared with current arrangements, the new CST would "end the intrusiveness of cost-sharing under CAP."[13] as well as reduce federal-provincial entanglement and other long-term irritants. As stated in the 1995 budget plan[14]

- Provinces will no longer be subject to rules stipulating which expenditures are eligible for cost-sharing or not.
- Provinces will be free to pursue their own innovative approaches to social security reform.
- Federal expenditures will no longer be driven by provincial decisions on how, and to whom, to provide social assistance and social services.

However, greater flexibility was to come at a price for the provinces, since the introduction of the new CST was to be accompanied by significant cuts in federal transfers over the next few years. Moreover, the new transfer was to retain the tax points/cash transfer characteristics of EPF and therefore some of its "irritants." Details of the new transfer were laid out as follows:

> The provinces will receive $29.7 billion in transfers under the existing programs for 1995-96, about the same as in 1994-95, to allow for a period of stability before change. Under the CST, funding will be reduced from what it would otherwise have been in 1996-97 by $2.5 billion to $26.9 billion. It will be further reduced from what it would otherwise have been in 1997-98 by $4.5 billion to $25.1 billion. While the reductions in major transfers are significant (4.4 percent), they are less than cuts to other federal government program spending.[15]

This immediately opened up the old debate over the value of the tax points as a transfer. Since the "cuts" by definition were to come from cash, the magnitude of these relative to the CST cash component was, in fact, much greater (on the order of 33 percent). In addition, it was proposed that the CST, in its first year, be allocated across provinces in accordance with 1995-96 provincial shares in total entitlements under EPF and CAP. Thus, the initial allocation formula carried forward the discrimination against the three "have" provinces resulting from the cap on CAP. Further, provinces were to remain subject to the general provisions of the *Canada Health Act* and the absence of residency requirements for welfare. The federal government's determination to maintain its role in health care was also reflected in its decision to quickly rename the new transfer the Canada Health and Social Transfer.

The 1996 budget introduced further measures to deal with three unresolved issues related to the new transfer arrangements: (i) preventing the erosion of the cash transfer; (ii) defining a permanent allocation formula; and (iii) providing revenue predictability for the provinces.

One of the problems with combining cash and tax points into a single block fund under the CHST was the risk that without real growth in entitlements, the cash component (and, therefore, federal leverage) would be subject to erosion over time, much as had previously been the case with EPF. To ensure that the cash transfers remained a significant component of CHST, it was announced in the 1996 budget that an $11 billion cash floor would be legislated to provide "an iron-clad guarantee that cash can never fall below $11 billion throughout the five-year arrangement."[16]

The 1996 budget also dealt with the outstanding issue of a permanent provincial allocation formula for the CHST by providing for a gradual shift toward equal per capita distribution: "Over the five-year arrangement beginning in 1998-99, each province's allocation will be further adjusted to more closely reflect its share of Canada's population. By 2002-03, current disparities in per-capita entitlements among provinces will be reduced by half."[17]

There are two important points to make regarding this allocation policy. First, the so-called disparities in provincial per-capita entitlements stemmed directly from the federal government's decision to roll previous transfer arrangements (EPF and CAP) into one block fund and to adopt the 1995-96 distribution of transfers by province as the benchmark for future allocation. Since previous EPF entitlements were already on an equal per-capita basis, this meant that the "provincial disparities" in per-capita CHST entitlements that did exist were a direct reflection of per-capita differences in 1995-96 CAP payments to the provinces. The disparities were thus both a function of each province's welfare caseload and level of benefits for that particular year and the cumulative effects of the cap on CAP since 1990. The second point is that in the process of moving from the 1995-96 benchmark to a semi-equal per-capita allocation, the CHST would remain a transfer that is neither fish nor fowl since it would be unrelated to expenditure needs, or population shares, or economic circumstances, or fiscal capacities. This formula would prove to be unsustainable and a source of growing acrimony on the part of the three "have" provinces.

The third element emphasized in the 1996 federal budget was that of revenue predictability. In laying out the parameters of a five-year arrangement for the CHST, Ottawa wanted to provide advance notice to the provinces to allow them to prepare for the severe reductions in federal transfers in store for them. As originally planned, there were to be significant cutbacks in total entitlements in 1996-97 and 1997-98, followed by a two-year freeze and then modest growth based on a three-year moving average of the rate of growth of GDP (lagged one year) minus 2 percent in 2000-01, minus 1.5 percent in 2001-02, and minus 1 percent in 2002-03. Total cash entitlements, as projected in the 1996 budget documents, are listed in the following schedule (Table 1).

Thus, for 1996-97 the cut in cash transfers amounted to just under $3.5 billion; for 1997-98 it was just over $2.5 billion.

The severity of the cuts was mitigated by the federal government's decision in 1998 to raise the CHST cash floor to $12.5 billion. Indeed, the 1998 budget marked a turning point for the federal government which, having

**Table 1: Entitlements under EPF/CAP and CHST
(in millions of dollars), 1996 Estimates**

Year	System	Total Entitlements	Cash Component
1995-96	EPF+CAP	29,735	18,538
1996-97	CHST	26,900	15,047
1997-98		25,100	12,489
1998-99		25,100	11,826
1999-00		25,100	11,129
2000-01		25,702	11,111
2001-02		26,512	11,180
2002-03		27,426	11,303

Note: Cash amounts include the value of the special Quebec tax abatements and reflect 1996 projections on the value of tax points.

Source: CHST Technical Backgrounder, Federal-Provincial Relations Division, Finance Canada, 1996.

reached its zero-deficit objective much sooner than anticipated, also announced future funding for the National Child Benefit and its plans for the Canada Millennium Scholarships.

THE HEALTH-CARE BUDGET

The most significant aspect of the first post-deficit federal budget in 1999 was its primary focus on health care. In the midst of federal-provincial negotiations on the social union and growing public pressure to resolve what was perceived as a crisis in the national health-care system, there had been much pre-budget speculation as to how Ottawa would re-inject funding into health care and ensure it received due credit for it. Grand schemes featuring new national programs for home-care or Pharmacare were among the rumoured possibilities. Only two weeks after the signing of *A Framework to Improve the Social Union for Canadians*, the federal budget announced with great fanfare that the provinces would receive an additional $11.5 billion in transfer payments over the next five years "specifically for health care."

The 1999 budget provided for an increase in CHST cash of $2 billion — thus raising the total cash transfer to $14.5 billion in each of 1999-2000 and 2000-01, and a further increase of $0.5 billion in 2001-02, thus raising the total cash transfer to $15 billion in each of 2001-02, 2002-03 and 2003-04.[18] These funds are to be earmarked for health care — a commitment the provinces have formally agreed to — and are to be divided on an equal per-capita basis across the provinces. The other significant element of the 1999 budget was the announcement that measures initiated in 1996 to reduce per-capita disparities in CHST entitlements by half by 2002-03 would be stepped up significantly in order to completely eliminate such disparities by 2001-02, at which point all provinces and territories will receive equal per-capita entitlements — cash plus the value of the associated tax points. As Figure 3 illustrates, this will be a particularly difficult transition for Quebec and Newfoundland. These two provinces, which currently have the highest ratios of welfare beneficiaries to population in the country, had benefited significantly from the previous cost-sharing arrangements under CAP, especially relative to Ontario — the province most affected by the cap on CAP.

Figure 4 depicts the evolution of cash transfers since 1982 and includes the projected increases announced in the 1999 budget. According to the budget papers, the $2.5 billion increase in CHST cash from $12.5 to $15 billion in 2001 brings *"what is regarded as the health component of the CHST* [our italics] *as high as it was before the period of expenditure restraint of the mid-1990s."*[19] While this may be the case (see Table 2 below), it is also true that

Figure 3: *Changes in Provincial CHST Entitlements Per Capita*

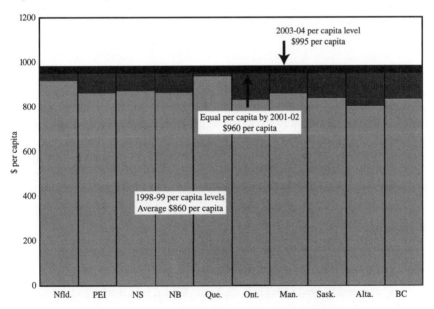

Source: Adapted from Department of Finance, *Budget 1999, Federal Financial Support for the Provinces and Territories* (Ottawa: Department of Finance, February 1999), p.16.

***Figure 4: Cash Transfers to the Provinces under EPF, CAP and
CHST (millions of dollars), 1982-2004***

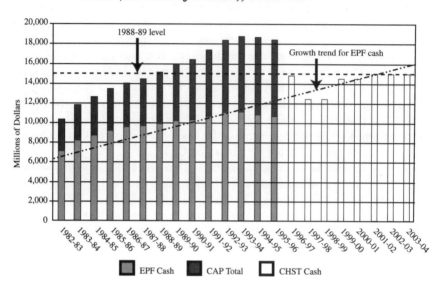

Source: Compiled from data provided by the Federal-Provincial Fiscal Relations
Division, Finance Canada and figures contained in the 1999 federal budget
documents.

the overall federal cash contribution to social programs under the CHST at
that point will be no higher than it was in 1988-89, in nominal terms (see
Figure 4).

As has traditionally been the case, however, the emphasis in the budget
documents is on the growth in entitlements (cash plus tax): "Together with
the value of CHST tax transfers ... federal support is expected to grow to
$31.4 billion in 2003-04. A new high for the CHST will be reached by 2001-
02 — surpassing where transfers stood prior to the expenditure restraint of
the mid-1990s."[20] To that effect, the federal government reiterates its claim to
the value of the EPF tax points as a *bona fide* federal transfer to the provinces
in support of health and postsecondary education programs:

> While the mechanism for delivering federal support differs under cash and tax
> transfers, both have exactly the same impact on federal and provincial finances.
> They represent foregone [sic] revenue to the federal government and increased
> revenue to provincial and territorial governments.[21]

Our analysis of the fiscal impact of changes in these funding arrangements
over time suggests a very different interpretation. The transfer of tax room

that occurred under EPF in 1977 meant that in the first few years under the new regime the provinces would be funding directly (i.e., through their own revenues) approximately 75 percent of the costs of health care and PSE, as opposed to 50 percent under previous cost-sharing arrangements. The EPF tax points did represent forgone federal revenues, but this was accompanied by a corresponding reduction in federal transfers to the provinces on the expenditure side of the ledger. Moreover, under block-funding not only would the remaining federal cash contribution no longer increase in line with program costs, it would also significantly erode in real terms over time due to federal constraints on growth in entitlements under EPF and substantial cuts under the CHST. As a result, the provinces' share of funding for these programs has continued to increase in subsequent years.

Nor does the federal government's argument about tax and cash transfers having the same impact on provincial finances stand up to scrutiny when viewed over time. As shown in Figure 5, the value of the EPF tax points will have roughly tripled between 1982-83 and 2003-04. The evolution of cash transfers as we have seen (Figure 4) has been quite different,[22] and there are no indications that this is about to change.

Figure 5: Value of EPF Tax Points (millions of dollars), 1982-2004

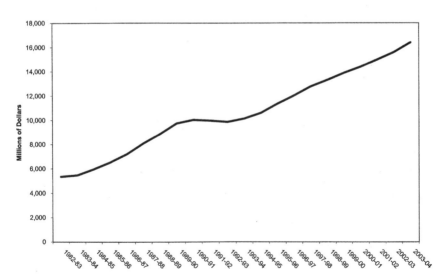

Source: Data provided by the Federal-Provincial Fiscal Relations Division, Finance Canada.

Figure 6 illustrates the growth in the combined value of the CHST cash transfer and the value of the EPF tax points for each year since its inception through 2003-04. The $2 billion increase in CHST cash in 1999-2000 is followed by a one-year freeze; the $0.5 billion increase in 2001-02 is followed by a two-year freeze. To the extent that there is growth, as argued in the 1999 budget, it is in the value of the tax points. As was pointed out earlier, for the provinces this does not constitute growth in transfers; rather it represents growth in their own-source revenues.

Figure 6: CHST Cash and the Value of Tax Points Combined (millions of dollars), 1996-2004

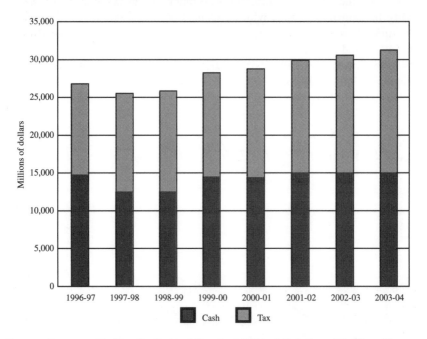

Source: Data provided by the Federal-Provincial Fiscal Relations Division, Finance Canada.

AN ASSESSMENT OF THE CHST AS AN INSTRUMENT OF SOCIAL POLICY

The most generous interpretation of the CHST is that it is the vehicle for maintaining a federal presence in funding provincial programs in health care, postsecondary education, and welfare, albeit at much lower levels. A less generous interpretation is that in the first year of cuts and transition to the CHST (1996-97), the $3.6 billion reduction in cash transfers (see Table 2) more than eliminated "what had been regarded as" the PSE component of EPF (estimated at $3.4 billion in 1995-96). As will be discussed further below, this would have been consistent with the directions proposed for PSE in the Axworthy Green Paper. The 1997-98 cuts (a further $2.4 billion) are then seen as cuts to health and welfare transfers.

From Figure 4 we observe that had EPF cash continued to grow on trend, the level of transfer would have been roughly equivalent to the entire cash transfer under the CHST by the year 2001-02 (see dashed trend line in Figure 4). Viewed from this perspective, it might be argued that the CHST does not embody any federal contribution toward provincial welfare expenditures.

As an alternative scenario, consider the implications for the growth of EPF if, instead of the combined tax point/cash transfer put in place in 1977, there had only been a tax point transfer to the provinces of equivalent value (inclusive of associated equalization). This would have doubled the number of tax points allocated to the provinces and would have generated roughly $30 billion in EPF revenues by the year 2001-02 (see Figure 5) — the same amount as total (cash plus tax) CHST entitlements projected for that year. Interestingly, a similar point is made in the 1999 budget documents where it is stated that: "[t]oday, as in 1977, approximately half the CHST is in the form of cash, while the other half is in the form of tax transfers."[23] Unfortunately for the federal government's case, this would also suggest that CAP somehow vanished along the way. Viewed this way too, the CHST fails to embody any federal contribution toward provincial welfare expenditures.

The point of this discussion is that while Ottawa still views the role of the CHST as providing "specific support to all provinces and territories for health care, PSE and social assistance and social services [to] help ensure these important programs are adequately funded,"[24] the fact remains that it has withdrawn significantly from the financing of these programs in recent years. The federal government's overall contribution now represents less than 15 percent of provincial expenditures in these areas. Even with the cash infusions announced in the 1999 budget, federal contributions will not rise above 1988-89 levels in nominal terms.

To illustrate the trends in federal funding for each of these three *policy* areas, Table 2 divides federal cash transfers into nominal education, health, and welfare components, respectively. As mentioned previously, this follows the practice by the federal government, since the inception of EPF in 1977, of tracking notional specific-purpose transfers, based on 1975-76 shares of 67.9 percent for health and 32.1 percent for PSE in the case of EPF. For the CHST, this nominal allocation is based on 1995-96 shares of EPF cash (57.6 percent) and CAP (42.4 percent) in the total cash transfer. Accordingly, we infer the PSE share of CHST to be 18.5 percent and the health share 39.1 percent.

Table 2: Notional Federal Cash Transfers for PSE, Health and Social Assistance (millions of dollars), 1982-2004

	Total EPF and CAP	Total EPF	EPF PSE	EPF Health	CAP Social Assistance	Total CHST	CHST PSE	CHST Health	CHST Health Supplement	CHST Social Assistance
1982-83	10,240	7,018	2,253	4,765	3,223					
1983-84	11,738	8,069	2,590	5,479	3,669					
1984-85	12,534	8,574	2,752	5,822	3,960					
1985-86	13,395	9,117	2,927	6,190	4,278					
1986-87	13,973	9,468	3,039	6,429	4,505					
1987-88	14,387	9,531	3,059	6,471	4,857					
1988-89	15,061	9,759	3,133	6,626	5,301					
1989-90	15,837	10,093	3,240	6,853	5,744					
1990-91	16,328	10,120	3,248	6,871	6,208					
1991-92	17,345	10,589	3,399	7,190	6,755					
1992-93	18,326	11,003	3,532	7,471	7,323					
1993-94	18,736	11,024	3,539	7,485	7,712					
1994-95	18,642	10,794	3,465	7,329	7,848					
1995-96	18,391	10,601	3,403	7,198	7,790					
1996-97						14,786	2,736	5,787		6,263
1997-98						12,444	2,302	4,870		5,271
1998-99						12,447	2,303	4,871		5,272
1999-00						14,500	2,313	4,892	2,000	5,295
2000-01						14,500	2,313	4,892	2,000	5,295
2001-02						15,000	2,313	4,892	2,500	5,295
2002-03						15,000	2,313	4,892	2,500	5,295
2003-04						15,000	2,313	4,892	2,500	5,295

Source: Authors' calculations.

Finally, for 1999-00 through 2003-04, the nominal "health transfer" is augmented by the "health supplements" announced in the 1999 budget. As noted in the budget documents, with the addition of the health supplements, transfers for health have been returned to mid-1990s levels. The table also suggests, however, that transfers for PSE and welfare remain well below these levels.

The supplementary funding arrangements for health care under the CHST, announced in the 1999 budget, would seem to signal a shift toward earmarked, conditional health grants. The budget documents emphasize that the increased CHST cash is "designated specifically for health care" and refer to the premiers giving their consent to that effect at the 4 February meeting of the first ministers. It is also stated that the provinces have agreed to renew their commitment to the five principles of medicare and to make information available about the health-care system as part of the Framework Agreement on the social union signed on that date. Earmarking increases in transfer payments for health care certainly flies in the face of the increased flexibility and reduced entanglement attributes originally associated with the move to block-funding under the CHST.

The federal government's insistence that the health-care supplement be allocated to provinces and territories on an equal per-capita basis is revealing as well. Although the provinces had been adamant that new federal funding should be channelled through existing transfer arrangements, the end result is that a whole new set of fiscal arrangements designated for health care has been superimposed on the old block-grant structure. As a result, the latter is now for all intents and purposes little more than a mechanism for distributing federal revenues across provincial governments to address the problem of vertical fiscal imbalance. In terms of maintaining the integrity of the social union, the one advantage this mechanism has over a simple transfer of tax room is the implicit super-equalization element carried over from EPF.

Finally, the linking of new funding for health care in the federal budget to commitments made by the provinces in the context of the Social Union Framework Agreement is also somewhat surprising, given Ottawa's commitment in the same document to "consult with provincial and territorial governments *at least a year prior* [our italics] to renewal or significant funding changes in existing social transfers" The immediate change to a three-year fast track toward equal per-capita CHST entitlements announced in the budget would certainly seem to qualify as a significant funding change, particularly for some provinces (see Figure 3). This move raises questions about the federal government's commitment to funding predictability either through the five-year arrangements announced in previous federal budgets or the new provision to that effect in the Social Union Framework Agreement.

THE STATE OF THE SOCIAL UNION

Our analysis has shown that changes to fiscal arrangements in the 1990s have fundamentally altered the scale, the function, and the allocation of federal social transfers to the provinces. These changes have occurred in the context of other reforms to social programs, which on the whole have had major consequences for the federal government's role in the social union. Most of these reforms can be traced back to the Axworthy Green Paper which, in hindsight, did set the stage for a major restructuring of social policy in Canada. The proposals with regard to PSE funding and social assistance are particularly relevant, as are the repercussions of the UI reforms that followed the release of this blueprint document.

POSTSECONDARY EDUCATION

On the topic of PSE funding policy, the Green Paper had acknowledged the precipitous decline in the EPF(PSE) cash transfer and proposed that the remaining cash be diverted from transfers to provinces and replaced by a system of expanded student loans and restructured grants to individuals. It was anticipated that the provinces would respond by passing on transfer cuts to PSE through corresponding reductions in grants to PSE institutions. It was further expected that institutions would adjust to these reductions by increasing tuition fees.

The Canada Millennium Scholarship Fund established in 1998 can be seen as consistent with the earlier proposals found in the Green Paper. The $2.5 billion endowment, which will be managed by an arm's-length foundation, will award postsecondary education scholarships, based primarily on financial need, over a ten-year period beginning in the year 2000.

The federal government's decision to introduce the Millennium Scholarships in 1998 following years of reductions in PSE transfers to the provinces has placed them in a position where they can either accept this program's underlying premise — that increases in tuition are appropriate, since students should bear a greater portion of the cost of their education — or reduce their own programs of student loans and bursaries by a corresponding amount and use the funds to increase university grants. Moreover, the annual funding to be derived from the $2.5 billion endowment ($300 million per year over a ten-year period) is relatively small compared to previous reductions (an estimated $1.2 billion since 1994) in fiscal transfers designated to PSE. The western premiers have recently called for full restoration of funding for PSE through the CHST.

The Millennium Scholarships were also introduced without prior consultation with the provinces, which again seems contrary to the spirit of the recent social union agreement calling for "advance notice being given *prior* [our italics] to implementing a major change in a social policy or program which will substantially affect another government"[25] and consultation with the provinces to identify potential duplication.

SOCIAL ASSISTANCE

On social assistance funding, the Green Paper emphasized the deficiencies and restrictions associated with CAP, especially the cost-sharing conditions that created a disincentive to innovations in program delivery, as well as the problems arising from the cap on CAP. A number of options were reviewed, including integrating income-support programs under a Guaranteed Annual Income scheme, replacing CAP with either conditional or non-conditional block-funding, and redirecting federal spending under CAP and the Child Tax Benefit[26] toward priority areas such as improving income support for low-income families with children.

The National Child Benefit (NCB), which came into effect in July 1998, is described as a new joint initiative of Canada's federal, provincial, and territorial governments to help children in low-income families, promote attachment to the labour market, and reduce government overlap and duplication. Effective July 1998, the federal government combined two existing programs — the former Child Tax Benefit and the Working Income Supplement — into one benefit, the Canada Child Tax Benefit (CCTB) available to families with incomes of up to $66,721 and added a new monthly benefit for low-income families (with revenues of less than $25,921 in the case of a two-child family), called the NCB Supplement.

The federal government had committed $850 million in new funding for the NCB by July 1998 and announced further increases of $425 million in July 1999 and an additional $425 million in July 2000. A key point is that the NCB Supplement is paid regardless of the family's source of income. While low-income working families keep the entire supplement to the CCTB, provinces and territories may reduce social assistance benefits by the same amount as the NCB supplement such that families on social assistance continue to receive at least the same federal and provincial/territorial basic income support as before. As part of the NCB initiative, provinces are to reinvest the social assistance savings in programs and services benefiting children in low-income families. The objective of the program is to remove barriers to moving from social assistance to employment by providing children's benefits outside the social assistance system.

According to *The National Child Benefit Progress Report*[27] released in the spring of 1999, provinces had reinvested about $225 million from adjustments to social assistance funding during 1998-99 (or an estimated $303 million per year on a full-year basis). New Brunswick and Newfoundland chose to maintain social assistance payments and invested an additional $9.9 million, an amount equivalent to what would otherwise have been available for reinvestment. The report indicates that provinces/territories have opted to provide new or enhanced support for low-income families primarily through additional child benefits and earned income supplements (31 percent of funding) and child/day-care services (39 percent). Some have also invested in early childhood services, children-at-risk services, and supplementary health benefits.

The NCB initiative is commonly cited as a prime example of cooperative federalism adapted to today's needs. The program is based on the concerted action of the two levels of government to address the problems of child poverty and the welfare trap. The overall policy results have been greatly enhanced by having each level of government play its appropriate role: in the case of the federal government that of income redistribution at a national level and for the provinces that of designing and providing programs and services that reflect local needs and priorities. To the extent that it reduces provincial expenditures on social assistance, it could be said that the NCB acts as a substitute for cost-sharing transfers under the former CAP. However, even with projected funding increases, the figures released in the progress report clearly indicate that the NCB by no means replaces previous federal contributions to social assistance programs under CAP.

THE WELFARE IMPACT OF UI REFORMS

There is an additional dimension to the move by the federal government to cut the cost-sharing link to provincial social assistance expenditures. As was mentioned earlier, there has been a significant increase in social assistance rates (SAR) in Canada in the past few decades as the long-term unemployed have come to represent the bulk of the caseload. With every recession the national SAR has experienced a dramatic hike and only recovered marginally in subsequent periods of recovery. At present, over 9 percent of the Canadian population is on welfare rolls, compared with 5 percent in the 1970s and 7 percent in the 1980s. With the SAR increasingly a function of economic cycles, the move to block-funding under the CHST has helped insulate the federal government from the fiscal effects of future recessions while making the provinces correspondingly more vulnerable in that regard. This situation has been further exacerbated by the cumulative changes brought to the Unemployment Insurance Program (UI) in the 1990s.

Following the release of the 1994 Green Paper, the federal government implemented a series of UI reforms whose overall effect was to tighten the eligibility requirements and the benefits available under the renamed Employment Insurance Program. The impact of these reforms has been significant. Whereas 75-80 percent of unemployed Canadians were UI beneficiaries in the 1980s, less than 40 percent qualified by 1997. In a recent study of the determinants of social assistance rates in Canada between 1977 and 1996, Arnau, Crémieux and Fortin estimate that cumulative changes to UI eligibility in the 1990s (including the 1990, 1994, and 1996 amendments) have resulted in more than a 20-percent increase in the population on provincial social assistance.[28] According to the authors' estimates, the resulting SAR increase translates into an additional $2.5 billion in welfare expenditures for the provinces on an annual basis. While these estimates do not fully take into account the counteracting effects of administrative changes[29] to provincial social assistance programs implemented since the mid-1990s, they do provide a sense of the magnitudes involved. Given federal spending reductions of $6 billion annually on UI and an estimated additional $2.5 billion reduction in federal transfers designated to social assistance since 1995-96, the extent of federal fiscal offloading to the provinces has been quite dramatic.

THE FUTURE OF FISCAL FEDERALISM

Beyond its immediate budgetary impact, the combination of UI reforms and changes in fiscal transfer arrangements has long-term consequences for the provinces which will not only bear the full cost of increases in their welfare caseload, but will also have to deal on their own with the problems associated with the long-term unemployed. This represents the most significant shift in federal-provincial expenditure responsibilities in decades. Yet this issue failed to be addressed in the context of the Social Union Framework Agreement even though it is at the very heart of the matter. It was also completely ignored in the set of fiscal arrangements laid out for the next five years. As we pointed out earlier, the new federal funding is strictly for health care, otherwise the growth in CHST entitlements stems only from the increase in the value of EPF tax points. As for the move to an allocation formula on an equal per-capita basis, it has been presented as necessary to redress the long-standing inequities created by the cap on CAP for the "have" provinces. In its imminent manifestation as an equal per-capita grant, the CHST does away with the arbitrary nature of a distribution tied to the cap on CAP and differences in welfare "need" as they existed in 1995-96. Yet, by its very nature, an equal per-capita distribution fails to reflect differences in welfare "need" as they exist in 1999-2000 and beyond. One would be hard-pressed to find the rationale for funding social assistance on such a basis.

In a recent paper, Coulombe observes that with a SAR of 3.2 percent in Alberta and 12.8 percent in Newfoundland in 1997 (see Figure 2), the amount of federal subsidy received under the new CHST formula by the social assistance beneficiary in Alberta will be four times that received by the beneficiary in Newfoundland.[30] The author also questions the merit of funding health care and PSE on an equal per-capita basis without regard to expenditure need when significant regional differences in demographics, urbanization, and other factors are bound to play an increasing role in the costs of provision of these services. He argues that the new funding formula signals the abandonment by the federal government of its primary role in the federation, which is to ensure that provinces are in a position to provide comparable levels of services at comparable levels of taxation and rejects the idea that equalization alone can fulfil that role.

The National Council of Welfare has also been strong in its condemnation of the CHST:

> The Canada Health and Social Transfer was the culmination of a series of social policy blunders made by the federal Finance Department in recent years. Subsequent announcements by the federal government have softened its original financial impact, but the transfer is still bad social policy and should be replaced entirely.[31]

In the same report, the Council has advocated a new package of financial arrangements for social programs, specifically: (i) the abolition of the CHST, to be replaced by four new "cash-only" deals in support of medicare, postsecondary education, welfare, and social services; (ii) legislation to prevent "arbitrary and unilateral" changes in these programs; and (iii) guarantees that provincial governments will respect minimum national standards for welfare.

One of the Council's concerns about the CHST as a single block fund had been that "provincial or territorial governments could theoretically use all the federal money for medicare and none for the other three areas." Yet another reason for separating funds advanced by the Council is related to setting appropriate escalators. The fund for medicare, for example, might be escalated according to economic growth or inflation. Welfare, on the other hand, would be better suited to an escalator such as one linked to unemployment by province which would ensure changes in the level of federal support in times of recession.[32]

When the CHST was introduced in 1995, we argued for a decoupling of health and welfare components of the transfer.[33] The issue in health-care funding having become, in our view, one of revenue-sharing between the two levels of government and maintaining a federal presence, we proposed that the federal government cede the remaining value of the EPF cash transfer to the provinces as a tax abatement. Thus, a given percentage of federal income tax revenues (the Canada Health Tax Abatement) would be earmarked for provincial health-care programs and allocated to the provinces in the same fashion as the "cash" component under EPF; the difference being that its value would grow in step with growth in the value of the income tax base. This would have provided a way to effect fiscal disentanglement, while maintaining a federal role in preventing increases in fiscal disparity across provinces.

With regard to social assistance, the Hobson-St-Hilaire proposal was for a block grant that is equalized for differences in need across provinces. The total federal commitment (the Canada Social Transfer) would be based on a fixed percentage of *standardized* provincial social assistance spending across all provinces with a built-in system of differential cost-sharing whereby those provinces with above (below) average "need" would receive greater (less) than average cost-sharing. The equalization factor would therefore take into account differences in economic circumstances across provinces, including the "have" provinces when their need for social assistance is above the national average.

However, as this chapter has shown, there has been a lot of water under the bridge (all the king's horses and all the king's men) with regard to the fiscal arrangements since 1995. Our reading of the 1999 budget is that the federal government believes that it has brought closure to the whole debate concerning its role in funding social programs nationally. The cuts in transfer payments to the provinces have come to an end; more federal money has been injected directly into health care while reaffirming Ottawa's role in this area; and the transition to equal per-capita funding is almost complete, thus stemming the tide of discontent among the "have" provinces. In many ways, one gets a sense of "case closed" from the perspective of the federal government.

More importantly, the events of the last few years suggest that a "virage"[34] has taken place and that fiscal federalism has *de facto* become more of an instrument of last resort for the federal government in its efforts to maintain a federal presence in the area of social policy. With budgetary surpluses now a reality, the federal government seems little inclined to either restore non-health-related social transfers to the provinces or reduce the tax room it occupies to reflect a diminished federal role in these areas. Rather, it seems more intent on developing new and highly visible federal initiatives in the areas of health, education, and child poverty. The Canadian Innovation Fund, the Millennium Scholarships, and the National Child Benefit initiatives and the measures related to health care and research in the last federal budget all signal a new approach to federalism. While gaining federal visibility is clearly at issue, there may also be benefits if the result is greater transparency and accountability to the public in terms of who is responsible for what programs. However, this new way of doing things will require even more consultation and cooperation between the levels of government to avoid conflict, overlap, and duplication. This is why there will be so much at stake as events unfold and the Framework Agreement on the social union gets put to the test.

CONCLUSION: FISCAL ARRANGEMENTS FOR A NEW
SOCIAL UNION

The federal government's decision not to discuss the issue of adequate funding of core social programs in the context of the social union negotiations —
except as a last-minute deal breaker — is unfortunate, as this represented a
unique opportunity for both orders of government to consider the fiscal parameters required to lay the groundwork for a new social union framework.
Instead, these issues were dealt with in the usual fashion (unilaterally and
with little consultation) as part of the annual federal budget process.

The 1999 budget restated the role of the CHST as providing support for
health care, postsecondary education, and social assistance and social services to "help ensure these important programs are adequately funded." After
nearly a decade of freezes and cutbacks in federal transfers, the announcement of an $11.5 billion cash infusion for health care through 2003-04 was
undoubtedly received with great relief in provincial capitals. In the budget
documents much was made of the fact that by 2003-04, "what is regarded as
the health component of the CHST [will be] as high as it was before the period of expenditure restraint in the mid-1990s." If this point of view is accepted,
then "what is regarded" as the postsecondary education and welfare components of the CHST remain well below what they were prior to the period of
expenditure restraint in the mid-1990s. Moreover, it is not clear how an earmarked, conditional health grant fits into the CHST's original scheme as a
general-purpose block fund for social programs that was meant to give provinces greater flexibility in program design and delivery and enable them to
allocate funds according to their own priorities.

Should we then also expect to see distinct block grants for PSE and welfare
in coming years? We have argued that the rationale and the main options for
reforming federal funding for PSE and social assistance were clearly outlined
in the Axeworthy Green Paper. In PSE, it may well be that the federal government wishes to shift away from fiscal transfers to the provinces to some form
of voucher system directed at students and more direct funding for research in
general. As for social assistance, new federal funding is being allocated to the
NCB with the objective of removing children from the welfare caseload and
toward some form of guaranteed annual income for low-income families. The
new, earmarked, and conditional health-care supplement has been artificially
superimposed on the CHST structure because it was the most straightforward
way to inject additional federal funding directly into the system. But at the
same time, the federal government is still considering new funding scenarios
for home care and community-based services. Finally, what remains of the
CHST is unrelated to expenditure need, policy objectives or economic circumstances. Rather than an instrument of social policy, the CHST is little

more than a mechanism for redistributing federal revenues across provincial governments. Thus, it is no longer a question of putting Humpty together again.

It is our view that the 1999 budget does not bring closure to the debate surrounding the CHST. In many ways, the last decade has been one of transition from the old social union framework, which was put in place in the postwar period and founded on a cost-sharing partnership between the levels of government in the areas of health, PSE, and welfare to a new social union framework which involves less fiscal entanglement and potentially more efficiency and transparency. But this is still a work in progress. The transition is not complete and one of the main issues that needs to be addressed is the structural shift that has occurred in federal-provincial expenditure responsibilities for core social programs.

In the early 1990s, a number of studies, including one by the Economic Council of Canada, showed that Canada was facing a situation of increasing fiscal imbalances, with the federal government's revenue growth potential well in excess of its projected spending, mainly due to its dominance of the fastest-growing revenue sources. For their part, the provinces faced the opposite scenario, essentially because of cost pressures related to social programs.[35] Since then, UI reforms and changes in fiscal transfer arrangements have clearly worsened the imbalance. For instance, under current block-funding arrangements, the health-care cost implications of an aging population will be for the provinces to bear. This is where proposals such as ours for a move to a tax abatement, or that by Bird and Mintz in this volume for a transfer of tax room to the provinces, could play an important role in providing the provinces access to a growing source of revenue to ensure adequate funding without increasing fiscal disparities.[36]

This would still leave one important issue unresolved, however, which is the need to address the implications of the end of cost-sharing of social assistance and recent EI reforms. The future cohesiveness and resilience of Canada's social union will hinge on the risk-sharing mechanisms in place in our federal system to absorb the fiscal impact of future recessions and provide adequate support for regions with higher than average poverty and unemployment. And this is where "fair-shares" federalism falls well short of the mark.

NOTES

1. See, for example, Thomas Courchene, "Fair-Shares Federalism and the 1999 Budget," *Policy Options* (April 1999):39-46.

2. Human Resources Development Canada, "Improving Social Security in Canada: A Discussion Paper," (the Axworthy Green Paper) (Ottawa: Supply and Services Canada, 1994).

3.   See, for example, Paul Boothe and Derek Hermanutz, *Simply Sharing: An Inter- provincial Equalization Scheme for Canada*, C.D. Howe Institute Commentary No. 128 (Toronto: C.D. Howe Institute, 1999).

4.   The discussion in this and subsequent sections on the evolution of federal- provincial fiscal relations draws heavily on Paul A.R. Hobson and France St-Hilaire, *Reforming Federal-Provincial Fiscal Arrangements: Toward Sustain- able Federalism* (Montreal: Institute for Research on Public Policy, 1993).

5.   This further devolution of tax room placed all provinces on a roughly equal footing with Quebec, which had secured additional tax room for itself under earlier provisions for opting-out of shared-cost programs. In addition, a portion of the PSE transfer had been in the form of a tax transfer.

6.   Quebec's cash transfer is reduced by the value of additional tax points granted to Quebec in lieu of cash transfer — the Quebec EPF abatement as it is labelled in the chart.

7.   The Quebec special abatements, gained under earlier opting-out provisions, are treated as cash transfers for purposes of this discussion. It should be noted that these special abatements are not eligible for Equalization.

8.   Stephan Dupré referred to this as being at the top of the list of the "Big Lies" of Canadian public finance. See *The Future of Fiscal Federalism* (Kingston: The Institute of Intergovernmental Relations, Queens University, 1995), p. 250.

9.   Inferred from National Council of Welfare, *Profiles of Welfare: Myths and Re- alities* (Ottawa: Minister of Public Works and Government Services Canada, 1998), p. 15.

10. Inferred from National Council of Welfare, *Another Look at Welfare Reform* (Ottawa: Minister of Public Works and Government Services Canada, 1997), p. 2.

11. See Hobson and St-Hilaire, *Reforming Federal-Provincial Fiscal Arrangements*.

13. Department of Finance, *Budget Plan* (Ottawa: Department of Finance, 27 Feb- ruary 1995), p. 52.

13. Ibid., p. 53.

14. Ibid.

15. Ibid.

16. Department of Finance, *Budget Plan* (Ottawa: Department of Finance, 6 March 1996), p. 57.

17. Ibid., p. 59.

18. In fact, a "CHST Supplement" of $3.5 billion was made available to the prov- inces effective 1999-00. This amount was accounted for in 1998-99 by the federal government through the establishment of a trust fund in the name of the prov- inces. It was "anticipated" that the provinces would draw down their shares "in a gradual and orderly manner" — $2 billion in 1999-00, $1 billion in 2000-01, and $0.5 billion in 2001-02. In addition to these amounts, CHST cash was to be augmented by $1 billion for the year 2000-01, $2 billion for the year 2001-02,

and $2.5 billion for each of 2002-03 and 2003-04, thus raising the notional cash transfer to $14.5 billion in each of 1999-00 and 2000-01 and to $15 billion in 2001-02. The actual transfer would be $15 billion in each of 2002-03 and 2003-04. See Department of Finance, *Budget 1999, Federal Financial Support for the Provinces and Territories* (Ottawa: Department of Finance, February 1999), p.13.

19. Department of Finance, *The Budget Plan 1999* (Ottawa: Department of Finance, 1999), p. 83.

20. Department of Finance, *Budget 1999, Federal Financial Support*, p.13.

21. Ibid., p.11.

22. It could even be argued that reductions in cash transfers to the provinces amount to the same thing as a reassignment of tax points from the provinces to the federal government. A reasonable estimate of the equalized value of one PIT point in 1997-98 is $900 million. The reduction in cash transfers between 1995-96 and 1997-98 (in excess of $6 billion) would, therefore, be roughly equivalent to the federal government grabbing PIT points.

23. *Budget 1999, Federal Financial Support*, p.11.

24. Ibid., p. 9

25. *A Framework to Improve the Social Union for Canadians*, an agreement between the Government of Canada and the governments of the provinces and territories, 4 February 1999.

26. The Child Tax Benefit (CTB) was established in 1993 to replace the former family allowance program and the deduction for child dependants under the PIT.

27. National Child Benefit, *The National Child Benefit Progress Report, 1999* (Ottawa: Minister of Public Works and Government Services Canada, 1999).

28. Philippe Arnau, Pierre-Yves Crémieux and Pierre Fortin, "The Determinants of Social Assistance Rates: Evidence from a Panel of Canadian Provinces, 1977-1996," unpublished paper, April 1998.

29. The model takes into account the effects of changes in provincial benefit rates for social assistance, but not those resulting from increased administrative stringencies which are of some importance in certain provinces (e.g., Alberta, Ontario, and British Columbia).

30. Serge Coulombe, "Le fédéralisme fiscal a-t-il un avenir avec une division par habitant du TCSPS?" Présentation au XXIVe Congrès de l'Association des économistes québécois, Hull, le 14 mai 1999.

31. National Council on Welfare, *Another Look at Welfare Reform*.

32. Ibid.

33. Paul A.R. Hobson and France St-Hilaire, "The CHST in Two-Part Harmony," notes for a presentation at the IRPP Roundtable on the CHST, Montreal, 2 December 1995.

34. French term to describe a major change in direction.

35. Economic Council of Canada, *A Joint Venture: The Economics of Constitutional Options, Twenty-Eighth Annual Review* (Ottawa: Economic Council Of Canada,

1991), pp. 57-126. See also G.C. Ruggeri, D. Van Wart, G.K. Robertson and R. Howard, "Vertical Fiscal Imbalance and the Reallocation of Tax Fields in Canada," *Canadian Public Policy/Analyse de Politiques* 19, 2 (1993):194-215

36.   Richard Bird and Jack Mintz, "Tax Assignment in Canada: A Modest Proposal," in this volume.

7

Federal-Provincial Small Transfer Programs in Canada, 1957-1998: Importance, Composition and Evaluation

François Vaillancourt

Ce chapitre porte sur les petits transferts fédéraux-provinciaux au Canada. Ceci mérite examen car ces transferts, définis comme tous les transferts sauf le TSC et la péréquation, représentent environ 20% des transferts fédéraux aux provinces. Nous nous penchons tout d'abord sur leur importance au Canada pour la période 1957-1998 et constatons un certain déclin. Nous examinons ensuite quels sont les programmes les plus importants au Canada (1977-1998) et par province (1997-1998). Nous constatons que les transferts dans les domaines du logement et de l'agriculture sont les plus importants au Canada mais que d'autres programmes tels ceux pour la pêche (Terre-Neuve) et les langues officielles (Nouveau-Brunswick) importent à une province en particulier. Nous concluons en évaluant sommairement quelques programmes.

INTRODUCTION

The purpose of this chapter is to examine federal-provincial small transfer programs, that is, those other than Equalization and the Canadian Health and Social Transfer (CHST) (Established Programs Financing [EPF]/Canada Assistance Plan [CAP]) programs.[1] This is of interest as there has been little analysis of these programs in recent years, yet in the aggregate they have amounted to $3 to 4 billion every year since 1987. Transfer programs in areas other than health, income support, and postsecondary education have long histories in Canada, starting with the 4H Club subsidies in 1900 and the railway grade crossing program in 1909. This chapter, however, is limited to an examination of the 1957-58 to 1997-98 period with the main focus on more recent years as more precise issues are addressed. The choice of the first year reflects the introduction of both the Equalization and hospital insurance transfer programs in that year. The choice of the last year reflects the availability of data (Public Accounts) at the time of writing.

The chapter is divided into three parts. The first part presents evidence on the absolute and relative importance of small transfers, using both dollar amounts and percentages of various indicators for the 1957-98 period. The second examines the composition of small transfers for Canada as a whole for the 1977-98 period and by province for 1997-98. The third puts forward evaluation criteria and uses them to assess the ten most important programs in 1997-98. The time period covered is reduced as we move from the first to the third part of the chapter, reflecting in part the availability of data for the issues under discussion.

IMPORTANCE OF SMALL TRANSFER PROGRAMS,
1957-58 TO 1997-98

This first part examines the importance of small transfers. We begin by presenting data at the national level in Figures 1 and 2. The main trends over the 1957-98 period are:

1. an increase in total cash transfers in nominal and real dollars until 1994-95, followed by a sharp drop with 1997-98 transfers equal to about 80 percent of the 1994-95 transfers (see Figure 1);[2]

2. a less stable pattern for small transfers which increased until 1966-67, then decreased until 1969-70, increased again in 1970-71, decreased for two years and so on until 1997-98. This irregular behaviour is readily visible in Figure 2. As a result, small transfers have the second highest coefficient of variation of the various types of transfers at 0.97; only CAP transfers are more volatile (1.03) while Equalization (0.9), CHST (0.88), EPF (0.84) and other (0.75) are less volatile. This variability is explained mainly by the introduction and end of various programs rather than by abrupt changes in existing programs; and

3. a reduction over time in the importance of small transfers as measured by the four ratios (Figure 2) although there are signs of a small increase from the mid-1990s onwards. This is not surprising if one examines the three trend regressions estimated using the following equation: Transfers = B_0 + B_1 t (all coefficients are significant at the 1 percent level) where B_0 is the constant and B_1 t the trend (the changes from year to year in the transfer examined). The results are shown in Table 1 below.

One sees that small transfers increase more slowly in nominal dollars over time than equalization or CHST and that the R^2 is smaller indicating more variability around the trend.

Figure 1: Federal Transfers to Provinces, Canada, 1975-1998 ($ 000,000, Nominal and Real)

1a (Nominal)

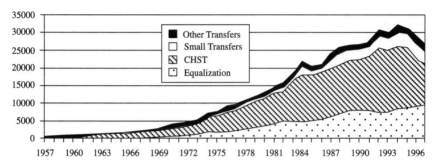

Source: Table A-1, items (1), (4), (5) and (6) in the Appendix.

1b (Real)

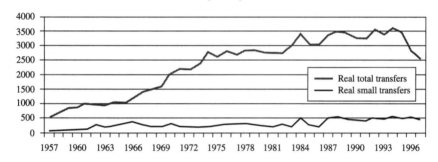

Source: Table A-1, items (8) and (9) in the Appendix.

Table 1: Trends in Transfers in Canada, 1957-1998, Regression Analysis

	Constant	Trend	R^2
Equalization	1,964	266	0.93
CHST	3,043	475	0.90
Small transfers	875	115	0.82

Source: Table A-1 and calculations by the author.

Figure 2: Importance of Small Transfers (ST), Four Ratios, Canada, 1957-1998

2a

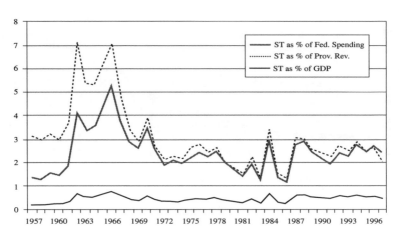

Source: Table A-1, items (13), (14) and (15) in the Appendix.

2b

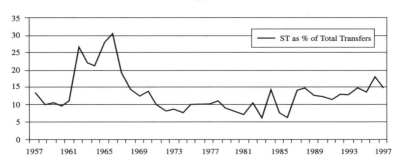

Source: Table A-1, item (12) in the Appendix.

Table 2 presents evidence at ten-year intervals on the amount of small transfers by province, on their importance in provincial revenues, which is also illustrated in Figure 3, and on the share of total small transfers received by each province.

These shares are presented for the full 1957-98 period in Figure 4. Figure 3 shows that in general, equalization-receiving provinces derive a greater share of their provincial revenues from small transfers than do Ontario, Alberta, and

Table 2: Small Transfers by Province (Nominal and Percentage) Canadian Provinces, 1957-58 to 1997-98

	1957-1958			1967-1968			1977-1978			1987-1988			1997-1998		
	$000,000	Prov. % in Total	% Prov. Revenues	$000,000	Prov. % in Total	% Prov. Revenues	$000,000	Prov. % in Total	% Prov. Revenues	$000,000	Prov. % in Total	% Prov. Revenues	$000,000	Prov. % in Total	% Prov. Revenues*
Nfld.	3.2	4.51	8.20	26.6	6.73	10.43	67.1	6.97	5.75	213.6	6.45	7.72	353.4	9.31	6.57
PEI	1.5	2.12	16.70	6.3	1.59	12.86	31.7	3.29	12.83	45.9	1.39	7.55	39.3	1.04	4.57
NS	4.2	5.92	6.50	42.9	10.85	12.22	48.1	5.00	3.31	143.7	4.34	3.88	140.3	3.70	3.66
NB	5.5	7.76	8.90	31.2	7.89	9.97	62.8	6.52	4.85	180.3	5.45	5.28	129.8	3.42	4.27
Que.	0.4	0.56	0.08	132.4	33.49	4.75	320.8	33.32	2.48	821.0	24.81	2.37	808.8	21.30	2.01
Ont.	17.8	25.11	3.00	85.8	21.70	2.42	133.3	13.85	1.04	909.5	27.48	2.29	1,081.2	28.48	2.61
Man.	4.5	6.35	6.10	18.5	4.68	4.34	73.1	7.59	4.54	172.7	5.22	3.24	264.4	6.96	3.54
Sask.	4.7	6.63	3.50	18.4	4.65	3.98	72.2	7.50	3.60	218.5	6.60	4.67	364.3	9.59	11.28
Alta.	7.2	10.16	2.90	16.2	4.10	2.28	77.9	8.09	1.20	289.6	8.75	2.26	352.2	9.28	1.98
BC	21.9	30.89	7.80	17.1	4.32	1.67	75.7	7.86	1.53	314.4	9.50	2.42	263.1	6.93	1.56
All provinces	71.0	100.00		397.8	100.00		970.2	100.00		3,378.3	100.00		3,899.4	100.00	

Note: *1995-96 results.
Sources: 1957-88, Perry ($) and Cansim (Revenues).
1997-98, Public Accounts.
1997-98, (2), Statistics Canada, 68-207 (1957), Financial Statistics of the Provincial Government.

Figure 3: Share of Small Transfers (%) in Provincial Total Revenues, Canada by Provinces, from 1957-58 to 1997-98

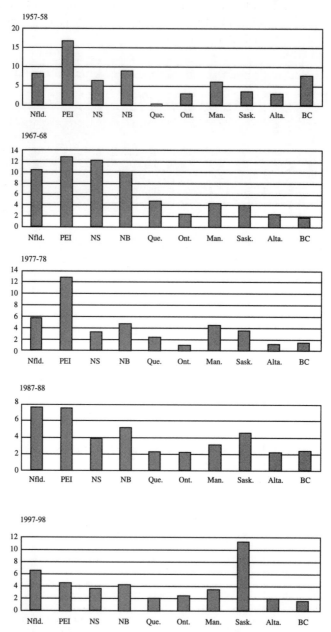

Source: Table 2.

British Columbia.[3] Figure 4 (and Table A2) shows that since 1990 the four Atlantic provinces each received a share of small transfers greater than their share of Canada's population, that Quebec received somewhat less, Ontario substantially less, Manitoba and particularly Saskatchewan more, and Alberta and, in particular, British Columbia less.

Figure 4: Provincial Shares of Small Transfers, Canada, from 1957-58 to 1997-98

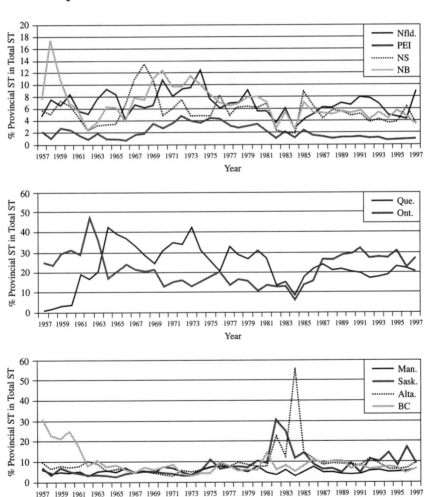

Source: Table A-2.

Figure 5 compares each province's share of small transfers for the 1990-97 period with their share of the population (1991-96) and with their share of Equalization payments (1991-96). It shows that the equalization-receiving provinces generally get more small transfers than their share of the population, but that this is not true for Quebec.

Figure 5: Share of Small Transfers (1990-97), Population (1991-96) and Equalization (1991-96), All Canadian Provinces

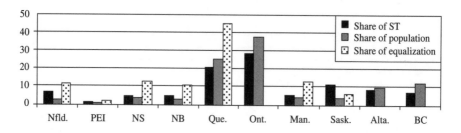

Sources: Table A2 in Appendix; Statistics Canada; Canadian Tax Foundation, *Finances of the Nation* (Toronto: Canadian Tax Foundation, 1995), and *The National Finances* (Toronto: Canadian Tax Foundation, 1991-1994).

THE COMPOSITION OF SMALL TRANSFERS, 1977-78 TO 1997-98

In this part we turn to the composition of small transfers for five select years. We limited ourselves to that period since Public Accounts information is available in comparable form for that period and the federal inventory of federal-provincial programs was published (almost annually) for the 1974-95 period, thus covering about the same years. A bird's eye examination of available documents shows a large number of programs (108 in 1987-88), some of which are extremely small, a fair number of which are extremely local in nature. Examples in 1987-88 range from the Canada-Manitoba agreement to correct damage to provincial lands due to beavers from a national park ($20,000 per year) to restoring St. Trinity Church in Saskatchewan ($9,000) and including others such as the Forges du Saint Maurice and the downtown Moncton renovation scheme. It is impossible to list them all, let alone describe or evaluate them in the space and time available.

We thus present, in Table 3, the ten most important programs in terms of spending for five years, 1977-78, 1982-83, 1987-88, 1992-93 and 1997-98, and also for all years for programs ongoing in 1997-98. We present the information by programs and not by department, since programs are sometimes moved from one department to another. We attempted to standardize program titles over time as much as possible.

The following is clear from Table 3: First, the most important program over time, Canada Mortgage Housing Corporation (CMHC) transfers, is not in the list for 1977-78. It shows up for the first time in 1982-83. This appears to be explained by a change in funding for the program from 1977-78 to 1982-83. It is now funded through a ministerial account and thus appears as a federal-provincial transfer and no longer as a Crown Corporation expenditure.

Second, if the three programs aimed at the agricultural sector are grouped, they account for 14.8 percent of cumulative spending, which puts them in a solid second place. Only the crop insurance and waterfowl program is mentioned in either 1977-78, 1982-83 or 1987-88; the two other programs are relatively recent in the field, which is formally a field of joint jurisdiction.

Third, the official language and vocational rehabilitation programs, ranked second and sixth overall, are long established programs that are renewed on a regular basis; fourth, the Saskatchewan Uranium Mine transfers is a stealth program that never shows up in the top ten for a given year but comes in eighth overall in the ongoing programs; and fifth, the regional and industrial development program underestimates regional economic spending, which is also found under region-specific agencies (ACOA, Quebec, Western Diversification).

An examination of the results for the five separate years shows that the most important program measured by spending is not the same for each of these years. The top-ranked program in 1977-78 ranks fifth in 1987-88 and drops off the chart in 1997-98. The number one program of 1987-88 is not on the 1977-78 or 1997-98 charts nor is the 1997-98 number two program on the 1977-78 or 1987-88 charts. Crop/revenue insurance for farmers remains in the top five throughout, whereas official languages and transportation programs lose grounds and the vocational rehabilitation program gains grounds. Of course, the national picture may obscure provincial differences. We thus present, in Table 4, for 1997-98, the top five programs by province. We note that CMHC is in the top five programs in all provinces — no other program has such a national presence; the Atlantic provinces use ACOA programs as well as programs specific to their needs such as the Northern Cod Program in Newfoundland and official language programs in New Brunswick. Also, the Prairie provinces make more use of agricultural programs than the other provinces.

François Vaillancourt

Table 3: Ten Largest Small Transfer Programs, Canada, Overall as of 1997-98, and in 1977-78, 1982-83, 1987-88, 1992-93 and 1997-98 (Nominal and Percentage)

1977-1978

Programs	Department	$ 000	% of Total 955,248	% Cumulative
Economic and Regional Expansion	Economic and Regional Expansion	365,898	38.3	38.3
Official Languages in Education	Secretary of State	222,516	23.3	61.6
Road Improvement	Transport	72,931	7.6	69.2
Crop Insurance	Agriculture	72,812	7.6	76.8
Vocational Rehabilitation of Disabled Persons	Health and Welfare	22,245	2.3	79.1
Legal Aid	Justice	19,611	2.1	81.2
Young Offenders Assistance	Health and Welfare	16,829	1.8	83.0
National Capital Commission	Urban Affairs	9,704	1.0	84.0
Fraser River Flood Control	Environment	5,809	0.6	84.6
Community Development	Indian Affairs and Northern Development	4,500	0.5	85.1

1982-1983

Programs	Department	$ 000	% of Total 5,375,924	% Cumulative
Economic and Regional Expansion	Economic and Regional Expansion	189,288	3.52	3.52
Official Languages in Education	Secretary of State	176,285	3.28	6.80
Crop Insurance	Agriculture	142,191	2.64	9.44
Canada Mortgage and Housing Corporation	Public Works and Services	118,101	2.20	11.64
Forestry Management	Environment	65,829	1.22	12.86
Vocational Rehabilitation of Disabled Persons	National Health and Welfare	55,554	1.03	13.89
Young Offenders	National Health and Welfare	41,205	0.77	14.66
Legal Aid	Justice	34,148	0.64	15.30
Road Improvement	Transport	26,188	0.49	15.79
James Bay Agreement	Indian Affairs and Northern Development	20,996	0.39	16.18

... continued

Table 3 *(continued)*

1987-1988

Programs	Department	$ 000	% of Total 3,378,291	% Cumulative
Canadian Jobs Strategy	Employment and Immigration	1,409,268	41.7	41.7
Canada Mortgage and Housing Corporation	Public Works	561,650	16.6	58.3
Official Languages in Education	Secretary of State	216,458	6.4	64.7
Crop Insurance	Agriculture	181,475	5.4	70.1
Industrial and Regional Development	Economic and Regional Expansion	113,341	3.4	73.5
Vocational Rehabilitation of Disabled Persons	Health and Welfare	92,658	2.7	76.2
Legal Aid	Justice	63,553	1.9	78.1
Additional Forestry Resource Agreement	Agriculture	63,486	1.9	80.0
Road Improvement	Transport	52,834	1.6	81.6
Forestry Resource Development Agreement	Agriculture and Agri-food	35,370	1.0	82.6

1992-1993

Programs	Department	$ 000	% of Total 10,743,962	% Cumulative
Canada Mortgage and Housing Corporation	Public Works	1,146,178	10.67	10.67
Gross Revenue Insurance Plan	Agriculture	679,253	6.32	16.99
Canadian Jobs Strategy	Employment and Immigration	526,041	4.90	21.89
Official Languages in Education	Secretary of State	267,405	2.49	24.38
Vocational Rehabilitation of Disabled Persons	National Health and Welfare	182,015	1.69	26.07
Crop insurance	Agriculture	173,391	1.61	27.68
Young Offenders	Justice	157,992	1.47	29.15
Legal Aid	Justice	89,467	0.83	29.98
Program for Older Worker Adjustment	Labour	75,950	0.71	30.69
Canada/Newfoundland Development Fund	Energy, Mines and Resources	52,467	0.49	31.18

. . . continued

Table 3 (continued)

1997-1998

Programs	Department	$ 000	% of Total 3,899,414	% Cumulative
Canada Mortgage and Housing Corporation	Public Works and Services	1,008,057	25.9	25.9
Terra Nova Offshore Petroleum Board	Environment	235,886	6.1	32.0
Vocational Rehabilitation of Disabled Persons	Human Resources Development	235,599	6.0	38.0
Crop Insurance and Waterfowl	Agriculture and Agri-food	206,073	5.3	43.3
Net Income Stabilization Account	Agriculture and Agri-food	203,177	5.2	48.5
Payments in Connection with the *Farm Income Protection Act*	Agriculture and Agri-food	192,109	4.9	53.4
Official Language in Education	Canadian Heritage	191,450	4.9	58.3
Young Offenders Assistance	Justice	150,000	3.9	62.2
Emergency Preparedness and Disaster Financial Assistance	National Defence	149,039	3.8	66.0
Canada-Ontario Infrastructure	Industry	119,701	3.1	69.1

Cumulative, Existing Programs in 1997-1998

Programs	$ 000	% Total	Cumulative	Number of 5 Years in Top 10
Canada Mortgage and Housing Corporation	14,017,138	29.6	29.6	4
Official Languages in Education	5,164,412	10.8	40.4	5
Regional and Industrial Development	3,791,740	7.9	48.3	1
Crop Insurance and Waterfowl	3,579,646	7.5	55.8	5
Gross Agricultural Income Assistance	2,474,906	5.1	45.5	1
Vocational Rehabilitation of Disabled Persons	2,448,724	5.1	50.6	5
Young Offenders Assistance	1,819,411	3.8	54.4	2
Saskatchewan Uranium Mines	1,788,214	3.7	58.1	0
Legal Aid	1,296,444	2.7	60.8	2
Net Agricultural Income Stabilization Scheme	1,047,137	2.2	63.0	1
TOTAL	47,736,000			

Note: The total is obtained by subtracting from the Public Accounts total, amounts for CAP, New Horizons (70,907,108) and Job Planning (6,674,329). These amounts are cumulative since the beginning of the relevant program in nominal dollars.

Source: *Public Accounts of Canada*, Volume II, Section entitled "Federal Provincial Shared Cost Programs."

Table 4: Top Five Transfer Programs by Province, 1997-1998

Newfoundland

Program	Department	Transfers	% of Total 353.4
Terra Nova Offshore Petroleum Board	Environment	235,886	66.8
Canada Mortgage and Housing Corporation	Public Works	20,816	5.9
Atlantic Canada Opportunities Agency: Coop Agreements – TAGS / ER	Industry	19,072	5.4
Newfoundland Agreement	Indian Affairs and Northern Development	10,907	3.1
Northern Cod Fisheries Retirement	Fisheries and Oceans	10,434	3.0

Prince Edward Island

Program	Department	Transfers	% of Total 39.3
Atlantic-Canada Opportunities Agency: Coop Agreements	Industry	13,556	34.5
Canada Mortgage and Housing Corporation	Public Works	7458	19.0
Atlantic Regions Freight Assistance Transition	Transport	4,823	12.3
Payments in Connection with the Farm Income Protection Act: Safety Net Companion Programs	Agriculture and Agri-food	2,606	6.6
Net Income Stabilization Account	Agriculture and Agri-food	2,084	5.3

Nova Scotia

Program	Department	Transfers	% of Total 140.3
Canada Mortgage and Housing Corporation	Public Works	45,361	32.3
Atlantic Regions Freight Assistance Transition	Transport	24,352	17.4
Strategic Capital Investment Initiative – Highways and Airports	Transport	19,643	14.0
Atlantic-Canada Opportunities Agency: Co-op Agreements	Industry	13,122	9.4
Vocational Rehabilitation of Disabled Persons	Human Resources Development	7,445	5.3

. . . continued

Table 4 *(continued)*

New Brunswick

Program	Department	Transfers	% of Total 129.8
Atlantic Regions Freight Assistance Transition	Transport	46,000	35.4
Official Language in Education	Canadian Heritage	16,201	12.5
Canada Mortgage and Housing Corporation	Public Works	14,193	10.9
Atlantic-Canada Opportunities Agency: Co-op Agreements	Industry	12,583	9.7
Highway Improvements	Transport	9,060	7.0

Quebec

Program	Department	Transfers	% of Total 808.8
Canada Mortgage and Housing Corporation	Public Works	180,003	22.3
Payments in Connection with the Farm Income Protection Act: Safety Net Companion Programs	Agriculture and Agri-food	105,824	13.1
Economic Development of Canada for the Regions of Quebec: Contribution to the Province of Quebec under the Canada Infrastructure Works Agreement	Industry	96,651	12.0
Vocational Rehabilitation of Disabled Persons	Human Resources Development	80,133	9.9
Cree-Kativik School Board (James Bay)	Indian Affairs and Northern Development	63,354	7.8

Ontario

Program	Department	Transfers	% of Total 1,081.2
Canada Mortgage and Housing Corporation	Public Works	417,756	38.6
Canada-Ontario Infrastructure	Industry	119,701	11.1
Social Services	Indian Affairs and Northern Development	97,264	9.0
Official Language in Education	Canadian Heritage	71,449	6.6
Vocational Rehabilitation of Disabled Persons	Human Resources Development	69,326	6.4

. . . continued

Table 4 *(continued)*

Manitoba

Program	Department	Transfers	% of Total 264.4
Joint Emergency Preparedness Program and Disaster Financial Assistance	National Defence	57,299	21.7
Canada Mortgage and Housing Corporation	Public Works	54,470	20.6
Crop Insurance and Waterfowl	Agriculture and Agri-food	45,220	17.1
Net Income Stabilization Account	Agriculture and Agri-food	32,041	12.1
Canada Infrastructure Works (Western Economic Diversification)	Industry	15,431	5.8

Saskatchewan

Program	Department	Transfers	% of Total 364.3
Canadian Environmental Assessment Agency: Saskatchewan Uranium Mining Development	Environment	82,809	22.7
Net income Stabilization Account	Agriculture and Agri-food	77,490	21.3
Crop Insurance and Waterfowl	Agriculture and Agri-food	62,412	17.1
Canada Mortgage and Housing Corporation	Public Works	50,756	13.9
Canada Agriculture Infrastructure	Agriculture and Agri-food	20,103	5.5

Alberta

Program	Department	Transfers	% of Total 352.2
Canada Mortgage and Housing Corporation	Public Works	78,912	22.4
Payments in Connection with the Farm Income Protection Act: Safety Net Companion Programs	Agriculture and Agri-food	51,502	14.6
Crop Insurance and Waterfowl	Agriculture and Agri-food	48,115	13.7
Net Income Stabilization Account	Agriculture and Agri-food	39,265	11.2
Western Economic Diversification: Infrastructure Works	Industry	23,477	6.7

. . . continued

Table 4 (continued)

British Columbia

Program	Department	Transfers	% of Total 263.1
Canada Mortgage and Housing Corporation	Public Works	96,527	36.7
Western Economic Diversification: Canada Infrastructure Works	Industry	46,903	17.8
Vocational Rehabilitation of Disabled Persons	Human Resources Development	25,253	9.6
Strategic Initiatives	Human Resources Development	17,342	6.6
Young Offenders Assistance	Justice	16,516	6.3

Note: The total amount in millions of dollars reported for each province is from Table 2.

Source: *Public Accounts of Canada*, Volume II – Part II (II) "Federal Provincial Shared Cost Programs" section.

A SUMMARY EVALUATION

A full evaluation of federal-provincial small transfers requires that criteria be established, each program be described in detail (formula, etc.) and, finally, that program characteristics be assessed with respect to the criteria. Since we do not describe each program in sufficient detail, the evaluation will be a summary one.

CRITERIA

One can assess federal-provincial transfers using various criteria as follows:

- first, one may want to assess the basis for state intervention in a given area such as the provision of private goods, such as housing or insurance programs. If one concludes that the state should not intervene, then the transfers are inappropriate;

- second, given that one accepts that the state is intervening, one may wish to argue that the distribution of power between the national/central and the subnational government is inappropriate and that it should be changed, doing away with transfers;

- third, accepting the existing division of powers, one may examine the need for transfers and the appropriate transfer mechanisms. We will evaluate the transfers from this third perspective.

Intergovernmental conditional transfer programs are appropriate from an economist's perspective when, for one reason or another, subnational units fail to produce a sufficient amount of publicly provided services or goods. The key reason for this is that there are external benefits to this provision that cannot be captured by the producing jurisdiction due to migration of individuals (postsecondary education) or contaminants (airborne/waterborne pollution) or public nature (on-air educational TV) of the service. A second reason may be that a given service may be seen as a merit good (i.e., a good that some individuals wish to see be consumed by others) by a majority of the national population but not by a majority in each subnational jurisdiction, leading again to underprovision.

PROGRAM DESCRIPTION

We now briefly describe the top ten transfer programs.

Canada Mortgage Housing Corporation. As of December 1996, there were 385,000 provincially (territorially) administered housing units (59 percent of the total CMHC stock) of which 204,000 (53 percent) are public housing units and 108,000 (28 percent), non-profit units. Major programs in the field of housing were: (i) non-profit housing: where owners of non-profit housing (which could be provincial or municipal housing) authorities received subsidies equal to the difference between admissible costs and rental income. This program was terminated in December 1993. Spending continues according to previous commitments; (ii) rent supplements where either CMHC or a provincial body administers the program, which pays out subsidies to landlords (private, co-ops, non-profit) for specific housing units. This program was also terminated in December 1993 with spending continuing due to previous commitments; and (iii) public housing where CMHC either lent up to 90 percent of the capital cost or paid 75 percent of the investment costs and losses to provincial government. This program was terminated in 1985 with spending continuing for previous commitments.

Official Languages in Education. This program helps finance some of the costs associated with minority language education (French outside Quebec, English inside Quebec) and with the teaching of the second official language. This program was introduced in 1970 following the recommendation of the Royal Commission on Bilingualism and Biculturalism. Agreements signed in 1970-71 were renewed in 1974 for five years, and extended annually until 1983 and then followed by a five-year agreement and a new federal-provincial protocol in 1997. Payments are mainly set on a per-pupil basis, but there is some specific project financing.

Regional and Industrial Development. These programs are negotiated with provinces and take into account their preferences and economic needs. Financing arrangements vary between 50/50 to 25/75.

Crop Insurance and Waterfowl, Gross Income Insurance and Net Income Stabilization. Agricultural income support was modified in 1991 with the *Farm Income Protection Act* which replaced the *Crop Insurance Act* and introduced both gross income insurance and net income stabilization account. This program requires participants to make contributions of up to 3 percent of eligible net sales (maximum $250,000) which in the 1995 stabilization years were matched (two-thirds federal, one-third provincial) by the participating governments. In Alberta, the federal government provides 100 percent of matching funds because of non-participation by the province.

These three programs all help protect the income of farmers indirectly (through crop insurance) or directly. They are negotiated on a provincial basis and require financing from farmers. Moral hazard and adverse selection issues are addressed in the federal-provincial agreements.

Vocational Rehabilitation of Disabled Persons. This program is now called the Employability Assistance for People with Disabilities Program. It provides employment counselling, training, and skills development funding for assistance, aids and devices, wage, and earnings supplements.

Young Offenders. This program was introduced in 1984, following changes in the *Delinquent's Act*, that meant that services previously funded under CAP were no longer funded, given that they were not deemed to be welfare services. Provinces faced additional costs due to various requirements such as larger segregated youth facilities.

Saskatchewan Uranium Mines. The title is self-explanatory.

Legal Aid. The title is self-explanatory.

EVALUATION

As Table 5 shows, the two economic reasons indicated earlier appear to play a small role in the justification of the ten largest small transfer programs. Issues such as history (CMHC), national security (Uranium) and overlapping jurisdiction matter more.

Given that these programs exist, a second question one can ask is: Are they well designed? To ensure this, the formulas used to fund the small transfers can be examined or an impact analysis can be carried out, that is, did the program attain the desired result without perverse effects? On the formula design issue, the following points can be made: (i) with respect to CMHC, the issue is irrelevant insofar as current transfers are the result of past decisions,

Table 5: Criterion Evaluation of Top Ten Programs

Program	Externalities	Merit Good	Jurisdiction	Other Justification / Comments
Canada Mortgage and Housing Corporation: • non-profit housing, • rent supplements, and • public housing	No	No	?	Post-WWII program self-perpetuating? Redistribution in kind?
Official Languages Education	No	Yes	P	Quebec + Ontario preferences?
Regional/Industrial Development	No	No	P	Reduce migration to occupy territory?
Agricultural	No	No	Joint-constitution	Avoids overlaps/inefficiencies?
Vocational Rehabilitation of Disabled Persons	No	No	P	?
Young Offenders	No	No	FP	?
Saskatchewan Uranium Mines	No	No	F	Strategic mineral?
Legal Aid	No	No	Joint	?

Source: Author's compilation.

that is, there is nothing one can do now to modify the end result; and (ii) the agricultural insurance programs appear to attempt to control for moral hazard and adverse selection. Examining the Canada-Quebec Crop Insurance Agreement, one finds, for example: a requirement that a minimum of 10 percent of producers be insured; very detailed coverage calculation taking into account the type of crop, experience, minimum/maximum yield and so on. Indeed, this level of detail justifies the use of regional/provincial agencies to carry out the program; a funding of 25 percent of insurance premiums and 50 percent of administrative costs by the federal government; a two-page appendix on "Recognition Requirements" that states that "The Canada and Quebec signatures shall be presented with equal prominence (i.e., same content, size, style and weight of type) side by side."

In the Official Language Act in Education Program, financing is based on (i) transfers per full-time equivalent student and (ii) project financing — it is

not 50/50 financing. The Employability Assistance for People with Disabilities Program is a 50/50 cost-sharing program with an annual ceiling ($168
million in 1997-98); and the Young Offender's Act and legal aid programs are
50/50 cost-sharing programs with an annual maximum. Thus, overall, one
sees the use of non-open-ended programs with either 50/50 funding or a per-
unit transfer. This is a reasonable design for this type of program.

CONCLUSION

My purpose was to establish the importance of small transfers, to describe
their make-up and to evaluate them. This, in retrospect, was an overly ambitious goal, especially given the absence of an existing literature on the various
small transfers. This chapter succeeds in establishing the quantitative
magnitudes of small transfers in Canada; it provides only a summary description of their make-up, and does not examine the degree of conditionality; it
evaluates them briefly. This is unfortunate since small transfers have accounted
for about 15 percent of federal transfers to provinces over the last five years
(1993-98), which is somewhat higher than in the first five years examined
(1957-62) which was 11 percent and slightly more than the average for the
1957-98 period, which is 13 percent. They are thus a permanent and fairly
important component of federal-provincial relations in Canada. They are of
particular interest in that the variability in their amounts and composition show
them to be a rapid response instrument for the federal government to specific
problems.

   Given the importance and complexity of small transfers, it is appropriate to
conclude by noting the need for more detailed research. This would allow us
to examine the appropriateness of existing arrangements and in particular to
assess if some programs could be integrated into large transfers (vocational
rehabilitation into CHST, for example) and if other programs are still appropriate.

NOTES

Paper prepared for the April 1999 Canadian Fiscal Federalism Conference of the Institute of Intergovernmental Relations, Queen's University. The author would like to
thank Sandrine Bourdeau-Primeau for research assistance, Harvey Lazar and one
anonymous referee for comments on an earlier version of this paper.

1.   The Territorial Formula Financing grant is not included as it is similar to Equalization.
2.   We do not consider tax points ceded to the province to be transferred although
      this value is used in calculating cash transfer under the EPF/CHST arrangement.
      Also note here that as indicated in Table A-1, the computation of the various
      transfers for 1996-97 and 1997-1998 uses a different source than the sole one
      used for the 1957-96 period. As a result, numbers may not be strictly compara-
      ble but trends and order of magnitudes are unaffected.
3.   In 1957-58, Quebec was an important exception to this generalization.

APPENDIX

Table A-1: Federal-Provincial Cash Transfers, Total and by Type, Nominal and Real per Capita %, Canada 1957-1998, $000,000 for Items (1) – (9)

Year	Equal. (1)	EPF (2)	CAP (3)	CHST (4)	Small Transfers (ST) (5)	Other Transfers (6)	Total Nominal (7)	Total Real (8)	ST Real (9)	ST per Capita Nominal $ (10)	ST per Capita Real $ (11)	ST as % of Total Transfers (12)	ST as % of Federal Spending (13)	ST as % of Provincial Revenues (14)	ST as % of GDP (15)
1957-58	136.0	34.6	39.7	74.3	71.0	246.7	528.0	528.00	71.00	4.27	4.27	13.45	1.36	3.14	0.21
1958-59	143.4	100.7	73.7	174.4	74.3	323.7	715.8	692.10	73.60	4.35	4.21	10.38	1.27	2.98	0.21
1959-60	183.0	196.8	90.7	287.5	95.7	335.8	902.0	844.18	91.50	5.47	5.12	10.61	1.57	3.24	0.25
1960-61	189.7	237.4	102.6	340	95.3	349.4	974.4	883.62	88.10	5.33	4.83	9.78	1.46	3.01	0.24
1961-62	164.7	332.9	143.3	476.2	129.2	378.9	1,149.0	1,004.51	115.03	7.08	6.19	11.24	1.87	3.69	0.32
1962-63	158.5	387.6	159.2	546.8	301.8	120.4	1,127.5	962.66	126.26	16.24	13.87	26.77	4.17	7.11	0.68
1963-64	156.2	445.6	171.8	617.4	247.5	100.3	1,121.4	930.25	209.10	13.07	10.84	22.07	3.35	5.41	0.52
1964-65	214.9	490.5	181.6	672.1	275.8	137.7	1,300.5	1,049.02	226.50	14.30	11.53	21.21	3.53	5.31	0.53
1965-66	273.4	421.2	147.2	568.4	372.9	118.3	1,333.0	1,029.72	293.40	18.98	14.66	27.97	4.53	6.15	0.65
1966-67	316.4	480.7	181.4	662.1	501.5	148.1	1,628.1	1,165.21	365.60	25.06	17.94	30.80	5.36	7.09	0.78
1967-68	544.8	698.4	363.7	1,062.1	397.8	78.4	2,083.1	1,401.53	271.80	19.52	13.13	19.10	3.76	4.72	0.58
1968-69	586.7	935.2	385.2	1,320.4	337.8	106.6	2,351.5	1,486.23	216.50	16.32	10.31	14.37	2.87	3.39	0.45
1969-70	675.3	1,177.6	414.0	1,591.6	339.2	112.3	2,718.4	1,587.55	200.80	16.15	9.43	12.48	2.61	2.92	0.41
1970-71	927.0	1,593.7	547.2	2,140.9	527.0	124.7	3,719.6	2,049.29	294.20	24.75	13.64	14.17	3.55	3.90	0.59
1971-72	1,052.5	1,970.7	654.1	2,624.8	418.1	156.8	4,252.2	2,201.49	215.00	19.04	9.86	9.83	2.47	2.68	0.43

... continued

Table A-1 (continued)

Year	Equal. (1)	EPF (2)	CAP (3)	CHST (4)	Small Transfers (ST) (5)	Other Transfers (6)	Total Nominal (7)	Total Real (8)	ST Real (9)	ST per Capita Nominal $ (10)	ST per Capita Real $ (11)	ST as % of Total Transfers (12)	ST as % of Federal Spending (13)	ST as % of Provincial Revenues (14)	ST as % of GDP (15)
1972-73	1,176.8	2,112.0	674.0	2,786	371.1	165.5	4,499.4	2,168.03	177.40	16.70	8.05	8.25	1.90	2.15	0.34
1973-74	1,517.1	2,239.8	702.3	2,942.1	457.8	280.8	5,197.8	2,335.01	204.40	20.35	9.14	8.81	2.11	2.28	0.36
1974-75	2,287.0	2,609	946.6	3,555.6	547.8	650.3	7,040.7	2,778.22	215.20	24.02	9.48	7.78	1.97	2.16	0.36
1975-76	1,921.6	3,071.3	1,230.7	4,302	757.0	573.4	7,554.0	2,619.68	260.70	32.71	11.34	10.02	2.19	2.61	0.44
1976-77	2,086.6	3,666.7	1,378.8	5,045.5	922.1	1,097.9	9,152.1	2,813.07	281.20	39.32	12.09	10.08	2.45	2.76	0.47
1977-78	2,383.5	3,921.8	1,352.1	5,273.9	970.2	851.5	9,479.1	2,687.28	278.60	40.89	11.59	10.24	2.26	2.43	0.45
1978-79	2,747.2	4,738.7	1,598.1	6,336.8	1,203.2	480.0	10,767.2	2,842.70	321.90	50.21	13.26	11.17	2.51	2.65	0.50
1979-80	3,321.4	5,328.7	1,653.2	6,981.9	1,049.7	463.7	11,816.7	2,846.93	257.00	43.37	10.45	8.88	2.02	2.05	0.38
1980-81	3,590.4	5,585.3	1,973.3	7,558.6	1,009.0	471.1	12,629.1	2,760.25	224.10	41.16	9.00	7.99	1.67	1.75	0.33
1981-82	4,478.2	5,909.9	2,337.5	8,247.4	1,013.5	601.5	14,340.6	2,765.82	198.30	40.83	7.87	7.07	1.42	1.52	0.28
1982-83	5,267.1	4,804.8	2,887.9	7,692.7	1,684.7	1,306.9	15,951.4	2,756.10	283.40	67.07	11.59	10.56	1.98	2.28	0.45
1983-84	5,358.4	7,665.5	3,359	11,024.5	1,114.4	766.2	18,263.5	2,975.97	184.00	43.93	7.16	6.10	1.20	1.37	0.27
1984-85	5,395.2	8,595.1	3,736.6	12,331.7	3,095.4	947.1	21,769.4	3,410.23	491.30	120.88	18.94	14.22	2.98	3.43	0.70
1985-86	5,155.8	8,663.9	3,876.1	12,540	1,543.5	1,137.3	20,376.6	3,070.16	235.80	59.73	9.00	7.57	1.37	1.60	0.32
1986-87	5,767.2	8,853	4,001.4	12,854.4	1,293.4	914.9	20,829.9	3,041.17	192.00	49.55	7.23	6.21	1.14	1.30	0.26
1987-88	6,386.2	8,800.3	4,245.7	13,046	3,378.3	1,086.5	23,897	3,358.00	482.80	127.72	17.95	14.14	2.80	3.09	0.61
1988-89	7,371.7	8,905.6	4,583.6	13,489.2	3,732.3	1,062.8	25,656.0	3,471.53	516.10	139.28	18.85	14.55	2.92	3.06	0.62
1989-90	8,155.1	8,829.2	4,885.3	13,714.5	3,362.6	1,213.3	26,445.5	3,432.04	444.40	123.24	15.99	12.72	2.44	2.58	0.52
1990-91	8,260.6	7,894.5	5,966.9	13,861.4	3,275.2	1,195.2	26,592.4	3,270.84	408.90	118.23	14.54	12.32	2.17	2.37	0.49
1991-92	8,075.1	8,830.6	6,130.3	14,960.9	3,144.9	1,117.3	27,298.2	3,229.77	378.80	112.19	13.27	11.52	1.95	2.27	0.47

1992-93	7,376.9	11,193.7	6,722.1	17,915.8	4,021.8	1,443.8	30,758.3	3,552.78	473.80	141.73	16.37	13.08	2.44	2.73	0.58
1993-94	7,755.9	9,610.3	7,219.2	16,829.5	3,836.6	1,247.4	29,669.4	3,368.38	444.00	133.67	15.18	12.93	2.28	2.50	0.51
1994-95	8,543.4	10,051.8	7,279.4	17,331.2	4,656.1	1,473.5	32,004.2	3,602.63	535.60	160.36	18.09	14.55	2.81	2.89	0.60
1995-96	8,800.6	9,605.8	7,184.5	16,790.3	4,244.7	1,210.8	31,046.4	3,451.45	481.80	144.60	16.08	13.67	2.47	2.51	0.53
1996-97	9,418.0	-	-	12,743	4,562.3	720.0	27,443.3	3,026.84	509.00	153.76	16.96	18.06	2.75	2.65	0.55
1997-98	10,000.0	-	-	10,504.0	3,899.4	681.1	25,084.5	2,619.10	429.40	129.93	14.17	14.63	2.41	2.07	0.46

Notes:

(2) EPF: Before 1977-1978, this is the sum of hospital insurance, medical care and postsecondary education transfers.

(3) CAP: Before 1965-1966, this is the sum of old age assistance, blind and disabled persons allowance and unemployment assistance.

(4) CHST: Before 1996-1997, this is the sum of EPF + CAP.

(5) Items vary across years: includes vocational training, natural resources (incl. agriculture), transportation, vocational education, natural resources, labour and employment and immigration, agriculture and primary industries, trade and industry, regional development, transportation and communications, agriculture, resource conservation and industrial development, natural resources (incl. agriculture and industrial development), protection, employment, housing, official languages services.

(6) Other Transfers: are total transfers (7) – (1 + 4 + 5) except in 1996-97 and 1997-98. They include items like statutory subsidies, share of utilities taxes, stabilization, etc. It is a balancing item.

Population: from 1957 to 1970: Cansim C892268, from 1971 to 1997: X100000.

Implicit price index, GDP: 1957-1993: Statistics Canada, 11-210; 1994-1997: Statistics Canada, 11-010.

Sources: Transfers:

1957-58 to 1995-96: "Financing the Federation, 1867 to 1995: Setting the Stage for Change," D.P. Perry; Canadian Tax Paper No. 102, 1997, Appendix Tables. 1996-97 and 1997-98: Computed by the Author, *Public Accounts of Canada*. Equalization and CHST figures are from Volume 1, p. 1.16, 1997-1998. Small transfers are the total from Vol. II-II, Section II. Other transfers are [Statistics Subsidies and Territorial Financial Arrangements – Youth Allowance Recovery] from Table 8.1 Finances of the Nation 1996 and 1997 to ensure coherence with the Perry numbers.

Federal Spending and Provincial Revenues:

1957-58 to 1960-61: Statistics Canada, 13-531, Tables 44 and 45.

1961-62 to 1991-92: Statistics Canada, 13-213, Tables 6 and 7.

1992-93 to 1996-97: Cansim D 25776 and D 26079.

1997-98: Computed by the Author, *Public Accounts of Canada*.

GDP:

1957-58 to 1960-61: Statistics Canada, 13-531, Table 1.

1961-62 to 1996-97: Cansim D 44959

1997-98: Statistics Canada, 11-010.

François Vaillancourt

Table A-2: Provincial Shares of Small Transfers, Canada, 1957-58 to 1997-98

	Nfld.	PEI	NS	NB	Que.	Ont.	Man.	Sask.	Alta.	BC
1957	4.8	2.1	5.8	7.7	0.6	24.9	6.1	6.6	10.1	30.7
1958	7.5	0.9	5.1	17.4	1.7	23.6	3.9	3.1	6.1	22.3
1959	6.5	2.7	7.3	10.7	3.1	29.4	4.6	6.7	7.8	21
1960	8.4	2.4	6.6	7	3.6	31.2	4.5	5.1	6.9	24.3
1961	5.6	1.5	4.8	5.7	19.1	28.7	4.9	4.1	7.9	17.9
1962	5.1	0.8	2.3	2.3	16.5	48	3	3.2	10.2	8.1
1963	7.7	1.8	3.2	3.9	20.7	35.2	4.8	3.2	8.6	10.5
1964	9.3	0.9	3.3	6.3	42.8	16.9	5.5	2.9	5	6.9
1965	8.4	0.9	3.5	6.1	39.4	20.5	4.7	2.3	5.9	8.2
1966	4.3	0.7	6.7	4	37.1	24.1	6.7	3.9	6.9	5.7
1967	6.7	1.6	10.8	7.8	33.2	21.5	4.7	4.6	4.1	4.3
1968	6.2	1.8	13.5	7.4	28.5	20.5	5.3	4.7	5.1	6.3
1969	6.6	3.5	10.5	11.1	24.5	21.3	4.8	5.4	4.3	5.6
1970	10.8	2.8	4.9	12.3	31.7	13	7.4	4.4	3.4	6.7
1971	8.1	3.6	6	9.7	35	15.4	6.8	4	2.8	8.3
1972	9.3	4.8	7.5	9.7	34.4	16.1	5.1	2.9	5.3	3.7
1973	9.6	4	4.8	11.5	42.9	13	3.1	2.8	5	2.7
1974	12.5	3.7	4.9	10	31	15.8	6	5.4	6	4.1
1975	7.7	4.6	4.8	8.2	25.1	18.3	7.5	11	6.9	4.4
1976	6.1	4.4	8.2	7	20.2	20.4	7.9	6.6	9.2	9.4
1977	6.9	3.3	4.9	6.5	33.1	13.7	7.5	7.4	8	7.8
1978	7	2.9	6.2	6.9	28.7	16.8	6.1	7.7	9.7	5.7
1979	9.2	3.2	6.4	7.8	27	15.7	5	7.4	8.3	6.6
1980	5.7	3.5	6.1	8	31.1	10.9	7.7	10.4	7.8	6.4
1981	5.7	2.2	6.8	7.1	26.9	13.9	4.6	9.5	8.1	12.9
1982	3.7	1.1	2.3	2.7	13.6	13	3.5	30.5	22.6	5.2
1983	6.1	2.1	1.9	5.6	15.2	13.4	6.1	25.3	12.9	8.3
1984	2.8	1.2	1.9	2.6	8.9	6.2	2.9	11.8	55.3	5
1985	4.3	2.5	8.8	7	17.6	14.1	5.1	14.5	14.4	8.2
1986	5.2	1.6	6.5	5.4	21.9	16	7.7	9.1	11.5	10.7
1987	6.3	1.4	4.3	5.3	24.3	26.9	5.1	6.5	8.6	9.3
1988	6.2	1.1	5.8	5.1	21.3	26.7	5.1	6.8	9.5	10.1
1989	7	1.3	5.6	5.7	21.9	28.7	4.2	4.9	8.6	10.2
1990	6.7	1.3	4.8	5.3	20.3	29.5	4	9.4	9.1	7
1991	7.9	1.4	5.1	5.7	19.8	32.5	4.4	4.9	7.2	7.8
1992	7.8	1.2	3.8	4.1	17.4	27.6	5.7	11.6	11.6	6.4
1993	6.9	1.3	4.1	5.4	18	28.1	6.3	10.1	9.4	7.1
1994	5.1	0.8	3.8	4.3	19.1	27.9	5.2	14.6	6.6	7.6
1995	4.8	0.9	3.9	5.7	23.5	31.2	5.3	8.4	6.1	6.8
1996	4.4	1	6.3	4.7	22.4	22.8	5.7	17.4	7.1	5
1997	9.1	1.1	3.6	3.4	20.7	27.7	6.8	9.3	9.9	6.6

Note: % may not add to 100.0 across columns due to rounding.

Sources:

1957-58 to 1995-96: "Financing the Federation, 1867 to 1995: Setting the Stage for Change," D.P. Perry; Canadian Tax Paper No. 102, 1997, Appendix Tables.

1996-97 and 1997-98: Computed by the Author, *Public Accounts of Canada.*

8

Poverty Trends and the Canadian "Social Union"

Lars Osberg

Ce chapitre soutient que les effets de la pauvreté doivent être similaires entre les provinces si on veut que le terme «union sociale canadienne» ait un sens pratique. On y compare l'intensité de la pauvreté entre le Canada et les États-Unis, de même qu'entre les provinces canadiennes, au début des années 1970 et entre 1994 et 1996. Même si, au plan statistique, l'intensité de la pauvreté au Canada et aux États-Unis n'était pas différente au début des années 1970, elle était beaucoup moindre au Canada qu'aux États-Unis en 1994. Au début des années 1970, l'intensité de la pauvreté variait considérablement entre les provinces canadiennes, tant avant qu'après avoir tenu compte des impôts et des transferts. Cependant, en 1994, toutes les provinces canadiennes partageaient une faible intensité de la pauvreté après impôts et transferts. En termes pratiques, on pourrait dire qu'une «union sociale» était présente entre les années 1973 et 1994. Toutefois, depuis 1994, la tendance s'est renversée. De 1994 à 1996, la pauvreté de la population non-âgée a augmenté, particulièrement chez les enfants âgés de moins de six ans en Ontario et en Nouvelle-Écosse. En conclusion ce chapitre, on présente certaines projections sur l'avenir de l'union sociale canadienne.

What is the practical meaning of a term like the Canadian "social union"?

How has the social union evolved in Canada in recent decades and how is it likely to evolve in future?

Why might it matter?

INTRODUCTION

This chapter takes the view that if a "social union" is to have practical meaning, it should find some concrete reflection in the outcomes that people actually experience — in particular, in the poverty outcomes that Canadians experience. This is not to say that other aspects of social policy are unimportant to a social union: social policy also affects the education, health care, and retirement incomes of non-poor Canadians. The public programs that provide these broader services are important to rich and poor alike, and the degree of commonality that people have in their personal experiences with these programs is important because a social union is presumably concerned with generating a national sense of shared experience and common destiny. Hence, services to the non-poor are clearly important.

However, because mitigating poverty is such a central issue for the welfare state, poverty outcomes are a particularly crucial and practical indicator of a social union. Poverty affects many Canadians directly[1] right now and the probability and depth of potential poverty affect the sense of economic insecurity with which many non-poor Canadians contemplate the future. If Canada is to be a meaningful social union one might therefore think that a basic objective of such a social union would be some commonality,[2] across provinces, of poverty outcomes and poverty mitigation.

The first part of this essay starts by asking how well the Canadian state has done over the period 1971 to 1994 in reducing the intensity of poverty to a common level in different areas of the country. Either by comparison with the United States, or in comparisons of provinces with each other, this period of roughly two decades saw a dramatic change in the effectiveness of Canada's tax/transfer system in reducing poverty intensity. However, the rapidity of the change also implies that such change is potentially vulnerable to equally rapid reversal.

The next section then outlines a few of the ways in which the federal government has withdrawn from anti-poverty policy in the period since 1994, and presents some evidence on recent trends in poverty intensity by demographic group. Although the provincialization of social policy has had relatively little effect on senior citizens, impacts on younger cohorts have been more significant. In particular, the poverty intensity of children under six years of age in Ontario and Nova Scotia has increased in recent years.

The third part is more speculative. It focuses on the possible future evolution of fiscal efforts to reduce poverty in Canada, in a more "provincial" environment where: (i) in the short term, the federal government faces political pressure to reduce further its anti-poverty initiatives from the official opposition and from major provinces; (ii) the federal government has effectively downloaded to the provinces much of the fiscal risk of any future recession; and (iii) there may be a secular trend to diminished saliency of pan-Canadian political sentiment.

TRENDS IN POVERTY INTENSITY IN CANADIAN PROVINCES

What trends have there been in recent years in poverty in Canada? The most commonly used statistic on poverty is the poverty rate, but since Sen in 1976, many authors have recognized that the poverty rate, by itself, is a poor index.[3] Simply counting the number of poor, as a percentage of all people, ignores any consideration of the depth of their poverty. As Myles and Picot have noted, some social policies transfer income to groups (such as single parents) whose incomes are well below the poverty line.[4] *Because* their incomes are so far below the poverty line, policy changes that affect these groups may have large impacts on their well-being, but not show up in the poverty rate statistics if few individuals are actually moved over the poverty line.

On the other hand, an index such as the average poverty gap ratio, which looks only at the average percentage shortfall of income below the poverty line, has the defect that it ignores the issue of how many people are poor. This chapter therefore uses the Sen-Shorrocks-Thon (SST) index of poverty intensity, which combines consideration of the poverty rate, average poverty gap ratio and inequality among the poor.[5] This chapter also takes the view that poverty in Canada should be assessed in terms of *Canadian* social norms, and therefore calculates the poverty rate and poverty gap for each individual with reference to a Canada-wide norm of living standards.[6]

What differences between provinces are meaningful? Since this essay will focus on the differences between Canadian provinces in poverty outcomes, it is essential to know when those differences are statistically significant and when they are not. Data on poverty are obtained from surveys of the population, and there is inevitably some statistical uncertainty in forming estimates of the characteristics of a population based on sample data. Osberg and Xu show how bootstrap estimation[7] can be used to establish the confidence intervals surrounding poverty estimates. Hence, this chapter reports both point estimates of poverty intensity and the 95 percent confidence band that surrounds such estimates, since we want to know when the differences between provinces are large enough to be statistically significant.

Overall, how much has the anti-poverty effectiveness of taxes and transfers changed in Canada in recent decades? Quite a lot, as it happens. Over the period 1971 to 1994, Canadian social policy followed a different trajectory than that of the United States.[8] As a result, Canadians have become accustomed to (and perhaps a bit sanctimonious about) the lower level of poverty to be observed in Canada, compared to the US. Figure 1 is based on Luxembourg Income Study data and plots the SST index of poverty intensity for Canada and the US from the 1970s to the 1990s. It is notable that although the 1994 data show a considerably greater intensity of poverty in the US than in Canada, this difference is of relatively recent origin.[9] In the early 1970s, Canada and the US were statistically indistinguishable in poverty intensity (indeed the point estimate of Canadian poverty in 1971 is actually a bit higher than the point estimate of poverty intensity in the US in 1974).

Lars Osberg

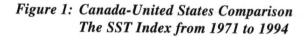

Figure 1: Canada-United States Comparison
The SST Index from 1971 to 1994

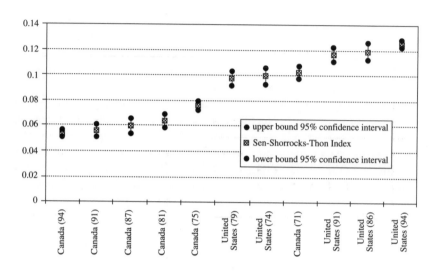

Notes:
Poverty Line=1/2 Median Equivalent Income–After Taxes and Transfers
Equivalence Scale=OECD (first adult=1, other adults=0.7, kids=0.5)

[95 percent confidence interval=mean +/- 2 standard deviations] of 200 bootstraps,
(income = money income of household after tax/after transfers).

Source: Luxembourg Income Study, Osberg and Xu, "International Comparisons of
Poverty Intensity: Index Decomposition and Bootstrap Inference," Working Paper
No. 97-03 (Halifax: Department of Economics, Dalhousie University, 1997).

How much similarity has there been across provinces in these trends?
Figure 2 also uses the Luxembourg Income Study database, but instead of
looking at Canada-wide outcomes in 1971, it compares Canadian provinces.
Since this chapter is interested in the impact of social policy on poverty, Figure 2 contrasts the level of poverty intensity "pre-fisc" (before taxes and
transfers) and "post-fisc"(after the impact of taxes and the receipt of transfer
payments).[10] The wide range of poverty intensity across Canadian provinces
in 1971 is notable, and it is particularly striking that Canadian provinces differed a good deal in poverty intensity, both before and after the impact of
taxes and transfers. Indeed, in 1971 poverty intensity *before* taxes and transfers in some Canadian provinces (Ontario, British Columbia, Alberta) was

Figure 2: Sen-Shorrocks-Thon Index of Poverty Intensity

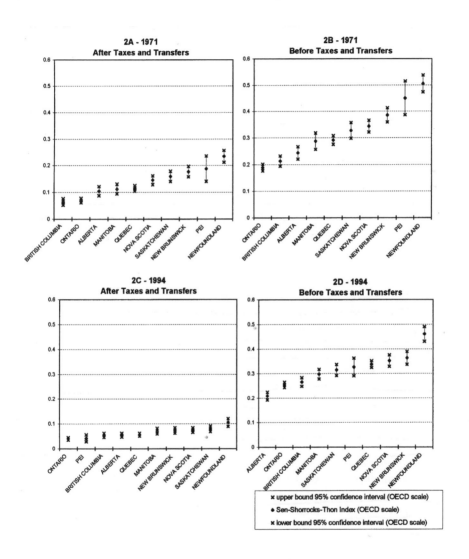

Notes:
Poverty Line=1/2 Median Equivalent Income
Equivalence Scale=OECD (first adult=1, other adults=0.7, kids=0.5)
Source: Luxembourg Income Study, author's calculations.

statistically indistinguishable from poverty intensity *after* taxes and transfers in several Atlantic provinces. Evidently, although the net impact of taxes and transfers within all provinces was a reduction in poverty intensity, in 1971 the tax/transfer system left poverty at a relatively high level and did little to equalize the experience of poverty across Canada.

By 1994, a very different picture in post-fisc outcomes had emerged. Panels 2c and 2d of Figure 2 present the SST index of poverty intensity (and its 95 percent confidence interval) for Canadian provinces in that year, pre- and post-taxes and transfers. Over all, the tax and transfer system produced a considerably lower national level of poverty intensity post-fisc in 1994 than in 1971. As well, it is notable that although pre-tax/transfer poverty outcomes continued to diverge substantially across provinces, by 1994 there was much more homogeneity in post-fisc poverty outcomes across Canadian provinces than in 1971. If mitigating poverty and substantial equalization of the life chances of Canadian citizens across provinces are indicators of the success of a social union, the 1994 data offer considerable reason for satisfaction.

SOCIAL POLICY CHANGE SINCE 1994

Although the data up to 1994 tell a hopeful story about the successes of the Canadian social union, 1994 was also a year that marked a major transition in social policy regimes in Canada.[11] "Since 1994, Canada has seen: (i) major revisions to the unemployment insurance (UI) system, and its replacement by the employment insurance (EI) system; (ii) replacement of the Canada Assistance Plan (CAP) by the Canada Health and Social Transfer (CHST); (iii) substantial devolution of authority to the provinces of in-kind service delivery such as social housing and training; (iv) major expenditure cuts in transfers to the provinces by the federal government; (v) substantial cuts in social assistance generosity in Ontario (and to a lesser extent in some other provinces).

The federal government has clearly been retreating from social activism and de-emphasizing poverty mitigation as a major goal of policy. As the pendulum swings toward greater provincial autonomy, in general, provinces now also have to rely much more on their own fiscal resources for social transfer expenditures.[12] Social assistance payments are no longer partially borne by the federal government, since cost-sharing under CAP has been replaced by block funding under the CHST, and provinces may differ in both fiscal capacity and inclination to reduce poverty.

In thinking about how poverty outcomes may have diverged across provinces, it is useful to distinguish between the outcomes experienced by different age groups. Improvements in the old age security system (Canada Pension Plan, the Guaranteed Income Supplement, and Old Age Security) occurred in the late 1960s and early 1970s and their impacts were phased in during the 1970s. The reduction in poverty among senior citizens which that produced has been a major success of Canadian social policy.[13] Because the old age security system is largely federal and has been mostly untouched in recent years there is likely to have been very little change across provinces in the poverty outcomes observed for senior citizens.

The experience of adults of working age, on the other hand, is more likely to vary across provinces. There have been different trends in local labour market conditions and the details of the UI/EI system have changed substantially. These changes interact in their effects on the working poor (and near poor) of different provinces, who have been differentially exposed to the impacts of changes in local unemployment and UI/EI regulations. Since provincial social assistance regulations for the working-age population have also changed in differing ways, they may also have experienced changes in social assistance benefit levels and accessibility. Since the poverty of children is determined by the poverty of their parents, child poverty outcomes are likely to have changed in different degrees in different provinces — and since the parents of very young children are likely to be the young adults who have been disproportionately affected by the labour market environment of the 1990s,[14] it seems useful to pay particular attention to the poverty of children under six.

Figure 3 examines changes in poverty intensity among people of different ages, in the different provinces of Canada from 1973 to 1994 and from 1994 to 1996. All figures embody the assumptions that: (i) family income is equally shared among all family members,[15] (ii) the OECD equivalence scale adequately captures the economies of scale in family consumption; (iii) the post-tax, post-transfer money income of the economic family measures family economic resources; (iv) the poverty line is drawn at one-half of the median equivalent income of all Canadians.[16] If these assumptions are granted, one can assign an equivalent income to each member of each economic family in the Survey of Consumer Finance,[17] and calculate the poverty intensity, rate of poverty and average poverty gap for four age groups: all persons aged 0 to 6, 0 to 17, 18 to 64, and 65 or over.

Figure 3A is consistent with the picture already painted in Figure 2: over the 21-year period, 1973-94, with the exception of British Columbia, all demographic groups in all provinces experienced a decline in poverty intensity. Notably, in all provinces other than Prince Edward Island and Newfoundland, the improvement for senior citizens was both greater than that for other demographic groups and much more uniform across provinces, possibly reflecting the greater federal role in old age security.

However, Figure 3B indicates a general trend since 1994 to stable or worsening poverty intensity. Although there has been little change in the poverty intensity of senior citizens, there have been especially large increases in poverty intensity among very young children in Ontario and Nova Scotia. And,

Figure 3: Improvement in SST Index – All Provinces

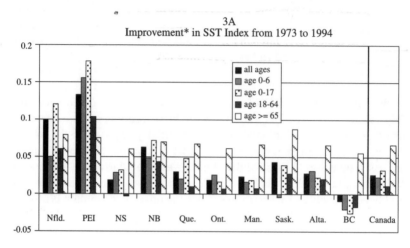

*Change in SST Index [1973-1994]

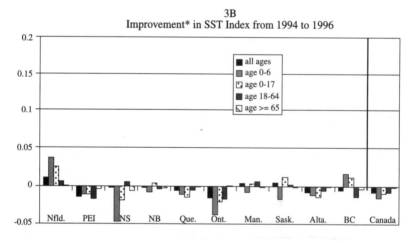

*Change in SST Index [1994-1996]

Notes:

Poverty Line=1/2 Median Equivalent Income–After Taxes and Transfers
Equivalence Scale=OECD (first adult=1, other adults=0.7, kids=0.5)

Poverty Line set at 1/2 the median equivalent income of economic families.

Source: Author's calculations from SCF.

although there has undoubtedly been an increase in the level of rhetorical concern with child poverty in recent years, the net effects of the actual policy measures adopted (e.g., the 21 percent cut in October 1995 in social assistance payments in Ontario) have not been consistent with that rhetoric. The increase in the poverty intensity from 1994 to 1996 among children under six in Canada's largest (and richest) province is especially notable.

LIKELY FUTURE TRENDS

The future trend of poverty outcomes in Canada will undoubtedly be affected by trends in household composition and stability, the ups and downs of aggregate demand in low-wage labour markets, and the impacts of regulatory, market, and technological changes on labour market structure and institutions. However, trends in social transfers are always particularly important for those who cannot rely on an adequate and stable stream of earnings. In thinking about likely future trends in poverty intensity in Canada, there is no escaping the central role of the adequacy of transfer payments.

Unlike some other federations (e.g., Australia), there is in Canada a substantial degree of divergence across provinces in pre-transfer/pre-tax poverty intensity. In the Canadian context, there is, in a sense, more for the federal government to do, if there is to be some commonality across provinces in citizenship rights and poverty outcomes, after taxes and transfers. However, there is no mistaking the direction of the political winds in the immediate future. The official opposition and the governments of the two largest provinces unite in the proposition that the federal government should play a diminished role in the tax/transfer system and in social policy, which is more or less the direction in which federal policy has moved in the last five years anyway. Provincial governments have been observed making rhetorical commitments to something called a "social union" but this appears to be code for restricting federal powers to impose conditions in cost-shared programs or to initiate federal social policy initiatives — the federal-provincial agreement on the social union is notably without any specific constraints on provincial decisions.[18]

Longer term trends can be decomposed into cyclical and secular components. Federal institutions (i.e., the Bank of Canada and the Department of Finance) retain sole control over monetary and fiscal policy in Canada, but the distribution of fiscal risk from business cycle fluctuations has shifted significantly in recent years. During the recessions of the early 1980s and 1990s, the federal government shared in the costs of cyclical downturn through its responsibility for unemployment insurance, and the cost-sharing of social assistance under the Canada Assistance Plan.[19] In those recessions, the vast majority of the unemployed got UI (paid for by the federal government) and

those who ran out of UI could sometimes go on social assistance, for which
the federal government paid 50 percent of the cost.

In the late 1990s, the situation is fundamentally different. A minority of the
unemployed are eligible for EI and any increase in social assistance costs
produced by a downturn in labour demand will be entirely borne by provincial treasuries. The shift to block funding of transfers to the provinces embodied
in the CHST means that the federal government's participation in increased
social assistance payments in a recession is now zero. Demands on the social
assistance system are likely to be more sensitive to future business-cycle downturns because the dramatic decline in eligibility for unemployment insurance
payments under EI[20] means that provincial social assistance programs will be
called on to carry the burden earlier, and to a far greater degree, than in past
recessions.

Furthermore, in addition to "recession proofing" its own fiscal situation at
the expense of the provinces, the federal government has backed away from
its commitment to the macroeconomic stabilization of output and employment, preferring a commitment to "price stability," with concomitant greater
likelihood of output and employment fluctuations.[21] Aggregate cyclical risk
has grown, and the provinces now have a greater share of that higher risk.

Provincial revenues from sales tax and income taxes are clearly vulnerable
to downturns in the business cycle: with the added wrinkle in Atlantic Canada
that Newfoundland, Nova Scotia, and New Brunswick have, by replacing their
provincial sales tax with the Harmonized Sales Tax, surrendered control of
both the rate and the definition of the tax base of one of their major revenue
sources.[22] In some provinces explicit legislation now ties governments to a
balanced budget and in all provinces there is heightened political sensitivity
to budget deficits. Hence, provincial expenditure cuts are a likely response to
any future recession. Of the four main headings of provincial government
expenditure (health care, education, debt payments, and social assistance),
social assistance is clearly the most vulnerable, since debt-servicing is sacro-
sanct, and there are broad and powerful coalitions supporting health and
education. There is thus reason to believe that the poor are increasingly at risk
in any future economic downturn.

During the 1930s, the inability of the provinces to cope with the fiscal burden of the Depression led to serious re-examination of federal-provincial
relations, which ushered in an era in which federal macroeconomic policy
aimed at minimizing downturns in output and employment, and federal programs shared the burden of cyclical downturns. That policy regime has now
been substantially dismantled, but nearly 60 years ago the Rowell-Sirois Commission expressed fairly clearly its rationale:

> The quality of education and welfare services is no longer a matter of purely
> provincial and local concern. In Canada today, freedom of movement and equal-
> ity of opportunity are more important than ever before, and these depend in part

on the maintenance of at least minimum national standards for education, public health and care of the indigent. The most economically distressed areas are the ones least capable of supporting these services, and yet are also the ones in which the needs are likely to be greatest. Whether the remedy lies in emigration from these areas or in the development of alternative means of livelihood, they must not be allowed to become backwaters of illiteracy and disease. Not only national duty and decency, if Canada is to be a nation at all, but equity and national self-interest demand that the residents of these areas be given average services and equal opportunities — equity because these areas may have been impoverished by the national economic policies which enriched other areas, and which were adopted in the general interest. Those whose interests were sacrificed have some claim that the partnership should work both ways. National self-interest demands it because the existence of areas of inferior educational and public health standards affects the whole population, and creates many grave and dangerous problems. More fortunate areas cannot escape the pressure on their standards and the effect on their people; in this case prevention, in both fiscal and human terms, is much cheaper than the cure.[23]

However, it is not clear that these lessons have been remembered.

In the new millennium, business-cycle fluctuations will interact with longer term secular trends in determining the degree of redistribution in Canada's tax/transfer system. Fundamentally, such redistribution is driven by a political sense of common membership in a national community (as Rowell-Sirois put it: "If Canada is to be a nation at all") and some expectation of the appropriate degree of sharing of aggregate output. The longer term question is whether a sense of national community in Canada can survive the barriers of geography, political decentralization, Quebec nationalism, regional alienation, the louder voices of the global entertainment industry, and the pervasive marketization of social policy. The issue is clearly somewhat circular, since the saliency of common institutions and the objective reality of a common situation underpin political support for pan-Canadian redistribution, and a decline in federal programs and an increase in the objective differences in outcomes between provinces undermines both, thereby accentuating the trend to greater provincialism.

Within the last three decades, two different patterns have been observed in Canada. In 1971, Canada had a similar overall level of poverty intensity as the United States and because pre-transfer poverty levels differed and because different tax and transfer systems were in place in different Canadian provinces, the provinces differed considerably in ultimate post-fisc poverty outcomes. In 1994, Canada had, overall, much less poverty than the United States and much greater commonality than in 1971 in the level of post-tax/transfer poverty intensity — the operation of the tax and transfer system meant that despite differing levels of pre-transfer poverty, Canadians in all provinces had in the end a much more similar chance and depth of poverty. In 1971, one could hardly say that there was a social union, but in 1994 a practical social union was in existence.

CONCLUSIONS

Which scenario is more likely for the future?

Who cares?

On balance, there would seem to be more likelihood than not that the federal
role in social policy will continue to shrink and that poverty outcomes will
continue to trend up and to diverge across provinces. The rhetoric of social
union may continue, but not the reality — at least for those under 65. The
direct impacts will clearly be felt primarily by the poor, who are a minority of
society, with very little political influence, and among senior policymakers
there may well be a diminished sense that this matters much.[24]

My own opinion is that this is a mistake. The prevalence and depth of poverty is of personal concern not only to those who are poor at any given time,
but also to the much larger number who will experience a spell of poverty at
some point in their lives, and to the even larger number who are anxious about
their probability of poverty. Even those people who are certain that they will
be affluent all their lives are affected, since growing poverty affects the general quality of urban life and undermines any residual sense of national
community. Having a sense of a larger identity to belong to seems to be important to many people, including the securely affluent, and there are many
economic costs to diminished social cohesion.[25] The maintenance of Canada's social union and an effective anti-poverty role matters, in many ways, but
it is unclear whether current trends will continue or not.

NOTES

Revised version of paper presented at the Symposium on Fiscal Federalism, Queen's
University, Kingston, Ontario, April 16-17, 1999. I would like to thank Lynn Lethbridge
for her excellent work as research assistant and the Social Sciences and Humanities
Research Council for its support under Grant No. 410-97-0802. Thanks also to Jim
Stanford and two anonymous reviewers for their helpful comments — errors remain-
ing are my responsibility.

1. The Appendix discusses measurement issues. The main body of this chapter
    uses the common practice, in the international literature, of drawing the poverty
    line at one-half the median equivalent after-tax/after-transfer income of indi-
    vidual Canadians (where household economies of scale are assumed to be
    captured by the OECD equivalence scale). This measurement choice implies a
    significantly lower poverty rate (11.57 percent in 1994) than the use of the Sta-
    tistics Canada Low Income Cut Off (15.9 percent in 1994). However, the issue
    this chapter focuses on is *trends* in poverty, which are much the same for all
    combinations of poverty lines and equivalence scales examined.

2. Note that "commonality" of poverty outcomes could be at either a high or low level of poverty. The issues of *whether* there is a social union, and *what type* of social union that may be, are analytically distinct.

3. Amartya K. Sen, "Poverty: An Ordinal Approach to Measurement," *Econometrica* 44 (1976):219-31. For surveys of the literature, see Aldi J.M. Hagenaars, "The Definition and Measurement of Poverty," in *Economic Inequality and Poverty: International Perspectives*, ed. Lars Osberg (Armonk, NY: M.E. Sharpe, 1991), pp. 134-56; or B. Zheng, "Aggregate Poverty Measures," *Journal of Economic Surveys* 11, 2 (1997):123-61.

4. John Myles and Garnett Picot, "Social Transfers, Earnings and Low-Income Intensity Among Canadian Children, 1981-96: Highlighting Recent Developments in Low-Income Measurement," unpublished paper (Ottawa: Statistics Canada, 1999).

5. The Sen-Shorrocks-Thon (SST) index of poverty intensity can be calculated as $I = (\text{rate})*(\text{gap})*(1+G(x))$ where "rate" is the percentage of the population with incomes below the poverty line (sometimes called the head-count ratio), "gap" is the average percentage gap between the incomes of the poor and the poverty line and $G(x)$ is the Gini index of inequality of the poverty gap among all people. In the main body of this essay, cash incomes are converted to "equivalent income" using the "OECD" equivalence scale ratios for households of different sizes. For further details on the SST index, and its trends over time in Canada, see Lars Osberg and Kuan Xu, "Poverty Intensity: How Well Do Canadian Provinces Compare?" *Canadian Public Policy/Analyse de Politiques* 25, 2 (1999):179-98; or Myles and Picot, "Social Transfers, Earnings and Low-Income Intensity Among Canadian Children, 1981-96." For international comparisons, see Lars Osberg and Kuan Xu, "International Comparisons of Poverty Intensity: Index Decomposition and Bootstrap Inference," Working Paper No. 97-03 (Halifax: Department of Economics, Dalhousie University, 1997). Also, Anthony F. Shorrocks, "Revisiting the Sen Poverty Index," *Econometrica* 63 (1995):1225-30.

6. The alternative point of view is that there is no such thing as "Canadian" society, and poverty norms should therefore be appraised with reference to local/provincial standard-of-living norms. Clearly, if this were the case, there would be no point at all in talking of a Canadian social union.
    In this version of the essay, the poverty line norm adopted is one-half the median equivalent income of all Canadian individuals, since this concept of poverty has been widely used in the international literature and can therefore be compared to international data. A disadvantage of this approach is that it does not recognize the differences in the cost of living that accompany residence in urban and rural areas. The Statistics Canada Low Income Cut Off (LICO), which builds in city size and urban/rural cost of living differentials, is unique to Canada and cannot be directly compared internationally. For results using the LICO, or the "LIS" equivalence scale (which are essentially identical), see the full paper at http://is.dal.ca/~osberg/home.html.

7. The idea behind bootstrap estimation is that of experimenting (by multiple random resampling of the survey micro data) with the implications of drawing somewhat different samples, from which to calculate the characteristics of the population. See Osberg and Xu, "Poverty Intensity: How Well Do Canadian Provinces Compare?" and "International Comparisons of Poverty Intensity."

8. See David E. Card and Richard B. Freeman (eds.), *Small Differences that Matter: Labour Markets and Income Maintenance in Canada and the United States* (Chicago: University of Chicago Press).

9. As well, it should be emphasized that the United States is a clear outlier in poverty intensity, and it is not really that hard to look good compared to the worst. Compared to other developed countries, Canada in 1994 was at the high end of a continuum, with a similar level of poverty as Spain or the UK, but clearly greater poverty intensity than Belgium, the Netherlands or the Scandinavian countries; for more details, see Osberg and Xu, "International Comparisons of Poverty Intensity."

10. In Figure 2, the poverty line is set at one-half the median of the relevant income concept — before tax and transfer or after tax and transfers.

11. Osberg and Xu compare poverty intensity within Canadian provinces in 1984 and for each year from 1989 to 1996; see Osberg and Xu, "Poverty Intensity: How Well Do Canadian Provinces Compare?"

12. The new national child benefit system does allow provinces to reduce social assistance payments to families in receipt of child benefits if the money is being spent on related programs.

13. Osberg discusses trends from 1971 to 1994 in the poverty and inequality outcomes of different birth cohorts of Canadians, and emphasizes that because many senior citizens depend on the same transfer programs, many have much the same income. This "spike" in the income distribution of senior citizens means that the poverty rate among the over 65 cohort *is* sensitive to choice of poverty line; see Lars Osberg, "Economic Growth, Income Distribution and Economic Welfare in Canada 1975-1994," *North American Journal of Economics and Finance* 8, 2(1997):153-66.

14. Osberg, Erksoy and Phipps discuss the impacts of the greater risk exposure of the youth cohort in the 1990s, due to higher unemployment and less generous unemployment insurance; see Lars Osberg, Sadettin Erksoy and Shelley Phipps, "How to Value the Poor Prospects of Youth in the Early 1990s?" *Review of Income and Wealth* 44, 1 (1998):43-62.

15. Sharif and Phipps note that the measurement of child poverty levels in Canada is quite sensitive to intra-family sharing assumptions. If, in all provinces, there is the same degree of intra-family inequality, the level of child poverty will change but not the interprovince differences reported above. However, if there are substantial differences across provinces in social norms with respect to the degree of inequality with which family resources are shared, the conclusions of Figure 3 with respect to child well-being may need to be revised; see N. Sharif and

Shelley Phipps, "The Challenge of Child Poverty: Which Policies Might Help?" *Canadian Business Economics* 2, 3(1994):17-20.

16. Note that this methodology implies a lower poverty rate and poverty gap than the use of the Low Income Cut Off, since the LICO is higher than half the median: see Note 1 and Appendix Table A-1. However, the main body of this chapter uses one-half the median equivalent income as the poverty line to keep comparability with the international literature on poverty. See Appendix A of the full version of the paper at http://is.dal.ca/~osberg/home.htmlfor calculations embodied using the Statistics Canada LICO as the poverty line and the corresponding equivalence scales.

17. Note that Figure 3 uses the Survey of Consumer Finance micro data directly, since 1994 is the most recent data for Canada available on the LIS. This necessitates a small change in definition from the poverty of households (LIS) to that of economic families (SCF): but there is no significant change in results. As well, 1971 is available in LIS but 1973 is the earliest SCF data available to us under the Data Liberation Initiative.

18. With the possible exception of residency-based policies which impede labour mobility, although the wording ["unless they can be demonstrated to be reasonable and consistent with the principles of the Social Union Framework"] would appear to have lots of room for interpretation.

19. In the 1990s' recession, federal participation in recessionary costs was greatly limited by the "Cap on CAP" which limited annual increases in Canada Assistance Plan transfers to Ontario, British Columbia, and Alberta to 5 percent — despite the fact that the recession hit Ontario hardest.

20. In 1997, the percentage of the unemployed receiving EI benefits was 25 percent. The beneficiary to unemployed ratio was significantly higher (at 42 percent), largely because a significant fraction of EI recipients work while on claim (and declare their earnings) and are therefore not counted as unemployed. The decline in UI/EI recipiency in the 1990s has been dramatic: the beneficiary-unemployed ratio in 1989 was 83 percent. See Human Resource Development Canada (HRDC), *An Analysis of Employment Insurance Coverage in Canada*, Research Paper No. W-98-35E (Ottawa: Applied Research Branch, HRDC, 1998), p. 56, Table 4.1.

21. See Federal Reserve Bank of New York, "Rigid Inflation Targeting Can Lead to Wide Swings in GDP Growth," *Research Update* (New York: Federal Reserve Bank of New York, July 1998).

22. Because federal transfers are either fixed sums per capita (CHST) or formula driven (equalization) and because the federal government retains control of the definition of the income tax base, the only major revenue parameter these governments now control is the provincial percentage rate of the income tax.

23. Canada. Report of the Royal Commission on Dominion-Provincial Relations (Rowell-Sirois), *Royal Commission on Dominion-Provincial Relations*, Book 2, *Recommendations* (Ottawa: Queen's Printer, 1940), p. 128.

24. See Frank L. Graves, Tim Dugas and Patrick Beauchamp, "Identity and National Attachments in Contemporary Canada," in *Canada: The State of the Federation 1998-99: How Canadians Connect*, ed. Harvey Lazar and Tom McIntosh (Kingston: Institute of Intergovernmental Relations, Queen's University, 1999), pp. 307-54.

25. A growing literature has begun to recognize the importance of social cohesion for economic growth; see Stephen Knack and Philip Keefer, "Does Social Capital Have an Economic Payoff?: A Cross-Country Investigation," *Quarterly Journal of Economics* (November 1997):1251-88. For a series of studies on the economic impact of social cohesion in a Canadian context, see Lars Osberg, *The Economic Implications of Social Cohesion* (Toronto: University of Toronto Press, forthcoming).

APPENDIX
Measurement Choices

The issue of where to draw the poverty line has been much debated over the years.[1] The main body of this chapter uses the common practice, in the international literature, of drawing the poverty line at one-half the median equivalent after-tax/after-transfer income of individual Canadians (where household economies of scale are assumed to be captured by the OECD equivalence scale). By this criterion, 11.57 percent of the population were poor in 1994. In using one-half the median, the poverty criterion of this essay is conceptually similar to what is now called the Low Income Measure (LIM) by Statistics Canada, which sets the 1994 poverty rate at 14.7 percent.[2] The difference arises because the Statistics Canada LIM uses pre-tax, post-transfer income (while we use after-tax, after-transfer income), calculates the median across households (we take the median across individuals), does not exclude people with negative incomes (we do), counts children as those under 16 (OECD uses 18), and uses an equivalence scale with much greater economies of scale in which additional adults count for 0.4 adult equivalents (OECD uses 0.7), and children count as 0.3 (OECD uses 0.5). By the more widely known (in Canada) Low Income Cut Off or LICO criterion, the poverty rate (after tax) was 15.9 percent in 1994 and 17 percent in 1996. See Table A-1 for the dollar values that correspond.

The sensitivity of the poverty rate at a point in time to the exact measure of the poverty line chosen is symptomatic of the ambiguity of definition of poverty for those just at the margin.[3] However, trends over time among the non-elderly, and the conclusions of this chapter, are not sensitive to these measurement choices. Because the dependence of many senior citizens on the same transfer programs implies that many have much the same (low) income, and because that "spike" in the income distribution of senior citizens lies between the LICO and one-half the median in 1994, poverty measurement among the over 65 cohort is more sensitive to measurement choices.[4]

Table A-1 presents the dollar values of the poverty line, in 1994 and 1996, which correspond to the conceptual choice of "Low Income Cut Off" or "one-half the median equivalent individual income" as the poverty line. Although these two conceptual choices generated much the same dollar poverty line for a four-person family in the late 1980s, they have diverged since then. In the period 1990-96, average real family income has fallen since consumer prices have risen faster than family money incomes. Because the LICO has been updated by the increase in consumer prices, while a poverty line drawn at one-half the median increases with family incomes, the LICO is now significantly higher than "one-half the median."

However, a major advantage of using the one-half the median equivalent individual income concept to draw the poverty line is the possibility of making international comparisons. An earlier version of this chapter (available on the web at http://is.dal.ca/~osberg/home.html) presented the numbers that correspond to Figures 2 and 3 in the text. The advantage of using the LICO is that it builds in consideration of the cost-of-living differences that go with residence in different urban or rural settings.[5] The disadvantage is that international comparability is lost, since the LICO methodology is unique to Canada.

In the international literature on equivalence scales, reference to the "LIS" scale is increasingly seen. This refers to the hypothesis that the number of equivalent adults in a household should be calculated as the square root of the number of household members. Are the results in the main body of the text sensitive to our use of the "OECD" equivalence scale? Figini notes that "OECD and other two-parameter equivalence scales empirically used show a similarity of results [in measurement of inequality] to one parameter equivalence scales with elasticity around 0.5,"[6] but that leaves open the possibility that in poverty-intensity calculations there may be differences due to equivalence scale choice. The paper posted on the Website presents the results obtained with the LIS equivalence scale, which are essentially identical to those in the main text.

NOTES

1. For surveys, see Hagenaars, "The Definition and Measurement of Poverty"; or Anthony B. Atkinson, *Poverty in Europe* (Oxford: Blackwell Publishers, 1998).

2. Statistics Canada, *Low-Income Measures (LIMs) 1996*, Catalogue No. 13-582-XPB (Ottawa: Household Surveys Division, Statistics Canada, 1998), p. 17.

3. See Michael C. Wolfson and J.M. Evans, *Statistics Canada's Income Cut Offs: Methodological Concerns and Possibilities: A Discussion Paper*, Research Paper Series No. 23 (Ottawa: Statistics Canada, 1989); and K. Short, T. Garner, D. Johnson and P. Doyle, *Experimental Poverty Measures: 1990 to 1997*, US Census Bureau, Current Population Reports, Consumer Income No. P60-205 (Washington, DC: Government Printing Office, 1999).

4. See Osberg, "Economic Growth Income Distribution and Economic Welfare in Canada 1975-1994."

5. The difference in housing costs between Metro Toronto and rural Ontario (or rural Nova Scotia) is a clear example of the importance of urban size to cost of living and since provinces differ in the relative importance of urban and rural areas, these have the potential to influence interprovincial comparisons. Note that interprovincial differences in cost of living, controlling for urban size, are much smaller than urban size differentials in cost of living.

6. Paolo Figini, "Inequality Measures, Equivalence Scales and Adjustment for Household Size and Composition," paper presented at the general conference of the International Association for Research in Income and Wealth, Cambridge, 1998, p. 2.

Table A-1: Poverty Lines – After-Tax LICO and one-half the Median Equivalent Income (OECD scale)

| | Low Income Cut-Offs | | | | | 1/2 Median Equivalent Income (OECD scale) | | |
| | Urban | | | | Rural | | | |
1994 # in household	>= 500,000	100,000-499,9991	30,000-99,999	< 30,000		1 adult	2 adults	3 adults
1	13,635	11,486	11,309	10,333	8,940	8,332	—	—
2	16,638	14,014	13,798	12,609	10,908	12,498	14,164	—
3	21,043	17,726	17,452	15,948	13,797	16,664	18,330	19,997
4	26,209	22,077	21,736	19,862	17,184	20,830	22,496	24,163
5	29,294	24,675	24,293	22,199	19,206	24,996	26,662	28,329
6	32,378	27,273	26,851	24,537	21,229	29,162	30,828	32,495
7 (or more-LICO)	35,462	29,871	29,408	26,874	23,252	33,328	34,994	36,661
8	—	—	—	—	—	37,494	39,160	40,827
1996								
1	14,240	11,996	11,811	10,792	9,337	8,590	—	—
2	17,376	14,637	14,411	13,169	11,393	12,885	14,603	—
3	21,977	18,513	18,227	16,656	14,410	17,180	18,898	20,616
4	27,373	23,058	22,701	20,744	17,947	21,475	23,193	24,911
5	30,595	25,771	25,372	23,185	20,059	25,770	27,488	29,206
6	33,816	28,484	28,044	25,627	22,172	30,065	31,783	33,501
7 (or more-LICO)	37,037	31,198	30,714	28,067	24,285	34,360	36,078	37,796
8	—	—	—	—	—	38,655	40,737	42,091

Sources: Statistics Canada – Catalogue 13-592-XPB. Survey of Consumer Finance, author's calculations.

III

Federal-Provincial Taxation Issues

9

The Tax on Income and the Growing Decentralization of Canada's Personal Income Tax System

Geoffrey E. Hale

Le récent accord fédéral-provincial qui permet aux provinces de prélever l'impôt sur les particuliers comme un «impôt sur le revenu» plutôt qu'un pourcentage de l'impôt fédéral de base provoquera sans doute les plus importants changements qu'a connu le système fiscal canadien au cours des trente dernières années. Ce chapitre analyse les changements proposés aux systèmes fiscaux provinciaux en fonction de la décentralisation des politiques fiscales et économiques canadiennes. Il présente les facteurs qui contribuent aux divergences entre les provinces en matière de politique fiscale de même que la dynamique et le contenu des réformes fiscales ou des réductions d'impôts proposées, à ce jour, dans cinq provinces: l'Alberta, la Saskatchewan, le Manitoba, l'Ontario et Terre-Neuve.

The recent federal-provincial agreement to allow provincial governments to redesign their personal income tax systems within specific limits promises to trigger the most significant changes to the Canadian tax system since the signing of the 1962 federal-provincial tax collection agreements and the federal tax reform bill of 1971.

Federal acceptance of the so-called "tax on income" proposal put forward by five provinces in December 1997 promises to accelerate what Dyck and Dahlby have called the continuing "provincialization of the Canadian fiscal system," while preserving a common personal income tax base and a shared tax collection system as central elements of the Canadian economic union.[1] These changes reflect several trends in federal-provincial fiscal and economic relations:

- the growing decentralization of fiscal and economic policies in Canada as provincial governments pursue a range of different economic strategies in response to growing regional and international competition, and the different agendas arising from very different provincial political cultures;

- the growing use of the tax system as a vehicle for policy innovation in response to changing economic and social conditions;

- the federal government's efforts to accommodate a growing diversity in provincial economic and social arrangements, while attempting to maintain its own leadership role in economic and fiscal policy; and

- growing interprovincial competition, especially at a regional level, for investment, employment, and skilled workers.

This chapter examines the changes that have been proposed to provincial income tax systems in the wake of the revisions announced in 1998 to the federal-provincial tax collection agreements. It addresses these changes in the context of the ongoing decentralization of Canadian fiscal and economic policies, factors contributing to divergent provincial fiscal and tax policies and the dynamics of federal-provincial relations. Finally, it reviews the dynamics and contents of tax reform and/or tax-reduction proposals that have emerged to date in five provinces: Alberta, Saskatchewan, Manitoba, Ontario, and Newfoundland.

THE TREND TO FISCAL DECENTRALIZATION

The re-emergence of the "tax on income" model, which enables provincial governments to design rate structures for their provincial income tax (PIT) systems independently of the federal PIT structure while maintaining a common definition of income and a unified system for tax administration and collection, reflects a broader trend toward the decentralization — or "provincialization" — of Canadian fiscal policy since the 1970s.[2]

The rapidly growing cost of provincial welfare states, and of related federal transfers to the provinces, has repeatedly forced Ottawa to introduce changes to its fiscal arrangements with the provinces in order to maintain some degree of control over its own fiscal priorities. The introduction of the Established Programs Financing program in 1977 was accompanied by a shift in personal and corporate income tax points intended to make provincial governments, at least those of the wealthier provinces, more fiscally self-sufficient by enabling them to finance a larger portion of their overall spending from their "own-source" revenues.

As a result, aggregate provincial government revenues (including federal transfers) have exceeded those of the federal government for more than 20 years, and provincial revenue sources have continued to grow marginally faster than those of the federal government.[3] Whether or not greater provincial self-sufficiency — a rather elastic concept subject to different interpretations — has been achieved is open to question. However, the decline of federal transfers as a percentage of provincial revenues (in most provinces) and the increasingly diverse political and economic priorities of provincial governments have contributed to a growing decentralization of fiscal policies. (See Table 1.)

These changes have done little to mitigate tax competition between the federal and provincial governments. As both senior levels of government share most major sources of revenues, the integration of federal and provincial tax systems makes each vulnerable to unilateral policy shifts by the other. Although the gradual broadening of the federal tax base following the partial deindexation of personal income taxes in 1985 allowed the provinces to reap windfall revenues, most provinces moved rapidly to offset the tax cuts introduced as part of the Mulroney government's tax reforms of 1987-88 by raising their own tax rates. In its turn, the federal government responded to the growth of provincial payroll and capital taxes, which cut into its own tax base, by warning the provinces that future increases in these areas would not be deductible from federal taxes. It also imposed the so-called "cap on CAP," which limited the growth of federal support for rapidly growing social assistance programs in Ontario, Alberta, and British Columbia.

Table 1: Federal Transfers as a Percent of Provincial Revenues

	1980-81	1989-90	1994-95	1997-98	1998-99
Canada	23.3	20.6	20.5	14.9	15.6
Newfoundland	49.4	48.7	48.3	52.1	49.1
PEI	50.6	44.4	40.9	37.1	52.5
Nova Scotia	47.9	40.5	42.6	39.5	39.3
New Brunswick	43.2	39.7	37.8	37.1	37.5
Quebec	26.6	21.3	20.3	14.3	17.5
Ontario	20.1	13.0	16.5	9.7	8.2
Manitoba	42.4	36.0	36.4	32.8	26.2
Saskatchewan	17.5	29.6	24.8	10.7	16.9
Alberta	8.3	15.1	11.9	6.6	7.9
British Columbia	18.0	15.5	12.6	9.1	10.5

Source: Canada, *Fiscal Reference Tables* (Ottawa: Department of Finance,1999); Nova Scotia, *Budget Highlights,* 14 October 1999.

These conflicts of the late 1980s and early 1990s, combined with the federal government's huge structural deficit and rapidly growing debt, undercut the federal government's ability to provide effective leadership in fiscal policy, reinforcing the Bank of Canada's already strong bias toward restrictive monetary policies and contributing to the length and severity of the recession of the early 1990s.[4] They help to explain federal Finance officials' caution in accommodating provincial proposals to exercise greater control over their own tax systems and their reluctance to accommodate proposed provincial innovations through the federal-provincial tax collection agreements — both in the early and mid-1990s.[5]

However, there have been two significant exceptions to this pattern. In 1985, federal Finance Minister Michael Wilson allowed his provincial counterpart in Saskatchewan to experiment with the introduction of a flat tax on net income — in effect, a form of provincial minimum tax applied on a relatively broad base. Manitoba and Alberta were allowed to follow suit in 1987. In 1996, Ottawa agreed to facilitate British Columbia's creation of a refundable child tax credit, in what became a prototype for the 1997 federal-provincial agreement leading to the introduction of the National Child Benefit.

Federal fiscal and tax policies during the Chrétien government's first term (1993-97) were characterized by a single-minded focus on the elimination of the federal deficit. The broader trend toward fiscal decentralization, or "provincialization," during this period was reinforced by Ottawa's decision to phase in reductions of its cash transfers to the provinces by almost 25 percent in return for giving the provinces greater flexibility in applying the new Canada Health and Social Transfer (CHST) to their fiscal priorities.

However, since balancing its budget in 1997-98, the federal government has pursued a very different approach to its relations with the provinces, negotiating specific general and bilateral agreements with provinces to link increased transfer payments to the achievement of specific federal objectives. This approach reflects the federal Liberals' clearly expressed desire to increase their political credit for tax and spending measures with Canadians, while maximizing the flexibility of the federal Department of Finance in balancing the political and economic demands of the government's broadly-based political coalition.[6]

While most provinces anticipated or paralleled the fiscal policies of the federal government in reducing their budget deficits and moving toward balanced budgets at different rates after 1993, they adopted very different paths in moving toward these goals.

DIVERGING PROVINCIAL FISCAL POLICIES

The decentralization of Canadian tax policies since 1997 has resulted from more than just the federal government's declining political leverage over the larger and wealthier provinces. It also reflects the growing diversity of provincial economies and the lack of synchronization among provincial economic cycles as by-products of Canada's integration into the continental and global economies.[7] These have resulted in very different political responses from province to province based on four major factors:

- the emergence of widely differing strategic visions for provincial economic development — and the role of provincial governments in these "province-building" strategies;

- the countervailing pressures of regional economic competition, both in tax levels and the levels of services provided by governments;

- the effects of different electoral cycles, often involving the tightening of fiscal constraints immediately following an election and a combination of increased spending and actual or promised tax reductions closer to an election; and

- the relative dependence of individual provinces on federal cash transfers, and their differing capacities to insulate themselves from their decline over the long term (see Table 1).

DIFFERENT APPROACHES TO ECONOMIC DEVELOPMENT

Province-building is not a new phenomenon in Canada. However, Canada's growing integration into the continental and global economies has contributed to a much stronger external orientation among most provincial economies. Most provinces now export more to other countries than to other parts of Canada. International exports now account for 41 percent of Canada's gross domestic product — ranging from a high of 52 percent in Ontario to a low of 30 percent in British Columbia.[8]

Virtually all provincial governments have sought to diversify their provincial economies, and to develop provincial economic strategies emphasizing regional comparative advantages. Some provinces, particularly New Brunswick, Quebec, and British Columbia, have sought to attract or retain business investment with a variety of incentives that can withstand challenges under World Trade Organization and North American Free Trade Agreement rules. Others, notably Ontario and Alberta, have significantly reduced their business subsidies, and sought to make their provincial tax systems more competitive with those of neighbouring American states and other international competitors.

Several provinces, particularly New Brunswick, British Columbia, Alberta, Prince Edward Island, and more recently, Ontario, have centralized control over property taxes levied to finance primary and secondary education costs. In most cases, this has been intended to balance greater budgetary control over provincial education costs, equity in funding between urban and rural areas and, in some cases, the perceived need to limit the growth of property tax rates in the name of economic development.[9] Many of these changes were closely linked to budgetary pressures as provincial governments struggled to balance their budgets in the mid-1990s.

Most provinces, regardless of ideological outlook, have taken steps both before and during the 1990s to reduce tax rates for lower income taxpayers, raise the income thresholds at which provincial income taxes are applied, and increase the progressivity of their provincial tax systems. These changes were usually justified on the grounds of fairness — particularly in sharing the burdens of deficit and debt-reduction policies introduced by most provinces during the early and mid-1990s. However, the extent and rapidity of tax reduction have been closely tied to the political outlooks of individual provincial governments and their relative emphasis on promoting private sector wealth creation rather than income redistribution and the extension of public services.

DIFFERENT ROADS TO BALANCED BUDGETS

Both federal and provincial governments faced massive deficits at the end of the 1991-92 recession. Provincial deficits totaled $26.3 billion on a financial management system basis,[10] about 3.8 percent of GDP. Managing deficits and balancing budgets became the central priority of virtually all provincial governments for the next several years — although they approached this challenge in several different ways.[11]

British Columbia, Newfoundland, New Brunswick, and Quebec limited spending growth at different times between 1992-93 and 1996-97, or made modest spending reductions, hoping to take advantage of economic growth to balance their budgets. Manitoba and Alberta made significant spending reductions, while avoiding tax increases. Saskatchewan and Nova Scotia combined significant spending reductions with "deficit-reduction" tax increases. After the 1995 provincial election, Ontario cut both spending and taxes in a bid to stimulate economic growth and reduce the direct role of government in the economy and society. (See Table 2 for provincial spending trends.)

Most provinces also used their deficit-reduction campaigns to restructure their tax systems, both by changing rate structures and the mix of various revenue sources. Most increased the progressivity of their provincial tax systems — adding a variety of surtaxes on middle and/or upper income earners. Five provinces have reduced their basic personal tax rates below 1988 levels (see Table A-1). Top marginal tax rates in all ten provinces, including federal and provincial surtaxes, are higher than they were in 1988, although these increases have been rolled back somewhat in most provinces since 1995 (see Table 3).

Table 2: Provincial Spending Trends, Real per Capita Spending (FMS, $1998)

	1992-93	1996-97	1998-99	1992/93-96/97	1996/97-98/99	1992/93-98/99
	1998 Constant Dollars			%		
Increased spending						
BC	6,407	6,573	7,473	+ 2.6	+13.7	+16.6
Nfld.	6,796	6,549	7,073	- 3.6	+ 8.0	+ 4.1
Modest spending reductions						
NB	6,640	6,539	6,590	- 1.5	+ 0.8	- 0.8
Que.	6,940	6,636	6,784	- 4.4	+ 2.2	- 2.3
Prov. average	6,533	6,043	6,241	- 7.5	+ 3.3	- 4.5
Significant spending cuts						
PEI	6,751	6,222	6,336	- 7.8	+ 1.8	- 6.1
Ont.	5,957	5,417	5,464	- 9.1	+ 0.9	- 8.3
Man.	6,855	6,196	6,191	- 9.6	- 0.1	- 9.7
NS	6,301	5,443	5,816	-13.6	+ 6.8	- 7.7
Sask.	6,937	6,017	6,318	-13.3	+ 5.0	- 8.9
Alta.	7,148	5,730	5,666	-19.8	- 1.1	-20.7

Source: Statistics Canada, "Provincial and Territorial General Government Revenue and Expenditure," *Public Sector Finance, 1995-1996,* Cat. No. 68-212 (Ottawa: Statistics Canada, 1999).

Table 3: Personal Income Taxes – Top Marginal Tax Rates by Province (in percent)

	1988	1995	1999
Newfoundland	47.3	51.3	52.9
Prince Edward Island	47.7	50.3	49.5
Nova Scotia	46.3	50.3	49.2
New Brunswick	47.3	51.4	49.7
Quebec	51.1	52.9	52.1
Ontario	46.1	53.2	48.7
Manitoba	47.5	50.4	49.0
Saskatchewan	48.4	51.9	50.8
Alberta	44.9	46.1	45.2
British Columbia	44.8	54.2	52.3

After 1996, most provinces relaxed their controls on spending to some degree and introduced a series of modest tax reductions as a way of "rewarding" taxpayers for the sacrifices resulting from deficit reduction (see Table A-2). Ontario and Alberta were "outliers" in this process. The Harris government chose the path of fiscal stimulus through tax reductions to offset provincial spending cuts — implementing its promised 30 percent reduction in basic personal income tax (PIT) rates between 1996 and 1998. It also announced plans for a further 20 percent cut in PIT rates over four years before its successful re-election campaign of 1999, while continuing to project a balanced budget in 2000-01. The Klein government in Alberta followed the most consistent policy of fiscal constraint, deferring tax cuts and applying 75 percent of its sizeable surpluses — which averaged $1.8 billion in the four years after balancing its budget in 1994-95 — to debt reduction.[12]

Arguably, the deficit- and tax-reduction strategies adopted by each government have tended to reflect its political philosophy and the political culture of each province rather than external economic pressures. For example, Ontario's high-profile emphasis on tax cuts before balancing its budget reflected as much of an ideological commitment to smaller, more frugal government as to increasing its economic competitiveness. Faced with a low tax regime in neighbouring Alberta, the Romanow government in Saskatchewan emphasized sales-tax reductions rather than lower income taxes after balancing its budget in 1994-95, while allowing overall provincial tax levels to grow relative to those of its neighbours (see Table 4). Quebec's decision to rely more on tax increases than spending reductions to balance its budget suggests that its social democratic political culture has greatly outweighed competitive pressures from Ontario's tax cuts in shaping the province's recent budgetary priorities.

While each government's political philosophy colours its budgetary priorities to some extent, these are also affected by the practical realities of the electoral cycle. Governments of all political stripes have tended to concentrate painful economic news in the early years of their mandates, while relaxing their purse strings (or in some cases, the rigours of proposed budget reductions) as the prospect of an election nears.[13]

Now that the federal and most provincial governments have balanced their budgets, both senior levels of government can look forward to a growing fiscal dividend of sorts. According to a study by the Royal Bank, the federal surplus could rise to about $26 billion by 2004-05, compared to about $16 billion at the provincial level.[14] Finance Minister Paul Martin's announcement of a multi-year personal income tax reduction plan, with incremental tax cuts averaging $3 billion in each of the next five years, is likely to have a significant effect on provincial revenues in the absence of further changes to provincial income tax systems.

However, as both levels of government scramble to maximize their fiscal flexibility, as well as the political credit to be obtained from lower taxes and

Table 4: Provincial Own-Source Revenues as Share of Gross Provincial Product

| | Own-Source Revenues | | | | | |
| | As Share of Provincial GDP % | | | As Percent of National Average | | |
	1992	1996	1998	1992	1996	1998
Newfoundland	20.1	20.3	18.4	120	120	108
Prince Edward Island	19.9	19.4	18.3	119	115	107
Nova Scotia	16.4	16.1	16.2	99	95	95
New Brunswick	18.3	20.1	19.1	110	119	112
Quebec	20.0	20.1	21.2	120	119	124
Ontario	13.7	13.9	14.5	82	82	85
Manitoba	17.5	18.5	18.6	105	110	109
Saskatchewan	18.4	18.4	19.2	110	109	112
Alberta	15.8	14.8	14.8	95	87	87
British Columbia	18.9	21.6	20.0	113	128	117

Source: Statistics Canada, "Provincial and Territorial General Government Revenue and Expenditure," Cat. No. 68-212.

higher spending on public services, the federal government cannot reduce its taxes under the present system without reducing the flexibility of provincial governments to set their own political and fiscal priorities. To avoid this problem, provincial finance ministers have persuaded the federal government to allow them greater flexibility in managing their own tax systems.

This has led to the revival of provincial proposals from the early 1990s to decentralize the personal income tax system, giving the provinces (and territories) greater flexibility to manage their own tax systems by allowing them to set their own rate structures on a common definition of income — the so-called "Tax on Income" system.

THE REVIVAL OF THE "TAX ON INCOME" PROPOSAL

Like most ideas for tax reform, current proposals to provide provincial governments greater flexibility in the design of their personal income-tax systems reflect years of discussion and debate among federal and provincial government officials.[15]

The "tax on income" concept, or TonI as it is known among senior tax officials, is intended to allow the nine provincial governments which have participated in the federal-provincial tax collection agreements since 1962 to set their own tax rates and brackets on a common definition of taxable income, while continuing to contract with the federal government for the collection and administration of personal income taxes.

Federal and provincial finance ministers agreed in principle on the proposed change in December 1997, delegating responsibility for the details of the new system to a federal-provincial committee of senior officials, which issued its report in October 1998.[16]

This agreement reflects the broader trend toward the "provincialization" of fiscal policy discussed earlier by allowing provincial governments to design tax-rate structures more responsive to local political and economic conditions while maintaining several features of the present system that are central features of Canada's economic union.

1. a common definition of taxable income, to be defined by the federal government;

2. a core system of tax preferences and expenditures based on the federal definition of income, which provide a common base of entitlements to all Canadians and which help to maintain the coherence of fiscal policies;

3. maintaining the centralized collection of personal income taxes and source deductions, thus avoiding the creation of separate tax-collection bureaucracies in each province and increased administrative and compliance costs to employers and individual taxpayers; and

4. allowing the new Canada Customs and Revenue Agency, successor to Revenue Canada, to administer different provincial tax initiatives:

    *   *free of charge* — if they mimic comparable provisions of the federal tax system,
    *   *at their incremental cost of administration* — if somewhat different from comparable federal provisions, but still provided for within the tax-collection agreements, and
    *   *at full cost recovery* — if outside policy harmonization agreements.[17]

These changes provide for a rationalization of provincial tax structures, which have become increasingly convoluted since the mid-1980s, as most provinces have introduced a series of surtaxes, flat taxes, and low income-tax credits in addition to the basic "tax on tax" levied as a percentage of federal income taxes payable (see Table A-1).

Several provinces, mainly in western Canada, sought to persuade the federal government to accommodate their revenue needs and differing tax policy objectives by allowing them to shift from the existing "tax on tax" system to a "tax on income" system as early as 1987.[18] During the early 1990s, federal and provincial officials worked together to develop options for resolving technical issues. A joint Discussion Paper relating to these issues was released in 1991.[19] However, growing pressures of other issues, particularly those related to controlling federal and provincial deficits, and the strong opposition of many tax professionals and business groups side-tracked further action on the tax on income for several years.[20]

Provincial tax officials, especially in Alberta and Manitoba, continued to work out the details of a feasible tax on income proposal for much of the mid-1990s, although the proposal languished in the absence of political support.[21] One senior tax-policy observer, noting the effects of unilateral federal actions on federal-provincial relations during the period, commented that "if the provinces were not simply to be subject to the whims of the federal tax base and tax rates, they had to gain somewhat greater control over the provincial tax situation."[22] However, they also recognized the political and economic benefits to their citizens of maintaining a common tax base and a common tax-collection system with the federal government, including:

- a common definition of what constitutes income for tax purposes;
- a common set of deductions that recognizes the importance of certain expenditures such as child care expenses, medical expenses, education costs and retirement planning;
- a common definition of residency, ensuring that taxpayers will be taxed fairly; and
- a common tax administration, allowing provincial residents to file only one tax return and follow a common set of tax rules.[23]

When the tax on income proposal resurfaced in 1997, both political and financial conditions had changed. The federal government, having balanced its budget, could look forward to the prospect of lowering its income taxes, with a corresponding impact on provincial tax revenues. The tax on income proposal would allow the provinces to shield their tax bases against erosion by unilateral reductions in federal tax rates, and prevent them from using federal tax cuts as an excuse to raise their own tax rates as they had following federal tax reforms in 1987-89. If provinces took advantage of the new system to reduce taxes, Ottawa could use this as an excuse not to accommodate provincial demands for increased transfer payments — arguing that most provinces already enjoyed all the potential revenue sources necessary to finance their public services.[24]

Another factor that may have served as a catalyst for federal consent to the decentralization of tax policies was Ontario's implicit threat to withdraw from the federal-provincial tax-collection agreements and to set up a separate

provincial income tax system.[25] Federal and Ontario officials had clashed repeatedly over provincial attempts to modify the Ontario tax system to
accommodate a series of changes related to the restructuring of the province's
public sector and to speed up Ottawa's remittance of taxes collected on behalf
of the provincial government. Other areas of conflict included Ottawa's refusal to collect Ontario's proposed "fair share health levy" as a separate,
graduated tax, while collecting supplemental "flat taxes" on behalf of Alberta,
Saskatchewan, and Manitoba, and administrative delays in implementing new
tax credits that could be accommodated within the tax-collection agreements.[26]
While previous Ontario governments had talked about withdrawing from the
tax-collection agreements, the Harris government's demonstrated willingness
to disregard established political conventions posed a far greater potential threat
to federal leadership and the coherence of national tax policies than the com-
paratively moderate proposals of the western provinces.

At the federal-provincial finance ministers' meeting in December 1997, five
provincial governments, led by Manitoba and Alberta, presented a renewed
tax on income proposal carefully designed to accommodate federal sensitivi-
ties. Paul Martin and his provincial colleagues approved the proposal in
principle, and delegated its implementation to a working group of senior officials which released its consensus report in October 1998. The federal
government agreed to accommodate provincial tax reform proposals consistent with the consensus tax on income report, with provisions for
implementation by 1 January 2001. In response, several provincial governments announced public consultations on provincial tax reforms: Alberta, after
its 1998 budget and four other provinces during 1999.

EMERGING PROVINCIAL TAX REFORM INITIATIVES

Four provinces — Alberta, Manitoba, Saskatchewan, and Newfoundland —
set up independent tax review commissions during 1998 and 1999 to receive
public comments on the tax on income proposal and to examine potential options for its implementation. All four provinces have announced their firm or
"likely" intentions to move to a "tax on income" system in 2001.

Ontario, which tabled an election-year budget promising sizeable tax cuts
in May 1999, left its options open before announcing its commitment to im-
plement "a tax on income" in late November. Prince Edward Island and New
Brunswick also announced plans to study the concept during the year. British
Columbia and Nova Scotia announced in February 2000 that they would adopt
TonI, while passing on "the full benefit of any federal income tax reduction."[27]
These proposals are likely to take shape during the coming year.

ALBERTA

Alberta has been the catalyst for much of the provincial tax reform process. Its approach to tax reform appears to reflect a mixture of home-grown political issues and ongoing concerns for the competitiveness of both Albertan and Canadian tax systems compared to those of neighbouring American states.[28] Due to its oil and gas revenues, Alberta's revenue and spending levels were consistently the highest of any province during the 1980s. However, falling energy prices led to huge deficits during the late 1980s and early 1990s, and subsequently to deep spending cuts (see Table 2). These cuts, along with growing economic diversification, permitted the Klein government to run consistent surpluses during the 1990s, even with highly volatile energy revenues.

The Alberta Tax Review Committee is the third body set up to examine issues of tax rates and structure in Alberta since 1993. The committee's mandate was relatively narrow: to examine the tax on income proposal, to suggest whether corporate tax changes were necessary to assist "knowledge-based industries," and to examine the impact of proposed tax changes on competitiveness, families, marginal rates, and the "work-welfare trade-off."[29] Provincial Treasurer Stockwell Day announced early in the committee process that the government would not accept any recommendation leading to the creation of a provincial sales tax or higher provincial taxes. The committee's membership included the chairs of previous provincial tax reviews, a leading academic tax expert, tax professionals, and two sitting members of the government's legislative caucus.

Two major themes emerged from the committee's public consultation process. There was broad support, particularly from the province's business community, for a single rate system — a major departure from the existing system of progressive income tax rates which has been the norm for federal and provincial income tax systems since the Second World War. Consultations also revealed strong support for measures to reduce the tax difference between single and dual income families in order to provide parents with greater choice in balancing the trade-offs between work and family needs.[30] Courchene has noted that these two objectives became mutually reinforcing as a single rate system — with high individual and spousal tax thresholds — is a simpler and politically less controversial way of reducing tax disparities between one and two income households with similar incomes than is the introduction of joint filing, as in the United States.[31]

The committee's report, released in October 1998, proposed acceptance of the tax on income system, a single rate tax of 11 percent on all income over a basic personal exemption of $11,620 (compared with the existing federal threshold of $6,456), and an equal spousal credit. The increased tax threshold was vital to ensure that the proposed single rate tax system would result in a net tax reduction for most Albertans — a critical condition for winning broad public support for the proposed changes.

The committee also recommended the elimination of Alberta's existing "deficit-reduction" surtaxes and its 0.5 percent flat tax on net income, and the indexing of basic exemptions to inflation. The costs of the tax reform proposals were later estimated by the government at $600 million: about 4 percent of its own-source revenues for 1998-99.[32]

The effect of the committee's report was to eliminate or substantially reduce the personal income taxes payable by lower income Albertans, and cut the top provincial marginal tax rate from 14.3 percent to 11 percent. The resulting combined federal-provincial marginal rate of 41.5 percent would be the lowest in Canada. Middle-income families with children would receive sizeable tax cuts; those without would face minimal changes. University of Calgary economist Ken McKenzie notes that, when all provincial taxes are taken into account, the single rate tax "will help solidify Alberta's position as the lowest taxed jurisdiction in the country."[33]

Stockwell Day announced the government's acceptance of the committee's report in his March 1999 budget and its decision to phase-in the proposed tax reforms between 2000 and 2002 subject to their "affordability" — its ability to generate continued surpluses. In October 1999, Premier Klein announced the elimination of the province's "deficit-reduction" surtax 18 months "early" in January 2000 and the implementation of the new single rate system in January 2001.[34]

Alberta's proposed tax reforms have been relatively uncontroversial within the province — reflecting its fiscal and cultural conservatism and the proverbial reluctance of taxpayers to "shoot Santa Claus." However, they prompted a significant response in neighbouring Saskatchewan, which appointed its Personal Income Tax Review Committee just before the Romanow government faced the voters in a general election.

SASKATCHEWAN

The Government of Saskatchewan has long supported the introduction of a parallel provincial "tax on income" system. However, until now, the Romanow government has shown a strong commitment to relying mainly on progressive taxes for revenue growth and reducing its reliance on consumption taxes. After balancing its budget in 1994-95, it reduced sales taxes in its 1997 budget in line with this commitment. However, while Saskatchewan's relative reliance on personal income tax revenues in recent years has been comparable to Alberta's and British Columbia's, (see Table 5), its relatively narrow economic base and sharply progressive tax rate system have given it the second highest average personal income tax rate of any province (see Table 6).

Table 5: Distribution of Provincial Own-Source Revenues By Revenue Source (in percent)

	Personal Income Tax	Corporate Income and Capital Taxes	Sales Tax	Social Ins. Taxes	Liquor and Gambling	Resource Income	Property Taxes
Canada	35	11	18	6	6	4	2
Nfld.	33	7	27	4	10	2	0
PEI	29	6	28	0	6	0	6
NS	37	6	27	0	10	0	0
NB	34	4	24	0	3	5	10
Que.	41	9	18	12	4	1	0
Ont.	34	15	23	6	6	1	0
Man.	35	9	20	5	9	1	0
Sask.	30	9	16	0	9	13	0
Alta.	30	11	0	4	8	15	7
BC	30	9	17	5	6	10	7

Source: *Provincial Budgets 1999-2000; Ontario Economic Outlook & Fiscal Review,* November 1999.

Table 6: Average Provincial Personal Income Tax Rates (in percent) – 1999*

Ontario	43.5	Prince Edward Island	59.7
Alberta	48.4	New Brunswick	60.8
British Columbia	53.7	Saskatchewan	66.8
Manitoba	56.6	Newfoundland	70.3**
Nova Scotia	57.2		

Notes: * Ratio of provincial to federal income tax revenues.
       ** Newfoundland has announced plans to reduce its basic tax rate, while introducing a system of graduated surtaxes.

Source: Saskatchewan Finance, Saskatchewan Personal Income Tax Review Committee *Report* (Regina: Saskatchewan Finance, 1999), p. 9.

Like Alberta, the Saskatchewan government set up a Tax Review Committee to review the tax on income proposal and make recommendations to guide its possible implementation. Unlike in Alberta, the committee was made up solely of tax experts, including its chair, University of Saskatchewan accounting professor and former senior Finance Ministry official Jack Vicq. The committee's mandate was to recommend changes to the province's tax system in order to promote "fairness in the tax system; support for the family; simplicity for both the tax filer and the Government; and competitiveness in attracting jobs and investment to Saskatchewan."[35]

The committee's consultation process was interrupted by a provincial election, which saw the Romanow government reduced to a legislative minority dependent on Liberal support. Premier Romanow used the NDP's campaign platform to promise tax reductions of up to $200 million — about 4 percent of the provincial tax base. This effectively broadened the committee's mandate and made it possible to recommend much larger reductions in PIT rates than would otherwise have been the case to make the province's tax system more competitive with Alberta's.

The Saskatchewan Tax Review Committee's report was clearly influenced by Alberta's proposed tax reforms, and by concerns raised during consultations that many upper income taxpayers were already moving to Alberta for tax-planning purposes. It recommended that the province's basic tax rate match the proposed Alberta rate at 11 percent, albeit with a lower income threshold. (See Table 7.) Concerns over work/family trade-offs were to be accommodated by equalizing the basic personal and spousal exemptions and eliminating the 2 percent flat rate income tax on net income over $10,000. Concerns over high marginal rates and taxpayer flight were to be addressed by increasing the ceiling on the new middle income tax bracket to $100,000 (from the current $59,000) and by matching Alberta's capital gains tax rate of 11 percent on profits from the sale of small businesses and family farms. As a result, Saskatchewan would sharply reduce the personal income tax gap with Alberta and have the second lowest top marginal rate of any Canadian province.[36]

As the price tag of the proposed reforms — about $427 million — was well outside the committee's fiscal terms of reference, it recommended an offsetting increase of $187 million in the sales tax base while lowering the sales tax rate from 6 percent to 5 percent and increasing provincial offsets provided to lower income families, seniors, and others.

This would result in the taxation of currently exempted products including restaurant meals, insurance premiums, entertainment, and non-prescription drugs. The proposed taxation of necessities such as utility payments and children's clothing — valued at about 25 percent of the proposed increase or about $68 annually for the average family — has been the most debated element of the proposed changes. Some have charged that this would effectively reverse

Table 7: Tax Competition on the Prairies

		Alberta		Saskatchewan	
		Current (1999)	Proposed (2001)	Current (1999)	Proposed (2003)
Basic exemption	($)	6,794	11,620	6,794	8,500
Spousal credit	($)	5,718	11,620	5,718	8,500
Inflation indexing		Ad hoc[1]	Automatic	Ad hoc[1]	Automatic
Basic tax rate[2]	(%)	7.98	11	11.18	11
Middle income rate	(%)	11.94	11	15.93	13
Threshold	($)	29,590	n/a	29,590	35,000
Middle income surtax	(%)	12.86	none	18.10	none
Threshold	($)	45,403		39,201	
Upper income rate	(%)	14.28	11	19.90	15
Threshold	($)	59,181		59,181	100,000
Top fed.-prov. marginal rate	(%)	45.2	41.45	50.8	45.45
Threshold	($)	63,704	63,704	63,704	100,000

Notes: [1] Changes to basic personal and spousal credits and tax rate thresholds adjusted at discretion of federal government, or by annual rates of inflation in excess of 3 percent.
   [2] Current rates include supplementary flat taxes.

Sources: Alberta Tax Review Committee; Saskatchewan Personal Income Tax Review Committee.

the government's high-profile decision of 1991 to scrap the harmonization of provincial sales taxes with the federal Goods and Services Tax.[37]

Initial feedback suggests that the Saskatchewan government is likely to accept the broad outlines of the Tax Review Committee report, although the precise timing and details of its implementation still remain to be determined at the time of writing.

MANITOBA

Manitoba has less fiscal flexibility than either Alberta or Saskatchewan in implementing provincial tax reforms. It currently depends on both personal income taxes and sales taxes for a larger share of its revenues than either of its Prairie neighbours (see Table 5). Its sales tax base is significantly broader than Saskatchewan's, precluding major revenue gains from base broadening.[38] Balanced budget legislation requires a province-wide referendum before increasing tax rates on several major taxes. While Manitoba's overall personal taxes on lower income individuals and families are comparable to or lower than Alberta pre-reform tax levels, its tax rates are also more sharply progressive.[39]

The newly-elected government of NDP Premier Gary Doer has committed itself to reducing property taxes, described by one official as "our biggest competitive disadvantage on the tax side,"[40] modest income tax reductions, and small business tax cuts over its mandate. Finance Minister Greg Selinger announced Manitoba's intent to introduce a tax on income system in December 1999. The rather political complexion and mandate of the province's "Lower Tax Commission," appointed by the outgoing Filmon government, has complicated the tax reform challenge facing the Doer government. Chaired by former Conservative Finance Minister Clayton Manness, the commission was given a broad mandate to review Manitoba's tax system, and recommend changes to the structures and mix of personal, business, consumption and family taxation. The commission's report, issued in February 2000, recommended increases in personal and family exemptions and credits and a two-rate tax system — 14 percent on all "non-sheltered taxable income up to $150,000, and 17 percent thereafter."[41] It also recommended replacing Manitoba's refundable income tax credits and rebates for lower and middle-income taxpayers, currently Canada's highest at $114 per head, with a system of targeted cash grants.[42] While the government is unlikely to respond to these proposals until its budget, expected in March 2000, the adoption of quasi-Alberta-style tax reforms by a NDP government would signal a major shift in Manitoba's political culture.

In January 2000, the Doer government reduced Manitoba's personal income tax rate from 48.5 percent to 47 percent of the basic federal tax. A comparable TonI structure, absorbing the province's existing flat tax and surtax, and using existing tax bracket thresholds, would result in the following rates as shown on Table 8.

While Manitoba's basic tax rate would be close to Saskatchewan's under such a system, it remains to be seen whether its government will be under significant pressure to follow its western neighbour in reducing tax rates for middle-income earners and broadening its application to taxpayers earning more than $60,000.

ONTARIO

Ontario already enjoys Canada's lowest provincial income tax rates. The Harris government promised further tax cuts in its pre-election budget of May 1999.

Table 8: Tax Reform Options in Manitoba

| | Extending Current Rate System | | | Lower Tax Commission | |
	Rate (%)	Threshold* ($)		Rate (%)	Threshold ($)
		(1999)	(2004)		
Basic tax rate:	10.00	6,794	8,000	14	7,700/11,000+
Middle income rate	16.22	29,591**	35,000	n/a	
Upper income rate	17.63	59,180	70,000	17	150,000

Note: * Assumes continued use of federal tax bracket thresholds.
   ** Single taxpayer; threshold increases with dependents.
   + Single individual $11,000; couple: $15,400; $3,300 for each extra child; to be indexed to inflation.

Sources: Government of Manitoba, *Final Report of the Manitoba Lower Tax Commission*, February 2000; Canada, *Budget 2000* (Ottawa: Department of Finance, 28 February 2000).

The province's basic tax rate was reduced from 40.5 percent of basic federal tax to 38.5 percent on 1 July 1999. The Tories' election platform promised to reduce this further to 32.5 percent by 2004 as well as reducing the education portion of property taxes by 20 percent — about $500 million.[43]

However, Treasurer Ernie Eves has been extremely vocal over what he views as a lack of federal commitment to the concept of "shared jurisdiction" in tax policy, particularly the federal government's reluctance to accommodate a series of social policy initiatives delivered through the tax system. Eves announced in November 1999 that Ontario would implement a tax on income that would "no longer be subject to hidden tax increases in the federal tax system."[44] He also announced plans to set up a Business Tax Review Committee to propose changes to the province's tax system. However, as the Canada Customs and Revenue Agency requires that the details of proposed changes be submitted by 31 March 2000 for implementation in the 2001 tax year, and Ontario budgets are usually tabled in May, it is unlikely that provincial tax reform proposals will be implemented before 2002.

Conversion of existing and promised provincial tax rates and the incorporation of existing surtaxes into a separate provincial rate structure would result in the following five-bracket tax structure by 2004.

Table 9: Ontario Tax-bracket Structure with Tax on Income

| | Rate | | Threshold* | |
	1999	2004	1999	2004
	(%)		($)	
Basic tax rate	6.72	5.53	6,794	8,000
Middle income rate	10.27	8.45	29,591	35,000
Middle income surtax	12.32	10.14	52,700	52,700
Upper income rate (before surtaxes)	13.75	11.31	59,180	70,000
Top tax rate	17.87	14.70	61,500	?

Note: * Assumes use of proposed federal tax thresholds (February 2000).

A more realistic expectation would be for Ontario to increase its basic personal exemptions and income thresholds as proposed in Saskatchewan so that the middle and upper income tax rates take effect at significantly higher levels than at present. Ontario is unlikely to compete with Alberta for the lowest top marginal rate among the provinces, but it is likely to ensure that tax rates *are* either lower or comparable for the vast majority of taxpayers earning less than $100,000 a year.

NEWFOUNDLAND AND ATLANTIC CANADA

The Atlantic provinces have personal income tax rates and overall provincial tax levels (except Nova Scotia) over the national average — despite depending on federal transfers for a disproportionate share of their revenues (see Tables 1 and 5). Despite sales tax reductions arising from the harmonization of their provincial sales tax bases with the federal Goods and Services Tax in 1996, they also depend more heavily than other provinces on general sales taxes.

Both New Brunswick and Newfoundland have expressed concerns over the impact of high marginal tax rates and the likely loss of provincial revenues as a result of expected federal tax reductions. Newfoundland's fiscal challenges have been complicated by its loss of 42,000 residents (about 7 percent of its population) between 1992 and 1999.

Newfoundland Premier Brian Tobin assigned responsibility for tax review to his Advisory Council on the Economy and Technology in August 1999. The council's November 1999 report recommended the creation of a tax on income system and reductions of provincial tax rates from 69 percent of the basic federal tax (BFT) to the equivalent of 59 percent of BFT over three years, to be financed in part by higher corporate income taxes on manufacturing, but not through budget deficits.[45]

Shortly thereafter, Tobin announced plans to cut the basic provincial tax rate by up to 28 percent over three years "if it is fiscally responsible to do so," along with the introduction of graduated surtaxes and the "likely" introduction of a tax on income in 2001. This would reduce Newfoundland's core personal income tax rate to 49 percent of the basic federal tax rate.[46]

New Brunswick has also announced its intention to reduce provincial tax rates and "study" the implementation of a tax on income. Prince Edward Island announced its intention to "assess the desirability of this fundamental change" in its 1999 budget.[47] While Nova Scotia's sizeable provincial deficit leaves it little room for tax cuts in the short term, the probable impact of federal tax reductions on its tax base and the competitive pressure of expected tax cuts in neighbouring provinces have prompted it to join other provinces planning to implement a tax on income system.

CONCLUSION

The spreading acceptance of the "tax on income" concept as a central feature of emerging provincial tax reforms reflects a series of pragmatic trade-offs both in relations between the federal and provincial governments and in the policy choices of provincial governments representing virtually the full spectrum of Canadian politics.

The federal government has recognized that to maximize its own fiscal and political discretion in making the most of the looming fiscal dividend, it must increase the political and administrative flexibility of the provinces in designing their tax systems, or face sharply increased demands for higher transfer payments to offset regional disparities and growing provincial health and education costs. The provinces — ever prone to demand more money from Ottawa while insisting on greater flexibility in its use — are ill-equipped to do so while most are in the process of reducing their own tax rates.

Despite sizeable tax cuts in Ontario, and growing regional competition on the Prairies and in Atlantic Canada to match the tax reductions of neighbouring provinces, internal political conditions appear to play a larger role in defining the distribution and rate levels of provincial taxes than external tax competition. The growing progressivity of federal and provincial tax systems — in which a large majority of voters receive more in services than they pay in taxes — along with the perception of tax reductions as a zero-sum game by many Canadians, effectively limit the tax-cutting dynamic in many provinces, especially those with strongly social democratic governments.[48]

The nature of specific provincial tax reforms will depend largely on the willingness and capacity of regional political leaders to take advantage of the current window of opportunity created by relatively buoyant economies and the federal government's willingness to accommodate widely varying provincial priorities within the tax-collection agreements.

NOTES

The author wishes to express appreciation to Harvey Lazar and an anonymous reviewer for their helpful comments, to a number of officials in federal and provincial finance departments and ministries for their insights and suggestions.

1. Dagmar Dyck and Bev Dahlby, "Alberta and the Provincialization of the Canadian Fiscal System," (Edmonton: Institute for Public Economics, University of Alberta, unpublished paper, 1999). The so-called "five-province report" was published as *Federal Administration of Provincial Taxes,* Annex 4, (Ottawa: Department of Finance, 2000). The federal-provincial consensus agreement is outlined in *Tax on Income, Report prepared by the Federal-Provincial Committee on Taxation for presentation to Ministers of Finance* (Ottawa: Department of Finance, 1998).

2. Dyck and Dahlby, "Alberta and the Provincialization of the Canadian Fiscal System; Thomas J. Courchene, "National vs. Regional Concerns: A Provincial Perspective on the Role and Operation of the Tax Collection Agreements," *Canadian Tax Journal* 47, 4 (1999):861-89.

3. Canada, *The Fiscal Balance in Canada* (Ottawa: Department of Finance, 1999).

4. Interview, former federal deputy minister of finance.

5. Federal officials suggest that this reluctance was the natural by-product of not wishing to introduce major, and possibly irreversible changes to the tax structure without working out both major policy and technical implications first. Provincial officials were more inclined to attribute federal "resistance" to the tax on income to their concerns over preserving federal control over the tax system. These debates were renewed when Ontario sought to introduce significant changes to its tax system after 1995.

6. Geoffrey E. Hale, "Managing the Fiscal Dividend: The Politics of Selective Activism," in *How Ottawa Spends: 2000-01,* ed. Leslie A. Pal (Toronto: Oxford University Press, forthcoming).

7. Courchene, "National vs. Regional Concerns," p. 862.

8. Bruce Little, "Q. Who supplies Canada's trading muscle? A: Ont...," *The Globe and Mail,* 13 December 1999, p. A10.

9. In Alberta, this has included elimination of the provincial business property tax on machinery and equipment in 1996-97, introduction of a uniform provincial education tax rate, and recommendations to average and cap property tax increases arising from rapid increases in property values. Alberta, *Treasury Annual Report for the Fiscal Year Ended March 31, 1997* (Edmonton: Alberta Treasury, 1997); Alberta. Education Property Tax Committee, *Interim Report* (Edmonton: Alberta Treasury, 4 October 1999). In Ontario, the 1998 budget introduced phased reductions of education taxes on commercial and industrial properties over average provincial rates. Ontario, *1998 Ontario Budget* (Toronto: Ministry of Finance, May 1998), pp. 90-93, 98.

10. The Financial Management System used by Statistics Canada applies consistent accounting rules to all levels of government, unlike the "public accounts" which

are subject to a variety of different accounting conventions from province to province.

11. Even the NDP government of British Columbia, the only government not to reduce its spending in real per capita terms between 1992 and 1996, was re-elected largely on the basis of its pretended success in balancing the budget — although the figures used to support this claim later turned out to be the product of very dubious accounting practices.

12. Canada, *Fiscal Reference Tables* (Ottawa: Department of Finance, September 1999), p.33. Alberta amended its *Fiscal Responsibility Act* late in 1999 to allow for spending of more than 25 percent of projected revenue windfalls for in-year spending initiatives and has announced major spending increases in coming years.

13. This truism is confirmed by Kneebone and McKenzie's analysis of the discretionary fiscal stance of nine provinces during the early and mid-1990s. Ronald D. Kneebone and Kenneth J. McKenzie, "Fiscal Policy in Canada," *Canadian Public Policy/Analyse de Politiques* 25, 4 (1999):488-92.

14. *The Fiscal Balance in Canada*; John McCallum, "Relative Power: Ottawa vs. the Provinces," (Toronto: *Royal Bank Economics*, September 1999).

15. Interviews, current and former Finance/Treasury officials of Manitoba, Saskatchewan, and Alberta governments.

16. *Tax on Income*, Report prepared for the Federal-Provincial Committee on Taxation for presentation to Ministers of Finance; Canada, *Federal Administration of Provincial Taxes* (Ottawa: 25 January 2000).

17. Munir A. Sheikh and Michel Carreau, "A Federal Perspective on the Role and Operation of the Tax Collection Agreements," *Canadian Tax Journal* 47, 4 (1999):845-60. Explanations of the detailed impact of this agreement on each province may be found in "Application of Framework for Federal Administration of Federal Taxes," *Federal Administration of Provincial Taxes,* Annex 5. (Ottawa: Supply and services Canada, 2000).

18. Saskatchewan, *Tax on Income: Discussion Paper* (Regina: Ministry of Finance, 1988).

19. Canada, *Personal Income Tax Coordination: The Federal-Provincial Tax Collection Agreements* (Ottawa: Department of Finance, 1991).

20. Interviews, federal Department of Finance and Alberta Treasury. Explanations for the breakdown in negotiations by federal and provincial officials reflect rather different perceptions by federal and provincial officials.

21. Interview, Government of Alberta.

22. Interview, member, Alberta Tax Review Committee. This theme surfaced over and over again in interviews with provincial officials.

23. Saskatchewan, "Redesign of Provincial Income Taxation," in *1999 Saskatchewan Budget* (Regina: Ministry of Finance, 1999).

24. Giles Gherson, "Martin to Tell Provinces He Needs Surplus," *National Post*, 9 December 1999, p. A7; A. Toulin, "Ministers Seek Tax Cuts that Won't Affect their Revenues," *National Post*, 9 December 1999, p. A7. Provincial officials

interviewed for this chapter suggest that federal officials tacitly encouraged the development of provincial tax on income proposals after 1996.

25. Ontario, *1999 Ontario Budget* (Toronto: Ministry of Finance, 1999), p. 35; Courchene, "National vs. Regional Concerns," pp. 867-68. This contention is strongly challenged by federal officials. However, it is inherently difficult to prove as no government would ever concede its willingness to accommodate such pressure tactics, thereby encouraging more of them.

26. Ibid. The Finance Department defends its position by noting that proposed provincial changes are often introduced on short notice, and that existing agreements often require consultation with other provinces on the potential effects of such changes on other provinces and on the economic union. It also notes changes made to accelerate revenue flows under tax-collection agreements. *Federal Collection of Provincial Taxes,* Annex 4 and Annex 6 (Ottawa: Supply and Services Canada, 2000).

27. "Province to Change Method of Collecting Income Tax," Press Release, Nova Scotia Department of Finance, 23 February 2000; "Province to Ensure Tax Cuts Go to Those Most in Need," News Release, British Columbia Ministry of Finance and Corporate Relations, 24 February 2000.

28. Interviews, Alberta Tax Review Committee.

29. Alberta Tax Review Committee, *Terms of Reference* (Edmonton: Alberta Treasury, 25 May 1998.)

30. Interviews, Alberta Tax Review Committee.

31. Courchene, "National vs. Regional Concerns," pp. 878-79. The Alberta proposal has subsequently been adopted as the basis for federal tax reform proposals advanced by the new Canadian Alliance. Monte Solberg, MP, "The Single Rate Tax," unpublished paper, 27 January 2000.

32. Alberta Tax Review Committee, *Final Report and Recommendations,* October 1998; Alberta, *Budget 99: Government of Alberta Fiscal Plan,* 11 March 1999, p.127.

33. Kenneth J. McKenzie, "O'Brien's Last Stand: An Examination of the Single Rate Tax," unpublished paper, (Edmonton: Institute for Public Economics, University of Alberta, 1999), p.11.

34. Alberta, Press Release (Edmonton: Premier's Office, 14 October 1999).

35. Saskatchewan, "Redesign of Provincial Income Taxation," March 1999.

36. Saskatchewan, *Report of the Saskatchewan Personal Income Tax Review Committee,* (Regina: Ministry of Finance, November 1999).

37. Interview, Government of Saskatchewan; Murray Mandryk, "A Reversal in Thinking for NDP," *Regina Leader Post,* 6 December 1999; *Report of the Saskatchewan Personal Income Tax Review Committee,* p. 61.

38. Interview, Government of Manitoba.

39. *Report* of Saskatchewan Personal Income Tax Review Committee, Tables 1, 2, 15, 16.

40. Interview, Government of Manitoba.

41. Manitoba Lower Tax Commission, *Final Report* (Winnipeg: Ministry of Finance, 10 February 2000), p. 11.

42. Ibid., pp. 50-52.

43. *1999 Ontario Budget* (Toronto: Ministry of Finance, May 1999), pp. 69-70, 84-88.

44. Hon. Ernie Eves, "Statement to the Legislature," (Toronto: Ministry of Finance, 30 November 1999), p.4.

45. Newfoundland, *Report of the Premier's Advisory Council on the Economy and Technology — Provincial Tax Review* (St. John's: Premier's Advisory Council, November 1999).

46. Newfoundland, "Multi-Year Tax Reductions Announced," (St. John's: Executive Council, 16 November 1999).

47. Prince Edward Island, "Budget Paper C: Personal Income Taxes," *The 1999 Provincial Budget* (Charlottetown: Department of Provincial Treasury, 6 April 1999), p. 4.

48. Michael Walker, "Why Polls Don't Tell the Whole Truth on Tax Cuts," *Financial Post,* 7 December 1999, p. C7; Ekos Research Associates, *Reinventing Government: Understanding Conflicting Priorities on Tax Cuts, Social Spending and Productivity* (Ottawa: Ekos Research Associates, 1999); Earnscliffe Research Associates, *Policy Priorities and Economic Assumptions* (Ottawa: Department of Finance, 1999); Earnscliffe Research Associates, *Themes, Taxes and Productivity* (Ottawa: Department of Finance, 1999).

APPENDIX

Table A-1: Personal Income Tax – Provincial Comparisons

		Basic Rate (as percent of Basic Federal Tax)		Surtax Rate (%)	Surtax Threshold ($)	Supplemental Flat Tax or General Payroll Tax?
Nfld.	1999	69.0		10	60,100	Payroll Tax (2.1%)
	1995	69.0		—	—	
	1988	60.0		—	—	
PEI	1999	58.5		10	50,400	No
	1995	59.5		10	92,777	
	1988	56.0		5	95,408	
NS	1999	57.5		10	80,600	No
	1995	59.5		10	78,288	
	1988	56.5		—	—	
NB	1999	60.0		8	98,200	No
	1995	64.0		8	93,071	
	1988	60.0		—	—	
Que.	1999	Separate Rate Structure				Payroll Tax (4.26%)
Ont.	1999	39.5	(1)	20	52,700	Payroll Tax
			(2)	56	61,500	(0.98/1.95%)
	1995	58.0	(1)	20	52,300	
			(2)	30	67,900	
	1988	51.0		10	86,051	
Man.	1999	48.5		2	30,000	Flat Tax (2%)[1]
	1995	52.0		2	30,000	Payroll Tax (2.15%)
	1988	54.0		2	30,000	

... continued

Table A-1 (continued)

		Basic Rate (as percent of Basic Federal Tax)		Surtax		Supplemental Flat Tax or General Payroll Tax?
				Rate (%)	Threshold ($)	
Sask.	1999	48.0	(1)	10	20,000	Flat Tax: (2%)[1]
			(2)	25	41,600	
	1995	50.0	(1)	10	12,900	
			(2)	25	40,400	
	1988	50.0		12	40,323	
Alta.	1999	44.0		8[2]	46,814	Flat Tax (0.5%)[1]
	1995	45.5		8	45,400	
	1988	46.5		8	43,168	
BC	1999	49.5	(1)	30	57,400	No
			(2)	49	80,900	
	1995	52.5	(1)	30	54,700	
			(2)	50	79,400	
	1988	51.5	—	—		

Note: [1]Net income threshold for Manitoba flat tax increased from $7,600 in 1988 to $8,391 in 1999 depending on number of dependents. Net income threshold for Saskatchewan flat tax: 1988: $10,000; 1995: $7,400; 1999: $10,000. Saskatchewan surtax levied on both provincial income and flat taxes. Taxable income threshold for Alberta flat tax increased from $9,550 in 1988 to $16,000 in 1999. Abolition proposed as part of shift to single rate tax in 2001.
[2]Alberta surtax abolished 1 January 2000.

Sources: Canadian Tax Foundation, *The National Finances: 1987-88* (Toronto: Canadian Tax Foundation, 1988); *Finances of the Nation, 1995* (Toronto: Canadian Tax Foundation, 1995); Alberta Treasury; Manitoba Department of Finance; Newfoundland Department of Finance (1999).

Geoffrey E. Hale

Table A-2: Provincial Tax Reductions 1995-1999

	Personal Income Tax	Corporate Income Tax	Retail Sales Tax	Payroll Tax
Newfoundland	*Post-1999[1] budget*		*1996 budget[2]*	*1999 budget* 1998 budget
PEI	1999 budget			
Nova Scotia	1998 budget 1996 budget		1996 budget[2]	
New Brunswick	1997 to 1999 budgets	1999 budget 1995 budget	1996 budget[2]	
Quebec	1999 budget *1997 budget*			1998 budget
Ontario	*1996 to 1999 Budgets*	*1998 budget*		*1998 budget* *1996 budget*
Manitoba	1999 budget 1998 budget	1999 budget		1998 budget 1997 budget
Saskatchewan	1998 budget	1995 budget	1999 budget 1997 budget	
Alberta	1999 budget 1998 budget			
British Columbia	*1999, 1998 & 1996 budgets*	*1999, 1998 & 1996 budgets*		

Notes: [1] Budgets presented in italics indicate that tax-reduction initiatives were announced prior to the balancing of the budget.
[2] Reduction of provincial sales taxes in conjunction with harmonization with federal Goods and Services Tax.

Source: Canada, *The Fiscal Balance in Canada* (Ottawa: Department of Finance, 8 December 1999), p. 10.

10

Tax Assignment in Canada: A Modest Proposal

Richard M. Bird and Jack M. Mintz

Des déséquilibres importants existent dans l'attribution des dépenses et des recettes au Canada. Le gouvernement fédéral prélève plus de recettes qu'il a de dépenses. Les municipalités comptent sur d'importants transferts des provinces. Les provinces jouent le rôle d'intermédiaires en recevant des transferts fédéraux qui, en gros, correspondent aux montants qu'elles transfèrent aux municipalités. L'attribution des impôts pose deux problèmes. Le premier en est un d'imputabilité, puisque le niveau de gouvernement responsable des dépenses n'a pas à porter l'odieux d'une augmentation des impôts face à l'électorat. Le second problème est que l'attribution défectueuse des impôts, laquelle produit des débordements horizontaux et verticaux, dénature la prestation privée et publique des biens et services. Ces deux problèmes d'imputabilité et d'attribution sont reliés au financement des dépenses de programme des municipalités, récemment transférées par les provinces, et aux taxes d'affaires déformantes des municipalités et des provinces dans une économie mondiale de plus en plus compétitive. Nous soutenons que la réattribution des impôts et les tentatives d'harmonisation ont atteint un cul-de-sac. Nous croyons plutôt que la solution aux problèmes d'attribution des impôts passe par une réforme fiscale provinciale et municipale. Nous soutenons que les gouvernements provinciaux devraient se retirer de certains champs fiscaux — taxes sur le revenus des entreprises, sur le capital et, peut-être, sur la masse salariale — au profit du gouvernement fédéral. Ces taxes devraient être remplacées par une taxe d'affaire sur la valeur. Une portion de cette taxe pourrait être versée aux municipalités pour leur permettre de réduire les impôts fonciers sur les propriétés non-résidentielles.

INTRODUCTION

"Who should tax, where, and what?" is how Richard Musgrave once characterized the question of tax assignment in a multi-level government.[1] This question has attracted increasing attention in recent years in Canada. Ip and Mintz, for example, suggested that the corporate income tax (CIT) should become entirely federal while the federal goods and services tax (GST) and excises should be replaced by appropriately increased provincial retail sales taxes and excises. Boadway went even further and proposed that the personal income tax (PIT) too should be entirely federal.[2] In contrast, Dahlby and

Ruggeri, Howard and Van Wart suggested that the PIT should be taken over entirely by the provinces, with the federal government taking over all provincial sales taxes (as well as the CIT).[3] In reviewing this discussion, Bird argued that it was most unlikely that either level of government would be willing to make any of these changes.[4] He suggested that the most likely scenario to prevail would be one in which both federal and at least some provincial governments would continue to levy PIT, CIT, and sales taxes. Bird agreed with Ip and Mintz that the tax-collection agreements worked fairly well for the PIT, but argued that the economic inefficiencies that resulted from less than perfectly integrated federal and provincial CITs could be viewed as simply one cost of our form of federalism.[5] Subsequently, Bird and Gendron, building in part upon Mintz, Wilson and Gendron and Gendron, Mintz andWilson, argued that the method of sharing the sales tax field as agreed between the federal and Quebec governments worked surprisingly well and indeed was preferable to the so-called "harmonized" sales tax (HST) adopted in several small provinces in 1998.[6]

As this very selective summary history shows, both authors of the present chapter have in the past discussed aspects of this subject with some, but by no means complete, agreement in the views expressed. Our aims in the present brief essay are three. The first is simply to revisit this subject and state our present, and basically joint, appraisal of the current situation with respect to tax assignment in Canada. The second is to suggest a new approach — our "modest proposal" (so named with due deference to Jonathan Swift's well-known prior use of this terminology!) — to this issue, encompassing local as well as federal and provincial taxation. Finally, we have attempted to move our proposal a bit closer to reality both by putting a little empirical flesh on our conceptual skeleton and by considering briefly a few of the additional questions that need to be taken into account in resolving these basic issues. The next three sections of the chapter take up these three aims in turn.

We do not, of course, think that we have by any means solved the fundamental fiscal conundrum of Canadian federalism in this brief essay. But we do hope at least to have introduced some new thinking into the arena and perhaps also to have been sufficiently provocative to stimulate others to rethink these matters as well.

WHERE ARE WE NOW?

Whether viewed from on high, essentially the position we adopt in this chapter or from the trenches in which taxpayers and officials live, the present assignment of taxes in Canada suffers from a variety of problems. The first and in many ways the most important problem is that there is a significant vertical imbalance between expenditures and revenues at all levels of government, with consequent implications for autonomy, efficiency, and accountability. The second major problem is that the present confused and confusing system results in significant costs — costs of administration, costs of compliance, and costs arising from tax-induced inefficient allocation of scarce resources. Our "modest proposal" essentially focuses on the second of these problems, but in the remainder of the present section we shall elaborate briefly on the origins and nature of both problems in order to set the stage for our proposed approach to resolving at least one of them to some extent.

Table 1 depicts the flow of revenues and expenditures to and between levels of government in 1996. As can be seen in this table, broadly speaking, the federal government collects about 2 percent more of gross domestic product (GDP) in revenues than it spends, other than on intergovernmental transfers, while the provinces as a whole collect about the same amount as they spend (net of transfers). What this means is that, in effect, the provinces as a whole pass on approximately the amount of the transfers they receive from the federal government — which constitute 20 percent of their net-of-transfer expenditures — to the municipalities, whose own revenues only suffice to cover a bit more than 50 percent of their expenditures.

Table 1: Own Revenues and Expenditures by Level of Government in 1996

Level of Government	Own Revenues (1)	Expenditures Less Transfers (2)	Own Surplus (3)=(1)–(2)	Received Transfers as % of Expenditures Net of Transfers (4)
	(% of GDP of Canada)			(%)
Federal	18.82	16.67	2.15	0.43
Provincial	17.50	17.49	0.01	20.03
Municipal	4.00	7.21	-3.21	52.01

Source: Based on Statistics Canada Cansim Time Series.

Table 2 looks more specifically at the allocation of tax revenues by level of government. While property taxes were collected almost entirely at the local level in 1995 outside of a few small eastern provinces — since then, more property taxes have accrued to the provincial level, especially in Ontario — all the other major sources of revenue are divided, in varying proportions, between the other two levels of government. The basic picture shown in Table 2 has remained broadly unchanged for the last 20 years although, as Figure 1 shows, provincial taxes had increased sharply in relative terms up to the mid-1970s.

Table 2: Tax Collections by Level of Government and Type of Tax in Selected Years

Type of Tax	Years	Federal	Provincial	Municipal	Total
		(% of total)			(% of GDP)
Personal Income Tax	1955	88.8	11.2	0.0	6.1
	1975	68.5	31.5	0.0	12.3
	1995	57.3	42.7	0.0	14.3
Corporate Income Tax	1955	95.5	4.5	0.0	4.5
	1975	73.4	26.6	0.0	4.4
	1995	69.2	30.8	0.0	2.6
Consumption Taxes	1955	69.6	30.4	0.0	8.3
	1975	51.4	48.6	0.0	8.6
	1995	41.1	58.9	0.0	9.7
Property Tax*	1955	0.0	0.0	100.0	3.0
	1975	0.0	0.0	100.0	3.2
	1995	0.0	0.0	100.0	4.5
Other	1955	1.3	74.7	24.1	0.3
	1975	0.7	93.8	5.5	0.6
	1995	7.0	65.2	27.8	1.0
Total Tax and Revenue	1955	70.0	16.2	13.8	22.2
	1975	55.2	33.7	11.1	29.1
	1995	48.9	38.1	11.1	36.1

Note: *Some property tax is collected by provinces and used to finance education or local services. See text for other discussion.

Source: Richard M. Bird and Duanjie Chen, "Federal Finance and Fiscal Federalism: The Two Worlds of Canadian Public Finance," *Canadian Public Administration* 41(1998):51-74, based on Statistics Canada Cansim Time Series.

Presented in this fashion, Canada appears to be a very peculiar country indeed, with the provinces in effect acting as an intermediary in redirecting federal revenues to municipalities and with all major taxes divided between the federal and provincial governments. Of course, this is by no means the only or even the most important story that can be told. Very important differences between various provinces are, for example, hidden in these aggregate numbers. Nonetheless, this brief account provides sufficient background

Figure 1: Tax Revenue as % of GDP by Level of Government 1950-1995

Source: Richard M. Bird and Duanjie Chen, "Federal Finance and Fiscal Federalism: The Two Worlds of Canadian Public Finance," *Canadian Public Administration* 41(1998):51-74.

against which to set out in a bit more detail the two major problems alluded to above.

IMBALANCE AND ACCOUNTABILITY

These problems fall into two classes: the broad issues of political economy connected with fiscal imbalance and the narrower, but not necessarily less important, issues associated with tax misassignment, as discussed further in the next subsection. From the perspective of efficient and effective government, broadly considered, the basic principles of tax assignment are simple: (i) each governmental unit should have adequate revenues to cover its expenditures, and (ii) each should also be able to affect its revenues by its own actions — for example, by altering tax rates, imposing new levies or abolishing old ones, changing tax bases, or exerting administrative effort. The extent to which the first of these principles is attained can be measured, roughly, by the aggregate data set out earlier. From this perspective, Canada scores very well in terms of the provincial level, at least in aggregate, and not very well at all with respect to the municipal sector.

Of course, matters would look much less healthy in this sense even at the provincial level if we consider what would happen if the provinces had to fund most of their current health and education transfers from, as an example, their own taxes on personal income rather than federal grants. Table 3 shows, by province, the percentage of provincial expenditures, including transfers to municipalities, that are financed out of their own current revenues, excluding transfers from the federal government. Similar ratios are shown, by province, for municipalities.

As this table shows, all provinces, even the richest, finance some of their expenditures from transfers, although with wide variation in the extent to which they are dependent on transfers. Similar variations in imbalance exist at the municipal level across provinces. The present system thus requires a significant flow of intergovernmental fiscal transfers in order not only to maintain vertical fiscal balance (between levels of government, especially at the provincial-local level) but also, more importantly, to maintain some degree of horizontal fiscal balance (between units of government at the same level).

Multi-tiered governments in principle work best when taxes and the benefits of public spending are as closely related as possible — when, that is, the citizens-voters-consumers residing in a particular political jurisdiction both pay for what they get from the public sector and benefit from the expenditures

Table 3: Own Revenues as % of Total Expenditures by Level of Government in 1995

Provinces	Provincial	Municipal
Newfoundland	58.75	61.44
Prince Edward Island	66.09	17.01
Nova Scotia	60.92	43.72
New Brunswick	68.25	59.38
Quebec	75.90	53.96
Ontario	76.10	66.40
Manitoba	74.01	55.38
Saskatchewan	83.33	70.62
Alberta	92.92	56.26
British Columbia	90.78	39.03

Source: Based on Statistics Canada Cansim Time Series.

made by the taxes they pay. Obviously, when citizens reside in several over-lapping jurisdictions (municipality-province-nation) this so-called "principle of fiscal equivalence"[7] suggests that they should pay taxes to each level corresponding to the benefits they receive from each jurisdiction. In this framework, the only rationale for intergovernmental transfers would be to restore this equivalence when, for example, some benefits flow ("spill over") from one jurisdiction to another or (negatively) when some taxes levied by one jurisdiction are in fact paid by ("exported to") persons residing in another jurisdiction. Moreover, such transfers would be horizontal, between provinces or municipalities, and not between levels of government.

If governments at all levels were indeed required to be more "self-financing" in this sense, differences in their capacities to raise revenues would, of course, affect tax burdens. Simply as an example, Table 4 illustrates the impact on provincial income taxes if Ontario alone were to become, in effect, "fiscally autonomous" by eliminating the (cash portion of) the CHST grant in 2003-04. (Other provinces would still receive some CHST grant.) This could be achieved if the federal government transferred 11.5 points under the personal income tax to Ontario (and, of course, other provinces). The result would be that, on average, the provinces would have to increase their PIT collections by 25 percent, with the largest increase being in Ontario. In reality, of course, such a change would lead to further adjustments in tax burdens and transfers for two reasons. First, as shown in Table 4, Quebec and the Atlantic provinces would have smaller increases in PIT revenues because each tax point is of lower value to them. Second, on the other hand, equalization payments, which are not shown in Table 4, would also increase, because the national average provincial PIT rate would increase, thus benefiting recipient provinces.

We are not recommending a major policy change for Canada along these lines. Nonetheless, it deserves to be emphasized that levying taxes on the basis that residents should pay for the benefits received from public services provided by the respective jurisdictions would minimize both horizontal and vertical spillovers. Horizontal spillovers may result in excessive levels of taxation since non-residents (= non-voters) in effect pay for services enjoyed by residents (= voters) to the extent taxes are exported.[8] Alternatively, the result may be too low a level of taxation for fear of loss of the tax base to other jurisdictions. Similarly, vertical spillovers may arise from the interdependence of tax decisions when different levels of government tax the same base — as in the case of the PIT — or if taxes at one level are deductible (e.g., the property tax from the CIT) or creditable at another level.[9] Still further spillovers may occur if one level of government incurs additional expenditure as a result of the tax policies of another. An example might be if high marginal rates imposed on low-income workers by one government reduced work incentives and hence increased the demand for welfare assistance from other levels of government.

Table 4: **Impact of Elimination of Cash Grant to Ontario and Increase the Tax-Point Transfer for the Year 2003-04**

Provinces	Current CHST (1)	Additional Tax Transfer (2)	New CHST (3)	Adjusted PIT (4)	Proportional Increase in PIT (5)
	($ Million)				(%)
Newfoundland	254	127	127	760	16.7
Prince Edward Island	68	35	34	177	19.5
Nova Scotia	463	277	186	1,384	20.0
New Brunswick	368	206	162	1,076	19.2
Quebec	3,649	2,492	1,157	12,063	20.7
Ontario	5,337	5,337	0	18,787	28.4
Manitoba	565	405	160	1,761	23.0
Saskatchewan	502	309	194	1,288	24.0
Alberta	1,347	1,323	24	5,059	26.2
British Columbia	2,385	1,603	781	6,827	23.5
Total	14,939	12,114	2,825	49,183	24.6

Notes: 1. "Current" refers to cash transfer under CHST made to each province as projected for 2003-04.
2. "Transfer" refers to a 11.5-point transfer of federal personal income tax to the provinces that would eliminate Ontario's cash grant.
3. "New" refers to the current cash grant reduced by the additional cash transfer [(3)=(1)-(2)].
4. Adjusted personal income tax excludes credits, surtaxes, and flat taxes as projected for the year 2003-04 for each province.
5. Additional tax transfer as percentage of adjusted PIT [(5)=100*(2)/(4)].

Source: Based on the 1999 budget projections from the Department of Finance for the fiscal year 2003-04.

Both horizontal and vertical spillovers reduce the accountability of governments. When governments can impose taxes that are, in effect, borne by other governments or non-residents, the economic cost of taxation is lower than it should be, and the result is likely to be excessive government spending. On the other hand, if spillovers result in the tax base moving to other jurisdictions, tax competition may make the perceived economic cost of taxation too high, thus resulting in too little government expenditure — although authors ranging from Brennan and Buchanan through McLure to Edwards and Keen have suggested that such tax competition may sometimes be useful in limiting the taxing power of governments.[10] Of course, those who argue this way have also generally been concerned about the possibility of excessive spending as a result of intergovernmental spillovers. Some have suggested that an important role for intergovernmental transfers may be precisely to offset such spillovers. Although the equalization system in Canada has reduced horizontal spillovers by lessening tax competition — and thus, some have argued, reinforcing the governmental "cartel" against taxpayers[11] — it has done so only at the expense of increasing vertical spillovers[12] since provincial governments that receive Equalization can increase taxes and reduce their tax base while being compensated with additional Equalization payments.

Finally, considerations of administrative efficiency and feasibility may dictate that higher (or lower) levels of government impose certain taxes or carry out certain expenditures even when it may not be strictly appropriate to do so on "equivalence" grounds. Vertical fiscal flows, such as those that dominate the scene in Canada, are in principle motivated largely by this consideration, at least with respect to those flowing to richer jurisdictions. (In practice, of course, such flows may be motivated by such nebulous but important concerns as "nationhood," "federalism," and so on.[13]) This "equalization" argument for some intergovernmental transfers may even be strengthened by our proposed approach to the tax assignment issue, as developed further below. In any case, grants from higher levels of government should — as is now generally the case — continue to be inframarginal so that subnational governments will clearly face the full tax price (at the margin) of the spending decisions for which they are responsible.

THE COSTS OF MISASSIGNMENT

The previous section focused on the balance (or imbalance) of revenues and expenditures resulting from the present tax assignment. The most critical problem in this respect clearly arises at the municipal level. The inadequate own-revenue resources of most Canadian municipalities give rise to a variety of other costs — costs that have likely been accentuated in recent years by the downloading of responsibilities that have, in at least some provinces (such as Ontario), accompanied the restoration of relative fiscal balance. The principal villain in this equation is the property tax, the only real source of "own" local revenue in Canada. This tax suffers from at least three defects. First, its inherent inelasticity with respect to economic growth in population and incomes (arising from both administrative and political factors) makes it a most inappropriate source of finance for much more elastic expenditures such as those on education and social assistance. Second, the politics and economics of property taxation are such as to induce local governments to attempt to load as much tax as possible on non-residential properties, preferably those with respect to which the incidence of the tax can be plausibly asserted to be on non-residents, thus providing exactly the wrong incentives to local political decisionmakers.[14] Attempts to constrain the political and economic distortions resulting from this inevitable tendency by "provincialization" of the property tax function (as has recently occurred in Ontario, for example) worsen the basic revenue-expenditure imbalance at the local level and tend to make local governments even less accountable. Third, insofar as it is a tax on a particular form of business input, essentially real property, increasingly heavy reliance on property taxes imparts an undesirable bias to business investment decisions.

Exactly similar problems to the last two just mentioned occur at the provincial level with respect to the corporate income and capital taxes. Such taxes are especially likely to generate the horizontal and vertical spillovers suggested above because capital is mobile. At present, the three provinces that collect their own corporate income tax (Alberta, Ontario, and Quebec) in total account for about 75 percent of the provincial tax base in this area.[15] The remaining provinces have a tax-collection agreement for the corporate income tax with the federal government. Although agreeing provinces can choose their own tax rates, the tax base is similar. Capital taxes, however, are neither subject to such an agreement nor harmonized.[16] Since much business activity is national, or multinational, the income and capital used as a tax base must be allocated among the provinces in some way. Even those provinces that collect their own corporate income tax have largely agreed to use a common allocation formula to determine their share of the tax base.[17] Since Canada does not have a consolidated return system, however, corporations can nonetheless minimize taxes by setting up separate corporations in each jurisdiction and then shifting income from one province to another, with the result that a province with a lower corporate tax rate can obtain a larger corporate income tax base. Table 5 shows precisely this inverse relationship between provincial corporate tax rates and corporate income as a proportion of capital, with Quebec having the lowest tax rate and the highest reported profitability per dollar of taxable capital.

Although some degree of tax harmonization has been achieved at the federal-provincial level with respect to income taxes, significant issues thus remain with respect to corporate income and capital taxes. The lack of harmonization imposes compliance costs and provides opportunities for tax minimization. In some instances, provinces have engaged in competitive bidding for specific projects — films and R&D projects provide illustrations. More generally, provinces continue to have considerable problems in dealing with corporate taxes. Most of the difficult and significant policy issues, such as those related to the treatment of international business income, have been left largely to the federal government. Moreover, businesses have been able to play off independently-collected provincial corporate taxes against other provincial corporate taxes, for example, by electing not to increase the cost basis of assets (in order to avoid capital gains taxes) in the province in which a vendor

Table 5: *Corporate Income Tax Rates and Ratio of Corporate Income to Assets by Province, 1999*

	Corporate Income Tax Rates		Corporate Income/Assets*	
	General (%)	Manufacturing (%)	Large (%)	Large and Small (%)
Quebec	9.2	9.2	6.8	10.0
Newfoundland	14.0	5.0	5.1	7.1
Ontario	15.5	13.5	5.9	7.0
Alberta	15.5	14.5	5.2	7.3
Prince Edward Island	16.0	7.5	5.0	9.3
Saskatchewan	17.0	10.0	4.8	7.4
Nova Scotia	16.0	16.0	4.7	6.5
British Columbia	16.5	16.5	4.0	6.2
Manitoba	17.0	17.0	5.2	7.0
New Brunswick	17.0	17.0	5.2	7.1

Note: * Corporate income is allocated by province. Assets are taxable paid-up capital by province (includes certain components). Large refers to business income subject to the general rate and large and small includes small business income. Assets used for calculations are the same in both cases.

Source: Department of Finance, *Equalization Tables 1999-2000* (Ottawa: Supply and Services Canada).

resides while declaring a higher cost basis (for depreciation purposes) in the province where the purchaser resides. Corporate taxes are hard enough for countries to enforce effectively in this globalizing world. They are even more difficult at the provincial level.

Since people are less mobile than capital, problems at the personal tax level are not so serious. Nonetheless, to the extent that both personal taxes and transfers are increasingly decided at the provincial level, the scope for beggar-thy-neighbour policies and inappropriate fiscal competition may well increase in this arena in the future. This has already been illustrated by Alberta's recent announcement that it is adopting a flat tax of 11 percent, which will give it the lowest top marginal tax rate in Canada, in order to attract skilled labour to the province.

Similar problems are already a matter of some concern with respect to consumption taxes, as evidenced by recent developments in the excise tax area (e.g., with respect to the evasion of tobacco taxes). Not only is cross-border shopping by consumers a problem but in addition interprovincial trade in general currently labours under additional and perhaps largely unnecessary costs as a result of Canada's uniquely complex sales tax system — with, in effect, four systems currently in operation in different parts of the country (the GST alone in Alberta, the HST in Nova Scotia, New Brunswick, and Newfoundland, the GST/QST in Quebec, and a GST and an RST in the other four provinces). As well, in those provinces in which the RST still operates — and even to a limited extent with the QST — a high share of sales tax revenues really come from business purchases and thus potentially give rise to interjurisdictional fiscal spillovers similar to those discussed earlier.[18]

PROPOSED SOLUTIONS OF THE PAST

In their never-ending quest to solve federal-provincial conflicts, Canadians have over the years considered a wide variety of approaches to improve the assignment of tax powers in Canada. Unless expenditure assignment is fundamentally changed, which we consider unlikely, the two most important solutions put forward have been to exchange tax fields and to improve the degree of tax harmonization in Canada.[19] While there is obviously some value to each of these approaches, we suggest that Canada has reached a dead-end in pursuing them.

Exchanging Tax Fields. Proposals to exchange tax fields, for example, have a long history. The Rowell-Sirois report suggested prior to World War II that the federal government should assume powers over the income and estate taxes in exchange for transfers paid to the provinces and the federal assumption of responsibility for unemployment relief. The Carter Commission in 1967 recommended that the federal government should assume responsibility for all income taxes and should eventually abandon the manufacturers' sales tax, leaving the provinces in control of retail sales taxes. More recently, as indicated earlier, other proposals have been made to transfer the sales tax field to the federal government with a transfer of personal income tax to the provinces, or vice versa.

The value of exchanging tax fields is that the inherent conflicts and spillovers resulting from independently chosen policies and the duplication of administration that arise from joint occupancy of tax fields could be minimized. Tax powers could be assigned to the level of government that can most efficiently operate the system, given the relative needs of different levels to raise revenue. Thus, for example, even though the VAT is most efficiently levied by a central government, Quebec has demonstrated that VAT can be administered at the provincial level with a small loss in efficiency and coordination — provided, of course, that the central VAT (which may also be provincially administered, as in Quebec) also applies in the province on essentially the same base.[20]

Nonetheless, proposals to exchange tax fields are invariably fraught with problems. Some tax fields tend to grow more quickly with the economy (e.g., income taxes) while others are more inelastic but stable (e.g., property taxes). Assigning stable tax fields to governments with growing expenditure needs will create a continuing vertical imbalance between expenditures and revenues. For this reason, a case can be made that the personal income tax should be assigned to the provinces. However, the abandonment of the personal income tax field would reduce the role of the federal government both with respect to redistribution in general and, through the interregionally redistributive role of the PIT, as an important way of reducing the risks faced by any one region.

Even if the newly assigned taxes matched expenditure responsibilities, any reassignment of taxes between levels of government will, of course, create transitional imbalances for each government. For example, if the sales tax field were given up by the federal government in favour of an equal-yield national transfer of personal income tax points from the provinces to the federal government, provinces with more consumption relative to income compared to the national average will be better off, while others would be worse off. The federal government could try to compensate the losing provinces with transfers or other adjustments, but it would need to recover the cost incurred from some expenditure program or tax. Similarly, each province — even those with gains in revenue — would need to decide whether to spend the funds or reduce some other tax. Tax reassignment thus requires all affected governments to adopt a new fiscal position and perhaps to undertake expenditure or tax reforms. If fiscal equilibrium is to be maintained the exchange of tax fields may thus require considerable cooperation among governments. It is not surprising that past proposals to exchange tax fields have failed to be adopted in Canada.

Tax Harmonization. Another approach to the tax assignment problem is to harmonize federal and provincial taxes when governments jointly occupy a tax field. Harmonization, in this sense, means that federal and provincial governments agree to use a common base — not necessarily with uniform rates — as well as employ a single administration for the collection of taxes. The tax-collection agreements for personal income, corporate income, and, more recently, sales taxes have generally followed these principles.

The benefit of such tax harmonization, especially when federal and provincial taxes are collected jointly by one administration, is that it clearly reduces both compliance costs faced by taxpayers and administrative costs for government. Harmonization that yields common tax bases also reduces economic costs of the tax system to the extent that it minimizes distortions to the free flow of goods, services, labour, and capital across provinces.

However, the cost of harmonization is that it limits the powers of governments to determine their own tax policies. In the past, tax agreements took the form that the provinces agreed to the federal base — as defined by the federal government — but were given some autonomy over rates and credits. In the case of the Harmonized Sales Tax agreement between the federal government and three Atlantic provinces, the parties have tied their hands in choosing the rate, a feature that is now being questioned by the new Nova Scotia government. Increasingly, as the powers of the provinces have grown, they have sought more autonomy over harmonized taxes by either considering operating their own tax (Ontario and the western provinces have considered operating an independent personal income tax system) or by seeking greater power over the determination of the tax base (such as through the newly-legislated federal tax-collection agency). Recently, the federal government offered more flexibility to the provinces by allowing them to collect their personal income tax as a percentage of income rather than federal tax paid. This helps decouple some aspects of federal and provincial personal income taxes, although the definition of income is still essentially determined by the federal government (albeit in consultation with the provinces). So far, only Alberta has taken up this offer but other provinces, including Ontario, are clearly interested in pursuing it.

Although personal income tax harmonization and moves to increase provincial autonomy been relatively successful, recent trends are to increase provincial powers. Corporate tax harmonization, even though most provincial revenues are collected by provinces with independent taxes, has so far resulted in provinces using essentially the same base — to some extent out of sheer necessity to collect revenues in today's complicated global world. Sales tax harmonization has been relatively less successful in some respects since six provinces have essentially rejected it and the harmonization agreements for the HST and the QST are different in certain important respects since Quebec has more flexibility. Prospects for further harmonization of the major taxes seem low at present. A new approach is needed.

A MODEST PROPOSAL

Our modest proposal is simply to ignore the never-ending federal-provincial battle on "who should tax what" and instead to focus on what needs to be done, and what can be done, to reform provincial-local finance. Somewhat miraculously, when we concentrate on this issue, it turns out that we can also to some extent resolve the former issue without having to deal with it explicitly. Let us now turn to how this miracle might be brought about, leaving for the next section some potentially important caveats and problems with the proposed solution.

Broadly, our proposal has two major components. The first component is to replace provincial corporate income and capital taxes by a new "business value tax." Although this proposal, which is developed in more detail below, would not directly affect federal-provincial vertical imbalance, it might facilitate more flexibility in coordinating federal and provincial personal income and sales taxes. The second component is concerned with what we view as the increasingly pressing problem of accommodating growing local revenue needs by establishing a new system of local business taxation, thus perhaps reducing the prevailing sharp vertical fiscal imbalance between these two levels of government to some extent. The next two subsections expand on these ideas.

A PROVINCIAL BUSINESS VALUE TAX

As noted earlier, there are many problems with such existing subnational taxes on business in Canada as the provincial corporate income and capital taxes and the local non-residential property tax. The general academic advice with respect to such taxes is simple: don't do it! As a rule, the scholarly world has looked at the distortions and problems arising from subnational business taxes, shuddered, and passed on to things of more interest. But this will not do, for two important and quite different reasons. First, there is in fact a good (benefit) case for some subnational taxation of business.[21] And, second, whether there is such a case on economic grounds or not, the political realities of governing in a democratic society are such that virtually any subnational government will want to impose such a tax.[22]

Since we are therefore likely to have to continue to live with such taxes at the provincial level, it is important to consider whether the problem is with the *idea* of the provinces taxing business or with the *way* in which we now do so. We suggest that the latter is true, and that most of the problems giving rise to concern arise because of either jurisdictional apportionment problems or the partial factor nature of the taxes. The second of these problems can largely be avoided with the form of business taxation suggested here, which moreover has the additional benefit of satisfying the reasons why such a tax may make sense more adequately than the existing provincial taxes on business. The first (apportionment) problem may then also prove easier to resolve than at present, as discussed later.

Basically, what may be called the "economic," as opposed to the "political economy" case, for local business taxation is simply as a form of generalized benefit tax. The idea is an old one. Where possible, specific public services benefiting specific business enterprises should be paid for by appropriate user charges. Where it is not feasible, however, to recoup the marginal cost of cost-reducing public sector outlays through user charges, some form of broad-based general levy on business activity may provide a useful substitute. Kitchen and Slack have estimated that on average about 40 percent of local (non-educational) expenditures benefit non-residential properties, although the share is less than 20 percent if education is taken into account.[23] Similarly, Oakland

and Testa have estimated the "business-related" share of combined state and local expenditures in the United States to be about 13 percent, although with considerable variation from state to state.[24] (This estimate assumes business receives no specific benefits from expenditures on education, which seems improbable.)

This argument, however, provides no support for taxing any one business input, whether labour (payroll tax) or capital (capital tax or corporate income tax). Instead, what this line of reasoning suggests is that a broad-based levy neutral to factor mix should be imposed, such as a tax on value-added. Indeed, as Sullivan has documented, the original conception of the VAT (by Thomas Adams) was as a business benefit tax.[25] More precisely, as Allan and then the Meade Report suggested — admittedly from rather different perspectives — the most appropriate form of VAT for this purpose would really be a VAIT, a "value-added income tax" or a VAT levied on the basis of income (production, origin) rather than consumption (destination).[26]

Compared to a conventional VAT, a VAIT, which we shall henceforth call a "business value tax" or BVT to avoid acronymic confusion, has three important distinguishing features. First, it is levied on income, not consumption: that is, it is imposed on the sum of profits and wages, or to put it another way, on investment income as well as on consumption.[27] Second, it is imposed on production, not consumption: that is, it is imposed on an origin not destination basis and hence, in effect, it taxes exports and not imports. And third, it is assessed by the subtraction (or addition) method on the basis of annual accounts rather than on a transaction or invoice-credit method.

Those who think taxes on exports, investment — and perhaps even on profits — are always and inevitably undesirable will no doubt reject this proposal out of hand. But those, like us, who think both that there is at least some justification for local business taxation and that, whether we like it or not, there will continue to be such taxes should not be so hasty. While the danger of tax exporting and, more importantly, "beggar-my-neighbour" tax competition suggest strongly that it might be advisable to place a floor, and perhaps also a ceiling, on such taxes, this form of business taxation is likely to be less distorting than such existing subnational taxes as the provincial CITs and capital taxes and the non-residential property tax.

Moreover, this is by no means solely a theoretical argument since there is already some important real-world experience with such taxes, for instance, in the state of Michigan (the SBT, or single business tax) and in Italy (the new regional business tax, the IRAP). The 1998 Italian reform is perhaps most interesting in this connection. An existing regional income tax levied mainly on business income (at a rate of about 16 percent), a tax on dividend distributions by corporations, a small net worth tax, and social contributions levied to finance a national health scheme were all replaced by an origin-based, value-added tax (IRAP). This new tax applies to wages, salaries, profits, rents, and interest. It is applied on a subtraction basis by taking the difference between gross receipts and purchases from other firms (including depreciation). IRAP applies to most firms at a uniform rate of 4.25 percent, although regional governments can add an additional percentage point to the rate if they so choose. IRAP is not deductible from the income tax but, a portion of the tax may be creditable against foreign taxes for foreign-owned companies (at least for US tax purposes).

A final preliminary word on our proposal, which is spelled out in more detail in the next section, may be useful, given the existence of a national VAT (the GST) in Canada. The apparent oddity of, in effect, having two different taxes on value-added resides largely in the potential similarity of the names. As Meade argued, if it makes sense to have taxes on consumption and on income, as it may, it may equally make sense to levy all or part of one or both taxes indirectly in the value-added form at the business level. As Bird and Gendron have recently argued, subnational VATs in the traditional (invoice-credit, consumption-type) form are, as shown by the QST, perfectly viable in Canada.[28] What we are now asserting is that it may equally make sense to levy a different form of VAT — the income-type, annual accounts-based variety, labelled here the BVT — at a low rate as a generalized tax on business activity. Moreover, as shown in the next section, while it would not be either feasible or desirable to impose a traditional VAT like the GST at the local level, it should be perfectly feasible to impose a BVT at the local as well as the provincial level.

PROVINCIAL-MUNICIPAL REVENUE-SHARING

As noted earlier, many of the economic problems with local property taxes arise because of the distortions introduced by taxing business property. As we have also noted, there is nonetheless a respectable and, in political economy terms, perhaps an imperative case for levying some form of local business tax. For exactly the reasons set out briefly in the last section, the BVT seems worth considering in this respect also.

Assume, first, that there is no provincial BVT: Would a local BVT make sense? It might in larger municipalities which could reasonably be expected to assess and collect such a tax and would have the incentive to do so because of the size of the local tax base that could be tapped. On the whole, however, a local BVT would really make most sense if there were already a provincial BVT in place, on which a (limited) local rate could be "piggy-backed." Many countries already have some form of local business taxation, for example, Germany (*gewerbsteuer*) and Japan (enterprise income tax), but most countries following the UK tradition rely primarily on business property taxes (United States, Australia, New Zealand, Ireland — though not, interestingly, any longer the United Kingdom itself). A local BVT, imposed as, say up to a

1-percent surcharge on the BVT base reported for provincial tax purposes (which is essentially just "sales less cost of goods purchased" or wages plus profits) by entities physically located within the taxing jurisdiction would seem to be a considerably more desirable form of local business taxation than any of these. Another approach might be for a province to levy the "local" BVT at a common rate, with the proceeds being shared among municipalities in accordance with some formula, although this would clearly be less desirable in terms of ensuring local fiscal accountability.

We therefore suggest that the present non-residential property tax should be reduced and replaced by a local BVT imposed as a surcharge on the provincial BVT base (which in turn would be equal to the provincial VAT base less imports plus exports). As mentioned earlier, limits can and likely should be imposed on local surcharges in order to prevent excessive locational distortions. The only other tax for which even this degree of local rate freedom might be possible and advisable would be a surcharge on the provincial personal income tax. In this case, however, the commuter problem within metropolitan areas would make such a tax unwieldy. To resolve this problem would require some kind of revenue-pooling and formula-sharing system, which would, of course, substantially reduce the accountability from local decisionmakers.[29]

THE "NEW MODEL" TAX SYSTEM

Under our proposal, the provincial government would impose a personal income tax (in tax-on-base form), BVT, and a VAT (preferably on the QST model) in addition to other existing taxes (such as excises and certain payroll taxes) and fees. Municipal governments would levy residential (and perhaps equal non-residential) property taxes, as well as perhaps a BVT surcharge (and user charges). What would be left for the federal government? It would now have full authority over the corporate income tax, as well as its own personal income tax and GST, and, of course, payroll and excise taxes. The federal government might also be involved, particularly in the smaller provinces in collecting the BVT, as it currently does with respect to the corporate income tax and the HST. Of course, the new Canada Customs and Revenue Agency may prove willing to collect even non-harmonized provincial (and local) taxes for a fee.

THE DEVIL IS IN THE DETAILS

Ideas are easy. Implementation is hard, and it is always easy to find problems with new suggestions, and reasons for remaining with the status quo. In this section of the chapter, we first sketch the proposed system and provide some illustrative quantitative calculations as to how it might work. We then discuss briefly a number of implementation issues which would need to be resolved if our modest proposal were to be implemented. No doubt many other such issues could be raised about various aspects of this proposal. We think, however, that the status quo is itself giving rise to increasing problems and that fully adequate technical solutions are as or more likely to be found to the problems with our system as to those with the existing system. In any case, as we have argued earlier, it is surely time to begin thinking of some new ideas in the eternal Canadian tax debate.

BVT TAX RATES: AN ILLUSTRATION

We calculate the BVT base as follows:[30]

> Business Value-Added = Revenues from the sales of goods and services
>   − purchases of current inputs (except labour)
>   − depreciation of capital expenditure
>   − royalties paid to the Crown.

Note that financial income is not included in the tax base. Nor is interest on borrowed funds deductible. Although we calculate the business value-added base on an "income basis" for the reasons given above, we discuss below some potential adjustments.

With respect to financial institutions and insurance companies, for example, a special regime would be necessary since most of their value-added would not be included in the tax base. Presumably, one would need to levy a combination of capital and payroll taxes on this sector, but we do not try to take this complication into account in our estimation of the value of the BVT tax base.

The potential BVT tax rates by province needed for revenue-neutral replacement of the taxes replaced in 1999 are shown in Tables 6a and 6b. These tables provide illustrative calculations for the BVT by province as a replacement for business income taxes, capital taxes, 5 percent of property tax revenues, and provincial payroll taxes (not including workers' compensation premiums).[31] Table 6a assumes that business value-added is apportioned to provinces according to their provincial share of national value-added, an appropriate way to allocate the tax base for businesses operating in more than one jurisdiction. However, since data at the provincial level do not allow us to separate public from private activities, these weights are distorted by giving more value-added to provinces with a larger public sector. We therefore provide a second set of calculations in Table 6b, based on allocating business value-added on the basis of the current formula used to allocate corporate income (for most businesses, one-half of the share of payroll and sales measured on a destination basis). This measure too is not quite right, because sales of establishments on a destination basis do not necessarily reflect value-added

Table 6a: Tax Rates of the BVT in Order to Replace 1999's Revenues from Current Business Taxes

Provincial Allocation of Business Value-Added Using Provincial Shares in Canadian Total Value-Added*

Provinces	Replace Business Income Taxes	Replace Business Income and Capital Taxes	Replace Business Income, Capital Taxes and 5% of Property Tax Revenues	Replace Business Income, Capital Taxes, 5% of Property Tax Revenues and Payroll Taxes
	(percentage)			
Total	2.7	3.7	4.1	5.7
Newfoundland	2.8	3.3	3.5	4.8
Prince Edward Island	1.5	1.6	1.9	1.9
Nova Scotia	1.1	1.6	1.9	1.9
New Brunswick	1.6	2.3	2.6	2.6
Quebec	1.8	3.8	4.1	8.0
Ontario	3.3	4.1	4.5	6.1
Manitoba	1.3	2.4	2.7	4.2
Saskatchewan	3.0	4.9	5.3	5.3
Alberta	3.5	3.6	3.9	3.9
British Columbia	2.5	3.2	3.5	3.5

Note: *Total Business Value-Added excluding royalties was taken from the series in J. Sargent *et al.*, "The Evolution of Business Taxes in Canada: Data and Estimates," Working Paper No. 97-17 (Ottawa: Technical Committee on Business Taxation, Department of Finance, 1998), Table A.3 and projected until 1999 using GDP growth rates. This aggregated Business Value-Added was allocated to the provinces using the 1994 shares of each province in the total value-added from the Provincial Economic Accounts. This total value-added is Net Domestic Income at factor cost and is composed by labour income, corporation profits before taxes, interest, and other investment income, accrued net income of farm operators, net income of non-farm unincorporated business and inventory valuation of adjustment.

Source: Based on the budget estimates from the Department of Finance for the fiscal year 1999-2000.

Table 6b: Tax Rates of the BVT in Order to Replace 1999's Revenues from Current Business Taxes

*Provincial Allocation of Business Value-Added Using Provincial Shares in
the Canadian Tax Base of the Business Income Tax**

Provinces	Replace Business Income Taxes	Replace Business Income and Capital Taxes	Replace Business Income, Capital Taxes and 5% of Property Tax Revenues	Replace Business Income, Capital Taxes, 5% of Property Tax Revenues and Payroll Taxes
		(percentage)		
Total	2.7	3.7	4.1	5.7
Newfoundland	3.9	4.6	4.8	6.7
Prince Edward Island	2.9	3.1	3.6	3.6
Nova Scotia	1.7	2.5	2.9	2.9
New Brunswick	1.9	2.8	3.1	3.1
Quebec	1.9	4.1	4.5	8.7
Ontario	3.1	3.8	4.2	5.7
Manitoba	1.8	3.2	3.6	5.7
Saskatchewan	3.6	6.0	6.5	6.5
Alberta	2.6	2.7	2.9	2.9
British Columbia	2.8	3.5	3.9	3.9

Note: *Total Business Value-Added excluding royalties was taken from the series in J. Sargent *et al.*, "The Evolution of Business Taxes in Canada: Data and Estimates," Working Paper No. 97-17 (Ottawa: Technical Committee on Business Taxation, Department of Finance, 1998), Table A.3 and projected until 1999 using GDP growth rates. This aggregated Business Value-Added was allocated to the provinces using the 1994 shares of each province in the total value-added from the Provincial Economic Accounts. This total value-added is Net Domestic Income at factor cost and is composed by labour income, corporation profits before taxes, interest, and other investment income, accrued net income of farm operators, net income of non-farm unincorporated business and inventory valuation of adjustment.

Source: Based on the budget estimates from the Department of Finance for the fiscal year 1999-2000.

in production. These weights tend to discriminate against provinces (e.g., resource provinces) that tend to export intermediate product to related establishments in other provinces that sell the product.

In any case, in both illustrative cases, if the BVT replaced only business income taxes, the average provincial BVT rate would be 2.7 percent. Ontario would have an above-average rate (in both cases) while several eastern provinces and Quebec would have a lower BVT rate. If the BVT replaced both business income taxes and capital taxes, the average provincial rate would increase to 3.7 percent, with above-average rates found in Saskatchewan, Quebec, and Ontario. Allowing the BVT to replace, in addition to business income and capital taxes, 5 percent of property taxes (a significant share of the non-residential property tax), the BVT rate would increase on average to 4.1 percent, with similar patterns of BVT rates across provinces as in the previous case. Finally, if provincial payroll taxes were also replaced, the average BVT rate would rise to 5.7 percent. Unsurprisingly, given its higher payroll taxes, the highest provincial rate on this base would be in Quebec (8 percent in Table 6a and 8.7 percent in Table 6b) while the lowest rate would be in Nova Scotia and New Brunswick in Table 6a (1.9 percent) or Nova Scotia and Alberta in Table 6b (2.9 percent).[32]

One important conclusion suggested by these calculations is that the BVT rate would need to be rather high, 5.7 percent on average, to replace business income, capital, some non-residential property, and provincial payroll taxes. Of course, all this shows is that subnational taxes on business are already high in Canada. Second, since rates would vary significantly across provinces, important issues with regard to tax avoidance, tax competition, and equalization of provincial tax revenues are raised, though again it should be remembered that all these issues already exist under the present system. On the other hand, there are a number of offsetting benefits from our proposal. Provincial business income taxes that are as high as 17 percent would be eliminated. Moreover, municipal governments would have access to a new form of taxation, reducing their reliance on the non-residential property taxes that reduce local accountability.

The calculations in Tables 6a and 6b are only illustrative. As discussed above, the weights used obviously need to be estimated with more refined data. Moreover, yet more federal-provincial discussions would undoubtedly be needed to determine how to allocate the tax base of firms that operate in more than one jurisdiction. And, of course, some (or all) provinces may wish to replace only business income and payroll taxes, leaving capital taxes and property taxes alone. Or they may wish to replace more property taxes and only part of payroll taxes. To keep the BVT rate from becoming too high, provinces might also choose to maintain some capital and payroll taxes in place. Our own preferred solution would be to give the highest priority to the elimination of business income taxes and a significant share of municipal non-residential property taxes. Political priorities may differ.

As a replacement for provincial corporate income and capital taxes, an income-based BVT would improve the tax system in several ways. First, such a tax would be more neutral than the current CIT and capital taxes, which discriminate against capital investment. Second, a BVT would be less susceptible to base erosion. The tax rate would be lower and corporate profits (gross of interest expenses) would be fully taxed and hence unaffected by the degree of debt financing. Third, the BVT base, although less cyclically sensitive than corporate income taxes, would be more sensitive to business cycles than the increasingly important capital taxes, which are essentially fixed payments that hit businesses hardest in cyclical downturns, when they are most financially vulnerable.

IMPLEMENTATION ISSUES

There are many implementation issues that would need to be considered by provincial governments if this proposal were to be adopted. Some issues would necessarily involve the federal government as well. While these issues are clearly important for governments to consider, none in our view is sufficiently difficult to solve to make the BVT impossible to achieve. We suggest below how some of these issues can be resolved.

Accounts-Base for Calculating the BVT. The BVT would be an accounts-based form of taxation. In principle, it could be operated similarly to the business income tax and even calculated using the federal income tax form as a basis for calculating the BVT. Taxable financial income would be deducted and interest expense added back to business income to calculate the BVT base. If the BVT used a method of calculating depreciation deductions different to the current corporate income tax, capital-cost allowances would also have to be added back to business income before allowing the BVT depreciation deduction. Some costs incurred to earn financial income may also be disallowed. This would require additional rules to disallow or apportion costs between non-financial and financial activities (e.g., fees paid to financial advisors). If the BVT rate is sufficiently low, presumably such measures could be simplified. Since the principle of the BVT is to tax income on an origin-basis, income from foreign activities could probably be ignored.

Nonetheless, there are several additional issues that need to be dealt with should a BVT be adopted. First, the BVT would likely exempt certain categories of income — non-profits, charities, Crown corporations, municipal government business activities, and Aboriginal bands — except to the extent that such income is already taxed under the corporate income tax. Some distortions would thus remain, as with business income taxes in general, although the rates of tax would be lower under the BVT than existing provincial corporate income tax rates. Second, as mentioned above, the deduction for depreciation expenses could be based on the current federal capital consumption allowance system or determined separately for the BVT, up to and including expensing capital.[33] The advantage of following the federal system is simplification. The disadvantage is that the federal depreciation system provides faster write-offs for capital costs in some cases compared to economic depreciation and inadequate deductions in certain other cases.[34] Third, as also noted earlier, a special capital and/or payroll tax regime would be needed for financial institutions and insurance companies, but such regimes already exist in most provinces.

Provincial Coordination Issues. Some coordination is needed among provinces to determine how much value-added is earned in each province. The federal government would need to play some role in assisting provinces to allocate BVT revenues, and, as in the case of the current tax-collection agreements, agree to collect the taxes on behalf of some provinces. Two explicit issues would need to be resolved. The first issue is that the tax base should definitely be as similar among provinces as possible — as in the case of the corporate income tax — to facilitate compliance and administration of the BVT. Provinces should thus have similar rules to measure the base, including rates of depreciation. Presumably, provinces could use tax credits, as they do now, that would allow them to differentiate their tax base if they so wish.

The second issue is to determine the allocation formula for business value-added. Businesses that operate in only one province would be taxed solely by that province. Value-added earned in more than one jurisdiction would need to be allocated to each province according to formula weights. The weights could be based on payroll, sales (on an origin basis) or capital (as determined by the undepreciated amount of capital), or some combination. As the weights used can have an important impact on BVT revenues received, as illustrated by Tables 6a and 6b above, provincial coordination in determining formula weights will be difficult. A logical starting point for these discussions might be the current method used to allocate corporate income. As Smith documents, such negotiations about who gets what tax base are by no means easy, but they have often reached successful conclusions in the past.[35]

Relationship with the Personal Income Tax. Under the current tax system, corporate and personal income taxes are roughly integrated (for distributed profits) at a combined federal-provincial corporate income tax rate of 20 percent through the combination of the dividend tax credit and the one-quarter exclusion of capital gains from taxable income. If the provinces eliminated their business income taxes and assessed an equal-yield BVT (at the average rate of 2.7 percent), these integration measures may need to be evaluated.

The simplest approach is to do nothing. The BVT replaces several taxes and the only one that matters for integration is the corporate income tax. To the extent that the BVT is in part a payment for benefits received, as suggested earlier, no integration is necessary.[36] One might take the view that the existence of the BVT together with the federal corporate income tax will create some opportunities for tax planning, but such problems are unlikely to be serious. At the top federal corporate income tax rate of 29.12 percent and a BVT rate of 5.7 percent, the combined rate on profits would be about 34 percent, instead of the current top rate of 43 percent. A shift to the BVT will thus improve integration of corporate and personal income taxes for larger corporations. Small businesses would still be taxed at the federal corporate rate of 13.12 percent and, if the 5.7 percent BVT were included, the total rate on profits would be about 19 percent. If the BVT rate is much lower than this, some adjustments to either the corporate income tax or integration at the federal level may be needed: for example, reductions in the dividend tax credit and the portion of capital gains income excluded from tax.

Integration is a more complicated issue with respect to salaries or interest expense. Under the federal corporate income tax such expenses are deductible from business income but fully taxed as income at the personal level. With the BVT, salaries, and interest expense would not be deductible, yet they are still fully taxed under the personal income tax. The combined personal income tax rate and provincial BVT rate, about 55 percent, would thus be greater on such income than the combined federal and provincial taxes on dividends and capital gains earned from investments in smaller firms, about 50 percent. There would thus be a small incentive to structure payments to small business owners in the form of dividends and surplus stripping. The incentive would be reduced, however, if the BVT were assessed at a low rate or there were a modest reduction in the dividend tax credit and capital gains exclusion.

Deductibility of the BVT from Federal Corporate Income Tax. At present, provincial capital, property and payroll taxes are deductible from the corporate income tax while provincial corporate income taxes are not. The deductibility of a BVT replacing some of these taxes from federal corporate income tax would be an important issue. Should the BVT not be deductible, the federal government would end up with greater corporate income tax revenues. Should all the BVT be deductible, the federal government would lose revenue. One way to resolve this issue, on average, would be to disallow deduction of that part of the BVT equivalent to the amount of provincial taxes that are currently not deductible.[37] Although this would prevent a windfall gain or loss in revenues for the federal government, given the different business tax mixes in different provinces, there would clearly be differential impacts across provinces. Solution of this problem would require difficult federal-provincial negotiations and perhaps, in the end, some supplemental federal funding to facilitate harmonization (as in the recent case of the Harmonized Sales Tax).

Crediting against Foreign Taxes. At present, provincial corporate income taxes paid by multinational companies operating in Canada may be credited against taxes of certain capital exporting countries — the United States, United Kingdom, and Japan, for example. A shift from provincial corporate income taxes to the BVT would result in some multinationals losing foreign tax credits, thereby increasing the tax cost of investments in Canada, although this would be partly ameliorated by the deductibility of the BVT in determinating foreign-source income earned by the parent in countries that tax such income.

As noted above, the issue of creditability of the BVT against foreign taxes has been important in Italy, where the IRAP, a similar tax, was recently adopted as a replacement for regional income and capital taxes. The Italian government has been able to achieve an agreement with the United States to allow a portion of their regional IRAP to be credited against US taxes paid by US parents on their foreign-source income earned in Italy. Canada would need to negotiate a similar agreement — a process which, like the intergovernmental negotiations mentioned earlier, might take quite some time to complete.

Equalization of Provincial Tax Revenues. If the provinces replaced taxes with the BVT, presumably the federal government would agree to include the BVT in the calculation of equalization payments to the have-not provinces. The current formula results in the federal government providing a grant to a province based on the difference between the national standard rate and the rate chosen by the province times the per capita tax base times the population. The BVT would be equalized by using the per-capita business value-added tax base to determine equalization payments.

Although our proposal is revenue-neutral in aggregate, it is by no means clear that the distribution of value-added to determine the national standard rate and provincial tax base would be the same as the distribution of the tax base for other taxes. Moreover, as shown in Table 6a and 6b, BVT rates might differ significantly across provinces depending on the weights used to allocate value-added. Thus, equalization payments made by the federal government would be affected for each province. We have not tried to determine the new amounts of equalization payments, but any significant change to provincial tax systems might result in some adjustments to the equalization system.

CONCLUSION

The modest proposal for provincial-municipal tax reform we have suggested is essentially based on three simple principles: (i) more attention should be paid to matching expenditure and revenue needs; (ii) more effort should be made to ensure that all governments bear significant responsibility at the margin for financing the expenditures for which they are politically responsible; and (iii) subnational taxes should not unduly distort the allocation of resources.

Our proposal focuses in particular on the third of these principles. It may also help with respect to the second principle to the extent it makes clearer the relative burdens of business taxation in the different provinces. It may even help with respect to the first principle, at least at the provincial-municipal level. Our primary aim, however, is to suggest a less harmful form of subnational business taxation. Provincial corporate income taxes, capital taxes, and payroll taxes, and municipal non-residential property taxes can introduce serious economic distortions in a variety of ways. Nonetheless, there is both an economic (benefit) case for some regional and local taxation of business and, it seems, often an overwhelming political need for local leaders to impose such taxes. The approach to this problem suggested here has been the introduction of what is in effect another form of value-added tax, called here the business value tax or BVT. Variants of such taxes already exist in the United States (the Michigan SBT and the New Hampshire BET) and Italy (the IRAP) and to some extent Germany (the *gewerbesteuer*). The theoretical case for such levies has been argued for decades[38] and concrete proposals along these lines have recently been made in the United States.[39]

Much more work remains to be done to develop the details of the scheme sketched here. For example, myriad details of design and administration need to be settled and the role and design of intergovernmental fiscal transfers needs to be reconsidered simultaneously, as does the appropriate and tolerable level of asymmetry in the application of the suggested principles to subnational governments of vastly differing size and competence. Nonetheless, we think there is a good case for at least some benefit taxation of business by provincial and local governments, and that a promising approach to this goal may lie in the introduction of a "business value tax" at a low and uniform rate. Such a tax will certainly not solve all the problems of establishing a sound and workable multi-tiered tax system on Canadian business, but it should move us at least modestly closer to this goal.

NOTES

We wish to thank Harvey Lazar and two anonymous referees for helpful comments and Fernando Bruna for very helpful research assistance.

1.   Richard A. Musgrave, "Who Should Tax, Where and What?" in *Tax Assignment in Federal Countries*, ed. Charles E. McLure (Canberra: Centre for Research on Federal Financial Relations, Australian National University, 1983).

2.   Irene Ip and Jack M. Mintz, *Dividing the Spoils: The Federal-Provincial Allocation of Taxing Powers* (Toronto: C.D. Howe Institute, 1992); Robin Boadway,

The Constitutional Division of Powers: An Economic Perspective (Ottawa: Economic Council of Canada, 1992).

3.   Bev Dahlby, "Taxation under Alternative Constitutional Arrangements," in *Alberta and the Economics of Constitutional Change*, ed. Paul Boothe (Edmonton: Western Centre for Economic Research, University of Alberta, 1992); Giuseppe C. Ruggeri, Robert Howard and Donald Van Wart, "Structural Imbalances in the Canadian Fiscal System," *Canadian Tax Journal* 41 (1993):454-72.

4.   Richard M. Bird, "Federal-Provincial Taxation in Turbulent Times," *Canadian Public Administration* 36 (1993):479-96.

5.   Bird, "Federal-Provincial Taxation in Turbulent Times," and Ip and Mintz, *Dividing the Spoils.*

6.   Richard M. Bird and Pierre-Pascal Gendron, "Dual VATs and Cross-Border Trade: Two Problems, One Solution?" *International Tax and Public Finance* 5(1998):429-42; Jack M. Mintz, Thomas M. Wilson and Pierre-Pascal Gendron, "Canada's GST: Sales Tax Harmonization is the Key to Simplification," *Tax Notes International* (1994):661-78; Pierre-Pascal Gendron, Jack M. Mintz and Thomas A. Wilson, "VAT Harmonization in Canada: Recent Developments and the Need for Flexibility," *International VAT Monitor* 7 (1996):332-42.

7.   Mancur Olson, "The Principle of 'Fiscal Equivalence': The Division of Responsibilities among Different Levels of Government," *American Economic Review* 59(1969):479-87.

8.   Jack M. Mintz and Henry Tulkens, "Commodity Tax Competition Between Member States of a Federation: Equilibrium and Efficiency," *Journal of Public Economics* 29(1986):133-72.

9.   Robin Boadway and Michael Keen, "Efficiency and the Optimal Direction of Federal-State Transfers," *International Tax and Public Finance* 3(1996):137-55; and Bev Dahlby, "Fiscal Externalities and the Design of Intergovernmental Grants," *International Tax and Public Finance* 3(1996):397-412.

10. Geoffrey Brennan and James Buchanan, *The Power to Tax: Analytic Foundations of a Fiscal Constitution* (New York: Cambridge University Press, 1980); Charles E. McLure, Jr., "Tax Competition: Is What's Good for the Private Goose also Good for the Public Gander?" *National Tax Journal* 39 (1986):341-52; and J.S.S. Edwards and Michael Keen, "Tax Competition and Leviathan," *European Economic Review* 40 (1996):113-34.

11. P.J. Grossman and Edwin G. West, "Federalism and the Growth of Government Revisited," *Public Choice* 79 (1994):19-32.

12. Michael Smart, "Taxation and Deadweight Loss in a System of Intergovernmental Transfers," *Canadian Journal of Economics* 31,1 (1998):189-206.

13. See, e.g., Thomas J. Courchene, *Equalization Payments* (Toronto: Ontario Economic Council, 1984).

14. Wayne R. Thirsk, "Political Sensitivity vs. Economic Sensibility: A Tale of Two Property Taxes," in *Tax Policy Options in the 1980s*, ed. Wayne R. Thirsk and John Whalley (Toronto: Canadian Tax Foundation, 1982).

15. Technical Committee on Business Taxation, *Report* (Ottawa: Department of Finance, 1998).

16. Peter E. McQuillan and E. Cal Cochrane, "Capital Tax Issues," Working Paper No. 96-8 (Ottawa: Technical Committee on Business Taxation, Department of Finance, 1996).

17. Ernest H. Smith, *Federal-Provincial Tax Sharing and Centralized Tax Collection in Canada*, Special Studies in Taxation and Public Finance No. 1 (Toronto: Canadian Tax Foundation, 1998).

18. C-Y Kuo, T. McGirr and S. Poddar, "Measuring the Non-Neutralities of Sales and Excise Tax in Canada," *Canadian Tax Journal* 36 (1988):655-70.

19. Another approach is to reassert the federal role in provincial fields through new conditional grants. See Emmett Hall, *Canada's National-Provincial Health Program for the 1980's* (Ottawa: Department of National Health and Welfare, 1980); and A.W. Johnson, *Giving Greater Point and Purpose to the Federal Financing of Post-Secondary Education and Research in Canada* (Ottawa: Secretary of State for Canada, 1985). Given our emphasis on the need to improve accountability — which includes letting provincial governments within their powers determine priorities freely — this solution is not further discussed here.

20. Bird and Gendron, "Dual VATs and Cross-Border Trade."

21. William H. Oakland and William A. Testa, "Can the Benefits Principle Be Applied to State-Local Taxation of Business," Working Paper Series No. 16 (Chicago, IL: Research Department, Federal Reserve Bank of Chicago, 1998).

22. Giancarlo Pola (ed.), *Local Business Taxation: An International Comparison* (Milano: Vita e Pensiero, 1991).

23. Harry M. Kitchen and Enid Slack, *Business Property Taxation*, Government and Competitiveness Paper 93-24 (Kingston, ON: School of Policy Studies, Queen's University, 1993).

24. William H. Oakland and William A. Testa, "Community Development-Fiscal Interactions: Theory and Evidence from the Chicago Area," Working Paper Series No. 16 (Chicago, IL: Research Department, Federal Reserve Bank of Chicago, 1995).

25. Clara K. Sullivan, *The Tax on Value Added* (New York: Columbia University Press, 1965); see Thomas S. Adams, "The Taxation of Business," in *Proceedings of the Eleventh Annual Conference on Taxation of the National Tax Association* (New Haven, CT, 1918), pp. 185-94.

26. C.M. Allan, *The Theory of Taxation* (London: Penguin Books, 1971); Meade Report. Institute for Fiscal Studies, *The Structure and Reform of Direct Taxes* (London: Allen & Unwin, 1978).

27. Note that if capital is expensed rather than depreciated, the VAT becomes a consumption-based rather than income-based tax.

28. Bird and Gendron, "Dual VATs and Gross-Border Trade."

29. The establishment/plant problem at the business level would require some kind of formula apportionment solution for the BVT, of course. Given the huge

discretionary power available to provincial governments with respect to local finance, however, such problems could presumably be resolved much more easily, if arbitrarily, among localities than among provinces.

30. In principle, the business tax could apply to both the corporate sector and to unincorporated business income. At the time of starting up the tax, however, it might be simplest to replace only the corporate income tax.

31. A 5-percent reduction in property taxes could provide a $1.5 billion dollar reduction in non-residential property taxes or about 10 percent of total property taxes paid by businesses. We did not choose a higher amount in order to avoid creating BVT rates that are too high. Of course, these calculations are only illustrative. Provincial governments could choose to reduce non-residential property taxes even further than provided here if they decide to keep some of the other revenue sources, such as part of capital taxes, instead.

32. Note that we are not suggesting increases in business taxation in any province: the rates shown in these tables are simply those needed to yield the same revenue as now collected from the existing taxes on business in the different provinces.

33. Of course, as noted earlier, the extreme of expensing turns the BVT into a consumption rather than an income tax.

34. See Technical Committee on Business Taxation, *Report*.

35. Smith, *Federal-Provincial Tax Sharing*.

36. It might also be argued that integration measures for domestic owners of businesses are ineffective in a small, open economy so such measures are not needed. Even in this case, however, some integration may be needed to minimize economic distortions resulting from tax planning. Moreover, the evidence is that Canada is not a small, open economy in equity markets — dividend and capital gains taxation impact on equity prices of companies and the cost of equity finance. See Technical Committee on Business Taxation, *Report*, ch. 7, for further discussion.

37. This is similar to the crediting arrangement recently accepted by the US Internal Revenue Service with respect to the Italian IRAP, as mentioned earlier.

38. Sullivan, *The Tax on Value Added*; Robert J. Bennett and Gunter Krebs (eds.), *Local Business Taxes in Britain and Germany* (Baden-Baden: Nomos Verlagsgessellschaft, 1988); and Richard M. Bird, "Why Tax Corporations?" Working Paper No. 96-2 (Ottawa: Technical Committee on Business Taxation, Department of Finance, 1996).

39. Oakland and Testa, "Can the Benefits Principle Be Applied to State-Local Taxation of Business?"

IV

Other
Orders of
Government

11

Provinces and Municipalities, Universities, Schools and Hospitals: Recent Trends and Funding Issues

Harry Kitchen

Ce chapitre étudie la décentralisation des responsabilités budgétaires des gouvernements provinciaux aux gouvernements municipaux, aux écoles primaires et secondaires (financées par les provinces), aux universités et aux hôpitaux au cours de la dernière décennie. Il conclut qu'il y a eu décentralisation des responsabilités en matière de dépenses et de financement des gouvernements provinciaux aux gouvernements municipaux dans presque toutes les provinces ou territoires. Au même moment, le désir des provinces de contrôler les dépenses des écoles locales a mené à la centralisation des finances des écoles dans la plupart des provinces. Cependant, la plus grande décentralisation a eu lieu dans le secteur universitaire où les transferts provinciaux ont chuté de 40% au cours de la dernière décennie. En comparaison, les transferts provinciaux aux hôpitaux ne font montre d'aucune tendance distincte; il y a eu augmentation des transferts dans certains cas et diminution dans d'autres. Enfin, ce chapitre étudie de nombreux enjeux de financement ayant gagné en importance à la suite des initiatives provinciales dans chacun de ces secteurs.

INTRODUCTION

Given this volume's questions about trends in fiscal decentralization, this chapter considers the extent to which decentralization of expenditure and funding responsibilities from the provinces to municipalities, schools (publicly funded elementary and secondary), universities, and hospitals (MUSH sector) has emerged over the past decade. More specifically, it provides an interprovincial and intertemporal comparison of similarities and differences in expenditure responsibilities and funding for the MUSH sector from the late 1980s to the late 1990s (data are not available on a consistent and uniform basis prior to the late 1980s). These data, then, are used as the basis for commenting on the issue of decentralization and the potential implications for funding public services in each of these sectors. The presentation is provided in three parts: first, municipalities and public schools (elementary and secondary) are combined under local government because one or both rely on property taxes in most provinces; second, universities; and third, hospitals.[1] The final section describes and considers emerging funding issues of relevance to each of these sectors.

INTERPROVINCIAL AND INTERTEMPORAL COMPARISONS

LOCAL GOVERNMENT EXPENDITURES

Expenditure responsibilities and revenue-generating opportunities for municipal governments and school boards (when combined, they are referred to as local government) are tightly controlled by provincial legislation and regulations. These controls mean that local governments are essentially "creatures of the province" and can or will do whatever it is that the province permits or requires them to do. While operating in this restrictive environment, there are interprovincial differences in both expenditure responsibilities and the extent to which local governments rely on the various revenue sources available to them. As well, there have been shifts in the provincial-local fiscal environment within some provinces over the past decade with most of the changes arising from provincial initiatives to decentralize spending responsibilities without the provision of additional provincial funds or direct access to provincial revenue sources.

Per capita expenditures are a measure of the level of municipal and school-board spending in each province. Expenditures as a percent of gross domestic provincial product (GDPP) reflect the relative importance of each of these sectors in the overall level of economic activity within a province. Municipal spending as a percent of consolidated provincial/municipal spending serves as a measure of the size of the municipal sector in the overall provincial/municipal government universe.

Tables 1 to 4 portray interprovincial similarities and differences in local government spending over the past decade. In particular, *per capita municipal spending* (Table 1) across the provinces in 1998 ranged from a low of $320 in Prince Edward Island to a high of $1,650 in Ontario; the Northwest Territories and the Yukon were higher at $2,788 and $1,934 respectively (column 3). Interprovincial differences (territorial figures are excluded in these comparisons because they tend to be outliers in most instances) are attributed to higher servicing costs in some areas, greater municipal needs in the more

Table 1: Municipal Expenditures, 1988 and 1998

Province/Territory (1)	1988 – Per Capita (2)	1998 – Per Capita (3)	1988 – % of GDPP (4)	1998 – % of 1997 GDPP (5)	1988/89 % of Provincial- Local Total (6)	1996/97 % of Provincial- Local Total (7)
	$	$	%	%	%	%
Newfoundland	563	648	4.0	3.2	9.2	8.5
Prince Edward Island	252	320	1.8	1.5	4.5	4.9
Nova Scotia	865	997	4.5	4.6	15.3	15.9
New Brunswick	551	744	3.3	3.3	10.0	9.5
Quebec	1,002	1,256	4.9	5.0	15.3	15.5
Ontario	1,181	1,650	4.6	5.4	20.1	19.7
Manitoba	871	1,211	4.5	4.7	13.8	15.0
Saskatchewan	814	1,008	4.5	3.7	12.3	12.1
Alberta	1,306	1,461	5.2	4.2	17.9	19.4
British Columbia	830	1,299	3.8	4.8	15.4	15.9
Yukon	1,177	1,934	3.6	3.8	9.8	9.9
Northwest Territories	1,816	2,788	5.5	6.4	10.2	11.4
Weighted Average	1,035	1,381	4.6	4.9	16.7	16.9

Note: Columns 2 and 3 are obtained by dividing total municipal expenditures by population for 1988 and 1998, respectively. Column 4 records 1988 municipal expenditures as a percent of 1988 gross domestic provincial product (an estimate of economic activity in each province). Column 5 records 1998 municipal expenditures as a percent of 1997 gross domestic provincial product because 1997 is the latest year for which GDPP data are available. Column 6 calculates local government expenditures for 1988 as a percent of consolidated provincial-local expenditures for the fiscal year 1988/89. Column 7 calculates local government expenditures for 1996 as a percent of consolidated provincial-local expenditures for the fiscal year 1996/97.

1988 is the first year for which data, over this period, are available in a uniform and consistent manner. 1998 is the last year and 1996/97 is the last year for consolidated provincial/local expenditures data.

Source: Calculated from Statistics Canada data, Financial Management Systems (FMS), mimeograph, September 1999. The data for 1996/97 and earlier are actual; 1998 are estimates.

highly urbanized provinces, and different municipal expenditure responsibilities across Canada. From 1988 to 1998, per capita expenditures by province displayed the greatest increase in British Columbia and Ontario (from a comparison of figures in columns 2 and 3).

When *municipal spending as a percent of GDPP* is observed, it amounted to 4.6 percent of GDPP for all of Canada in 1988 and 4.9 percent in 1998 (columns 4 and 5), a slight increase in relative importance but at a level less than for the period from the early 1970s to the mid-1980s.[2] When these percentages are compared across provinces, municipal spending grew in relative importance in six provinces with the largest increases occurring in British Columbia and Ontario. The largest proportionate decrease was in Alberta.

Finally, when *municipal spending as a percent of consolidated provincial-local spending* is observed, it was 16.7 percent of the total in 1988-89 (column 6) and 16.9 percent in 1996/97 (column 7) for all of Canada. Six provinces recorded an increase with the largest occurring in Alberta (from 17.9 to 19.4

Table 2: School Board Expenditures, 1988 and 1998

Province/Territory (1)	1988 – Per Capita (2)	1998 – Per Capita (3)	1988 – % of 1988 GDPP (4)	1998 – % of 1997 GDPP (5)
	$	$	%	%
Newfoundland	894	1,060	6.4	5.3
Prince Edward Island	756	980	5.4	4.5
Nova Scotia	784	901	4.7	4.1
New Brunswick	0	0	0.0	0.0
Quebec	863	981	4.2	3.9
Ontario	964	1,247	3.8	4.1
Manitoba	854	1,084	4.4	4.2
Saskatchewan	828	1,064	4.6	3.9
Alberta	872	1,091	3.4	3.1
British Columbia	698	925	3.2	3.4
Yukon	0	0	0.0	0.0
Northwest Territories	317	473	1.0	1.1
Weighted Average	852	1,063	3.8	3.8

Notes and Source: Same as for Table 1.

percent) and Manitoba (from 13.8 to 15 percent). Four provinces recorded a decrease, with the largest occurring in Newfoundland (from 9.2 to 8.5 percent).

School board spending, the other part of the local government universe, amounted to 3.8 percent of GDPP in 1988 and 1998 (columns 4 and 5 of Table 2). School boards do not exist in New Brunswick and the Yukon; here, the province and territory assume responsibility for funding all school expenditures. Where school boards exist, however, their expenditures fell as a percent of GDPP in seven provinces and rose in three over the decade with the largest proportionate increases coming in British Columbia and Ontario. School board expenditures in 1998 ranged from a low of $901 per capita in Nova Scotia to a high of $1,247 in Alberta with the average being $1,063 (column 3).

Since municipal responsibilities differ from province to province, Table 3 records the *relative importance of municipal expenditures by function* for each of the provinces and territories for 1998. The more notable points that may be extracted from this table are:

- Social services are almost entirely a provincial funding responsibility in every province except for Ontario and Manitoba where they account for a notable portion of municipal spending. Nova Scotia is moving toward complete removal of social service funding from the local property tax base.

- Nova Scotia is the only province where municipalities are responsible for funding a noticeable portion of education expenditures: school boards and/or the province handle(s) *all* spending in the other provinces/territories.

- Health expenditures are the responsibility of the provinces/territories except for relatively small expenditures made by municipalities in some provinces for preventative health-care programs.

- Expenditures on transportation (roads, streets, snow removal, and public transit), protection (police and fire), and environmental (water, sewage, and solid waste collection and disposal) services account for over 50 percent of all municipal expenditures in every province/territory except for Ontario (it is lower here because of large municipal funding for social services).

- Expenditures on recreation and cultural services account for between 7 and 20 percent of the municipal total everywhere.

- Debt charges (for capital projects only because municipalities are not permitted to borrow for budgeted operating deficits) show considerable variation ranging from a high of almost 17 percent of the total in Newfoundland to a low of slightly more than 1 percent of the total in the Yukon and Northwest Territories.

Table 3: Distribution (in percent) of Municipal Government Expenditures[1] by Province and Territory, 1998

Municipal Services	Nfld.	PEI	NS	NB	Que.	Ont.	Man.	Sask.	Alta.	BC	Yukon	NWT	Canada
General administration	13.9	13.8	6.9	9.5	11.9	9.0	12.1	13.2	10.9	9.6	22.1	17.4	10.1
Protection	8.7	23.7	16.6	23.6	17.7	14.3	16.5	15.3	13.9	18.3	10.2	4.8	15.7
Transportation	25.5	23.2	16.5	21.3	22.9	17.4	20.6	29.8	28.0	14.5	24.1	16.6	19.9
Health	0.0	0.0	0.1	0.2	0.0	4.6	4.7	1.0	1.6	3.0	0.2	5.4	2.8
Social services	0.1	0.0	10.9	0.0	0.8	25.1	7.6	0.7	1.7	0.2	0.0	5.0	12.2
Education	0.0	0.0	15.6	0.0	0.1	0.0	0.0	0.0	0.0	0.0	0.0	0.0	0.4
Resource conservation	0.5	1.2	0.5	2.2	1.9	1.4	2.1	6.6	3.2	1.2	1.3	0.6	1.8
Environment	21.4	17.0	17.6	22.5	16.1	12.7	14.8	15.7	13.5	22.1	16.8	27.2	15.2
Recreation/culture	11.5	15.5	7.4	13.8	11.7	8.9	10.6	14.0	14.0	17.5	20.4	15.4	11.3
Housing	0.6	0.0	0.6	0.1	3.3	1.7	0.4	0.1	0.5	0.7	0.0	2.8	1.7
Regional planning	1.1	1.4	2.8	1.4	1.8	1.1	1.5	0.9	2.7	1.9	3.0	3.0	1.6
Debt charges	16.6	4.1	4.4	5.2	11.6	3.2	9.0	2.1	9.9	9.5	1.4	1.2	6.8
Other	0.0	0.0	0.0	0.0	0.1	0.6	0.1	0.5	0.0	1.5	0.4	0.5	0.5
TOTAL	100.0	100.0	100.0	100.0	100.00	100.0	100.0	100.0	100.0	100.0	100.0	100.0	100.0
1998 school board exp. as a % of 1998 municipal plus school spending	62.1	75.4	47.5	0.0	43.8	43.0	47.2	51.4	42.7	41.6	0.0	14.5	43.5

Note: [1] For a description of specific municipal services included in each of these functions, see Appendix A.

Source: Same as Table 1.

Table 4: Distribution (in percent) of Municipal Government Expenditures by Province and Territory, 1988

Municipal Services	Nfld.	PEI	NS	NB	Que.	Ont.	Man.	Sask.	Alta.	BC	Yukon	NWT	Canada
General administration	13.6	10.8	7.7	8.2	13.1	8.7	12.0	11.2	8.0	7.7	18.7	24.1	9.9
Protection	6.6	18.3	12.2	23.3	14.4	15.0	15.7	15.0	11.8	19.0	14.1	5.8	14.8
Transportation	28.0	26.1	11.4	23.6	22.5	21.6	25.4	29.3	29.2	15.3	29.0	15.9	22.3
Health	0.0	0.0	0.1	0.9	0.1	2.9	2.0	2.6	1.2	5.0	0.3	0.8	2.0
Social services	0.0	0.0	23.3	0.0	0.5	14.6	5.6	1.7	1.9	0.3	0.0	2.2	7.4
Education	0.0	0.0	12.9	0.0	0.3	0.0	0.0	0.0	0.0	0.0	0.0	0.0	0.4
Resource conservation	0.4	0.7	2.7	2.3	1.3	2.4	1.8	2.1	2.7	2.2	0.7	0.2	2.1
Environment	21.2	12.3	12.4	17.3	15.9	14.2	13.7	16.8	11.8	15.0	16.4	27.9	14.6
Recreation/culture	9.7	21.0	9.2	12.5	9.7	11.2	11.9	14.8	13.3	16.1	15.8	15.9	11.6
Housing	0.6	0.0	0.6	0.7	2.6	2.3	0.3	0.0	0.3	0.8	0.2	1.5	1.8
Regional planning	2.3	2.2	1.6	1.3	1.9	1.9	2.7	2.5	2.5	2.4	1.4	2.3	2.1
Debt charges	17.4	7.6	5.5	9.8	14.1	4.1	8.4	3.9	17.4	15.2	3.4	2.3	9.5
Other	0.2	0.9	0.2	0.0	3.7	1.2	0.4	0.1	0.0	1.0	0.0	1.3	1.6
TOTAL	100.00	100.0	100.0	100.0	100.00	100.0	100.0	100.0	100.0	100.0	100.0	100.0	100.0
school board exp. As a % of local expenditure	61.4	75.0	51.0	0.0	46.3	44.9	49.5	50.4	40.0	45.7	0.0	14.9	45.2

Notes and Source: Same as Table 1.

Table 4 illustrates the relative importance of expenditures by function and province for 1988. When the information in this table is compared with the information in Table 3, the following may be noted for the period from 1988 to 1998.

- Transportation, protection, and environment were the three most important expenditure functions over the period 1988-98.

- Overall, expenditures on social services have increased in relative importance (primarily driven by Ontario) although they have declined in Nova Scotia.

- Debt charges have declined in relative importance everywhere except for Manitoba where they have increased marginally.

Tables 3 and 4 (bottom row) also record *school board expenditures* as a percent of municipal plus school spending in each province for 1988 and 1998. In particular:

- There was a small proportionate decline in school-board spending as a percent of municipal plus school spending from 1988 to 1998: from 45.2 to 43.2 percent.

- Interprovincially, expenditures by school boards in Prince Edward Island account for the highest percentage of all local spending while those in British Columbia, Alberta, Ontario, and Quebec account for the lowest (recall that New Brunswick and Yukon do not have school boards).

LOCAL GOVERNMENT REVENUES

Local government revenues are separated into municipal revenues (Tables 5 and 6) and school board revenues (Tables 7 and 8). *Municipal revenues* consist of grants (conditional and unconditional) and funds generated from own sources including property taxes and user fees with small sums coming from investments and a miscellaneous collection of amusement taxes, licences and permits, and fines and penalties. Tables 5 and 6 note the relative importance of the major revenue sources available to municipalities for 1998 and 1988, respectively. From these two tables, the following observations may be drawn.

Own-source revenue (OSR) for all of Canada grew dramatically in relative importance from 1988 to 1998 — from slightly more than 77 percent of municipal revenue (Table 6) to almost 85 percent (Table 5). Interprovincially, OSR declined in two provinces (Quebec and Manitoba) while it increased in the other eight with the largest increases occurring in Newfoundland, Nova Scotia, New Brunswick, Ontario, and Alberta.

This increase in OSR was singularly driven by a substantial increase in *property taxes* rising from 48.6 percent of all municipal revenues in 1988 to

Table 5: Distribution (in percent) of Municipal Government Revenue[1] (excluding school board revenue) by Province and Territory, 1998

Revenue Source	Nfld.	PEI	NS	NB	Que.	Ont.	Man.	Sask.	Alta.	BC	Yukon	NWT	Canada
Property taxes	54.1	60.2	70.4	53.2	68.5	56.4	43.3	53.6	42.6	52.4	46.9	14.4	56.7
Other taxes	1.7	0.5	0.2	0.4	0.3	1.1	1.8	4.5	1.3	3.0	1.8	0.5	1.2
User fees	15.6	28.4	15.9	22.1	15.4	19.5	20.8	24.1	30.4	26.7	19.7	29.2	20.7
Investment income	1.7	2.3	2.8	0.7	1.9	3.7	5.8	7.5	13.3	8.2	4.7	1.3	4.9
Other	0.6	1.6	0.4	0.6	2.4	0.6	0.8	1.0	1.3	0.5	0.7	0.3	1.1
Own-source revenue	73.7	92.9	89.7	77.0	88.5	81.4	72.5	90.8	89.0	90.8	73.8	45.7	84.6
Unconditional grants	8.5	3.2	2.6	13.7	1.3	3.6	6.3	4.6	1.4	1.5	9.4	6.7	2.9
Conditional grants	17.8	3.9	7.8	9.3	10.1	15.0	21.2	4.6	9.6	7.7	16.9	47.6	12.4
Federal	4.0	1.6	0.5	2.2	0.2	0.6	1.1	0.5	0.8	1.0	0.0	0.9	0.7
Provincial	13.8	2.3	7.3	7.1	9.9	14.4	20.1	4.1	8.8	6.7	16.9	46.8	11.8
Total grants	26.3	7.1	10.3	23.0	11.5	18.6	27.5	9.2	11.0	9.2	26.2	54.3	15.4
TOTAL	100.00	100.0	100.0	100.0	100.00	100.0	100.0	100.0	100.0	100.0	100.0	100.0	100.0

Note: [1]For a more detailed listing of revenues reported in each source, see Appendix B.
Source: Same as Table 1.

Table 6: Distribution (in percent) of Municipal Government Revenue (excluding school board revenue) by Province and Territory, 1988

Revenue Source	Nfld.	PEI	NS	NB	Que.	Ont.	Man.	Sask.	Alta.	BC	Yukon	NWT	Canada
Property taxes	41.9	50.0	58.0	41.7	68.8	41.7	44.5	48.1	36.3	48.0	31.7	16.6	48.6
Other taxes	1.9	0.5	0.6	0.5	1.0	1.3	2.2	3.9	1.0	2.5	1.4	0.8	1.4
User fees	12.6	30.7	10.8	18.9	16.5	20.0	17.7	21.4	26.5	23.7	13.9	33.8	20.0
Investment income	1.9	3.7	3.7	1.2	3.0	5.1	8.3	6.7	12.8	10.1	4.1	2.1	6.0
Other	0.4	1.2	0.8	0.6	2.0	0.7	1.0	1.4	1.4	0.5	0.6	0.2	1.1
Own-source revenue	58.8	86.1	73.7	63.0	91.3	68.8	73.7	81.3	78.0	84.9	51.8	53.6	77.1
Unconditional grants	18.2	12.2	4.6	26.5	0.5	7.3	7.8	10.1	6.8	4.3	8.1	9.2	5.8
Conditional grants	23.0	1.7	21.6	10.5	8.3	23.8	18.5	8.6	15.2	10.8	40.2	37.2	17.1
Federal	3.1	0.2	0.4	1.6	0.2	0.9	1.2	0.3	0.5	1.1	1.0	0.3	0.7
Provincial	19.9	1.5	21.2	8.9	8.1	23.0	17.3	8.2	14.7	9.7	39.1	36.9	16.4
Total grants	41.2	13.9	26.3	37.0	8.7	31.2	26.3	18.7	22.0	15.1	48.2	46.4	22.9
TOTAL	100.00	100.0	100.0	100.0	100.00	100.0	100.0	100.0	100.0	100.0	100.0	100.0	100.0

Notes and Source: Same as Table 1.

Table 7: Distribution (in percent) of School Board Revenue by Province and Territory, 1998

Revenue Source	Nfld.	PEI	NS	NB	Que.	Ont.	Man.	Sask.	Alta.	BC	Yukon	NWT	Canada
Property taxes	0.0	0.0	0.0	0.0	13.7	39.4	29.7	44.4	4.6	0.0	0.0	22.9	21.3
Grants-in-lieu	0.0	0.0	0.0	0.0	0.2	0.6	2.3	1.3	0.3	0.0	0.0	0.0	0.4
Business taxes	0.0	0.0	0.0	0.0	0.0	0.0	0.0	2.3	0.0	0.0	0.0	0.0	0.1
Other	0.0	0.0	0.0	0.0	0.0	0.0	0.0	0.0	1.0	0.0	0.0	0.0	0.0
Total property related	0.0	0.0	0.0	0.0	13.9	40.0	32.0	48.0	5.8	0.0	0.0	22.9	21.8
User fees	1.8	0.3	2.1	0.0	7.9	1.4	3.2	3.0	4.4	2.2	0.0	2.9	3.1
Investment income	0.2	0.0	0.1	0.0	0.0	0.0	0.2	0.7	0.4	0.7	0.0	0.9	0.1
Other	0.2	0.0	0.0	0.0	0.0	0.1	0.0	0.0	0.1	0.1	0.0	0.0	0.1
Own-source revenue	2.2	0.3	2.2	0.0	21.8	41.5	35.4	51.7	10.7	2.9	0.0	26.7	25.1
Conditional grants													
Federal	1.0	0.0	0.0	0.0	0.2	0.3	0.2	0.0	0.0	0.3	0.0	1.6	0.2
Provincial	96.8	99.7	80.6	0.0	77.8	58.2	64.4	48.3	89.3	96.8	0.0	71.7	74.7
Municipal	0.0	0.0	17.2	0.0	0.2	0.0	0.0	0.0	0.0	0.0	0.0	0.0	0.0
Total grants	97.8	99.7	97.8	0.0	78.2	58.5	64.6	48.3	89.3	97.1	0.0	73.3	74.9
TOTAL REVENUE	100.00	100.0	100.0	0.0	100.00	100.0	100.0	100.0	100.0	100.0	0.0	100.0	100.0

Source: Same as Table 1.

Table 8: Distribution (in percent) of School Board Revenue by Province and Territory, 1988

Revenue Source	Nfld.	PEI	NS	NB	Que.	Ont.	Man.	Sask.	Alta.	BC	Yukon	NWT	Canada
Property taxes	5.3	0.0	0.0	0.0	4.1	43.0	21.5	39.2	29.3	27.3	0.0	21.1	26.8
Grants-in-lieu	0.4	0.0	0.0	0.0	0.0	0.5	2.8	1.3	1.3	0.6	0.0	0.0	0.6
Business taxes	0.0	0.0	0.0	0.0	0.0	6.5	0.0	1.9	0.0	0.0	0.0	0.0	2.8
Other	0.0	0.0	0.0	0.0	0.0	0.9	0.0	0.0	2.1	0.0	0.0	0.0	0.6
Total	5.7	0.0	0.0	0.0	4.1	50.9	24.3	42.4	32.8	27.9	0.0	21.1	30.7
Licenses, permits	0.0	0.0	0.0	0.0	0.0	0.0	0.0	0.1	0.0	0.0	0.0	0.0	0.0
User fees	1.6	0.3	2.5	0.0	7.6	1.7	3.6	3.1	4.6	3.3	0.0	2.2	3.8
Investment income	0.1	0.3	0.7	0.0	0.0	0.0	0.4	1.1	0.6	0.7	0.0	4.6	0.2
Other	0.1	0.0	0.0	0.0	0.0	0.1	0.1	0.0	0.1	0.0	0.0	0.0	0.0
Own-source revenue	7.5	0.5	3.2	0.0	11.7	52.6	28.4	46.7	38.0	31.9	0.0	27.9	34.8
Conditional grants													
Federal	0.4	0.0	0.0	0.0	0.3	0.1	0.3	0.0	0.1	0.4	0.0	0.0	0.2
Provincial	92.1	99.5	96.8	0.0	87.7	47.2	71.3	53.3	61.9	67.7	0.0	72.0	65.0
Municipal	0.0	0.0	0.0	0.0	0.3	0.0	0.0	0.0	0.0	0.0	0.0	0.0	0.1
Total grants	92.5	99.5	96.8	0.0	88.3	47.4	71.6	53.3	62.0	68.1	0.0	72.1	65.2
TOTAL REVENUE	100.00	100.0	100.0	0.0	100.00	100.0	100.0	100.0	100.0	100.0	0.0	100.0	100.0

Source: Same as Table 1.

56.7 percent by 1998. Interprovincially, the largest increases in dependence on property taxes have occurred in Ontario. For some time, there has been considerable variation in the extent to which municipalities across Canada rely on property taxes. In 1998, for example, property taxes across provinces ranged from a high of 70.4 percent of all municipal revenues in Nova Scotia to a low of 42.6 percent in Alberta. The Northwest Territories was the lowest at 14.4 percent and is a clear outlier in this comparison. At the same time, user fees across Canada have grown slightly in importance: from 20 percent of all revenues in 1988 to 20.7 percent by 1998. As with property taxes, there is considerable variation in the relative importance of user fees — they accounted for 30.4 percent municipal revenues in Alberta (the highest) and for 15.4 percent in Quebec (the lowest) in 1998. Finally, from 1988 to 1998, user fees increased in all but three provinces (Prince Edward Island, Quebec, and Ontario).

In addition to own-source revenues, municipalities rely on provincial, and to a lesser extent, federal *grants*. In 1988, grants accounted for 23 percent of all municipal revenue in Canada. By 1998, this had fallen to slightly more than 15 percent: a decrease of eight percentage points in relative importance. Over this time, municipalities in nine of the twelve provinces/ territories experienced a decrease in their relative reliance on grant revenues (although of differing magnitudes) while municipalities in the other three witnessed an increase (Quebec, Manitoba, and the Northwest Territories). As for changes in their composition, conditional grants provided about 17 percent of all municipal revenues at the beginning of the period and 12.4 percent by the end of the period. Unconditional grants fell from slightly less than 6 percent of all municipal revenues in 1988 to slightly less than 3 percent by 1998. By 1998, the interprovincial comparison indicated that municipalities in Manitoba and Newfoundland received the largest percentage of revenues from grants (27.5 percent and 26.3 percent respectively) while municipalities in Prince Edward Island received slightly more than 7 percent (the lowest). Finally, municipal grants come almost entirely from the provinces: the federal government provides very little in the way of grant support.

School boards in all provinces and territories where they exist are responsible for funding elementary and secondary schools with revenues generated from a combination of grants (almost entirely provincial) and own-source revenues (primarily property taxes). Tables 7 and 8 depict the distribution of school board revenues for 1998 and 1988, respectively. In some provinces, significant changes have occurred in school board financing over the past decade. In particular, the complete or partial provincialization of school financing in Alberta, British Columbia, and Ontario has reduced the extent to which school boards in these provinces now have access to local property taxes; for example, school boards in Alberta now generate less than 6 percent of their funds from local property taxes, whereas they generated about one-third of their revenues from this source in the late 1980s. Similarly, school boards in British Columbia used to receive between 25 and 30 percent of their funds from property taxes; now they get nothing, although they have the right to access local property taxes but only after approval through a local referendum. In 1998, the provincial government in Ontario removed a school board's power to set its own property tax rates (see discussion below). Changes in these three provinces over the past decade have contributed to a nine percentage-point reduction in the relative importance of school board property taxes for all of Canada and an offsetting increase in the relative importance of provincial grants. At the moment, only Manitoba and Saskatchewan remain with traditional property-tax-supported school boards, a dramatic change from the funding system of 20 years ago.

Property Taxes

Since the property tax is the only significant tax of any direct importance to municipalities and school boards, Table 9 records per capita levels of property taxation by province for 1988 and 1998 (columns 2 and 7, respectively); total property tax revenues as a percent of all provincial and local taxes (columns 3 and 8); and the percentage breakdown of property taxes that are collected by municipal governments, provincial governments, and school boards (columns 4 to 6 for 1988 and columns 9 to 11 for 1998). From this table, the following is apparent:

- Wide variation exists in the level of per capita property taxes across Canada: Atlantic Canada's levels are considerably lower than those for Quebec, Ontario, and western Canada.

- For all of Canada from 1988 to 1998, property taxes accounted for the same percentage of provincial and local tax revenues: 24.9 percent (comparison of columns 3 and 8).

- Interprovincially, property taxes as a percent of all provincial and local taxes fell in four provinces and rose in six over the past decade.

- In every province and territory, the property tax is shared between the municipal sector and the province and/or school boards.

- Provincial involvement in property taxation is linked to the province's direct interest in taxing property to fund the costs associated with elementary and secondary schooling (PEI, NB, Manitoba, Alberta, BC, and since 1998, Ontario). The general practice is for provinces to stay away from provincial property taxes if local school boards have the power to tax property.

- At the moment, Manitoba and Saskatchewan are the only two provinces that permit school board taxation in any significant way. School

Table 9: Per Capita Levels of Property Related¹ Taxation and Its Relative Distribution to the Municipal, Provincial and School Board Sectors, 1988 and 1998

Province/Territory (1)	1988					1998				
	Per Capita Level (2) $	Property Taxes as a % of All Provincial & Local Tax Revenue (3) %	Percent of All Property Taxes Collected By:			Per Capita Level (7) $	Property Taxes as a % of All Provincial & Local Tax Revenue (8) %	Percent of All Property Taxes Collected By:		
			Municipal (4) %	Provincial (5) %	School Boards (6) %			Municipal (9) %	Provincial (10) %	School Boards (11) %
Newfoundland	258	11.3	80.2	0.0	19.8	371	11.1	96.0	4.0	0.0
Prince Edward Island	300	14.0	37.6	62.4	0.0	558	16.6	43.6	56.4	0.0
Nova Scotia	477	18.6	100.0	0.0	0.0	739	21.3	91.9	8.1	0.0
New Brunswick	428	16.7	52.2	47.8	0.0	774	21.8	52.0	48.0	0.0
Quebec	666	19.4	94.6	0.0	5.4	1,184	20.3	71.0	17.6	11.4
Ontario	992	28.1	50.0	0.1	49.9	1,575	28.2	58.1	9.5	32.4
Manitoba	783	24.6	48.7	24.0	27.3	1,162	25.5	46.3	23.7	30.0
Saskatchewan	757	28.9	51.3	0.1	48.6	1,249	25.5	39.6	17.3	43.2
Alberta	813	32.0	56.9	7.9	35.2	1,085	26.1	58.4	36.3	5.3
British Columbia	775	26.9	51.3	23.3	25.4	1,125	26.0	54.6	45.4	0.0
Yukon	503	22.2	74.9	25.1	0.0	1,072	25.2	87.3	12.7	0.0
Northwest Territories	451	24.7	67.2	17.7	15.1	638	24.6	64.0	18.7	17.3
Weighted Average	797	24.9	61.6	5.2	33.2	1,273	24.9	60.3	19.1	20.6

Note: ¹ Property and related taxes include real property taxes, development charges, lot levies, special assessments, business taxes, land-transfer taxes and grants-in-lieu of taxes.

Source: Same as Table 1.

boards in Quebec, the Northwest Territories, and Alberta raise small amounts of revenue from property taxes but they are highly dependent on provincial funding. Elsewhere, elementary and secondary school funding is entirely the responsibility of the province.

PROVINCIAL-LOCAL FISCAL RELATIONSHIPS: HAS
DECENTRALIZATION OCCURRED?

While there is interprovincial variation in municipal and school board revenues and expenditures, there remains the issue of whether or not there has been a trend toward decentralization from provincial to local governments over the past decade. The short response is that there has been a move toward decentralization across the country. For example, the size of the municipal sector in Canada, when taken as a percentage of gross domestic provincial product, increased from 4.6 to 4.9 percent over the period from 1988 to 1998. At the same time, federal spending as a percent of GDPP declined from 23 to 19 percent (when debt expenditures are ignored, the decline went from 17 percent to 13.9 percent) and provincial spending fell from 21.3 to 20.6 percent (removal of debt expenditures reduced these percentages to 18.7 percent and 17.6 percent, respectively),[3] suggesting that decentralization of expenditure responsibilities to municipalities has occurred. At the same time, provincial grants to municipalities have declined leaving the municipal sector with the necessity of generating more own-source revenue to meet its increasing expenditure commitments. In particular, provincial grants, for Canada as a whole, accounted for slightly more than 15 percent of all municipal revenues in 1998, down from almost 23 percent a decade earlier. This decrease of eight percentage points in their relative importance was offset by a corresponding increase of eight percentage points in the relative importance of property taxes for funding municipal services — from slightly less than 49 percent of municipal revenues in 1988 to almost 57 percent by 1998. Interprovincially, the largest decrease in the relative importance of grants, and correspondingly the largest increase in the importance of property taxes, occurred in Ontario, the Yukon, Newfoundland, Nova Scotia, and New Brunswick. User fees, the other major component of municipally generated own-source revenue, changed very little in terms of revenue generated over this period.

While this move to proportionately less reliance on provincial funds and greater reliance on own-source revenues may be interpreted as a move to provincial decentralization of increased funding responsibilities to municipalities, it has not been accompanied by a freedom for municipal governments to spend as they wish. They remain "creatures of the province" and are frequently required to use these additional locally generated revenues to meet provincially determined expenditure standards and goals. Perhaps the most obvious example of this is in Ontario where the province implemented a number of initiatives in 1998 that have dramatically changed the provincial-municipal fiscal environment. These are discussed below.

At the same time as changes have taken place in provincial-municipal relations, there has been a movement across the country toward greater centralization of school finances (Alberta, British Columbia, and Ontario, being the most recent). With the exception of Manitoba and Saskatchewan, school boards have either lost their taxation powers or been severely restricted in their access to locally generated property tax revenues. This increased provincialization of schools has essentially eliminated school boards as governing units. While continuing to be composed of elected representatives, they have become arms of the provincial government. They do not have (significant) taxing authority; they are given a budget by the province and it is their responsibility to determine how to spend it. This increased provincial involvement on the funding side has been driven largely by a determination of the provinces to gain control over school spending.

UNIVERSITIES

Table 10 records provincial transfers per capita to universities for 1998 by province along with trends in the relative importance of these transfers over the period from 1988-98. For all of Canada, per capita transfers equaled $176 in 1988 (column 2) with Prince Edward Island incurring the highest level at $241, and Ontario and Alberta, the lowest at $150 and 158, respectively.

In current dollars (column 3), per capita transfers declined by 22 percent overall from 1988 to 1998. This decline was driven largely by the large decreases in British Columbia (32.2 percent), Alberta (30.4 percent), and Ontario (29.3 percent). Four other provinces also experienced decreases, although less significantly, while the three remaining provinces actually increased per capita transfers; specifically, Saskatchewan increased their transfers by 25.7 percent per capita; Manitoba by 12.6 percent; and Prince Edward Island by 5.5 percent. When inflationary increases are removed from these transfers (column 4), however, every province recorded a decrease with the most significant declines occurring in British Columbia (48.3 percent), Alberta (46.8 percent) and Ontario (45.1 percent). For all provinces combined, per capita spending in constant dollars fell by almost 40 percent.

Perhaps the simplest way of viewing the extent to which provincial transfers to universities have changed over time and across provinces is to take them as a percent of provincial government expenditures or as a percent of gross domestic provincial product. As a percent of provincial government spending, provincial transfers on average accounted for 2.8 percent of all spending (column 5) in 1998. Provincial governments in Prince Edward Island

Table 10: Changes in Provincial Transfers to Universities by Province from 1988 to 1998

Province (1)	Per Capita Transfers			As Percent of Provincial Spending		As Percent of Provincial GDP	
	In 1998 Dollars (2)	Percentage Change from 1988 to 1998		In 1998 Dollars (5)	Percentage Point Change in Relative Importance from 1988 to 1998 (6)	1998 Transfers as Percent of 1997 GDPP (7)	Percentage Point Change in Relative Importance from 1988 to 1998 (8)
		Current Dollars (3)	Constant Dollars (4)				
	$	%	%	%	%	%	%
Newfoundland	224 (3)	-15.6	-33.0	3.2	-1.6	1.1	-0.8
Prince Edward Island	241 (1)	5.5	-15.7	3.8	-0.5	1.1	-0.5
Nova Scotia	198 (6)	-8.2	-24.5	3.4	-0.9	0.9	-0.4
New Brunswick	206 (5)	-7.1	-26.5	3.1	-1.2	0.9	-0.4
Quebec	209 (4)	-16.1	-33.8	3.0	-1.3	0.8	-0.4
Ontario	150 (10)	-29.3	-45.1	2.7	-1.9	0.5	-0.3
Manitoba	191 (7)	12.8	-14.7	3.1	-0.1	0.7	-0.1
Saskatchewan	235 (2)	25.7	-2.7	3.7	0.4	0.9	-0.2
Alberta	158 (9)	-30.4	-46.8	2.8	-1.0	0.5	-0.4
British Columbia	177 (8)	-32.3	-48.3	2.4	-3.4	0.6	-0.5
Canada	176	-22.0	-39.5	2.8	-1.6	0.6	-0.4

Note: Figures in parenthesis in column 1 indicate provincial ranking. The percentages in columns 2 and 3 record the percentage change in per capita expenditures from 1988 (first year for which data were provided on a consistent and uniform basis) to 1998 for current and constant dollars respectively. The percentage point changes in columns 6 and 8 record the change in the proportion of provincial spending (column 6) and GPP (column 8) accounted for by postsecondary education from 1988 to 1998. A plus sign indicates an increase and a negative sign a decrease.

Source: FMS data provided by Statistics Canada.

(3.8 percent), Nova Scotia (3.4 percent), and Newfoundland (3.2 percent) devoted the largest percentage of their spending to universities while British Columbia (2.4 percent), Ontario (2.7 percent), and Alberta (2.8 percent) devoted the least. Observing this percentage change over the period from 1988 to 1998, one notes that transfers to universities have become a lower spending priority in all provinces except for Saskatchewan. On average, they fell from 4.4 percent of provincial spending in 1988 to 2.8 percent by 1998 with the largest proportionate decreases occurring in British Columbia (from 5.8 percent to 2.4 percent of total provincial spending) and Ontario (from 4.6 percent to 2.7 percent). Saskatchewan was the only province where transfers to universities increased as a percentage of provincial spending (from 3.3 percent of provincial spending to 3.7 percent) over this period.

If transfers to universities are taken as a percentage of provincial gross domestic product (column 7), one gets a similar picture — Ontario, Alberta and British Columbia's transfers were the lowest — 0.6 percent or less of GDPP in 1998. Newfoundland and Prince Edward Island's transfers were highest at 1.1 percent of provincial GDP. When these percentages are compared with those for 1988 (column 8), every province recorded a decrease in the percentage of GDPP directed at transfers to universities over the decade, further evidence of reduced provincial funding for this sector.

Three key trends have surfaced in Canadian universities. First, there has been a significant decline in real government support for universities (see Table 10). Second, reductions in the real value of operating grants have forced universities to raise tuition fees. As a result, undergraduate fees since 1990-91 have more than doubled in all provinces (Table 11) except for Prince Edward Island, New Brunswick, and British Columbia.[4] The largest increase has occurred in Alberta where average tuition fees for undergraduate arts students have almost tripled from $1,244 to $3,658 (columns 2 to 4). These rising tuition fees have become an increasingly important source of revenue for Canadian universities. In 1997-98 (most recent year for which data are available), tuition fees represented almost 20 percent of university revenues (column 5), up from 8 percent in 1980-81. During the same time period, the proportion of operating revenues represented by government contributions declined from almost 75 percent to slightly more than 55 percent.[5] Student fees as a percentage of revenue were highest in Nova Scotia at 28.2 percent, followed by Ontario at 23.6 percent. Universities in these two provinces have depended less heavily on revenue from government grants and contracts when compared with other provinces; for example, in 1997-98, government funding represented just over 47 percent of total university revenue in both provinces. Quebec universities, by comparison, received the highest proportion of revenue from government grants and contracts (67.8 percent), with students contributing a provincial low of 13.6 percent of total university revenue.[6]

Table 11: Average Undergraduate Arts Tuition Fees¹ and their Contribution to University Revenues by Province throughout the 1990s

Province (1)	Tuition Fees in 1990-91 (2)	Tuition Fees 1999-2000 (3)	% Increase in Tuition Fees from 1990/91 to 1999/2000 (4)	Contribution of Fees to University Revenues in 1997-98⁴ (5)
	$	$	%	%
Newfoundland	1,344	3,300	145.5	20.4
Prince Edward Island	1,840	3,480	89.1	21.1
Nova Scotia	1,943	4,113	111.7	28.2
New Brunswick	1,898	3,329	75.4	21.7
Quebec²	902	2,387	164.6	13.6
Ontario	1,653	3,872	134.2	23.6
Manitoba	1,415	2,940	107.8	18.2
Saskatchewan	1,526	3,164	107.4	17.2
Alberta	1,244	3,658	194.1	18.7
British Columbia³	1,727	2,470	43.0	16.3
Average	1,496	3,379	125.9	19.5

Notes: ¹ Using the most current enrolment data available, average tuition fees have been weighted by the number of students.
² Fees for both in- and out-of-province are included in the weighted average calculation.
³ Fees at both public and private institutions are included in the weighted average calculation.
⁴ Last year for which these data are available.

Source: Statistics Canada, "University Tuition Fees," *The Daily*, 25 August 1999; and "University Finances," *The Daily*, 13 September 1999.

Third, rising tuition fees have led to increasing student debt. In 1990-91, 98,878 students owed an average of $6,810. Five years later, the number of students carrying debt had increased to 148,731 with an average debt level that had risen by 13.4 percent to $7,725.[7] To offset repayment problems associated with rising student debt, universities and governments have increased the amount of assistance for needy students; for example, in some provinces, a portion of higher tuition fees must be directed to student assistance programs.

In summary, the declining role of provincial transfers and the increasing reliance on tuition fees reflect a trend to privatization, or perhaps more accurately, user pay. In an indirect way, this is a form of decentralization.

HOSPITALS

Table 12 records per capita provincial transfers to hospitals by province along with the changing pattern of these transfers from 1988 to 1998. In 1998, per capita transfers were highest in Manitoba ($1,032) and lowest in Saskatchewan ($748) with the average for Canada being $809 (column 2). On average, per capita transfers in nominal terms increased by more than 23 percent (column 3) from 1988 to 1998. Removal of the inflationary component of this increase, however, indicated that per capita transfers actually fell by 4.5 percent for Canada (column 4) with the largest provincial decreases occurring in Alberta (by 21.2 percent) and Quebec (by 10.7 percent) and the largest increases in Prince Edward Island (by 45.4 percent) and Manitoba (by 13.6 percent).

In 1998, transfers to hospitals, on average, absorbed 13 percent of provincial spending (column 5) — a percent that barely exceeded the 1988 figure (by 0.2 percent). Interprovincially in 1998, Manitoba (16.6 percent), Alberta (14.8 percent), and Ontario (14.7 percent) devoted the largest percentage of provincial spending to hospital transfers while British Columbia (10.5 percent) devoted the least. At the same time, interprovincial differences in the pattern of transfers over the past decade may be noted (column 6). British Columbia (down 2.7 percentage points), Newfoundland (down 0.9 percentage points), and Quebec (down 0.8 percentage points) spent proportionately less in 1998 when compared with 1988 while Prince Edward Island (up 4.5 percentage points), Manitoba (up 3.9 percentage points), and Saskatchewan (up 2.3 percentage points) spent proportionately more.

As a percentage of GDPP (column 7), Newfoundland (4.2 percent) and Manitoba (4 percent) spent the most while Alberta (2.4 percent), Ontario (2.6 percent) and Saskatchewan (2.7 percent) spent the least. On average, provincial spending on health amounted to 2.9 percent of GDPP at both the beginning and end of the period.

From the evidence provided, there is no apparent or clear conclusion as to the extent of decentralization and its pattern across provinces. Some provincial governments have increased transfers to hospitals while others have decreased them. Furthermore, to draw conclusions based on data that capture the situation up to 1998 is unlikely to reflect the current situation. For example, the 1999 federal budget increased transfers to the provinces for funding hospitals and health care. At the same time, many provincial budgets announced that there would be increased transfers for health care and hospitals. These initiatives, when implemented, will likely increase per capita spending and

Table 12: Changes in Provincial Transfers to Hospitals by Province from 1988 to 1998

Province (1)	Per Capita Transfers			As Percent of Provincial Spending		As Percent of Provincial GDP	
	In 1998 Dollars (2)	Percentage Change from 1988 to 1998		In 1998 Dollars (5)	Percentage Point Change in Relative Importance from 1988 to 1998 (6)	1998 Transfers as Percent of 1997 GDPP (7)	Percentage Point Change in Relative Importance from 1988 to 1998 (8)
		Current Dollars (3)	Constant Dollars (4)				
	$	%	%	%	%	%	%
Newfoundland	847 (2)	17.9	-6.4	12.0	-0.9	4.2	-0.9
Prince Edward Is.	823 (5)	82.0	45.4	13.0	4.5	3.8	0.6
Nova Scotia	787 (8)	15.3	-5.1	13.5	-0.1	3.6	-0.4
New Brunswick	832 (4)	21.5	-3.8	12.6	-0.6	3.7	-0.4
Quebec	786 (9)	13.2	-10.7	11.6	-0.8	3.1	-0.3
Ontario	804 (6)	31.5	2.3	14.7	1.5	2.6	0.3
Manitoba	1,032 (1)	50.3	13.6	16.6	3.9	4.0	0.4
Saskatchewan	748 (10)	40.1	8.4	11.8	2.3	2.7	-0.3
Alberta	836 (3)	3.2	-21.2	14.8	1.2	2.4	-0.8
British Columbia	788 (7)	30.7	-0.1	10.5	-2.7	2.9	0.1
Canada	809	23.2	-4.5	13.0	0.2	2.9	0.0

Note: Figures in parenthesis in column 1 indicate provincial ranking. The percentages in columns 2 and 3 record the percentage change in per capita expenditures from 1988 (first year for which data were provided on a consistent and uniform basis) to 1998 for current and constant dollars respectively. The percentage point changes in columns 6 and 8 record the change in the proportion of provincial spending (column 6) and CGPP (column 8) accounted for by postsecondary education from 1988 to 1998. A plus sign indicates an increase and a negative sign a decrease.

Source: FMS data provided by Statistics Canada.

the proportion of provincial spending and GDPP directed at health care and, in some provinces, reverse the downward trend of the past few years.

FUNDING ISSUES

This pattern of reduced provincial grant funding for municipalities — substantial decreases in the real value of operating grants for universities and in some provinces, hospitals — has created a fiscal environment in which changes have emerged or are likely to emerge in the way in which the MUSH sector funds or will fund its services in the future. The importance of these changes and the public debate surrounding them, however, should not be diminished in the presence of 1999 federal and provincial budgetary announcements to increase funding for universities and hospitals over the next few years.

The intention in this section is to identify and describe funding issues in the provincial/ MUSH universe that are likely to become increasingly more important as Canada enters the millennium. Further, to provide a framework for discussing these services, this debate should be conducted, partially at least, within the context of a "benefit-based" model of government finance. In this model, the evaluation concentrates on decision-making and funding responsibilities, not production and delivery. MUSH sector services may be delivered in a number of ways: by the governing unit itself, by contracting out to another governing unit, or by contracting with the private sector. This separation of decision-making responsibility and funding from service production and delivery corresponds to what Osborne and Gaebler argue is the need for governments to concentrate more on "steering" (policy-making) and less on "rowing" (service delivery).[8]

BENEFIT-BASED MODEL FOR FUNDING PUBLIC SERVICES

The underlying principle of the benefits model is straight forward — those who benefit from publicly funded services pay for them. In this model, economic efficiency is achieved when the user fee, price or tax per unit of output equals the extra cost of the last unit consumed. Charges applied in this fashion are efficient for funding services where the beneficiaries can be clearly identified and the costs correctly derived. Prices or taxes serve to ration output to those who are willing to pay and they act as a signal to suppliers (local governments or their delivery agents), a signal that indicates the quantity and quality of output desired. Setting a correct price or tax per unit, then, is essential if efficiency is to be achieved. At the same time, it is critical that costs be calculated correctly and incorporated into the price: an incorrect calculation of costs will lead to incorrect prices or taxes.

Accountability is enhanced where there is a close link between the quantity consumed and the price or tax paid per unit of consumption. In this way, individuals/taxpayers are able to determine whether the benefit from the last unit consumed is worth the price or tax paid for its consumption and in a position to apply pressure on politicians to improve the efficiency with which services are provided or to reduce or expand their output.

Fairness within the benefits model is achieved because those who consume public services pay for them, just as someone who benefits from a private good pays for it. Concerns about the tax burden on low-income individuals, on the other hand, should be addressed through income transfers from provincial or federal governments and social assistance programs targeted to individuals in need. It is far more equitable and efficient to handle income-distribution issues through income transfers or targeting than to tamper with charging or taxing mechanisms to accommodate these concerns.[9]

The benefits model is most easily approximated where services do not generate spillovers or externalities; where the services are not designed as being mainly income redistributional;[10] where individuals can be excluded from consuming the service; and where precise measurement of output and costs can be calculated. When these conditions cannot be approximated, the benefits-based model may not be applicable. In its place, it may be appropriate to employ a model that is based on some kind of ability-to-pay criteria. Any ability-to-pay-based model, however, is almost certain to be inferior to the benefits-based model for evaluating the funding of services such as those provided by the MUSH sector, primarily because of the role that user fees (or taxes that approximate them) play or could play in funding these services.

Municipalities

The recent trend where the municipal sector everywhere has increased its reliance on property taxes and, in some provinces user fees, because of declining grants may be evaluated after the role for municipalities in funding and service responsibility has been determined. Municipalities should not be responsible for funding programs specifically directed toward the redistribution of income among individuals (social services, for example). These functions are better performed by the federal and provincial/territorial governments.

At the same time, municipalities should not be viewed as strictly service agencies, specifically charged with funding only those services where the benefiting properties are clearly and unequivocally identified and where user fees could be employed everywhere. Municipal governments are much more than this: they provide a range of local public services whose collective benefits (police protection, local roads, streets, sidewalks, street lighting, etc.) are enjoyed by the residents within its jurisdiction. To fund these services, user fees are inappropriate. In their place, an ideal tax would be one that is imposed on local residents (or exported to the same extent services are), with necessary adjustments through the use of grants to account for externalities (that is, benefits from these services that spill over into neighbouring communities).[11] While there is no clear-cut basis for determining the appropriate local tax base for funding local services with collective benefits, arguments in defence of property taxes can be made.[12] First, income and consumption taxes are currently in the domain of provincial and federal governments. To utilize these taxes as a complete substitute for property taxes would place additional pressure on their tax base, although they may be used as a supplement to property taxes.[13] Second, given that no single tax or no two taxes are deemed to be entirely fair and distortion free, there is considerable merit in a provincial or national tax system that employs a mix of taxes. Included in this mix is the property tax. After all, a tax on property may serve to achieve important social and economic policy objectives that could not be achieved by other taxes.[14]

Provincial grants are also important for funding municipal services. Specifically, conditional grants should be used for partial or full funding of services generating spillovers and for services in which the province has an interest (to ensure uniform or minimum standards, for example). Unconditional grants are provided to municipalities to ensure that minimum service levels may be funded without the imposition of excessively high tax rates on local taxpayers.

In the benefits-model framework, user fees are appropriate for funding services where specific beneficiaries can be identified. Property taxes are important for funding those services that generate collective benefits to the residents of the local community but for which specific users cannot be identified. Unconditional grants are useful where municipalities have an inadequate fiscal capacity for meeting their expenditure commitments and conditional grants are necessary for meeting part of the costs of those services generating spillovers.

Increased reliance on property taxes, and user fees in some provinces over the past decade is a direct result of the declining relative importance of provincial grants. Is this funding trend for municipal services desirable? The answer differs from province to province, primarily because of differing service responsibilities. Where municipalities are only responsible for funding services benefiting local residents, increased reliance on user fees and property taxes is efficient, fair, and accountable. Currently, user fees are employed for funding water and sewer services in almost every municipality in Canada. Indeed, they should be. As well, they are growing in importance for funding solid waste, public transit, and recreation in many municipalities. Finally, there may be an argument for considering them for some components of library services, police, and fire protection.[15]

At the same time, increased reliance on municipal property taxes for funding local public services is desirable if they are used to fund local services that provide collective benefits to residents of the community. If, on the other hand, the services are income redistributional in nature (social services in Ontario and Manitoba), there is no solid argument in support of local funding. This should be the responsibility of the federal or provincial governments. For services generating spillovers (arterial roads, social housing, land ambulance, for example), local property taxes should be expected to fund only a portion of the cost with the remainder coming from provincial grants to capture the value of the benefits spilling into neighbouring jurisdictions.

Reference to Tables 3 and 5 illustrates the current range of services for which municipalities are responsible across the provinces and the extent to which they rely on own-source revenues and provincial grants. In provinces where municipalities are not responsible for social services and social housing (see Table 3) which is all but Ontario and to a lesser extent, Manitoba, greater reliance is placed on own-source revenues. For example, provincial responsibility for social services and social housing in Prince Edward Island, Nova Scotia (while the 1998 figures for Nova Scotia in Table 3 show that municipalities have some responsibility for social services, they have almost been phased out and will be completely phased out in the next year or two), Saskatchewan, Alberta, and British Columbia leaves municipalities with responsibility for funding services that primarily benefit residents of the local community (see Table 3). In particular, municipalities in these provinces generate around 90 percent of all revenues from own sources — property taxes and user fees, primarily (see Table 5). In these provinces, there is a fairly close adherence to the benefits model. Municipalities in Ontario, by comparison, differ significantly from the benefits model because they are required to use property taxes to fund social services, social housing, and a variety of other services whose benefits are not confined to residents of the local community. Indeed, a number of provincial initiatives implemented in 1998 moved municipalities further from the benefits model and it is these changes that are described and examined in the next section.

Ontario: A Distinct Society. Following the provincial election in 1995, the Ontario government moved toward the implementation of a number of changes in its funding arrangements with municipalities and schools (elementary and secondary). This initiative was driven primarily by the province's explicit determination to take control of school spending, spending which it suggested had grown out of control over the past few years because of insufficient constraint exercised by local school boards. To achieve this, it implemented a uniform province-wide education tax rate on residential properties with the rate set at a level that would generate approximately one-half of the property tax previously collected from residential properties for education purposes.

For commercial and industrial properties whose owners continue to pay about the same total amount of property tax for education, the province has taken a different approach. From each municipality, it requisitions a fixed dollar amount from commercial properties and a fixed dollar amount from industrial properties. Here, tax rates are unlikely to be the same across municipalities — they depend on the assessment base and the amount of revenue to be collected. Since this policy direction has removed all taxation powers from local school boards, it has been the focus of considerable criticism, especially from the various teachers' associations in Ontario.

To offset this increase in the province's share of school funding and to meet the provincial objective of initiating changes that were revenue neutral, the province transferred to municipalities increased funding responsibility for a wider range and variety of services with very little (if any) say in service standards (social housing, 50 percent of land ambulance, downloaded provincial highways, and so on). As well, all municipalities now pay for policing and for local property assessment which is operated through a provincial non-profit corporation with standards set by the province. Finally, most municipal grants will be phased out over the next two or three years. Throughout this entire process, it has been impossible to find a solid rationale for the transfer of these new funding responsibilities to the municipal sector. It appears to have been driven by a single desire on the part of the province to meet their revenue-neutrality objective.

At the same time, the province implemented policies to reduce the number of municipalities (more than 225 municipal governing units have been eliminated through mergers and amalgamations) and municipal politicians, primarily through tying some provincial grant assistance to municipalities that restructured through amalgamations, mergers, or annexations. Similarly, the province legislated fewer school boards (through mergers and amalgamations), fewer school trustees with a stipendiary limit for their services of $5,000 per year per trustee (significantly lower than previously paid in many school boards) and reduced decision-making power.

Not surprisingly, these changes have generated significant criticism. Municipal officials argue that the initiatives are not revenue neutral and that once transition funding is over, large property tax increases will be necessary to meet the increased responsibilities. Indeed, this appears to be happening. Tables 5 and 6 record the extent to which the municipal sector has increased its reliance on property taxes over the past decade: from 41.7 percent of all municipal revenues in 1988 to 56.4 percent in 1998. This is translated into a per capita increase in property taxes of $469 over the same period — from $1,181 to $1,650 (Table 1). The province has countered that this need not be the case since municipalities could save money through further reorganization and restructuring, including implementation of new ways of delivering services.

Given that this debate is very much in the political arena, the question remains as to whether or not these recent provincial initiatives will improve the
efficiency, accountability, and fairness of municipal finance. While this may
not be determined until the new system is in place and has been functioning
for some time, there are normative arguments suggesting it will not. In addition to property taxes continuing to fund a range of services providing collective
benefits to the local community, they are now used to fund an expanded range
of services that are income redistributional (social welfare and social housing); that generate benefits (spillovers) for non-residents (land ambulance,
arterial roads, and highways); and where minimum standards are set by the
province (social services, social housing, land ambulance, and provincially
downloaded highways). This further decoupling of property taxes from funding municipal services that benefit primarily residents provides an incentive
for reduced efficiency, less accountability, and greater inequity. To reverse
this pattern, however unlikely the possibility, the province should move in the
direction of using local property tax revenues for funding a narrower range of
services than currently is the case.

Public Schools

In addition to provincial grants, elementary and secondary schools are financed
from property taxes raised by school boards, municipalities, or provincial
governments (Table 13) in every province and territory except for Newfoundland. While property taxation is widely used as a funding source for public
schools, school boards in Manitoba and Saskatchewan are the only ones left
with any notable property taxation powers. The provincialization of schooling in the rest of the country has effectively removed most, if not all, significant
decision-making from local officials. In spite of this trend where school boards
are becoming an arm of the provincial government, there are at least two issues that should be addressed. First, is there a role for local funding of schools
and should this funding come from property taxes on both residential and
non-residential properties? Second, is there a role for provincial property tax
funding of schools?

Is There a Role for Local Funding? While the public education system provides direct benefits to its students, current practice is not to charge students
directly for this service.[16] This is defended on the following grounds: first,
since one cannot measure the value of the direct benefit going to each student,
one cannot set a correct price or tax per unit for the service; second, since
education provides benefits for more than the direct users (spillovers), public
sector funding is required in order to approach an allocatively efficient level
of output; third, because students are required to attend school up to a specified age and to take courses prescribed by provincial authorities, forcing each
student (through the parent or guardian) to pay for this service may impose
severe income distributional consequences on the poorer of them.

Table 13: Property Tax Structure for Funding Public Schools by Province and Territory

Newfoundland	Property taxes are not used to finance public schools.
Prince Edward Island	The province funds 100 percent of education costs from general revenues. Included in these revenues is the money generated from a province-wide property tax, although it is not earmarked for education.
Nova Scotia	Public schools are financed from general revenues of the province (there is no provincial property tax) and from a uniform property tax rate set by the province and imposed on municipalities. Municipalities also have the option of increasing the local tax rate to fund optional programs.
New Brunswick	All public education costs are funded from general provincial revenues — included in these revenues is a provincial property tax on all properties but the property tax is not earmarked specifically for schools.
Quebec	The province is almost entirely responsible for financing school boards from general revenues (no provincial property tax exists). Local school boards have the authority to levy a property tax but it can not exceed $0.35 per $100 of assessed value unless referendum approval is obtained from the taxpayers within the school district. School boards use local property taxes only to finance the maintenance of school facilities.
Ontario	Education is funded from a combination of provincial grants and an education tax rate on property that is set by the province, collected by the municipality and remitted to school boards. The education tax rate on residential/farm and multi-residential properties is uniform across the province. For commercial and industrial properties, the province requisitions a fixed dollar amount in each municipality.
Manitoba	Provincial funding comes from the general revenues of the province and from the proceeds of a province-wide property tax for education. The provincial tax rate applied to residential property is less than the rate assigned to other properties. Local revenues come almost entirely from property taxes on commercial, industrial, and residential properties.
Saskatchewan	Provincial funding comes from general revenues while school divisions generate revenues from property taxes collected from residential and non-residential properties.
Alberta	The province is responsible for funding education. About half of its funding requirement is supported from general provincial revenues and the remainder from a uniform province-wide tax rate on residential, commercial, industrial, and agricultural property. The tax rate on non-residential property is higher than that on residential and agricultural property. If school boards wish to spend more than their provincial grant, they must seek taxpayer approval through a referendum and the additional spending is restricted to a maximum of 3 percent of school budgets.
British Columbia	Schools are funded entirely by provincial grants generated from provincial government revenues which include provincially imposed commercial, industrial, and residential property taxes (property taxes account for about 30 percent of total funding). Although the provincial government sets the rate for school property taxes, there is no necessary connection between school property taxes and provincial grants to school districts. If school boards wish to spend more than their provincial grant, the board must seek local taxpayer approval through a referendum for additional expenditures to be financed through local property taxes.
Northwest Territories	Education mill rates may differ by property class.
Yukon	The government levies a territory-wide school tax which accounts for about 5 percent of school revenue.

Source: *1998 Finances of the Nation* (Toronto: Canadian Tax Foundation, 1999), ch. 6; *Tax Practices Across Canada Manual* and *Appeals Procedure Manual* (Mississauga: Canadian Property Tax Association Inc., 1999); and Harry Kitchen, *Property Taxation in Canada* (Toronto: Canadian Tax Foundation, 1992).

In addition to direct benefits, the local education system provides collective benefits for residents of that community. To illustrate, it is not uncommon for residential property owners to move from one neighbourhood to another, or one town or city to another, so as to benefit from a better quality of education. Given that collective local benefits exist, local funding for a portion of school expenditures may be appropriate, although the proportionate funding split between the local community and the province remains an unresolved issue.

If one adheres to the benefits model, there is merit in a finance system that assigns some direct responsibility for funding to local residents. Accountability and allocative efficiency may be advanced because of the more direct link between the level of government raising the revenue and the level of government making the expenditure. The flexibility and autonomy of local school boards, districts, or divisions, may also be enhanced through access to locally generated revenues from the residential sector, allowing them to accommodate more easily the desires of the local community.

Given the arguments in support of local funding and, therefore, property taxation since it is the only tax available at this level, there is a further issue of whether non-residential (commercial and industrial) and residential properties alike should contribute or whether this contribution should come from only one of these sectors. Making a case for local funding from the commercial and industrial sector is far more difficult than for the residential sector. For example, there is no question that commercial and industrial property owners benefit from a well-educated and highly skilled labour force. This benefit, however, tends to be linked to the education system across the entire province and not directly to the expenditures made in a particular school jurisdiction.[17] As long as the local education system provides no collective or direct benefits to local commercial and industrial property owners, the imposition of non-residential property taxes to fund a portion of local education costs is both inefficient and unaccountable. It is inefficient because the commercial/industrial sector pays taxes for services that primarily benefit the residential sector.[18] This type of cross-subsidization has the potential for leading to an oversupply of services for the residential sector. Further, it lacks accountability, since those who pay are not the recipients of the service for which they have paid.

While there is a solid argument for not funding schools from a local property tax on non-residential property, such cannot be claimed for a local tax on residential property. Further, the arguments against the taxation of commercial and industrial properties for funding local schools should not be confused with the arguments in support of province-wide property taxation of non-residential properties for school purposes. They are quite different as is noted below.

Provincial Property Taxation of Non-residential Property? As long as non-residential property is taxed to finance education, there may be good reasons to pool non-residential assessment and assign the tax revenues to the province.[19] For example, it is unlikely that the local commercial/industrial sector directly benefits from the local education system although it is almost certain to benefit from a province-wide system.[20] Furthermore, if the local tax is exported or partially exported, much of the burden is likely to be borne by residents of other taxing jurisdictions and the initial intent, which was to tax the local non-residential sector, will not be achieved. As well, a uniform province-wide tax on business may be desirable on allocative efficiency grounds. Otherwise, industrial or commercial location may well be based on the tax rather than other economic considerations.[21]

Province-wide pooling of non-residential assessment would also have the advantage of injecting more "wealth neutrality" into the funding system in those provinces that currently do not have it. British Columbia,[22] for example, has a scheme of this type and it has been recommended for Ontario.[23] This eliminates the situation where a school board located in an industrially or commercially rich area, can raise more tax revenue without raising the tax on residential property when compared with an area where the commercial/industrial mix is relatively low.

Universities

Whereas municipalities and schools are financed primarily by a partnership of provincial and local governments, the current partnership at the university level is a federal-provincial one. It is a complex partnership, since it involves not only the costs of educating students, but also the broad agenda of research and development, as well as federal and provincial support for an extensive range of other programs involving training and contract services. While recognizing a variety of arguments and concerns within each of these areas,[24] this discussion concentrates on what has become a highly controversial and debatable issue; specifically, decreased provincial funding and increased tuition fees.[25]

While increases in tuition fees have met with criticism, almost all of it from current students, a few faculty members and university administrators, there has been and continues to be debate over whether fees should constitute a much larger or much smaller share of the direct cost of a university education. Decisions regarding tuition fees impact on such critical issues as private versus social benefits (rates of return) of higher education, accessibility, and participation rates (the percentage of a particular age cohort attending universities), and policies related to student financial aid.

Tuition and Private versus Social Benefits. Recent trends toward greater reliance on tuition fees in funding universities begs the question of whether this is a fair, accountable, and efficient way of partially financing universities. Students who graduate with a degree from a university benefit directly through higher incomes, increased social status, enhanced life-long learning, better health, more efficient budgeting, higher returns on investments, and so on.[26] Some of these are more measurable than others. The external benefits, while recognized widely, are very difficult to quantify. External benefits include the enhancement of democratic institutions, adaptability to change, lower welfare costs, greater community health, tolerance, and a more sophisticated class of leaders in society. The only quantifiable factor is the lower welfare costs due to lower unemployment for graduates and the additional tax revenue that stems from higher lifetime earnings.

Based on a number of Canadian studies which estimated the rates of return up to the late 1980s,[27] the only consensus to emerge was that the high private rates of return to postsecondary education made it very attractive for the individual to invest in higher education. These estimated rates of return, however, did not capture the unmeasurable benefits to society and hence they underestimated the real social return to expenditures made on postsecondary education. A more recent study[28] claims that the private rate of return for university graduates in Ontario has remained relatively stable over the period from the 1980s through the early 1990s at 13.8 percent for male graduates and 17.6 percent for female graduates. Whether similar net benefits will emerge as tuition fees continue to increase is an open question, but there is ample evidence that a university education continues to generate higher rates of return. In part, this is one of the reasons why there are continued calls for greater use of benefits-based funding of university education.[29]

Tuition, Accessibility and Participation Rates. A primary argument against raising tuition fees is the belief that access will be limited because of costs. "Access" is not easily defined in this context. Does improving access mean creating an environment that will increase the participation rate of 18 to 24 year olds? Does it mean creating an environment that will encourage more high school graduates from low-income families to attend university? Or does it mean expanding the number of students from under-represented groups in universities?

One of the most exhaustive studies[30] of postsecondary enrolment in Canada concluded that the percentage of 18 to 24 year olds enrolling in postsecondary institutions increased as tuition, in real terms, rose. Other studies, however, have found that as tuition increased, enrolment declined.[31] The abolition of tuition fees in 1984 in Australia appears to have had little impact on the overall social composition of students attending university.[32] One of the most recent papers on tuition fees and accessibility in Canada argues that low tuition does not enhance accessibility and only serves to limit the effectiveness of universities. A much more sensible policy would be to raise fees and provide direct assistance to those who need it.[33] In general, price response, or elasticity, studies show that relatively modest tuition increases have little impact on overall university participation rates and little effect on traditional age, middle- or high-income participants.[34]

There is clearly no consensus on this issue, however. The level of parents' education is perhaps the strongest single influence on a student's decision whether to enrol in a university program.[35] Future increases or decreases in tuition fees may be more a matter of the public pressure related to the overall increase in government expenditure and the public's tolerance for higher taxation or deficits. In the current climate, provincial governments are moving in the direction of higher fees; however, if these fees are to continue to rise, government and university assistance programs will have to play an increasingly important role in public policy.

Tuition and Student Aid. Financial aid to students has changed noticeably in the 1990s: there has been a major shift away from grant support to student loans. This increased reliance on loans has had a dramatic effect on student debt, so much so that some provinces require universities to provide more institutional grants for needy students. Ontario, in particular, requires universities to set aside a portion (now 30 percent) of increased tuition revenue for student-support programs. As well, the Ontario government created the Student Opportunity Trust Fund (in 1997) — a program where the province matches all private sector contributions raised by universities that are targeted to student assistance. This move toward target funding is on the rise and is an attempt by provinces to maintain control over part of university spending. Targeted funding, however, is not only restricted to the provinces. The federal government has created the Canada Millennium Scholarship Fund to provide scholarship support to needy students (beginning in 2000). While the details of this recent federal initiative to provide scholarship support directly to students have not been fully worked out, the program could be designed as a voucher scheme. The idea of education vouchers has been around for a long time and several Canadian studies on financing education have examined the benefits and drawbacks of such a scheme.[36] In its simplest form, a federal higher education voucher would involve each individual who has completed secondary school receiving a "line of credit" applicable at any university at any time in their lives. This would add an element of the market system to higher education.[37] Vouchers meet the criteria of efficiency and accountability. Further, the equity criteria is enhanced if vouchers embody a premium for students from low-income families or those with insufficient means to pay the full cost of education. For the federal government, the political value of a voucher system is obvious; each year, students would receive a letter of credit from the federal government indicating precisely the value of their education/ training voucher. Accountability would be "up front."

Recent moves toward higher tuition fees has, as expected, spawned a number of proposals to reform the existing system of student financial assistance. One reform that has received considerable attention is a contingent repayment loan (CRL) where the repayment of funds borrowed for education is based on the borrower's future ability to repay the loan. The idea is founded on an argument that imperfect capital markets lead to an underinvestment in education and training. Further, it has been debated and discussed by commissions, governments, and scholars for some time.[38] Like the voucher, the CRL may be any value up to the total direct cost of education or training. The major difference is that the repayment depends upon the individual's level of income after completing or after attending university. The attractiveness of the scheme is that it can be incorporated into an income tax form. As long as the individual is in school, no repayment would be required and the interest on the loan could be paid by the federal and/or provincial government. The program could be universal with no means test, a reform that the Macdonald Commission in its review of postsecondary education suggested was overdue.[39]

Hospitals

Over the past two or three years, every provincial government has been confronted by doctors, nurses, patients, and ordinary citizens criticizing cutbacks in hospital care. Horror stories about clogged emergency rooms and ambulances being diverted from hospital to hospital while trying to admit patients has elevated health care to the top of public policy concerns. To alleviate some of these concerns and to remain popular with the voting public, federal and provincial governments alike have recently introduced budgets announcing increased funding for hospitals, and health care more generally. Is this the answer? Will increased public funding resolve citizen concerns? The most hardened sceptic would argue, in all likelihood, that this is not the answer. Change must be made, but how? Should user fees be introduced, in spite of the federal government's explicit opposition to them?

Hospitals and User Fees. As has been noted above, efficiency and accountability in the provision of public services is enhanced when consumers are charged a per-unit fee, price or tax that covers the additional cost of the service consumed. Failure to adopt this type of pricing policy for services where specific beneficiaries can be identified, then, leads to over-use and abuse. In the words of one local hospital administrator when commenting on crowded hospital waiting rooms and emergency wards, "failure to impose user fees, modest as they may be, is like having a free bar at a wedding." Obvious as it may seem and in spite of solid economic arguments in support of user fees,[40]

Canadian governments have steadfastly resisted their implementation. In addition to political concerns that citizens may reject their party at the ballot box, it is argued that user fees will lead to a two-tiered health-care system — one level for the rich and one for the poor. As well, concerns have been expressed that the poor would not be able to pay for expensive medical services. While these arguments cannot be dismissed or ignored, there are potentially serious problems by not implementing user fees to cover a portion of the cost of hospital services. First, it is a well-known economic axiom that whenever a service is provided free of charge or for a fee that is less than its marginal social cost, it will be overconsumed and society will be expending more resources on the provision of this service than is allocatively efficient. Second, there is the moral hazard problem — provision of free medical services reduces the incentive for individuals to live healthy life styles and to take care of themselves, especially if they can get free medical assistance during illness. Third, it may help prevent some of the well-known abuse created by patients who frequent emergency rooms on an ongoing basis. Fourth, there is a potential financial crunch. With our changing demographic pattern and the financial burden that this will place on the hospital system over the next few years, one has to ask whether the country can afford not to introduce user fees to protect this system.

Finally, to alleviate concerns that the poor will not have access or will not be able to afford it, income distributional issues are better handled through income transfers via the tax system and targeted programs to the poor. Indeed, attempts to handle redistribution concerns through inadequate and inefficient pricing may well result in less overall distribution than might otherwise be attained.[41]

CONCLUSION

From the evidence provided in this chapter, one can conclude that there has been a decentralization of spending and funding responsibilities from provincial to municipal governments over the past decade in almost every province/ territory. As a percent of gross domestic provincial product, the size of the municipal sector across Canada has grown while the size of the federal and provincial sectors has fallen. This increase in municipal expenditure responsibilities has coincided with a reduction in provincial grants, leaving the municipal sector with the necessity of generating more own-source revenue, almost entirely through property taxes, to meet its increasing expenditure commitments.

While this move to proportionately less reliance on provincial funds and greater reliance on own-source revenues may be interpreted as a move to provincial decentralization of increased funding responsibilities to municipalities, it has not been accompanied by a freedom for municipal governments to spend as they wish. They remain "creatures of the province" and are frequently required to use these additional, locally generated revenues to meet provincially determined expenditure standards and goals. Perhaps the most obvious example of this is in Ontario where the province implemented a number of initiatives in 1998 that have dramatically changed the provincial-municipal fiscal environment.

At the same time, there has been a movement across the country toward greater centralization of school finances (Alberta, British Columbia, and Ontario being the most recent). With the exception of Manitoba and Saskatchewan, school boards have either lost their taxation powers or been severely restricted in their access to locally generated property tax revenues. Although continuing to be governed by elected representatives, the provincialization of schools means that school boards are little more than an arm of the provincial government. They do not have (significant) taxing authority; they are given a budget by the province and it is their responsibility to determine how to spend it. This increased provincial involvement on the funding side has been driven largely by a determination of the provinces to gain control over school spending.

While the decrease in provincial transfers to municipalities has been criticized by local officials and a handful of citizens as being unfair and somewhat draconian, it has been far less dramatic than the decreases in provincial transfers to universities. In real terms (that is, constant dollars), transfers to universities have declined by almost 40 percent over the past decade. In fact, universities in every province have experienced a decrease in the real value of provincial transfers, although the magnitude of this decrease has varied. Furthermore, the proportion of provincial spending devoted to transfers declined everywhere, with the exception of Saskatchewan. This decline in the funding role played by provincial transfers and the increasing reliance on tuition fees reflects a trend to privatization, or perhaps more accurately, user pay. In an indirect way, this is a form of decentralization.

When provincial transfers to hospitals in real terms are examined over the past decade, there is no apparent or clear conclusion as to the extent of decentralization and its pattern across provinces. Some provincial governments increased transfers (in constant dollars) to hospitals while others reduced them. Furthermore, to draw conclusions based on data that capture the situation up to 1998 is unlikely to reflect the current situation. For example, the 1999 federal budget increased transfers to the provinces for funding hospitals and health care. At the same time, many provincial budgets announced that there would be increased transfers for health care and hospitals.

This decreasing role played by provincial transfers to the MUSH sector has been motivated in virtually every instance by each province's desire to eliminate its operating deficit, to restrict the growth in or reduce its accumulated debt while simultaneously cutting taxes. To achieve these objectives, provinces have responded, partially at least, by reducing provincial transfers and hence cutting direct provincial funding for services provided by this sector.

Reduced provincial grant funding for municipalities — substantial decreases in the real value of operating grants for universities and in some provinces, hospitals — has created a fiscal environment in which changes have emerged in their funding. Furthermore, there is nothing to indicate a change in direction in the near future. If anything, there is likely to be a greater emphasis on direct funding by users or consumers. Municipalities will increase their reliance on property taxes and user fees; the provincialization of public schools will not diminish; tuition fees will rise to account for an increasing proportion of university revenues; and user fees are likely to be introduced for hospitals or an increasing array of hospital services and the health-care sector more generally. On this latter point, it might require a change in the conditions of the *Canada Health Act* so that federal transfers to the provinces, under the CHST, would not decline in the presence of user fees.

While the recent funding pattern and its continuation into the future may incur significant criticism from a wide range of individuals, it may be economically fair, efficient, and accountable. For instance, efficiency may be improved if the price or tax per unit of output equals the extra cost of the last unit consumed. Accountability may be enhanced because of the fairly close link between the quantity consumed and the price or tax paid per unit of consumption. Greater fairness may arise as long as those who benefit from the services pay for them. Finally, to overcome the criticism that the use of benefits-based taxation for funding these services is unfair to the poor and restricts their opportunity for consuming them, income-support programs will have to be a part of the picture. For users of municipal services, schools, and hospitals this may include social-assistance programs targeted to specific individuals. For university students, it may include an expansion of scholarships and bursaries plus the introduction of a contingent repayment loan program where the repayment of funds borrowed for education purposes is based on the borrower's future ability to repay the loan.

NOTES

The author wishes to acknowledge helpful and constructive comments on an earlier draft from two referees and the editor of this volume. Any errors or omissions, however, remain the responsibility of the author.

1.   To stay within the traditional MUSH sector, the discussion concentrates on hospitals and not on Regional Health Authorities and the multitude of issues surrounding them.

2.   See Harry Kitchen, *Local Government Finance in Canada* (Toronto: Canadian Tax Foundation, 1984), ch. 2.

3. Calculated from FMS data provided by Statistics Canada.

4. British Columbia has frozen tuition fees for five consecutive years; Quebec's tuition fees are frozen at $1,668 for residents of the province but higher fees are imposed on out-of-province students.

5. Statistics Canada, "University Tuition Fees," *The Daily*, 25 August 1999; and "University Finances," *The Daily*, 13 September 1999.

6. Ibid.

7. Statistics Canada, "Student Debt," 30 July 1999.

8. David Osborne and Ted Gaebler, *Reinventing Government: How the Entrepreneurial Spirit is Transforming the Public Sector* (Reading, MA: Addison-Wesley Publishing Co., 1992).

9. For a discussion of these programs, see Robin Boadway and Harry Kitchen, *Canadian Tax Policy* (Toronto: Canadian Tax Foundation, 1999), chs. 8, 9.

10. While some elements of income redistribution are inherent in almost all public services, income redistributional services include welfare payments, children's aid, social housing, and income transfers to name the most obvious.

11. Under this view, user fees or charges are retained for funding those services whose costs and benefits can be assigned to specific properties or individuals (water and sewers, and a portion of transit and recreation, for example). For an excellent discussion of the benefits model of local finance, see Richard M. Bird, "Threading the Fiscal Labyrinth: Some Issues in Fiscal Decentralization," *National Tax Journal* 45, 2 (1993):207-27.

12. A discussion in support of property tax funding for local public services which provide benefits of a collective nature to the local community is found in John Bossons, Harry Kitchen and Enid Slack, "Local Government Finance: Principles and Issues," an unpublished paper for the Ontario Fair Tax Commission, Toronto, 1993; Almos Tassonyi, "The Benefits Rationale and the Services Provided by Local Governments," an unpublished paper for the Ontario Fair Tax Commission, Toronto, 1993; and Paul A.R. Hobson, "Efficiency, Equity and Accountability Issues in Local Taxation," in *Urban Governance and Finance: A Question of Who does What,* ed. Paul A.R. Hobson and France St-Hilaire (Montreal: Institute for Research on Public Policy, 1997), pp.113-31, especially 117-18.

13. In Manitoba, for example, municipalities receive a share of provincial personal and corporate income taxes.

14. See Neil Brook's commentary on the Ontario Fair Tax Commission's report entitled *Fair Taxation in a Changing World* (Toronto: University of Toronto Press, 1993) in the report at pp. 1019-23.

15. Harry Kitchen, "Pricing of Local Government Services" in *Urban Governance and Finance: A Question of Who does What,* ed. Paul A.R. Hobson and France St-Hilaire (Montreal: Institute for Research on Public Policy, 1997), pp.135-68, especially 160-62.

16. Private schools, by comparison, charge tuition fees.

17. Timothy Bartik, "Business Location Decisions in the United States: Estimates of the Effects of Unionization, Taxes and Other Characteristics of States," *Journal of Business and Economic Statistics* 3 (1985):59.

18. Harry M. Kitchen and Enid Slack, *Business Property Taxation*, Government and Competitiveness Project Discussion Paper No. 93-24 (Kingston: School of Policy Studies, Queen's University, 1993).

19. British Columbia, *Report of the Royal Commission on Education: A Legacy for Learners* (Victoria: BC Government, 1988).

20. Bartik, "Business Location Decisions in the United States," p.18.

21. Harry Kitchen and Douglas Auld, *Financing Education and Training in Canada* (Toronto: Canadian Tax Foundation, 1995), ch. 4.

22. See "Financing Public Schools: Issues and Options, A Discussion Paper," Victoria: Education Funding Review Panel, 1992.

23. Ontario. Ministry of Education, "Alternative Methods of Financing Elementary and Secondary Education in Ontario," 1984; and Macdonald Commission, *Report on the Financing of Elementary and Secondary Education in Ontario*, 1985; and more recently in the report of the Ontario Fair Tax Commission, *Fair Taxation in a Changing World* (Toronto: University of Toronto Press, 1993), ch. 32.

24. Kitchen and Auld, *Financing Education and Training in Canada*, chs. 5-10.

25. For a detailed examination of the role of tuition fees in the overall framework of university and college finance, see David A.A. Stager, *Focus on Fees: Alternative Policies for University Tuition Fees* (Toronto: Council of Ontario Universities, 1989).

26. For a complete discussion of the theory on the social and private rates of education, see W.W. McMahon, "Consumption and Other Benefits of Education," in *Economics of Education; Research and Studies*, ed. G. Psacharopoulos (New York: Pergamon Press, 1987); and W.W. McMahon and A.P. Wagner, "Expected returns to Investment in Higher Education," *Journal of Higher Education* 16, 2(1981):274-85.

27. For a summary of these, see Kitchen and Auld, *Financing Education and Training in Canada*, ch. 7.

28. D.A.A. Stager, "Returns to Investment in Ontario University Education, 1960-1990 and Implications for Tuition Fee Policy," *The Canadian Journal of Higher Education* 26, 2 (1996):1-22.

29. Nancy Olewiler, "Let's Use Benefit Taxes More," *Policy Options* 19,10 (1998):24-27, p. 27.

30. John Vanderkamp, *Canadian Post-Secondary Enrolment: Causes, Consequences and Policy Issues*, Final Report for the Review of Demography (Ottawa: Ministry of Health and Welfare, 1988).

31. There are a large number of studies on this topic which have been summarized and compared in a paper by Leslie and Brinkman. See L. Leslie and P.T. Brinkman, "Student Price Response in Higher Education," *Journal of Higher Education* 58 2(1987):181-204.

32. D.S. Anderson and A.E. Vervoon, *Access to Privilege: Patterns of Participation in Australian Post-Secondary Education* (Canberra: ANU Press, 1983).

33. See Benjamin Levin, "Tuition Fees and University Accessibility," *Canadian Public Policy/Analyse de Politiques* 16, 1(1990):51-59.

34. Robert Clift, Colleen Hawkey and Ann Marie Vaughan, "A Background Analysis of the Relationships Between Tuition Fees, Financial Aid, and Student Choice," unpublished paper, February 1998, pp. 5-6.

35. Stager, *Focus on Fees*, p. 64.

36. For strong arguments against vouchers, see Tim Sale, "The Funding of Post-Secondary Education in Canada: Can the Dilemma Be Resolved?" Working paper No. 28 (Ottawa: Economic Council of Canada, 1992), p. 34.

37. Peter M. Leslie, *Canadian Universities and Beyond: Enrolment, Structural Change and Finance* (Ottawa: AUCC, 1980).

38. The discussion by Friedman is found in Milton Friedman, "The Role of Government in Public Education," in *Economics and the Public Interest*, ed. R.A. Solo (Rutgers University Press, 1955). Examples of the ongoing discussion include: Ontario, Commission on Post-Secondary Education in Ontario, *The Learning Society* (Toronto: Queen's Printer, 1984); Carnegie Commission on Higher Education, *Quality and Equality: New Level of Federal Responsibility for Higher Education* (Hightown, NJ: McGraw Hill, 1968); Nova Scotia, Royal Commission on Post-secondary Education, *Reports* (Halifax: The Commission, 1985); D. Auld, "Paying for Post-Secondary Education," *The Toronto Star*, 7 July 1992. Detailed discussions of the capital markets argument and repayment of student loans can be found in Stager, *Focus on Fees*, ch. 7; and Edwin G. West, *Higher Education in Canada* (Vancouver: The Fraser Institute, 1988), ch. 8.

39. Canada, The Royal Commission on the Economic Union and Development Prospects for Canada, *Report* (Toronto: University of Toronto Press, 1985). In the commission's words, the income contingent repayment plan, "removes the necessity to consider whether or not a student could be supported by his or her parents ... feature does not require any 'needs' test before the loan is granted, since repayment will be tailored automatically to post-education income, and not to current needs," p. 751.

40. Olewiler, "Let's Use Benefit Taxes More," p. 27.

41. Richard M. Bird, *Charging for Public Services: A New Look at an Old Idea* (Toronto: Canadian Tax Foundation, 1976), p. 104.

APPENDIX A
List of Municipal Government Services

Protection   –   courts of law, correction and rehabilitation
                 –   police
                 –   firefighting
                 –   regulatory measures

Transportation and Communications
                 –   roads and streets
                 –   snow and ice removal
                 –   parking
                 –   public transit

Health   –   hospital care
                 –   preventive care

Social Services
                 –   social welfare services

Resource Conservation and Industrial Development
                 –   agriculture
                 –   tourism
                 –   trade and industrial development

Environment   –   water
                 –   sewer
                 –   solid waste collection and disposal
                 –   recycling

Recreation and Culture
                 –   recreation
                 –   culture

Housing   –   housing

Regional Planning and Development
                 –   planning and zoning
                 –   community development

Debt Charges –   interest payments

APPENDIX B
List of Municipal Government Revenues

Own-Source Revenues

    1.   Property Taxes
- real property
- developers contributions and lot levies
- special assessments
- grants-in-lieu of taxes
- business property taxes

    2.   Other Taxes
- amusement taxes
- licences and permits

    3.   User Fees
- for water and sewage
- rentals
- concessions and franchises

    4.   Investment Income
- profits from own enterprises
- interest and penalties from taxes

    5.   Other
- fines and penalties

Total Grants

    1.   Unconditional
- no strings or conditions attached to receipt of these grants

    2.   Conditional
- strings or conditions are attached to receipt or acceptance of grants

12

Funding an Aboriginal Order of Government in Canada: Recent Developments in Self-Government and Fiscal Relations

Michael J. Prince and Frances Abele

La mise en oeuvre d'un ordre gouvernemental pour les Autochtones au Canada est un lent processus de changements constitutionnels qui est non seulement défini par les jugements des tribunaux et la constitution écrite, mais aussi par les ententes financières, les programmes sociaux et les traités. Les principes et les pratiques de même que les problèmes et les possibilités du fédéralisme fiscal pour les Autochtones sont étudiés dans ce chapitre. Les idées de la Commission royale sur les peuples autochtones relativement à la réforme fiscale y sont présentées, de même que le plan d'action du gouvernement fédéral sur les Autochtones, Rassembler nos forces, lequel est une réponse à la Commission. En ce qui concerne les pratiques établies et les possibilités, cinq types d'arrangements financiers — allant de l'augmentation graduelle à la transformation de l'autorité et de l'autonomie des gouvernements autochtones — sont examinés. Afin d'explorer plus en détails les problèmes et les possibilités auxquels font face les gouvernements autochtones, les politiques fiscales visant deux situations spécifiques — les Autochtones vivant en milieu urbain ou hors-réserve et le traité Nisga'a qui vient d'être ratifié — sont présentées. Ces deux situations constituent des formes institutionnelles distinctes et nouvelles d'autonomie gouvernementale et illustrent à la fois les obstacles et les opportunités qu'offre le fédéralisme fiscal. Le rôle marginal des chefs autochtones nationaux dans les structures et les processus du fédéralisme exécutif est aussi examiné dans le contexte de la déclaration de Calgary de 1997 sur l'unité nationale et de l'entente sur l'union sociale de 1999. Les auteurs affirment que la réalisation complète de l'autodétermination autochtone exigera une réforme importante de la pratique actuelle du fédéralisme fiscal et des relations intergouvernementales. Les modes de financement des gouvernements autochtones sont et demeureront fort divers, tout comme la forme de ces gouvernements.

INTRODUCTION

This chapter examines recent examples of the evolution of Aboriginal self-government and intergovernmental fiscal relations in the current extremely fertile context of innovation and development. Our approach is a mixture of description, evaluation, and prediction. We describe the salient conclusions and recommendations for fiscal and governance reform in the 1996 report of the Royal Commission on Aboriginal Peoples (RCAP) and the federal government's initial reply. We assess the overall patterns in self-government and fiscal relations that are emerging across the country. And we forecast what the issues are likely to be over the next few years in the context of the federal Aboriginal Action Plan and the Social Union Framework Agreement. Matters of policy, key concepts, and jurisdiction are considered in the second section, and we offer some observations concerning the overall patterns of change in funding arrangements in section three. Two cases of Aboriginal governance and fiscal arrangements, urban and off-reserve Aboriginal People in the provinces, and the Nisga'a Treaty, are discussed in section four. Here we identify areas where further reform and innovation are necessary. In the next section, we consider the interrelationship between recent developments on national unity, the social union, and executive federalism on the one hand, and Aboriginal national representation on the other.

Our central argument is that the full realization of Aboriginal self-government will require significant revisions to fiscal federalism and some innovations yet to be identified. Existing fiscal arrangements are suitable for some First Nations, perhaps, but not for others.[1] As self-government arrangements evolve and the new institutions develop and adapt, it is becoming clear that the emerging "system" for funding Aboriginal governments will be extremely heterogeneous, as are the emerging governments themselves.[2] However diverse the elements of the system will be, it is important that they be fair to all and consonant with the constitution, legislation, and policy.

Since the 1980s, the machinery in provincial and territorial governments for managing Aboriginal affairs has grown, exhibiting considerable diversity as well. Federal institutions for consultation, program delivery, and policy support have changed a great deal. With signs of a third order of government, we believe a new concept and model of federalism is emerging in Canada. In light of this it is unfortunate that in the larger process to redefine the social union, Aboriginal issues in general and Aboriginal-federal-provincial-municipal fiscal relations more particularly have been marginal to current debates. Neglect of these matters, while the basic outline of the new fiscal social contract is being developed, risks the creation of "no-win" situations for Aboriginal and other governments, and exacerbation of general public concern of the implications of Aboriginal self-government.

THE EMERGENCE OF AN ABORIGINAL ORDER OF GOVERNMENT

In his last major work on federalism, the distinguished political scientist Donald Smiley argued that Canadian politics would come increasingly to revolve around forces other than those demarcated by provincial boundaries, thus challenging the strength of the provinces. One set of forces Smiley noted were pan-Canadian institutions and processes — the organization of the federal government and bureaucracy, national party leadership conventions, and the *Charter of Rights and Freedoms*. Other sorts of influence identified were spatially-delineated forces other than provincial: local governments, the local organizations of political parties, and territorial-defined groupings of rights-holders — specifically, official language minorities and Aboriginal Peoples. At the time he was writing in the mid-1980s, Smiley did not regard Aboriginal self-government and land claims as "very important in the total structure of political power in Canada."[3] He did, however, view Canadian federalism as being in a process of continual transition and predicted that "considerable progress towards an enhanced range of aboriginal self-government is likely in the foreseeable future."[4]

Since then, a number of developments suggest that the progress Smiley anticipated is evident. There has been a significant devolution of responsibilities for the management and delivery of health and social services to First Nations. Various other functions, in such areas as environmental protection, are in the process of being devolved. New treaties and agreements have been reached with Inuit and Cree in northern Quebec, Inuvialuit in the Mackenzie Delta area, the Inuit of Nunavut, the 17 Yukon First Nations, and the Nisga'a and Sechelt in British Columbia, establishing jurisdictions and their land and resource bases. Other Aboriginal nations are relatively close to agreements.[5] Concurrently, Supreme Court of Canada decisions continue to affirm and specify Aboriginal treaty rights.[6] Aboriginal groups and leaders, and some of their issues and concerns, played a notable part in the Charlottetown Accord, the unsuccessful effort at constitutional reform in the early 1990s. The Royal Commission on Aboriginal Peoples was established in 1991, reporting in late 1996 with 440 recommendations in five compelling volumes to which the federal government is, if only partially, responding. Several key decisions by the Supreme Court of Canada have been made on Aboriginal rights and title, prompting the federal government in 1995 to recognize in public policy the inherent right to govern by Aboriginal Peoples.

Aboriginal governments have existed in Canada for decades,[7] though their citizens generally have viewed them as not fully adequate. The Chief and Band Council arrangements created by the *Indian Act* in status Indian communities have numerous shortcomings, not the least of which is that the "constitution" provided by the Act is usually in conflict with the governing institutions characteristic of the original political culture. After a century of *Indian Act*-imposed institutions, however, in many places both the original governing traditions and the imposed ones have their advocates.[8] In such settings, the shape of government in the future is not yet evident. Metis have a land base only in the Metis Settlements of Alberta[9] but through the Metis National Council they have advanced proposals for Canada-wide self-government. It is likely that

Metis land and self-government rights will become considerably clearer over the next several years, as senior judicial attention turns to these questions. For all Inuit except those who live in Labrador, self-government arrangements are in place. It remains for the residents of Nunavut and Nunavik (a public regional government in northern Quebec) to work with the new institutions to build strong governments and strong societies. Just which, if any, self-governing arrangements will serve the growing number of Aboriginal People living in the cities remains largely an open question.

The public orders of state, the federal and provincial governments, are not similar — that is, the federal order consists of one big government; the provincial order consists of ten provincial governments (and three quasi-provinces or provinces-in-waiting). The Aboriginal order would consist of even more governments, which would be even more heterogeneous. One might ask whether such a varied institutional landscape could properly be referred to as a separate, Aboriginal order of government. At present, the answer is, probably not. But the trend seems clear. Various forms of Aboriginal self-government have been negotiated, each with specific areas of jurisdiction and specific fiscal relationships to their citizens and to federal and provincial governments. More Aboriginal governments will come into being.

In a sense, the emergence of an Aboriginal order is a slow-moving constitutional change, of the sort that created the unwritten part of the Canadian constitution. All constitutional change does not proceed by formal amendment, nor should it. A good example is the evolution of the social union; another example is the building of institutions and taxation capacity for First Nations.

Table 1 outlines a selection of key developments over the past decade or so in establishing legislative and institutional underpinnings of the fiscal role of First Nation governance. The amendment of the *Indian Act* in 1988 gave First Nations explicit power to levy property taxes and, in particular, to tax non-Native interests in reserve lands. The Indian Taxation Advisory Board's (IATB) establishment in 1989 made it the first Aboriginal-controlled institution involved in the exercise of the minister of Indian affairs decision-making powers under the *Indian Act*. By 1997-98, 78 First Nations in seven provinces had taxation laws generating annual revenues of over $26 million. Since the amendment of the *Indian Act*, over $100 million have been raised by First Nations. The IATB has processed over 530 bylaws covering property taxation, assessment, rates, expenditure, business licensing, financial administration, telephone companies, and related matters. This trend not only illustrates capacity development but also the diversity in strengthening governance that we have already mentioned. Only 12 percent of all First Nations (78/633) have chosen this real property taxation route to date, and two-thirds of these First Nations (53/78) are located in British Columbia.

This table illustrates the nature and face of change for one large group of people, status Indians, in one important aspect of their relationship to fiscal

Table 1: *Legislative and Institutional Developments in Building the Taxation Capacity of First Nations in Canada, 1988 -1999*

Year	Development
1988	Bill C-115, amendment to the *Indian Act* giving First Nations the power to levy property taxes.
1989	Formation of the Indian Taxation Advisory Board (IATB).
1990	Bill C-65, *Indian Self-Government Act* requires British Columbia provincial government and its municipalities to vacate property tax jurisdiction on reserves when a First Nation passes a section 83 bylaw to avoid double taxation.
1994	Aboriginal Payments-in-Lieu of Taxes Program between IATB and Ontario Hydro so that First Nations receive grants in lieu of taxes, like municipalities, for hydro assets located on their land.
1995	First Nations Finance Authority established.
1996	First Nations Tax Administrators' Institute established associated with the University of Victoria.
1997	Centre for Municipal-Aboriginal Relations opened, sponsored by the IATB and the Federation of Canadian Municipalities.
	First Nations Gazette, the formal vehicle for giving legal notice to the general public of First Nations legislation, is launched.
	Federal legislation allows the Cowichan Tribes of Indians and the Westbank First Nation to impose taxes on the sale of tobacco products on their reserves by status and non-status persons.
1998	Memorandum of Understanding signed between the Assembly of First Nations and the Certified General Accountants' Association of Canada to implement a joint Accountability Project that will increase the accounting and auditing knowledge and skills of First Nations.
1999	The Quebec government and the Kahnawake First Nation reach a five-year agreement on tax exemption and tax collection.

Sources: Indian Taxation Advisory Board, various issues of their newsletter, *Clearing the Path,* available at www.itab.org, and Assembly of First Nations.

federalism — taxation. Similar patterns can be demonstrated for other Aboriginal groups and other fiscal matters. By such means is the new order emerging.

FINANCING ARRANGEMENTS FOR ABORIGINAL GOVERNMENT: PERSPECTIVES AND PRACTICES

The *Report of the Royal Commission on Aboriginal Peoples,* and the federal reply to it, *Gathering Strength,* both emphasize the importance of fiscal reform and express similar ideas concerning funding arrangements for Aboriginal governments. In addition, we identify five types of fiscal relations that either exist in current practices or in the form of policy proposals.

THE RCAP PERSPECTIVE

The RCAP final report emphasized the central importance of fiscal arrangements to determining a new relationship between Aboriginal and public governments in Canada.

Financing was presented as one of the fundamental ingredients of effective and good governance, closely intertwined with the two other basic attributes of legitimacy and power. As the commissioners observed, Aboriginal Peoples as a well as other Canadians and the federal and provincial governments want to have confidence in and support the fiscal arrangements. This legitimacy of financing depends on the adequacy and stability of funds, the accountability for and control over transferred funds, as well as the effectiveness in meeting the needs of Aboriginal citizens and communities. The legal and formal authority of any form of governance, Aboriginal or otherwise, needs fiscal resources to realize the capacity to act, to make and enforce laws, and to deliver programs and services.

On the current state of fiscal capacity and policy arrangements, the Royal Commission noted that Aboriginal governments are highly dependent on federal funding that has often been conditional, discretionary and, therefore, unpredictable over time. Embedded in this critique is a set of preferred features for financing Aboriginal governments. To support political autonomy and policy planning, a significant proportion of funding should be unconditional, predictable, and relatively stable through time. What the commissioners had in mind was the formula-funding approach in the fiscal arrangements between the federal and territorial governments. These arrangements are based on a set of indicators and reviewed every five years. Reporting requirements should be fairly simple and not necessitate elaborate administrative rules and structures. These criticisms are familiar ones. The solutions have been proposed before, by the Penner report in 1983, the last time Aboriginal fiscal issues were examined at length at the federal level.[10]

The RCAP expressed five objectives for financing Aboriginal governments. Financial arrangements for Aboriginal governments should advance and support the following fundamental goals:

- *Self-reliance* by encouraging the development of independent sources of revenue;
- *Equity* in the distribution of resources among and between Aboriginal governments and between Aboriginal and non-Aboriginal People as a whole;
- *Efficiency* in the use of limited resources for service delivery;
- *Accountability* for the use of public funds and for revenue decisions; and
- *Harmonization and cooperation* with adjacent jurisdictions with respect to program and service standards, and tax policies.

In essence, these goals are criteria for designing fiscal arrangements. They stress the principles of fiscal autonomy through own-source taxing authority, fiscal equity, program and management efficiency, public accountability, and economies of scale. The RCAP vision on financing recognizes that transfer payments from the federal and provincial governments will be needed, but to a lesser extent over time. The hope is that many Aboriginal governments would become largely self-financing in the long term through access to own-source revenues. Transfer payments ought to be freed from many of the restrictions on their use and accountability; and reporting requirements for Aboriginal governments should be no more onerous than those for the federal and provincial governments. The RCAP also recommended that new financing arrangements should provide opportunities for individual Aboriginal communities to aggregate their collective interests with neighbouring Aboriginal and/or non-Aboriginal jurisdictions. Whatever measures of cooperation in service delivery arrangements may take place, the level of services should be equalized so that programs delivered by Aboriginal governments meet the standards of comparable public services in adjacent public jurisdictions.

THE FEDERAL GOVERNMENT'S PERSPECTIVE: RESPONSE TO RCAP AND
VISION OF TREATIES

Gathering Strength: Canada's Aboriginal Action Plan, released in 1997, is the federal government's response to the Royal Commission, self-described as "a framework for new partnerships with First Nations, Inuit, Metis, and Non-Status Indians. It is a first step toward more effective working relationships between the Government of Canada and Aboriginal people."[11] Initially, the second Chrétien government had three social priorities: jobs, youth, and health care. In the wake of the RCAP report, Aboriginal issues were added as the fourth priority and *Gathering Strength* became a horizontal policy initiative, not simply a departmental one by Department of Indian Affairs and Northern Development (DIAND).[12]

More a course correction than a radical shift in federal policy, the action plan is very much about self-government and self-reliance. The plan has four core objectives: renewing partnerships; strengthening Aboriginal governance; developing a new fiscal partnership; and supporting strong communities, people, and economies. Our focus in this chapter is on the second and especially the third of these objectives. Strengthening Aboriginal governance is expressed in the federal government working with Aboriginal People, the provinces and territories, as well as other partners, to develop "practical, sustainable governance arrangements for Aboriginal people that are built on legitimacy, authority and accountability." Steps to do this include funding for Aboriginal women's organizations to assist greater participation of women in self-government processes and cost-shared Metis enumeration. Closely related to this aim is the objective of developing a new fiscal relationship.

Stronger Aboriginal governments obviously need fiscal autonomy and fiscal capacity. Echoing the RCAP, the federal government's action plan states that new fiscal relations mean arrangements that are "stable, predictable and accountable and will help foster self-reliance." The document mentions a number of specific measures:[13]

- Multi-year funding arrangements to increase the capacity of First Nations governments to spend according to community priorities. (DIAND reports the transfer of about $1 billion to nearly 300 First Nations in 1996-97 under multi-year funding arrangements.)

- Reform to the processes for negotiating and implementing the multi-year funding arrangements. ("The overall aim will be to ensure that programs and services provided by Aboriginal governments and institutions are reasonably comparable to those provided in non-Aboriginal communities.")

- Consolidation of funding from different government departments into one funding arrangement. The only venture mentioned is a joint pilot project of Health Canada and DIAND.

- Establishment of joint fiscal-relations tables for the development of mechanisms for financial government-to-government financial transfer systems.

Six principles are evident in various sections of the action plan that pertain to the strategy of a new fiscal relationship.[14] These principles include: creating stable and predictable relations with multi-year funding arrangements, reducing administrative burdens by harmonizing federal fiscal reporting requirements across departments, and ensuring accountability to community members as well as to maintaining accountability to funding governments. Further principles include: enhancing the internal generation of own-source revenue, strengthening the capacity to collect and analyze data on program performance and service results, and expanding access to investment equity and capital for Aboriginal businesses and communities.

With some adaptation, these principles are seen to apply not only to First Nations but also Metis, off-reserve groups, and Aboriginal groups in the North. Although DIAND has statutory responsibility only for status Indians and Inuit (as well as in a different sense, all territorial residents), *Gathering Strength* mentions the needs of two groups usually explicitly excluded from the department's ambit: Indians who do not live on reserves and Metis.

> [T]he government has looked specifically at the unique requirements of Metis and off-reserve Aboriginal groups. The government will seek to create multi-year funding arrangements with these groups and to harmonize federal fiscal reporting requirements across federal departments wherever possible, while maintaining the principle of accountability. These initiatives will contribute to creating a more stable and predictable environment for Metis and off-reserve Aboriginal groups, and should lessen the administrative burden that they face.[15]

To implement these principles, steps identified in *Gathering Strength* directly relevant to financial matters include:

- new financial standards comparable to those for other governments in Canada, including a system of public accounts and consolidated audits that comply with generally accepted accounting principles;

- support for Aboriginal governments wanting to increase their level of financial independence by helping First Nations to develop their own sources of revenues, including taxation;

- Statistical Training Program for Aboriginal groups in order to improve data collection methods and routine information exchange between the federal government and Aboriginal governments; and

- an Aboriginal Peoples Survey following the 2001 Census of Canada to improve data collection.

The Royal Commission identified treaties as the central mechanism for restoring relations of mutual respect and fair dealing between Aboriginal and non-Aboriginal People. This view is rooted in the historical role played by treaties and in their status as constitutional documents by virtue of section 35 of the *Constitution Act, 1982*. Treaties — both historical and modern ones — are affirmed by the federal government as a key vehicle for addressing Aboriginal issues, implementing the inherent right of self-government. Comprehensive claims agreements are recognized to be modern treaties. For groups that do not have a treaty but wish to enter into such a relationship, the federal government's vision appears to be that of a treaty package with several components.[16] These components embrace defined rights and powers over land and resources, defined rights and formal recognition of governance, an expanded land-base to the First Nation reserve that is recognized, plus a capital infusion and new fiscal relationship.

The federal perspective is that there will be a new government-to-government comprehensive fiscal transfer relationship rather than an *Indian Act* financial transfer arrangement. Funding should be flexible, stable, and sustainable for the long term. While the general principles on fiscal provisions may be included in a treaty and therefore will receive constitutional protection, the details on funding levels and program and taxation terms will not. Typically, fiscal financing agreements will be for five years with a defined process for renewal.

Accountability is mentioned here as well, as a matter of concrete concern to First Nations and to government:

> Any new fiscal relationship must ensure that all Aboriginal governments and institutions are accountable to their members through frameworks built on the recognized principles of transparency, disclosure and redress common to governments in Canada. This includes the progressive implementation of government budgeting, internal controls, reporting and auditing standards.
>
> Accountability to both community members and the Government of Canada will be enhanced through regular reporting of results against defined criteria and periodic evaluation of the effectiveness of financial arrangements with Aboriginal governments.[17]

Accountability for resource allocation and programming decisions is to be to Aboriginal citizens, likely addressed in an internal constitution that deals with transparency, disclosure, and redress provisions. Accountability to the transfer government(s) continues to exist for program and financial standards comparable to other governments. This will involve information-sharing and reporting on agreed-upon program terms and conditions. Whatever financial arrangements are negotiated with any one First Nation, Tribal Council or other Aboriginal group must be workable for other situations in the national context. Factors considered in negotiating the fiscal matters in a treaty take in the cost of proposed government institutions, the location and accessibility of the lands, and the population and demographic characteristics.

Ultimately, the fiscal capacity of an Aboriginal government under a new treaty must be adequate to provide public services at levels comparable to those in that region of the province. Treaty groups will continue to have access to existing and new Aboriginal federal programs that are not assumed under a fiscal agreement. The federal vision of a treaty sees financing of Aboriginal governments as a shared responsibility among the federal, provincial, and Aboriginal governments. The financial component of any treaty is guided by the principle of affordability for all three parties. Recognition of the legal authority of an Aboriginal government does not automatically create specific financial obligations for the federal or the provincial government party to a treaty. On the other hand, the new authorities obtained by a treaty will include taxation powers and exemptions for government and the ability to borrow. Moreover, resource-related benefits within First Nation lands would probably include new opportunities for employment and revenue generation.

The federal perspective also holds that the revenue capacity of Aboriginal governments, especially own-source revenue (OSR), must be directly integrated into fiscal transfer agreements. OSR should come into effect over a phase-in period to allow for the transition to self-government. The aim is that reliance on transfers, where feasible, will be reduced over time, and that the incentive to raise OSR will be promoted rather than discouraged or penalized under fiscal agreements. A treaty has the potential to increase the capacity to generate and attract capital, conduct business on an equal footing, and manage natural resources throughout the territory.

CURRENT PRACTICES, PILOT PROJECTS AND POSSIBILITIES: A CLASSIFICATION

Surveying the state of Aboriginal fiscal federalism in Canada, five types of financial arrangements can be noted in the form of policy proposals or established practice. These are: customary DIAND funding arrangements, adaptations to transfer payments and arrangements, economic development measures focused on capital and contracts, new fiscal arrangements in part or in whole, and framework policies on a sectoral or national basis.

First, are the existing financial arrangements with First Nation/Indian band governments primarily from DIAND. These arrangements include Comprehensive Funding Arrangements, Alternative Funding Arrangements (AFA), Flexible Transfer Payments (FTP), Contributions, and Self-Government Funding Agreements (SGFA). In general these arrangements, still quite prevalent among First Nations, are restrictive funding authorities with limited powers, autonomy and local accountability.[18] In addition, there are funding vehicles such as the On-Reserve Housing Policy launched in 1996 and the Innovative Housing Fund announced in 1999 to address urgent housing needs on reserves across the country.

Second, there are modifications and adaptations to these existing arrangements. The introduction of SGFAs in the mid-1980s, for the Cree-Naskapi and the Kativik regional government in Quebec, and the Sechelt Indian Band in British Columbia were innovations in fiscal relations for their day. These reforms were followed in the later 1980s by AFAs and FTPs which both sought to modernize the DIAND-Indian band relationship. More recently, in the later 1990s, a new device, the Financial Transfer Agreement (FTA), has been introduced. Hailed by DIAND as a "more modern fiscal relationship," the FTA is a five-year arrangement to support long-term planning and greater flexibility in program design and allocation of funds in line with community priorities. It is adjustable to reflect changes to the First Nation's population and covers a wide range of programs and services. Accountability to First Nation members is strengthened by FTAs incorporating the principles of transparency and disclosure in the delivery of programs, and redress of grievances between the Nation's leadership and its members. Ministerial responsibility to Parliament and First Nations people remains intact. As of March 1999, 13 First Nations in Saskatchewan had signed FTAs. In the Yukon, the seven self-governing First Nations have been allocated funds, as part of the capacity development theme under *Gathering Strength*, to work on gathering population statistics, and designing financial systems and auditing standards required for the self-government.

The transfer of program management responsibilities for Aboriginal friendship centres and cultural education centres to their respective national organizations is an another example of this kind of adaptation. Still other examples include a pilot project between DIAND and Health Canada to create a simplified consolidated funding agreement for First Nations governments; and a project among First Nations, DIAND, and the accounting industry to develop financial statements that are credible and understandable to community members and other organizations.

Third, are measures by federal departments and agencies to invest funds in, and award contracts to Aboriginal businesses. Through its Opportunity Fund, the federal government is seeking to increase business equity funding for First Nations' enterprises. Furthermore, through its Procurement Strategy for Aboriginal Business, 39 federal departments and agencies have awarded contracts to Aboriginal business worth $50 million in 1997 alone.[19] Such measures are explicitly aimed at strengthening economic development and self-reliance of Aboriginal communities and, in turn, Aboriginal governance and fiscal capacity. Aboriginal business arrangements do not just benefit the immediate partners in material ways. Such arrangements can build bridges across cultures, forging trust and fostering greater understanding between Aboriginal and non-Aboriginal communities; they assist the wider land claims and treaty processes; and they send positive signals to investors that stable and productive economic environments are being created.

Fourth, are fundamentally new fiscal arrangements in whole or in part for a particular First Nation and their members whether they reside on- or off-reserve. An example of a new component arrangement is the five-year tax agreement reached in March 1999 between the Quebec government and the Kahnawake Nation. This Mohawk First Nation will be able to charge tax-like levies on non-native people within the reserve, equivalent to the provincial sales tax, without applying that same fee to natives. The proceeds will remain within Kahnawake. Off their territory, Kahnawake Mohawks will be able to purchase goods and services for personal consumption tax-free when using special magnetic identification cards. "The system will be computerized and the data shared with provincial authorities" and any taxes collected in advance on tobacco, gasoline, and alcohol "will be remitted directly to the band council rather than individuals." Grand Chief Joseph Norton called the agreement, "another step in a very historic process. I must pay tribute to the Quebec government for their willingness to take risks." According to the Quebec finance minister, "It will make everything transparent and make it harder for the minority to fraud the system."[20] The Quebec government will also pay $2 million a year in user fees in recognition of the commuters that daily cross the reserve on three different provincial highways. An example of a new fiscal arrangement in whole is the fiscal relations and powers contained in the Nisga'a Treaty, which we examine in some detail in the next part of this chapter.

Fifth, are sectoral arrangements, accords with national Aboriginal organizations and, ultimately, a Canada-wide fiscal framework. The first two are emergent practices in Aboriginal fiscal policy, while the third is a dream espoused by the RCAP. Establishing fiscal relation tables in certain provinces, between the federal and provincial governments, such as in Saskatchewan, represent a sectoral approach to financial issues. These tables aim to develop government-to-government financial transfer systems for First Nation governments. The agreement between the federal Department of Human Resources Development Canada and the Inuit of Tapirisat of Canada, for the 1999-2004 period, illustrates the role of national accords in Aboriginal fiscal relations. Under the principles and goals of this accord, Aboriginal Human Resource Development Agreements will be signed with Inuit organizations across the country for the design and delivery of labour market programs and services at the local community level.[21]

The last aspect of this final type of financial arrangement is the most ambitious and least developed at present. It relates to the proposal by the RCAP that a Canada-wide fiscal framework be negotiated by representatives of the federal government and provincial and territorial governments, and national Aboriginal Peoples' organizations. Such a process would involve 14 public governments and at least five national Aboriginal organizations, and such a framework would have to be negotiated simultaneously alongside treaty negotiations and other Aboriginal policy initiatives. We will comment on the prospects for this proposal in the final section of the chapter within the current context of the social union and fiscal federalism more generally in Canada.

These five types of financial arrangements interrelate in a number of ways. Most focus on individual First Nations or Aboriginal groups, though the economic development measures and the RCAP vision of a Canada-wide fiscal framework are more national in nature. Each has a mix of strengths and weaknesses, risks and opportunities for Aboriginal governments and public governments. The first types of arrangements offer gradual capacity development and piecemeal reform within the administrative controls and policy structure of the *Indian Act*. For the later kinds of fiscal relations, a policy context other than the Act is taken as the starting point, with sharper breaks from past federal government practices. Reform here would involve not just unconditional financing for programs and services, but the equivalent of an equalization program and perhaps tax-collection agreements.

Table 2: Aboriginal Fiscal Relations: Practices and Possibilities

Types of Financial Arrangement	Focus	Extent of Reform	Degree of Fiscal Autonomy	Contribution to self-government	Impact on Canadian Federalism
Existing arrangements DIAND-First Nation	Band level	Minor modifications	Limited/ restrictive	Little to modest	None
Adapted arrangements (SGFA, FTP, AFA,* transfer of program funding)	Band, First Nation, Organization (Friendship Centres)	Variable, but dynamic	Potential to grow; no emphasis on "own source"	Gradual capacity building	None
Investment in Aboriginal business	Businesses; financial sector	Potential to change economic circumstances	Variable but not large (grants and guarantees)	Transforming economic relations, separate from political change	Minimal
New component arrangements	First Nations' territories and members wherever they reside	Potential major breakthrough	Taxation power; potential to be large	Extends some governance powers over non-First Nation members on FN territory	Could be large; province is agent of change
Sectoral arrangements; Canada-wide	Government-to-government; government-to-Aboriginal National Organizations	Transfer of responsibility and funding	Potential to be large	Could be transformative	Very great potentially; not much in existence

Note: * These acronyms refer to Self-Government Funding Agreements, Flexible Transfer Payments, and Alternative Funding Arrangements.

Altogether, the five types represent a spectrum of possibilities on the present Aboriginal policy agenda. The types range over an increasing emphasis on own-source revenues that could include taxation, investment, borrowing, business fees and royalties, and proceeds from gaming and lotteries. They range from a low to a high level of fiscal autonomy and authority for Aboriginal governments. They also differ in terms of the degree of change and innovation. Several of these types can and do co-exist within particular First Nations or Tribal Councils. Some funding types, however, would be uneasy partners as they are built on different philosophies of governance and Aboriginal-public government relations. The appropriateness of a particular fiscal transfer or set of fiscal transfers for any given Aboriginal government relates to various considerations such as the capacity and willingness of the community and the transfer government. The RCAP view, for instance, is that individual First Nations or Indian bands are too small to reasonably exercise the right of self-government. Given the remarkable diversity among Aboriginal governments and groups across Canada, several forms of fiscal relations will continue to exist for a long time.

EXISTING FISCAL ARRANGEMENTS IN TWO SITUATIONS

Emerging forms of Aboriginal self-government range from the "public government" model of the new territory of Nunavut, through the regional public government of Nunavik, reserve-based First Nation governments with varying levels of autonomy and funding arrangements, to visions of urban self-government. Also, there are the innovative composite forms of Aboriginal and public government created by modern treaties in, for example, Yukon and the Nisga'a territory. For reasons of space, our attention is on two differing situations: (i) the circumstances of urban and off-reserve Aboriginal People in the provinces; and (ii) the governing and fiscal arrangements created by the Nisga'a Treaty.

Each situation illustrates a distinctive and relatively new institutional expression of Aboriginal self-government, and each creates particular challenges and opportunities for fiscal federalism. We provide a brief description and analysis of each in turn, identifying instances of innovation.

URBAN AND OFF-RESERVE ABORIGINAL PEOPLE

Almost everyone recognizes that fiscal arrangements and program delivery for the over 50 percent of Aboriginal People who live in cities (and the over 70 percent who do not live on reserves) are inadequate, complicated, unsuitable, and frequently unfair. There is less consensus on who is responsible for sorting the matter out, and who bears primary fiscal responsibility.

At the level of high policy, the federal government through the Ministry of Indian Affairs and Northern Development recognizes that Metis, non-status, and status people living off-reserve, are all Aboriginal People who are entitled to certain specific services, just as are status Indians living on reserves. For example, the federal response to the RCAP report, *Gathering Strength* was issued by the minister of Indian affairs and northern development, but includes commentary on Metis, Inuit, and off-reserve matters. At the level of active program development and service delivery, with a very few exceptions,[22] the Department of Indian Affairs and Northern Development continues the long-standing practice of funding services on reserves and for Inuit, only.

The fiscally driven distinctions among Aboriginal People create a myriad of problems. Aboriginal Peoples are categorized into unequal classes for funding and programming purposes. The consequences of this balkanization are several. It excludes different groupings of Aboriginal People from accessing established programs and services. It creates hierarchies and thus divisions among First Peoples. This balkanization also creates competition ("petty politics") for representation of off-reserve First Nation people among various Aboriginal leaders and their organizations, and complicates enormously the ability of urban-based and off-reserve Aboriginal communities and municipal authorities to collaborate on such matters as local service provision agreements. Furthermore, as more and more modern treaties are signed, the old distinctions between status and non-status Indians could well become less salient. And, of course, the 1982 entrenchment of existing Aboriginal and treaty rights recognized the bearers of these rights as "Indians, Inuit and Metis" — a provision that puts considerable pressure on DIAND's focus on status Indians only.

There are influential research and advocacy groups who seek to represent the interests of urban Aboriginal People, in a status-blind or at least status-neutral way. For many years, the Native Friendships Centres have provided services to all Aboriginal People (and, for that matter, other local residents) without regard to status or ethnicity. Through the National Association of Friendship Centres, the people active in this movement have advocated for Aboriginal People in cities and towns. Newer organizations that are also having an important effect include the Centre for Municipal-Aboriginal Relations, the Aboriginal Council of Winnipeg, Aboriginal Capital Corporations, perhaps the National Aboriginal Housing Association, and the Institute of Indigenous Government.

For many Aboriginal Peoples, and many leaders, it is hard to see how constitutional amendments and the existing treaty negotiating processes can address the urgent problems of the cities: unemployment, homelessness, youth prostitution, violence, and drug addiction. These linked social problems arise from racism, inadequate education systems, poverty on and off reserve, and (for some communities) several generations of social dislocation. They require immediate amelioration, as well as longer-term, big-P political solutions.[23]

The federal government has created the possibility of the negotiation of tripartite agreements on self-government, engaging with provincial and territorial governments, and provincial or territorial Aboriginal organizations. Although in the Maritimes, in British Columbia, and in the north there has been considerable interest in the possibilities for simplifying service delivery and achieving some stability, these discussions are hardly progressing. Participants report that a major stumbling block is federal-provincial jousting over jurisdiction and responsibilities. The federal government representatives are mandated to avoid all funding commitments off-reserve, even for status Indians. The provincial government representatives must guard against federal off-loading, and ensure that they make no open-ended commitments that could strain their much smaller resources. Negotiators on both sides have no control over the policies that so hamper their ability to make progress.

The 1990s cutbacks in many areas of federal expenditure have tended to exacerbate reserve/off-reserve or status/non-status inequities. The Canada Mortgage and Housing Corporation (CMHC) Rural and Native Housing Program, for instance, was cut. This program provided housing for Aboriginal People on and off-reserve. What has survived is funding for housing for status Indians, administered to an ever-increasing degree by band governments. Faced with burgeoning populations on reserves and relatively small and decidedly limited levels of funds, even bands who wished to assist off-reserve people would be hard pressed to do so.

The impact of the CMHC cutbacks on Inuit have been documented in a report prepared by Pauktuutit, the Inuit Women's Organization:

> Inuit do not live on reserves and have to compete with other non-Aboriginal Canadians for social housing. In 1993, the federal government eliminated its portion of cost-shared funds to the Government of the Northwest Territories, the Government of Quebec and the Government of Newfoundland and Labrador for the construction of new social housing units. This action ... has had an extremely negative impact on the Inuit housing crisis.

> ...Overcrowding, inadequate and unsafe housing conditions, and the lack of basic facilities including running water and indoor plumbing, all contribute to increased incidences of communicable diseases, increased infant mortality and shorter life spans for many Inuit ...

> [Overcrowding] can leave residents of a household with little respite from the chronic high unemployment rates, the breakdown of the traditional culture and the general stresses associated with being frustrated and living in poverty.[24]

Cuts in just one program area have exacerbated an already difficult social condition.

Most funding for services for urban non-status Indians, Inuit, and Metis is project funding made available for specific and predefined purposes by one of several federal departments. On occasion provincial governments contribute or fund other ventures. While such funding — for drug counselling, training, family violence protection, among other purposes — is probably helpful, it is rarely stable. The instability of funding is itself a very expensive feature of current arrangements for urban Aboriginal People. Negotiations over funding quite often delay the commencement of programs so that a hasty beginning jeopardizes their implementation. These days, projects are frequently housed in Aboriginally controlled and staffed policy or service delivery organizations that are themselves operating on an inadequate financial base. Usually there is no non-governmental funding. Staff in these organizations devote a great deal of their energies toward learning of new program opportunities, negotiating for funding, and reporting on how that funding was spent, while rarely enjoying the capacity to administer a service over a sufficient period of time in which to learn from experience and improve their practices. In fact, the need to justify activities to funders on a very short time frame (even three-year funding commitments are rare) can lead these organizations to overlook or actively avoid confronting "soft spots" in their delivery.

Given the different circumstances off-reserve and in the cities, it is obvious that innovative and cooperative fiscal regimes are required. These regimes must be adequately resourced, for the absolute numbers of people and their needs are great. Even if different institutions for different ethnic groups are appropriate to local circumstances (as, for example, on the prairies Metis and Treaty Indians wish and require separate service delivery mechanisms) *levels* of funding must surely be status-blind.

Two system-wide areas of reform require urgent action. First, federal and provincial jurisdictional "marching orders" for negotiators should be clarified at the policy level. The Royal Commission on Aboriginal Peoples argued for the following regime:[25]

1. The federal government should assume the full cost of establishing self-government on the extended territories that result from treaty negotiations, *and* off a land base.

2. Existing programs on reserves should continue to be the responsibility of the federal government until the programs would be assumed by Aboriginal governments, after which time funding would be a matter of generally negotiated fiscal arrangements.

3. The cost of programs off-reserve, in excess of provincially available funding levels would be borne by the federal government.

4. Parallel arrangements should be made for Metis.

5. Provincial and territorial governments should be responsible for off-reserve services ordinarily available to other provincial or territorial residents.

As the commission noted, these principles establish clear lines of responsibility, thus enhancing democratic government, and they follow the traditional lines of constitutional responsibility. We note further that to *clarify* responsibilities does not amount to *writing a blank cheque*: there are many areas of governmental responsibility where available funding limits activity below the optimum levels.

Clarification of responsibilities should go some distance toward introducing more stable funding regimes for service delivery. In the shorter term, devolution of responsibilities and funding should aim for longer renewal horizons and provide funding for internal program review and improvement.

THE NISGA'A TREATY: GOVERNANCE AND FISCAL ARRANGEMENTS

British Columbia is the only province in Canada in which the majority of its Aboriginal Peoples have not signed treaties. The Nisga'a Treaty, recently ratified by the provincial and federal legislatures, is the first modern-day treaty in the province. Nisga'a have been actively seeking a treaty for over 120 years.[26] The recent treaty negotiation process extended over 20 years and while it may not serve as a precise template for other treaties, the Nisga'a settlement is an important guide and symbol. As the treaty is ratified and implemented, the Nisga'a will enter an eight to twelve year phase-out period, after which Nisga'a citizens will be fully taxed. The Nisga'a Treaty is also noteworthy because the internal governance structure is a genuine federal system and because a variant of the equalization principle, a cornerstone of modern Canadian federalism, is enshrined in the fiscal arrangements.

The Nisga'a are a relatively large First Nation with about 6,000 members, most of whom live in urban centres. The governance structure is moving from a two-tier system of a Tribal Council and four Indian Bands to a three-tier system of the Nisga'a Lisims (or central) Government, four Village Governments and three Urban Locals for Nisga'a citizens who live off the territory. The Nisga'a have substantial experience with policy and management, having operated a Health Board, Board of Trustees of a School District, a Family Law Program, and a Child and Family Services Program for a number of years.

Three basic principles lie behind the governance structure and jurisdictional model of the Nisga'a Treaty.[27] First, the *Indian Act* no longer applies. Second, the treaty is comprehensive in that all potential jurisdictions are included and it is constitutional in that the rights therein receive section 35 protection in the *Constitution Act, 1982*. Third, federal and provincial constitutional division of powers remains intact; and fourth, that the Nisga'a's structure is a federal system with a single written constitution. Detailed descriptions of at least 26 areas of jurisdiction are contained in the treaty. Nisga'a lands will not be reserves within the meaning of the *Indian Act.* Instead, they will become Nisga'a Land owned communally by the Nisga'a nation with title vested in the Nisga'a government. In turn the Nisga'a government will have the authority, in accordance with the treaty and their constitution, to create or transfer interest in Nisga'a Land without the consent of the federal or provincial governments.

In the treaty are several innovative and distinctive governance features. One concerns the process and financing of the process for determining membership as Nisga'a citizens. Under the treaty, the burden of demonstrating eligibility will be on the applicant. An Enrolment Committee will be established by the Nisga'a central government comprising eight Nisga'a persons, two from each of the four Nisga'a tribes. This committee will consider each application and either accept or reject it. The treaty provides for an Enrolment Appeal Board of three members, at least one appointed by the federal government. The federal and provincial governments will pay the reasonable and necessary costs of the committee and the board for an initial enrolment period of two years. After that, the Nisga'a central government will bear all costs associated with enrolment/citizenship, and the committee and board will be dissolved.

A treaty chapter on dispute resolution expresses the principles of intergovernmental cooperation, the resolution of conflicts through meeting, sharing information on issues, and notifying the other parties of intended actions. Dispute resolution procedures of consultation, conciliation, mediation, arbitration, and even judicial proceedings in the Supreme Court of British Columbia are set out. The parties to the treaty can call on technical advisors or create working groups or expert panels, as felt necessary, to reach a resolution, and the costs associated with such procedures will be shared on an equal basis between the participating parties. The treaty also provides that the Nisga'a constitution will initially include an amending process that requires an amendment be approved by at least 70 percent of Nisga'a citizen's voting in a referendum conducted for that purpose.

Key fiscal principles underlie the treaty as well. Law-making jurisdictions are not linked to funding obligations by the federal or provincial governments. Funding of Nisga'a governments and governance institutions is a shared responsibility among the three parties who all share the objective of reducing Nisga'a reliance on fiscal transfers. The Nisga'a government's own-source revenue capacity is taken into account in determining fiscal arrangements and payments; at the same time, there is a commitment to comparable public service levels in the northwest region of British Columbia.

From a constitutional perspective, the Nisga'a fiscal arrangements fall into two broad categories. As shown in Table 3, many of the fiscal matters are included as provisions in the treaty, thus receiving constitutional protection within the meaning of section 35 of the *Constitution Act, 1982.* At the same time, a number of other fiscal matters are non-treaty provisions and therefore do not create an Aboriginal or treaty right. Both categories establish and regulate the workings of fiscal relations. The real effect of this distinction is that those items that are constitutionalized are perhaps more stable and binding over the long term, perhaps even "sacred" from an Aboriginal viewpoint. The other items are guided more by federal laws such as the *Income Tax Act, Excise Tax Act,* and *Indian Act,* provincial laws such as the *Motor Fuel Tax Act,* and by Department of Finance policy decisions. For example, Nisga'a governmental institutions will be exempt from a range of Canadian taxes as long as the institutions operate as public bodies exercising the functions of a government at all times during the year within Nisga'a Lands.

Table 3: Nisga'a Fiscal Arrangements

Treaty Provisions	*Non-Treaty Provisions*
• Capital transfer payments • Negotiation loan repayment • Fisheries funds • Direct taxation power • Own-source revenue capacity • Capital taxation exemption • Citizen enrolment	• Fiscal Financing Agreements • Grants-in-lieu of property taxes • Tax administration agreements • Tax treatment of Nisga'a government institutions • Transitional tax treatment • Nisga'a taxation of real property

Capital transfer payments entail $190 million from Canada and British Columbia to the Nisga'a central government paid in annual instalments over 15 years. The payments will be adjusted to a federal price index to compensate for inflation, and will not be included in calculating the Nisga'a own-source revenue capacity. The negotiation loan repayment deals with repayment of the negotiation loans made by the federal government to the Nisga'a Tribal Council, including interest that has accrued. Fisheries Funds refer to $10 million from Canada to establish the Lisims Fisheries Conservation Trust, along with an obligation by the Nisga'a government to contribute a certain amount, plus $11.5 million for other fisheries-related activities.

On taxation, the Nisga'a central government has the jurisdiction to make laws in relation to direct taxation applicable to Nisga'a citizens on Nisga'a Land for Nisga'a government purposes. This power is granted with the proviso though that it does not limit the powers of the federal or BC provincial government to levy taxes. The treaty also specifies that the Nisga'a's own-source revenue capacity will be phased in over a 12-year period. Further, the

Nisga'a government will not be subject to capital taxation, including real property taxes and taxes on capital and wealth. This exemption does not apply, however, to the taxation of interests in Nisga'a Lands nor to the dispositions of any capital by Nisga'a governments. Likewise, private non-governmental activities and for-profit endeavours will be subject to federal and provincial taxation.

Section 87 of the *Indian Act* will no longer apply to Nisga'a citizens in respect of transaction (sales) taxes eight years after the treaty, and in respect of all other taxes 12 years after the treaty has been put into effect. The manner in which Nisga'a taxation will be coordinated with existing federal and/or provincial tax systems will be subject to future bilateral or multilateral negotiations. The three parties (Canada, British Columbia, and Nisga'a) commit to attempt to reach agreements in relation to grants, between them, in lieu of property taxes. Within 15 years of the effective date of the treaty, the Nisga'a government may request the federal and British Columbia governments to negotiate and seek to reach agreement on adjusting the tax powers and exemptions available to the Nisga'a government in light of land claim agreements subsequently reached.

The Nisga'a accord also includes a Fiscal Financing Agreement (FFA). Similar to federal-provincial fiscal agreements, this one lies outside the treaty itself and thus does not have constitutional status and rigidity. Every five years, or at such other periods as the three parties agree, a FFA will be negotiated. A three-way arrangement, there will be an annual transfer of $32.1 million to support program and service delivery in a wide range of fields. Over 90 percent of this funding is already allocated to the Nisga'a by federal and provincial departments. The funding is to be provided to the Nisga'a governments at both levels of the system. A localized version of the equalization principle is expressed in the purpose of the Nisga'a FFA, namely, "to enable the provision of agreed-upon public services and programs to Nisga'a citizens and, where applicable, non-Nisga'a occupants of Nisga'a Lands, at levels reasonably comparable to those prevailing in Northwest British Columbia." Note there is no mention of the other side of the equalization concept, that is, at reasonably comparable levels of taxation. The intent and hope is that the Nisga'a governments will contribute in an increasing fashion to the cost of program and service provision over time.[28]

THE SOCIAL UNION, ABORIGINAL GOVERNANCE, AND FISCAL FEDERALISM

In recent processes to renew the federation and reform the social union, Aboriginal issues and Aboriginal Peoples have generally been marginal, despite the efforts of Aboriginal leaders to gain access to, and a place within these structures of executive federalism. Consider, for example, the 1997 Calgary Framework for Discussion on National Unity, and the 1999 Social Union Framework Agreement. Triggered by the 1995 federal cuts to health and social transfer payments and the results of the 1995 Quebec referendum, the premiers undertook to articulate a vision of Canada, values and social programs. The Calgary Framework was such a declaration drafted by and agreed to by the premiers (except for Quebec) and territorial leaders in September 1997. The declaration was presented not as a deal among the governments but rather as an expression of ideas and principles for keeping Canada together and as a basis for any future constitutional discussions. These principles are shown in Table 4.

Table 4: The Seven Principles of the Calgary Framework for Discussion on National Unity

1. All Canadians are equal and have rights protected by law.

2. All provinces, while diverse in their characteristics, have equality of status.

3. Canada is graced by diversity, tolerance, compassion, and an equality of opportunity that is without rival in the world.

4. Canada's gift of diversity includes Aboriginal People and cultures, the vitality of English and French languages, and a multicultural citizenry drawn from all parts of the world.

5. In Canada's federal system, where respect for diversity and equality underlines unity, the unique character of Quebec society, including its French-speaking majority, its culture, and its tradition of civil law, is fundamental to the well-being of Canada. Consequently, the legislature and Government of Quebec have a role to protect and to develop the unique character of Quebec society within Canada.

6. If any future constitutional amendments confer powers on one province, these powers must be available to all provinces.

7. Canada is a federal system where the federal, provincial, and territorial governments work in partnership while respecting each other's jurisdictions. Canadians want their governments to work cooperatively and with flexibility to ensure the efficiency and effectiveness of the federation. Canadians want their governments to work together particularly in the delivery of social programs. Provinces and territories renew their commitment to work in partnership with the Government of Canada to best serve the needs of Canadians.

The Calgary Declaration was a premiers-led initiative that sought to reach out to the people of Quebec within the context of a broader expression of Canadian values and goals. The intent also was to draft a declaration that, in the words of Premier Romanow of Saskatchewan, was "[n]ot weighed down by a vast array of other interests seeking constitutional space in Canada."[29]

Aboriginal leaders understandably reacted with dismay over what was both included in the declaration and what was not there. At a meeting in Winnipeg in November 1997, national Aboriginal leaders presented to the premiers and territorial leaders a consensus statement of five participating National Aboriginal Organizations. These were the Assembly of First Nations, Congress of Aboriginal Peoples, Metis National Council, the Inuit Tapirisat of Canada, and the Native Women's Association. Their consensus statement outlined a framework of principles for a discussion of relationships between federal, provincial, and territorial governments and Aboriginal governments and peoples. These are listed below in Table 5.

The premiers and territorial leaders agreed to receive and consider the Winnipeg statement. They also joined with the Aboriginal leaders in calling on the federal government to recognize their treaty, constitutional, and fiduciary obligations toward Aboriginal People, to acknowledge its responsibility to provide programs and services for all Aboriginal People and to end its policies of off-loading these responsibilities to other orders of government. These are not difficult words for provincial and territorial leaders to support since they basically say that Ottawa should assume most if not all the spending responsibilities associated with Aboriginal Peoples across Canada. In contrast, the long-standing federal position is that it has primary but not exclusive responsibility for First Nations on reserve and Aboriginal Peoples north of 60 degrees, and that the provinces have primary, but not exclusive, responsibility for off-reserve Aboriginal Peoples. Without any real compromise on these policy stances by both the federal and provincial orders, the ability to build sustainable Aboriginal communities, particularly in urban areas will be seriously frustrated.

According to Premier Romanow, the national Aboriginal leaders,

> suggested ways to improve the Calgary Declaration. At the same time, they made it very clear to us that they supported the Declaration's "open hand" to Quebec and are anxious that the Premiers' initiative succeed. Their contribution was so constructive that I have sometimes taken to calling our consultation document the Calgary-Winnipeg Declaration.[30]

In a press release, the premiers and territorial leaders also acknowledged that in any future constitutional review process affecting Aboriginal rights and interests they will support the participation as equal partners of the five national Aboriginal organizations.[31] Tellingly, no similar commitment was made with respect to the social policy renewal process playing out in the

Table 5: *The Winnipeg Consensus Statement by National Aboriginal Organizations: A Framework for Discussion on Relationships between Federal, Provincial and Territorial Governments and Aboriginal Governments and Peoples*

1. The Government of Canada has the historic and primary fiduciary responsibility to all Aboriginal Peoples as evidenced by constitutional, treaty and Aboriginal rights.

2. The Aboriginal Peoples of Canada have, and enjoy, the inherent right of self-government, a right recognized in Section 35 of the Canadian Constitution and in agreements between the federal government and institutions and governments of the Aboriginal Peoples and in tripartite and other agreements amongst federal, provincial, territorial, and Aboriginal governments and peoples.

3. Provincial, territorial, and federal governments and Aboriginal governments and peoples should seek to work together to resolve issues of resource-sharing and management in a manner that will promote economic and social development with certainty and public acceptance without extinguishing or diminishing Aboriginal rights, treaty rights, and Aboriginal title.

4. The re-balancing of Canadian federalism must always be undertaken and accomplished in a manner that does not derogate from the Aboriginal and treaty rights and jurisdictions of the Aboriginal Peoples of Canada. It also must not diminish, in any way, the fiduciary and constitutional responsibilities of Canada and its capacity to honour its commitments and obligations to all Canadians, including the Aboriginal Peoples. There must be a willingness to enter into partnerships rejecting federal off-loading to the provinces and to Aboriginal governments and peoples in favour, rather, of joint efforts to maximize best possible uses of available resources.

5. Canada is a federal system in which federal, provincial, and territorial governments and Aboriginal governments and peoples work in partnership while respecting each other's jurisdictions, rights, and responsibilities. Nothing in the Calgary communiqué can minimize or derogate from that principle or from existing Aboriginal and treaty rights.

6. References in the Calgary communiqué to Aboriginal Peoples and cultures as one part of Canada's "gift of diversity" must not negate the uniqueness of the place of Aboriginal Peoples in Canada, a relationship that finds affirmation in the treaties and part II of the Canadian constitution.

7. The Aboriginal Peoples of Canada, the first peoples to govern this land, enjoy their own status and rights, including the equality of Aboriginal men and women, and have the right to ensure the integrity of their societies and to strengthen their relationships with their lands. The role of Aboriginal Peoples in the protection and development of their languages, cultures, and identities is recognized and supported by Canadians.

8. All governments must be committed to promoting and strengthening identifiable social, political, and economic developments which will lead to improved education, housing, and infrastructure and to stronger and healthier Aboriginal communities and people, particularly the young and those with special needs.

country at the time. This was apparent in December 1997, when the first ministers (with the exception of the premier of Quebec) agreed to mandate their lead social policy ministers to commence negotiations on a framework agreement for Canada's social union that would apply to federal, provincial, and territorial governments.

In May 1998, in Quebec City, five National Aboriginal Organizations (the Assembly of First Nations, Inuit Tapirisat, Congress of Aboriginal Peoples, Metis National Council and Native Women's Association of Canada[32]) held an Aboriginal Summit, prior to meeting with federal and provincial and territorial Aboriginal affairs ministers, the first such meeting in four years. The five Aboriginal leaders released another consensus document. In part, the Quebec statement reaffirmed the principles of the Winnipeg declaration; in part, it commented favourably on the recommendations of the Royal Commission on Aboriginal Peoples; and, in part, it argued for inclusive Aboriginal participation at all levels in changes to the social policy renewal process including seats on the federal/provincial/territorial Ministerial Council on Social Policy Renewal.[33] Again this final claim was not adopted.

In early February 1999, days before the first ministers agreed to the Framework Agreement on the Social Union, the National Chief of the Assembly of First Nations, Phil Fontaine, wrote to the prime minister calling on the federal government "to ensure that the interests and rights of First Nations peoples are included and protected in any new intergovernmental arrangements." In his open letter, Chief Fontaine reminded the prime minister and the premiers of the shared agreement among the federal, provincial and territorial governments and Aboriginal organizations at the Quebec City meetings the year before, that "the needs of and resources for Aboriginal peoples are considered in appropriate future federal-provincial-territorial agreements or arrangements."[34] Yet leaders from neither the Assembly of First Nations nor the other national Aboriginal organizations were direct parties to the social union and health accord negotiations.

Later, in a meeting in Regina in March 1999, between the leaders of the five national Aboriginal organizations and six premiers and two territorial leaders, support was expressed for their involvement in the implementation of the new social union agreement "wherever such implementation has implications for aboriginal union." The premiers and representatives of the five Aboriginal organizations issued a call for the prime minister to hold a first ministers and Aboriginal leaders meeting to discuss the Royal Commission's recommendations and, by implication, the federal government's action plan, *Gathering Strength*.[35] The premiers and leaders of the territories did not, however, endorse a proposal by Fontaine that a companion agreement be created to the social union deal, one that would give Aboriginal organizations a formal role in participating in any future negotiations between the federal and provincial and territorial governments.

These episodes, we believe, are not random events but rather reflect deeper structural features of Canadian federalism and Aboriginal politics. We mention five such features here and some policy questions they raise. All are worthy of further research and debate. One feature of our federalism, noted already, is the age-old difference between the federal government on the one side and the provinces on the other, regarding the financial responsibilities of each order for meeting the needs and rights of Aboriginal Peoples in Canada. How can this buck-passing be resolved? A second issue is the mixed opinions and tepid support for including Aboriginal national leaders at the conference table of future intergovernmental talks and negotiations on social policy, economic, and fiscal matters. Will it require the consent of all governments, or just Ottawa and six provinces representing at least two-thirds of the population, to invite Aboriginal leaders to the table? A third issue concerns the tax-exempt status of registered Indians. Under the *Indian Act*, the personal property of status Indians or bands situated on reserves is exempt from retail taxation. Should tax-exempt status be granted to urban-based and/or their organizations, if just for a transition period, to facilitate capacity-building? Will all First Nations engaged in treaty negotiations be expected and be willing to forego their traditional tax exemptions as have the Nisga'a?

A fourth feature is the competition between Aboriginal organizations, at the national level and between national and regional organizations, in representing certain constituencies of Aboriginal Peoples, especially the urban-based population.[36] Which leaders, then, of which Aboriginal organizations are to be included in intergovernmental meetings, and for whom do they speak? Lastly, a fifth feature relates to the inherent differences between executive federalism as typically practised by federal and provincial/territorial leaders and the consensual decision-making commonly practised by Aboriginal governments and communities. Ponting and Gibbins perceptively observed several years ago, "If Indian governments were to join this intergovernmental process, they would have to negotiate on behalf of their constituents without having to worry about subsequent ratification from individual bands, tribal associations or provincial organizations. Thus the price of admission to executive federalism and effective participation in the intergovernmental process will be a substantial loss of autonomy."[37]

If, however, the social union agreement indicates a willingness and ability among governments to somewhat democratize executive federalism, then the terms and conditions of participation by Aboriginal leaders and the ratification of any agreements could, themselves, be open to discussion and negotiation. The price of admission to executive federalism, in other terms, need not be fixed.

To guide the redesign of fiscal relationships among the orders of government, the Royal Commission on Aboriginal Peoples called for a forum convened under the authority of the first ministers of federal, provincial, and territorial governments and leaders of national Aboriginal organizations. Along with treaty renewal and new treaty making, the redistribution of land and resources, and the clarification of spheres of shared and independent jurisdiction, the Royal Commission's vision was of a Canada-wide framework agreement on financial matters.

This leads us back to Smiley's thesis that Aboriginal governance may weaken or impair the power of the provinces in the federal system. In the light of the features and issues just enumerated, we are not convinced that this is necessarily so or that it is an either/or situation. Provincial governments are direct parties to treaty negotiations; virtually all provincial laws remain paramount; all provinces have developed some government structure for managing Aboriginal affairs; and most funds for self-government will come from Ottawa not from provincial capitals. Furthermore, the certainty that will come from settled treaties will generate economic benefits for local and provincial economies, and the probability of a Canada-wide framework on macro fiscal relations seems a distant dream. That we live in an era of political decentralization there can be little doubt.

NOTES

1. It is difficult to generalize meaningfully about the hundreds of different circumstances of First Nations and Aboriginal communities, but it is very important to have an overview. For useful analyses concerning (status) First Nations' circumstances, see Terry Goodtrack, "Financial Accountability in Aboriginal Governments," unpublished Master of Arts Thesis, Carleton University, 1997; Daniel J. Caron *et al.*, *Evaluation Report for the Evaluation of the Long Term Impacts of Alternative Funding Arrangements* (Ottawa: Evaluation Directorate, Policy and Consultation, Indian and Northern Affairs Canada, 1993).

2. In a rich 1989 analysis, David Hawkes and Allan Maslove made a similar observation, and proposed a framework for developing policy that is in its general lines still useful today. David Hawkes and Allan Maslove, "Fiscal Arrangements for Aboriginal Self-Government," in *Aboriginal Peoples and Government Responsibility: Exploring Federal and Provincial Roles,* ed. David Hawkes (Ottawa: Carleton University Press, 1989).

3. Donald V. Smiley, *The Federal Condition in Canada* (Toronto: McGraw-Hill Ryerson, 1987), p. 191.

4. Ibid., p. 73.

5. In May 1999, Inuit in Labrador signed a Land Claims Agreement in Principle with federal and provincial negotiators; the Micmac Nation of Geseg signed a framework agreement for negotiating self-government with the federal and Quebec governments; and the minister of Indian affairs and northern development signed the Nisga'a Final Agreement prior to its consideration by Parliament. For details on these, and other recent developments, see www.inac.gc.ca/news.

While instances of progress and momentum are evident, some treaty tables are struggling and risk falling apart, resulting in litigation rather than negotiation. Either way, to settle all outstanding land claims and treaty processes across Canada will take many, many more years.

6.   There are too many important cases to cite, but we mention two recent decisions that have had far-reaching implications: *Delgamuukw v. R.* [1997] S.C.C.; *R. v. Marshall* [1999] S.C.C.

7.   Frank Cassidy and Robert L. Bish, *Indian Government: Its Meaning in Practice* (Lantzville: Oolichan Books and The Institute for Research on Public Policy, 1989).

8.   An interesting discussion of this matter appears in Brian Maracle, *Back on the Rez.: Finding the Way Home* (Toronto: Penguin, 1997).

9.   Fred W. Martin, "Federal and Provincial Responsibility in the Metis Settlements of Alberta," in *Aboriginal Peoples and Government Responsibility*, ed. Hawkes.

10. For detailed discussion of the Penner report and of the main funding arrangements between Indian Affairs Canada and First Nation governments as they evolved through the early 1980s to the mid-1990s, see Michael J. Prince, "Federal Expenditures and First Nation Experiences," in *How Ottawa Spends 1994-95: Making Change*, ed. Susan D. Phillips (Ottawa: Carleton University Press, 1994), pp. 261-99.

11. *Gathering Strength: Canada's Aboriginal Action Plan* (Ottawa: Supply and Services Canada, 1997), p. 3.

12. The development of what came to be the *Gathering Strength* report, earlier in draft form called "Charting a New Course," was overseen by a committee of deputy ministers and supported by a committee of assistant deputy ministers drawn from several federal departments and agencies.

13. *Gathering Strength*, p. 20.

14. We drew these from *Gathering Strength*, pp. 19, 22, 29, and 34.

15. *Gathering Strength*, p. 22. A reviewer of our chapter pointed out that the original constitutional responsibility for "Indians and the lands reserved for Indians" identified in the *British North America Act* (now *Constitution Act, 1982*, 91(24)) does not differentiate between status and non-status.

16. The following discussion is based on *Gathering Strength*, internal documents, and confidential conversations with federal government officials. The interpretation of this vision is, of course, our own.

17. *Gathering Strength*, pp. 20-21.

18. For a review of these financing arrangements, see Prince, "Federal Expenditures and First Nation Experiences."

19. *Gathering Strength*, p. 29.

20. Tu Thanh Ha and Erin Anderssen, "Quebec Mohawks Win Special Treatment," *The Globe and Mail*, 31 March 1999, pp. A1-A2

21. The Nunavut Territorial government is currently funded under the same institutional auspices as the former Northwest Territories government, out of which Nunavut was created, and roughly the same as applies to Yukon Territory and the new Northwest Territories. For background on Nunavut's first Formula Financing Agreement, see www.icon.gov.nu.ca

22. One important exception is federal participation (with the city and the province) in funding the impressive Aboriginal Centre being constructed in north Winnipeg, as a centrepiece of downtown revivification.

23. *Report of the Royal Commission on Aboriginal Peoples,* Vol. 4, *Perspectives and Realities* (Ottawa: Supply and Services Canada, 1996), ch. 7, "Urban Perspectives."

24. Pauktuutit Inuit Women's Organization, *Inuit Women: The Housing Crisis and Violence,* paper prepared for Canada Mortgage and Housing Corporation, Ottawa, n.d., p. 1.

25. *Perspectives and Realities,* pp. 519-621.

26. Daniel Raunet, *Without Surrender, Without Consent: A History of the Nisga'a Land Claims* (Vancouver: Douglas and McIntyre, 1996). The Nisga'a ratified the final agreement in November 1998 and the provincial legislature of British Columbia ratified the treaty in April 1999. The federal Parliament began considering the treaty in October 1999, when the federal government tabled legislation entitled, *The Nisga'a Final Agreement Act.*

27. This discussion is based on a review of the Final Agreement itself as well as related information about the treaty. For more details, see the Websites of the Nisga'a Tribal Council at www.ntc.bc.ca and the Department of Indian and Northern Affairs at www.inac.gc.ca/subject/agree/nisga/index.html

28. For a wider discussion, see Bert Waslander, "Government Expenditures on Aboriginal People: The Costly Status Quo," *Canadian Tax Journal* 45(5):959-78; and Brian Scarfe, "Financing First Nations Treaty Settlements," in *Prospering Together: The Economic Impact of the Aboriginal Title Settlements in B.C.,* ed. Roslyn Kaunin (Vancouver: The Laurier Institution, 1998), pp. 275-304.

29. Roy Romanow, "Notes for Remarks," Canada Seminar at Harvard University, Boston, Massachusetts, 23 February 1998, p. 9, available at http//www.gov.sk.ca/premier/harvard.html.

30. Ibid., p. 13.

31. See the Press Release, 18 November 1997, available from the Government of Manitoba at http//www.gov.mb.ca/cgi-bin/print...y/relation.html.

32. There are actually three national organizations representing Aboriginal women. Besides NWAC, there is Pauktuutit, the Inuit Women's Organization and the Metis National Association of Women. Quite frequently but not always, NWAC is included with the AFN, MNC and ITC, at the exclusion of the other two.

33. "Statement of the Aboriginal Summit," Quebec City, 19 May 1998 available at http//:www.scis.gc.ca/cinfo98/83061640a_e.html.

34. Phil Fontaine, National Chief, Assembly of First Nations, "Letter to the Prime Minister," 2 February 1999, p. 1, available at http//www.afn.ca/press/ LetterToPm.html.

35. Canadian Press, "Premiers Back Aboriginals Over Stake in Social Union," 23 March 1999. Also see David Roberts, "Premiers Agree to Mull Native Role in Social-Union Talks," *The Globe and Mail*, 23 March 1999, p. A4. The six premiers present at the meeting were from the provinces of British Columbia, Alberta, Saskatchewan, Manitoba, Ontario, and Nova Scotia. Together, these six jurisdictions contain about 70 percent of the overall population and 82 percent of the Aboriginal population of Canada, according to the 1996 Census. This combination of provinces and population would, with a consensus, meet the requirements for a possible new intergovernmental accord based on the federal spending power.

36. Roberts, "Premiers Agree to Mull Native Role in Social-Union Talks."

37. J. Rick Ponting and Roger Gibbins, "Thorns in the Bed of Roses: A Socio-Political View of the Problems of Indian Government," in *Pathways to Self-Determination: Canadian Indians and the Canadian State*, ed. Leroy Little Bear, Menno Boldt and J. Anthony Long (Toronto: University of Toronto Press, 1984), p. 131.

V

A Comparative Perspective

13

Federal Financial Relations:
A Comparative Perspective

Ronald L. Watts

Une étude comparative des relations financières dans les fédérations montre qu'il existe d'énormes variations attribuables aux différences quant à la diversité interne des sociétés visées, à leurs institutions politiques et au caractère de la décentralisation. Il demeure que toutes les fédérations ont vécu des déséquilibres horizontaux et verticaux qui ont requis d'importants transferts fédéraux, bien qu'on observe des différences quant à la forme, à l'étendue et au caractère conditionnel de ceux-ci. La caractéristique centrale des relations financières intergouvernementales dans toutes les fédérations a été le processus sous-jacent de négociation politique, bien que la nature véritablement «intergouvernementale» de ces négociations ne soit pas partout pareille. De manière générale, les relations financières intergouvernementales dans les fédérations dépendent beaucoup plus des différences en termes de société, d'économie, de culture politique, de valeurs et d'institutions politiques entre celles-ci que de la théorie économique normative.

INTRODUCTION

At a time when the financial arrangements within the Canadian federation are under review, there is some value in considering the patterns of intergovernmental financial relations in other federations in the contemporary world.

At the outset it should be noted that the comparison of financial arrangements in federations may provide insights but also requires caution.[1] There is no single pure model of federalism that is applicable everywhere. Indeed, the basic notion of involving the combination of shared-rule for some purposes and regional self-rule for other purposes within a single political system so that neither is subordinate to the other has been applied elsewhere in different ways to respond to different circumstances. One cannot therefore just pick models off a shelf. Even where similar institutional arrangements have been adopted, different circumstances may lead them to operate differently, a classic example being the different operational outcomes of similar procedures for formal constitutional amendments in Switzerland and Australia.[2]

Nevertheless, as long as these cautions are borne in mind, there is a genuine value in undertaking comparative analyses. Indeed, many of the problems in federal financial relations that we face in Canada are common to those in many other federations. Comparisons may help us in several ways: they may help to identify options that might otherwise be overlooked, and they may allow us to foresee clearly the possible consequences of particular changes to arrangements being advocated. Through identifying similarities and differences they may draw attention to certain features of our own arrangements whose significance might otherwise be underestimated. Comparisons may suggest both positive and negative lessons: we can learn not only from successes but also from the failures of other federations and of the mechanisms and processes they have employed to deal with federal financial relations.

A major theme of this chapter is that in considering the dynamics of financial relations within federations, it is necessary to consider the broader context in which these financial relations operate. Federal financial relations cannot be considered purely analytically and technically in isolation from the social fragmentation and diversity and the political institutions with which they interact. The particular dynamics and specific intergovernmental financial arrangements will vary with the degree and kinds of social fragmentation and with the political structures and processes within which they operate. For instance, the degree and kinds of social diversity (linguistic, ethnic, religious, cultural, and historical), whether this diversity is territorially distributed or non-territorial, and whether the different forms of diversity are reinforced by being cumulative or moderated by being cross-cutting will have significant influence. The kinds of federal political and constitutional arrangements, such as the degree of legislative and administrative decentralization, the allocation of taxing powers, expenditure responsibilities, and the scope for financial transfers, the extent of intergovernmental collaboration, interaction and autonomy, and the degree to which the governments of the constituent units participate in or influence central policy-making varies significantly among federations affecting their financial intergovernmental relations. Thus, different combinations of interacting factors tend to require their own distinctive form of intergovernmental financial relations to increase or sustain decentralization.[3] Technical financial solutions which do not take account of how they interact with the social and political context are likely to be counter-productive. This chapter therefore emphasizes the importance of attempting to understand how intergovernmental financial relations have worked in different social and political contexts.

Some common elements affecting federal financial arrangements considered will be: patterns in the allocation of revenue resources and powers to different orders of government; patterns in the allocation of expenditure responsibilities and powers to different orders of government; the size and nature of vertical and horizontal imbalances and the role of transfers adjusting these; equalization transfers; and the political processes and institutions established for adjustment of intergovernmental financial relations.

THE ALLOCATION OF REVENUE RESOURCES AND POWERS

The allocation of revenue resources and the degree of their decentralization within federal systems is important for two reasons: first, the financial resources available enable or constrain the various orders of government in the exercise of their legislative and administrative responsibilities; and second, taxing powers represent important levers enabling the particular governments to which they are assigned to influence or regulate the economy.

A common characteristic of the allocation of taxing powers in nearly all federations is that the majority of major revenue sources have been assigned to the federal government.[4] Even where some tax fields are placed under concurrent jurisdiction or shared, the federal governments have tended to predominate because of the federal power to occupy a major portion of the field of concurrent jurisdiction and because of the federal power to determine the level of taxes from which proceeds are shared with the governments of the constituent units. Several factors have contributed to this pattern. One has been the widespread assumption that policies for economic development are likely to be more coherent if handled by federal governments. A second is that the concentration of resources in the federal government is seen as necessary if it is to perform the redistributive role usually expected where there are substantial regional economic disparities. A third has been the influence of Keynesian theories concerning policies for economic stability and development prevalent at the time that many of the current fiscal arrangements were developed in these federations. The emphasis upon central Keynesian policies has varied considerably, however, being much stronger in the non-European federations, and it has waned considerably in recent years.[5] A fourth is the mobility of tax bases that is more easily accounted for at the federal level than at the provincial or state level. A fifth is that in federations in which the constituent governments have significant independent taxing power, such systems are often considered to face substantial problems of tax coordination in terms of federal-state and interstate relations.[6] While some federations such as the United States, Switzerland, and Canada have accepted the costs of considerable independent taxing powers for their constituent units as an important element supporting their political autonomy, many other federations have tended to concentrate major taxing powers under the federal government and to rely on other means such as constitutionally guaranteed shares of federal tax proceeds or the use of intergovernmental grants as the major way of decentralizing revenues.

In addition to taxation, there are two other important sources for governmental funds. The first is public borrowing, a source open to both orders of government in most federations, although foreign borrowing in some cases (most notably Austria, India, and Malaysia) has been placed under exclusive federal jurisdiction. In the case of Australia, all major public borrowing by both orders of government is coordinated through the operation of the intergovernmental Loan Council with specified voting rules. For many decades the strong federal taxing powers gave the federal government a dominant position in negotiations through its ability to underwrite the coordinated borrowing. In recent years the influence of the Australian Loan Council has declined, however. It still plays a coordinating role, but the states have been left much freer to borrow externally. The second source is the operation of public corporations and enterprises, the profits of which may serve as a source of governmental income. In most federations this has been a source of revenue open to both orders of government, but the scope for such revenue has

Table 1: Federal Government Revenues Before Intergovernmental Transfers as a Percentage of Total (Federal-State-Local) Government Revenues

	1986	1996
Malaysia	87.2	89.9
Spain	87.9	84.0*
Austria	71.6	72.8†
Australia	74.4	69.1
United States	64.7	65.8
India	68.2	64.6*
Germany	64.5	64.5
Canada	48.4	47.7‡
Switzerland	48.1	44.7‡
European Union	0.9	1.2

Notes: * These figures are for 1994.
          † These figures are for 1995.
          ‡ These figures are for 1993.

Source: Ronald L. Watts, *The Spending Power in Federal Systems: A Comparative Study* (Kingston: Institute of Intergovernmental Relations, Queen's University, 1999), p. 52.

varied depending on the degree of constitutional decentralization of legislative and administrative responsibilities.

The range of variation among federations in the degree of centralization of revenue resources has varied enormously. As Table 1 indicates, a comparison of federal government revenues before intergovernmental transfers as a percentage of total (federal-state-local) revenues in a representative group of federations in the mid-1990s ranged from 89.9 percent in Malaysia to 44.7 percent in Switzerland, Canada being the second most decentralized at 47.7 percent.

THE ALLOCATION OF EXPENDITURE RESPONSIBILITIES AND POWERS

Broadly speaking, the allocation of expenditure responsibilities and powers in federations corresponds to the legislative and administrative jurisdiction assigned to each government within a federation.[7] The extent of decentralization of these responsibilities and powers in a federation is heavily influenced by the degree and character of its social diversity and fragmentation leading to pressures for regional self-government over a substantial range of matters, and thus is often considerably greater than the decentralization of revenue resources.

In this respect three points need to be noted. First, where the administration of a substantial portion of federal legislation is constitutionally assigned to the governments of the constituent units, as in Switzerland, Austria, Germany, India, and Malaysia, the constitutional expenditure responsibilities of the regional governments have as a consequence been significantly broader than would be indicated by the distribution of legislative jurisdiction taken alone.

Second, expenditure requirements of different areas of legislative and administrative responsibility may vary significantly, and therefore, the expenditure requirements of regional governments may depend on which responsibilities have been assigned to them. For instance, in relative terms the provision of services such as health, education, and social services usually involves much higher expenditures than jurisdiction relating to functions which predominantly take the form of regulation.

Third, in most federations the spending power of each order of government has not been limited to their constitutionally specified legislative and administrative jurisdiction. Governments have usually been understood to possess a *general* spending power, either as a result of judicial review and convention in the older federations or explicitly in the constitutions of many of the newer federations.[8] Federal governments have often used this general spending power to pursue their own objectives in areas of state or local jurisdiction, for instance, by providing conditional cash transfers or matching grants to induce state or local governments to provide services or meet standards they otherwise could not afford. This federal "golden lead," as it is sometimes referred to in Germany, while widely used in many federations, has often been contentious, being viewed as a way of distorting state or local priorities and subverting their autonomy. This has particularly been the case where the federal spending on matters within regional authority has been commenced uninvited and then subsequently withdrawn unilaterally. Not only in Canada but in the United States such unilateral withdrawals of assistance have led to charges of "off-loading" and of "fend-for-yourself-federalism."

In the United States a trend that has occasioned considerable contention has been the imposition upon the states by Congress of unfunded mandates which has led some commentators to ascribe the label of "coercive federalism" to these federal-state relations.[9] It has been suggested that the reduction in Canada of federal transfers in the field of health during the 1990s has in effect represented a "quasi unfunded mandate."[10]

An important issue in the federal exercise of its general spending power in areas of state or provincial jurisdiction is the role, if any, that the governments of the constituent units are able to play in the design or withdrawal of such programs, either through formal representation in the federal institutions (of which the most effective example is the German Bundesrat which is composed of ministerial delegates from the Länder and has a veto on all legislation affecting the Länder, including financial arrangements) or in intergovernmental negotiations. By comparison with other federations the role of the Canadian provinces in the past in policy-making relating to the exercise of the federal spending power has been considerably less than their German and Swiss counterparts, but the highly developed processes of consensual intergovernmental negotiations in Canada has given them a role comparable to that of the Australian states and more than that of the states in the United States of America.[11]

While on the subject of spending powers, it should be noted that governments of the constituent units for their part have in a number of federations such as the United States and Australia, like Canada, used their own general spending power to establish trade and promotion offices outside the federation even when no constitutional jurisdiction in external affairs was specified.

As in the case of revenue allocations among governments within federations, there has also been enormous variation among federations in the degree of overall expenditure centralization or decentralization, although in virtually every case expenditure distribution has been considerably more decentralized than revenue allocation. This variation in distribution of expenditure responsibilities reflects the different intensities in pressures for decentralization arising from the particular character of diversity or fragmentation within each federation. Among a representative group of nine federations, federal

Table 2:   ***Federal Government Expenditures after Intergovernmental Transfers as a Percentage of Total (Federal-State-Local) Government Expenditures***

	1986	1996
Malaysia	82.4	85.6
Austria	70.5	68.8†
Spain	79.4	68.5*
United States	56.0	61.2
India	47.3	54.8*
Australia	52.7	53.0
Germany	35.7	41.2
Canada	41.4	40.6‡
Switzerland	35.0	36.7†
European Union	2.1	2.5

Notes: † These figures are for 1995.
     * These figures are for 1994.
     ‡ These figures are for 1993.

Source: Ronald L. Watts, *The Spending Power in Federal Systems: A Comparative Study* (Kingston: Institute of Intergovernmental Relations, Queen's University, 1999), p. 53.

government expenditures after transfers ranged in the mid-1990s from 85.6 percent in Malaysia to 36.7 percent in Switzerland, the comparable figure for Canada being 40.6 percent (see Table 2). In each case this was substantially less than the proportional allocation of revenues before transfers listed in Table 1.

VERTICAL AND HORIZONTAL IMBALANCES AND THE ROLE
OF TRANSFERS

Given the pattern noted in the preceding two sections whereby the degree of decentralization of expenditure responsibilities has been considerably greater than the decentralization of revenue-raising powers, virtually every federation has been faced with the need to correct the resulting vertical financial imbalance. A further reason for the constant need to correct vertical imbalances is that no matter how carefully political leaders initially attempt to match revenue resources to expenditure responsibilities, over time the financial significance and proceeds of different taxes and other revenue sources and the significance and relative costs of expenditure responsibilities assigned to the constituent units of government tend to change in unforeseen ways. Consequently, all federations have found it necessary to adjust these imbalances regularly over time.

A second kind of imbalance which has almost always required correction has been the horizontal imbalances that occur when the revenue capacities of different constituent units within a federation vary so that they are not able to provide their citizens with services on the same level with comparable tax levels. In addition to horizontal revenue imbalances among the constituent units, there can also be interstate imbalances on the expenditure side. Differences in expenditure needs may arise from variations or changes in population dispersion, urbanization, social composition or age structure, and the cost of providing services affected by such factors as the scale of public administration, the particular physical and economic environment, and the distinct cultural and social practices. Thus, as in the case of correcting vertical imbalances, most federations have felt a need to make regular adjustments to correct for horizontal financial imbalances.

At the most general level there are three ways in which vertical and horizontal imbalances in federations may be corrected. One is by relocating the assignment of revenue sources to the different orders of government in order to better match the actual total cost of their expenditure responsibilities. A second is by reallocating expenditure responsibilities carried out by each order of government in order to better match the actual proceeds from the revenue sources assigned to them. Some federations have pursued either or both these paths, but in practice political pressures and realities have usually confined such adjustments to a modest level. The third approach, and the most common within federations, has been to accept the pressures for greater decentralization of expenditure responsibilities than of revenue sources, and to reduce the vertical and horizontal imbalances by substantial transfers from the federal government to the regional units of government. These intergovernmental transfers have taken a variety of forms: specified shares of particular federal taxes, unconditional block grants, and specific-purpose conditional grants, with the particular mixture of these varying from country to country. The size and significance of these intergovernmental transfers have also varied greatly among federations, depending in large measure on the size of the imbalances resulting from the dominant political and social pressures for centralization or non-centralization within each federation. For example, as Table 3 indicates, in a representative group of nine federations in the mid-1990s, intergovernmental transfers as a percentage of total state or provincial revenues ranged from 77.6 percent in Spain to 17.9 percent in Malaysia, the Canadian figure being 19.8 percent.

Not only the size, but the particular forms of intergovernmental transfers relied upon in a given federation are significant because of their effect upon the ability of the federal government to influence the way they are used and

Table 3: *Intergovernmental Transfers as a Percentage of Provincial or State Revenues*

	1986	1996
Spain	77.4	77.6*
Austria	31.9	43.6†
Australia	54.4	40.7
India	44.0	39.4*
United States	20.5	29.6*
Canada	20.1	19.8‡
Switzerland	21.7	18.9†
Germany	15.5	18.3
Malaysia	29.5	17.9

Notes: * These figures are for 1994.
  † These figures are for 1995.
  ‡ These figures are for 1993.

Source: Ronald L. Watts, *The Spending Power in Federal Systems: A Comparative Study* (Kingston: Institute of Intergovernmental Relations, Queen's University, 1999), p. 53.

the amount of resulting degrees of dependency or autonomy for the governments of the constituent units. Where conditions are attached to the federal transfers, especially if the conditions are detailed or matching requirements are attached to them, this may provide a lever for a federal government to influence strongly the priorities and policies of state or provincial governments in the exercise of their own responsibilities. To avoid undermining the autonomy of the governments of the constituent units, transfers in some federations have taken the form of unconditional transfers, either set percentages of certain federal tax proceeds or unconditional block grants. Most federations have employed a mix of conditional and unconditional transfers, but the mix has varied enormously. Indeed the proportion of federal transfers which were in the form of conditional transfers in the mid-1990s varied from virtually 100 percent in the United States to 23.5 percent for those Autonomous Communities in Spain with "high level" responsibilities.[12] The comparable figure for Canada if the Established Program Financing and Canada Health and Social Transfer (CHST) semi-conditional cash transfers are included in the category of unconditional transfers was 6.8 percent of total cash transfers.[13] The conditions attached to these semi-conditional grants in Canada have been far less precise and specific than the conditional transfers in most other federations and therefore for comparability it seems best to treat them as unconditional. One measure of the impact of conditional grants upon the autonomy of the governments of the constituent units is the proportion of total state or provincial revenues (after transfers) that these conditional cash transfers constitute. Here too, there is a considerable range: 29.6 percent in the United States, 21.6 percent in Australia, 18.2 percent in Spain, 15 percent in India, 12.3 percent in Switzerland, 12.2 percent in Malaysia, 9.8 percent in Germany, and 1.2 percent in Canada (although if the semi-conditional CHST cash transfers are classified as conditional the figure would be 11.9 percent).[14]

Arguments have been advanced in support of, or against, both conditional and unconditional transfers. In the United States the prevailing emphasis has been on the principle of financial responsibility and accountability. This is based on the view that Congress, which has the nasty task of raising the bulk of the taxes, should, in the interest of accountability to the taxpayer, be the body that controls the use of these funds by the governments to which they are transferred. Consequently, in recent decades, conditional grants have predominated in the federal transfers in the United States. Countering this has been the concern to which more attention has been paid in some other federations, that conditional grants are likely to undermine the autonomy of the regional governments that represent the interests of distinct minorities or regional groups by inducing these governments to undertake expenditures not necessarily in tune with their own priorities. Furthermore, in those federations that, unlike the United States, have parliamentary executives responsible and accountable in the states or provinces to their own legislatures, it has been argued that in the case of unconditional transfers administrative accountability for expenditure is achieved by means of the executive accountability to their own legislatures. This perhaps helps to explain why conditional transfers as a percentage of total federal transfers are lower in all the parliamentary federations than in the United States or Switzerland, both of which have fixed-term executives with a separation of powers between the executive and the legislature.[15]

EQUALIZATION TRANSFERS

Systems of "equalization" transfers to correct horizontal imbalances arise from a commonly held view in federations, that all citizens wherever they live should be entitled to comparable services without having to be subject to excessively different tax rates. Furthermore, equalization transfers have usually been regarded as particularly important because disparities among regions within a territorially diverse society have almost invariably had a corrosive effect upon political cohesion within a federation. Indeed, for this reason, in most European federations, equalization transfers have been labelled "solidarity" transfers.

The extent and form of equalization has, as with other aspects of federal financial arrangements, differed enormously from federation to federation.[16] Several points should be noted. First, the *extent* of equalization transfers varies considerably. Most federations, with the exception of the United States, have some formal equalization scheme, but the scope of such transfers has been greater in countries such as Germany, Canada, and Australia than in others such as Switzerland. Second, in all but the German case where a large component of the equalization transfers takes the form of interstate transfers, equalization has been achieved by differential federal transfers to the regional governments to compensate the poorer units. Third, in most cases, as in Canada, the effort to correct horizontal imbalances has focused primarily on adjusting for the differential revenue capacities of the regional units, but in some, most notably in Australia, historically there was an effort to account as well for differential expenditure needs.[17] Fourth, the determination of equalization transfers to regional units of government has varied. There are those that are based on an agreed formula or formulas, as in Switzerland, Canada, Germany, Austria, Malaysia, Belgium, and Spain, although in some cases the process of agreement on a formula has in fact been dominated by the federal government. In others, such as Australia, India, and South Africa, the allocations have been largely based on the recommendations to the federal government of standing or periodic independent commissions which may themselves use a variety of formulas to arrive at their recommendations.

The question is sometimes raised whether there is a relationship between the degree of decentralization within a federation and the need for equalization arrangements. For instance, it could be argued that the more decentralization there is, the more it is likely that financial disparities among the constituent units will be significant, and hence the greater the need for equalizing mechanisms. But in practice that does not always appear to be the case. Indeed, as Bird has rightly noted, the extent of equalization in different federations does not seem to be directly related either to the extent of regional disparities or any other simple causal factor.[18] Two general factors would appear to affect this pattern. The first is the importance of the prevailing political culture and the degree to which it emphasizes equality of citizens and uniformity of services available to them. The second is the degree to which greater decentralization within a federation is itself the result of social fragmentation producing stronger pressures for regional distinctiveness, autonomy, and resistance to dependency upon federal funding aimed at inducing uniformity. Thus, it would appear that equalization in federations has varied in terms of the tolerance of their citizens to lack of uniformity and horizontal imbalances. For example, egalitarian Australians, blessed with relatively modest interstate disparities in revenue capacity compared to many other federations, have over the years gone to great lengths in their efforts to equalize. In this respect Germany has been similar, although the absorption of the new eastern Länder added some new stresses in the 1990s. On the other hand, the United States, with relatively large interstate disparities but no formal, systematic equalization scheme at all, appears to have a much greater tolerance for horizontal imbalances. Switzerland and Canada, two of the most decentralized federations and influenced by their linguistic, religious, and cultural diversity, lie somewhere between these extremes. Clearly a major factor affecting variations in the tolerance for horizontal financial imbalances in different federations is the relative value placed in their prevailing political cultures upon equity as opposed to non-centralization and regional autonomy.

PROCESSES AND INSTITUTIONS FOR ADJUSTING
FINANCIAL RELATIONS

As already noted, the values of revenue resources and the costs of expenditure responsibilities inevitably change over time. Consequently, adjustments are constantly required to reduce vertical and horizontal imbalances. As a result a major feature of intergovernmental financial relations in all federations has been the regular process of political bargaining between governments. Federal-regional conflicts, conflicts between rich and poor regions, conflicts between different interests in different regions, and conflicts between political parties, have all had to be accommodated in these processes.[19]

The nature of the political institutions within which this bargaining takes place is, thus, a fundamental factor shaping the dynamics of intergovernmental financial relations within a federation. Because in a federal system both the federal and regional units of government have their own constitutional powers empowering each to deal directly with its citizens in the exercise of its legislative, administrative, and taxing authority; and each is directly elected by its citizens, adjustments in practice inevitably involve a process of intense political bargaining between governments.

The dynamics of this intergovernmental bargaining are affected by the extent to which governments at each level are characterized by a separation of executive and legislative powers or by fused parliamentary executives. In the former case, as in the United States, Switzerland, and the Latin American federations, intergovernmental bargaining is diffused through a variety of channels with the federal legislature providing the ultimate arena for reconciling interests. In parliamentary federations on the other hand, the common tendency to predominance of their executives in their legislatures has meant that the primary arena for intergovernmental financial negotiations has been through the processes of "executive federalism" focusing upon the executives representing the federal and regional units of government. This character of intergovernmental financial relations is not unique to Canada but is generally typical of all parliamentary federations.[20]

In terms of the actual procedures for adjusting intergovernmental financial relations four patterns can be identified.[21] In Australia, India, Papua New Guinea, and South Africa, although in different forms, standing or periodic expert commissions have been given the primary task of determining the distributive formulas and recommending these to the federal parliament. Nevertheless, this occurs within a context where there is considerable political intergovernmental deliberation on financial issues, as, for example, took place in the past in the Australian annual financial Premiers' Conferences and since the tax reform of 1999 in Ministerial Council meetings. A second pattern is the constitutional provision for an intergovernmental council composed of federal and state representatives as the primary forum to reach agreement on financial arrangements, the Malaysian National Finance Council being an example. A more narrowly restricted example is the Australian Loan Council, a constitutionally established intergovernmental body which can make decisions regarding public borrowing binding on both federal and state governments. A third pattern is that found in Germany, Switzerland, Austria, the United States, and Belgium where grants to states are determined by the federal government, but there is some effective participation of state governments, legislatures or interests within the federal institutions. Among examples are the state representatives in the German Bundesrat who take part in approving financial matters affecting the states, the cantonal legislators with dual membership in the federal parliament in Switzerland, the representatives in the federal second chamber elected by state or community legislatures in Austria and Belgium, and the direct election of senators on a state-wide basis in the United States and Australia. A fourth pattern is that found in Canada where the determination of the major components of intergovernmental financial arrangements is under the control of the federal government whose legislature contains no provision for effective representation of provincial governments or interests as a result of the Senate's lack of legitimacy. Not surprisingly, because of the importance of intergovernmental financial issues, the result has been that federal-provincial financial relations have been the subject of extended discussion in the extra-parliamentary arena of innumerable committees of federal and provincial ministers and officials, and the source of much political polemics between federal and provincial governments.[22]

In virtually all federations, but most notably Australia, India, Germany, and Canada, a variety of intergovernmental councils, commissions, and committees have been developed to facilitate the adjustment of financial arrangements. Australia has perhaps gone the furthest in developing such institutions with the Premiers' Council over the years playing a key role in the discussion of financial issues, the Loan Council (a body established by constitutional amendment in 1927 and empowered to make decisions binding on both levels of government) coordinating federal and state borrowing, and the independent Commonwealth Grants Commission, a standing body that since

1933 has advised the Australian federal government on equalization and "relativities" relating to federal transfers to the states. In Germany, the Bundesrat and its committees, because of its unique character and powers as a federal second chamber composed of the Land executives and with a veto on all federal legislation affecting the Länder, has played a key role in intergovernmental deliberations relating to the adjustment of financial relations. In other federations, including Switzerland and Belgium, periodic commissions have from time to time advised governments on the adjustment of intergovernmental financial relations.

CONCLUSIONS

From the comparative examination of federal finance in federations some broad conclusions may be drawn. First, there is an enormous range of variations in the financial arrangements within federations. These are related to differences in the degrees of internal social diversity and hence in degrees of constitutional and political non-centralization and emphasis upon provincial autonomy, and also to the degree of provincial or state representation within the institutions for federal policy-making.

Second, all federations have experienced major vertical and horizontal financial imbalances requiring substantial federal transfers in order to adjust for these. Related to this is the fact that all federations have been marked by considerable overlap and interdependence in the performance of their relative functions, especially because of their cost and regional significance in the area of social policy and programs. Disentanglement and independent jurisdiction of the different orders of government combined with adequate and independent revenue sources for each government may have a seductive appeal as a way of ensuring the federal principle that neither order of government should be subordinate to the other. But in practice it has proved simply impossible to divide functions in federations into watertight compartments, particularly in the realm of revenues and expenditures. This has made necessary, in virtually all contemporary federations, an acceptance of the interdependence and interpenetration of the functions of different orders of government, not the least in the distribution of revenues and expenditure responsibilities, of regular adjustments of financial arrangements, and of the use of the federal spending power to facilitate flexibility.

Third, in terms of overall longitudinal trends relating to fiscal federalism as an instrument of decentralization, it would appear that in the period 1950-80 most federations in the developed world underwent a pattern of decentralization both in terms of government revenues and expenditures.[23] Central government receipts in Canada, the United States, Australia, Austria, Germany, and Switzerland as a percentage of total government receipts declined to the point where on average the figures for 1980 were 94 percent of those in 1950 (the Canadian figure exhibited one of the sharpest drops, arriving at 72 percent). Central government expenditures as a percentage of total government expenditures also declined in these federations in 1980 to an average of 84 percent of those in 1950 (the comparable Canadian drop being to 76 percent). In the period 1986-96 the pattern in different federations was less consistent, some exhibiting a relatively stable pattern or even a slight reversal, but with modest further decentralization of both receipts and expenditures in Australia, Switzerland, and Canada (see Tables 1 and 2). During this latter period intergovernmental transfers as a percentage of provincial or state revenues increased in the United States, Germany, and Austria, but declined in Australia, Switzerland, and Canada (see Table 3).

Fourth, a fundamental feature of the dynamics of intergovernmental financial relations in all federations has been the underlying process of intergovernmental political bargaining. These processes therefore have been heavily influenced by the relative strength of the social and political pressures arising from the particular character of internal diversity or fragmentation within each federation and by the particular political structure and processes established by their constitutional frameworks. As Bird has noted, in such a context what has mattered most in intergovernmental financial relations has been the character of the political bargaining, who determines the rules for that bargaining, and how those rules are changed.[24]

Fifth, the extent to which political bargaining relating to issues of federal finance has been truly "intergovernmental" has varied among federations. The degree to which there are provisions for the representation of regional governments or interests in the institutions of federal policy-making has been a factor with Canada providing the least in this respect. Thus, federal-provincial bargaining on financial matters has had to focus in Canada, more than in any other federation, upon the extra-parliamentary processes of executive federalism to influence federal policy-making affecting financial matters. The processes of executive federalism have been significant in other federations such as Germany and Australia, but the representatives of the Länder in the German Bundesrat and of state interests in the directly elected Australian Senate provide additional channels for state interests to influence federal policy-making.

Sixth, among federations Canada clearly stands out in its emphasis upon provincial autonomy. Next to Switzerland, it is the most decentralized in terms of the allocation of pre-transfer revenues and of post-transfer expenditure responsibilities, as indicated in Tables 1 and 2. Furthermore, the relatively low degree of conditionality of most federal transfers to the Canadian provinces, a substantial portion of which takes the form of semi-conditional CHST transfers which contain much less specific conditions than those in most other federations including Switzerland, has been a product of the emphasis upon provincial autonomy and of the role of Quebec within the Canadian federation. A feature that further distinguishes Canada from Switzerland is the degree of asymmetry exemplified by such arrangements as the Quebec Pension Plan and the *Framework for the Social Union*. The Canadian situation has also been influenced by the extent to which the constitution emphasizes the exclusive legislative powers of each order of government with fewer constitutionally concurrent areas of jurisdiction than in any other contemporary federation.[25]

Seventh, generally the pattern of intergovernmental financial relations has reflected the particular character not only of the economy but also of the society, political culture, values, and political institutions in the federation concerned, rather than being derived from normative economic theory. Thus, for instance, the emphasis in their intergovernmental relations upon equity and equalization in Australia, upon uniform social benefits and inter-locking federal-state relations in Germany, upon a complex balance of cooperative intergovernmental and autonomous cantonal and local decision-making in Switzerland, and upon a multitude of non-systematic grant programs within the United States each reflects the particular predominant political culture and reality within these federations. Similarly, the Canadian federal financial relations have reflected the political character of the Canadian federation with its emphasis upon the autonomous action of each order of government. These variations are not surprising since the dynamics of financial arrangements in federations depends so much on the processes of political bargaining within each federation.

NOTES

1. See, for instance, R.M. Bird, "A Comparative Perspective on Federal Finance," pp. 293-322, esp. pp. 293-98 and R. L. Watts, "Comment: The Value of Comparative Perspectives" pp. 323-28 both in *The Future of Fiscal Federalism,* ed. K.G. Banting, D.M. Brown and T.J. Courchene (Kingston: School of Policy Studies, Queen's University, 1994).

2. R. L. Watts, *Comparing Federal Systems*, 2[d] ed. (Kingston: McGill-Queen's for the School of Policy Studies, Queen's University, 1999), p.2.

3. Some authors have preferred to use the term "non-centralization" to "decentralization" in relation to federations on the grounds that the latter implies a hierarchy with power being devolved from the top as is typical of decentralized unitary systems whereas the former infers a constitutionally structured dispersion of power representing better the character of a federation. (See for instance, D.J. Elazar, *Exploring Federalism* (Tuscaloosa: University of Alabama Press, 1987), pp. 34-36. However, because the term decentralization is in such widespread public use, it will normally be used in this chapter.

4. For an outline of the actual distribution of taxing powers and revenue sources in 12 federations, see Watts, *Comparing Federal Systems*, pp. 43-44 and 126.

5.   See also the Quebec Tremblay Commission critique of Keynesianism in shaping policy.

6.   Bird, "A Comparative Perspective on Federal Finance," pp. 305-08.

7.   For an outline of the actual distribution of legislative and administrative jurisdiction in 12 federations, see Watts, *Comparing Federal Systems*, pp. 35-41 and 125-30.

8.   For a fuller comparative analysis of the spending power in federal systems, see R.L. Watts, *The Spending Power in Federal Systems: A Comparative Study* (Kingston: Institute of Intergovernmental Relations, Queen's University, 1999).

9.   John Kincaid, "From Cooperative to Coercive Federalism," *The Annals of the American Academy of Political and Social Science* 509 (May 1990):139-52, esp. pp. 148-50; J. Kincaid, "From Cooperation to Coercion in American Federalism: Housing, Fragmentation and Preemption 1780-1992," *The Journal of Law and Politics* 9, 2(1993):333-430.

10.   An interesting suggestion made to the author by François Vaillancourt.

11.   Watts, *The Spending Power*, pp. 54-56.

12.   Ibid., p. 56.

13.   If the EPF and CHST semi-conditional transfers were categorized as conditional, the Canadian figure would have been 67.4 percent of cash transfers. The source for the Canadian figures is *Finances of the Nation* (Toronto: Canada Tax Foundation, 1996), Table 8.1. For the other federations, see Watts, *The Spending Power*, p. 56.

14.   Watts, *The Spending Power*, p. 57.

15.   Ibid., p. 56.

16.   Watts, *Comparing Federal Systems*, pp. 50-53 and Table 12. See also Bird, "A Comparative Perspective on Federal Finance," pp. 301-05; B. Dafflon, *Fédéralisme et solidarité: Étude de la péréquation en Suisse* (Fribourg: Institut du Fédéralisme, 1995); U. Exter, "Financing German Federalism: Problems of Financial Equalization in the Unification Process," *German Politics* 1, 3 (1995): 22-37.

17.   See D.M. Brown, *Equalization on the Basis of Need,* Reflections Paper No.15 (Kingston: Institute of Intergovernmental Relations, Queen's University, 1996), also the various reports of the Commonwealth Grants Commission in Australia.

18.   Bird, "A Comparative Perspective on Federal Finance," pp. 301-03.

19.   Ibid., p. 310.

20.   R. L. Watts, *Executive Federalism: A Comparative Analysis* (Kingston: Institute of Intergovernmental Relations, Queen's University, 1989).

21.   Watts, *Comparing Federal Systems,* pp. 53-54 and Table 13; and Bird, "A Comparative Perspective on Federal Finance," pp. 304-05.

22.   Bird, "A Comparative Perspective on Federal Finance," pp. 304-05.

23.   See, for instance, Richard Bird, *Federal Finance in Comparative Perspective* (Toronto: Canadian Tax Foundation, 1986), pp. 17-18.

24. Bird, "A Comparative Perspective on Federal Finance," pp. 311-12.

25. Watts, *The Spending Power*, pp. 58, 65.

VI

Chronology

14

Chronology of Events July 1998 – December 1999

Estée Garfin and Felina Arsenault

An index of these events begins on page 427

4 July 1998 *Western Canada*	The annual conference of western premiers wraps up in Yellowknife. The leaders of the western provinces and territories release a final statement demanding that the federal government restore money previously cut from the transfer payments for education, health care, and social services. Now that the federal government has reduced its deficit the premiers would like to see the money returned to the transfer payments. Another topic of discussion at the conference is the proposed social union. The provinces have tabled a proposal to work with Ottawa in setting national standards for social programs, determining funding, and making arrangements for dispute resolution. Social union negotiations will resume in a few weeks.
9 July 1998 *Fisheries*	Federal Fisheries Minister David Anderson announces that negotiations between Canada and Alaska over salmon fishing have failed. BC Premier Glen Clark has been very critical of Anderson's negotiations, saying that he has "sold out" to the Americans in other deals cut with Washington State and expects more of the same with the Alaskan negotiations. The BC government is urging Ottawa to tax American fishing vessels traveling through Canadian waters and to prohibit US navy testing on Vancouver Island.

13 July 1998
Environment

Alberta's Premier Ralph Klein states that Alberta will not ratify the Kyoto Accord, which Canada has agreed to sign. The accord calls for a large reduction in the emission of fossil fuels. Klein criticizes the accord for being too strict, saying that it will damage Alberta's economy, which is largely dependent on the fossil fuels industry.

15 July 1998
Aboriginal Peoples/
Nisga'a

In British Columbia, agreement is reached between the Nisga'a people, the province, and the federal government to settle a land claim that is over a hundred years old. The BC government hopes that this deal will act as a template for future settlements of native land claims. The treaty grants the Nisga'a 1,992 square kilometres of land, ownership of the resources on the land, and self-government. Premier Clark plans to allow a free vote when the treaty is tabled in the legislature. Despite the excitement of the negotiators, there is much dissent. The Gitanyow and Gitxsan native bands claim that much of the territory granted to the Nisga'a in the agreement traditionally belongs to the Gitanyow and Gitxsan. In addition, the Reform Party and the provincial Liberal Party say that the agreement creates another level of government, grants too many powers to the Nisga'a, and creates racial inequality. Some have been calling for a provincial referendum on the treaty. An official ceremony will be held in the Nisga'a territory on 4 August 1998.

15 July 1998
Aboriginal Peoples

A law suit is launched by the Cree in the Superior Court of Quebec against the federal and provincial governments and the forestry industry. The Cree of northern Quebec argue that the forestry industry has been using logging practices that are not environmentally safe and have been violating the Cree's land rights. The law suit seeks full environmental assessments by both orders of government and a share of the logging profits and jobs.

15 July 1998
Senate

Reform Party member Deborah Hanly announces her bid for one of the two senators-in-waiting positions in Alberta. Premier Klein has been lobbying Ottawa to begin Senate reform which will include the move to an elected Senate. To this end, Klein announced in April that Alberta will elect two senators-in-waiting to take up any of Alberta's six Senate seats that may become vacant. Alberta is not expected to have a Senate seat vacancy until 2001. So far only the Reform Party has put forward nominations for the senators-in-waiting election race.

15 July 1998
Health

A report is released by the Canadian Institute for Health Information indicating that Canada has one of the lowest rates of organ donation among industrialized countries. The federal and provincial governments are working together to develop a national plan to increase Canada's rate of organ donation.

27 July 1998
Saskatchewan

Saskatchewan and the federal government agree to spend $40 million on economic development focusing on job creation, business incentives, and diversification of the province's economy. Manitoba and Alberta have developed similar accords with the Canadian government.

31 July 1998
Political Parties

Nominations for the federal Progressive Conservative Party leadership race close with five nominees: Joe Clark, Michael Fortier, David Orchard, Brian Pallister, and Hugh Segal. The leadership vote will be held 24 October.

6 August 1998
Nova Scotia/
Newfoundland

Nova Scotia Premier Russell MacLellan announces that a dispute with Newfoundland over an ocean floor border will go to arbitration. The controversy concerns hydrocarbon potential in the ocean bed. MacLellan is criticized by opposition MLAs for legitimizing Newfoundland's unfounded claim to the area.

6-7 August 1998
Premiers' Meeting

The annual Premiers' Conference takes place in Saskatoon. All of the leaders, including Quebec's Premier Lucien Bouchard, pledge to work together to negotiate with Ottawa for a new social union. In addition, the premiers and territorial leaders unanimously agree that the focus of new spending should be health care and demand that the federal government increase spending on health. The conference concludes with the leaders making a list of demands on the federal government: to continue negotiating with the provinces concerning hepatitis C compensation; to create a national transportation plan; to consult the provinces on future international trade agreements and to protect the rights of Canadians in a more strident manner; and to eliminate Employment Insurance (EI) premiums for youth and reduce EI premiums for other workers.

17 August 1998
Environment

Ottawa announces that it will go ahead and ratify the Kyoto Accord concerning fossil fuel emissions without the support of the Alberta provincial government.

20 August 1998
Separation

The Supreme Court of Canada hands down its decision concerning Quebec secession. It states that Quebec cannot unilaterally secede, but that if a "clear majority" of people in Quebec vote yes to a "clear question" on secession, then the Government of Canada would be obliged to negotiate the terms of separation with the province. These negotiations would have to respect what the court termed the fundamental characteristics of Canada: the rule of law, federalism, democracy, and respect for minorities. The court, however, did not indicate what would constitute a "clear" question or a "clear" majority. It suggested that these are political questions which must be resolved by elected officials. Both the federalists and the separatists claim this decision as a victory. The federalists say that this means that Quebec would not be able to dictate the terms under which it would leave Canada. The separatists say that this decision gives Quebec the right to separate from Canada.

28 August 1998
Senate

Jean Forest, an Alberta senator, steps down from the Senate for personal reasons. This leaves an unexpected vacancy among Alberta's six Senate seats. Alberta Premier Ralph Klein pressures the prime minister to choose a candidate by election in Alberta rather than by appointment.

4 September 1998
Fisheries

Quebec Premier Bouchard criticized the recent fishing quotas instituted by the federal government in the fishing communities of eastern Quebec. Federal Fisheries Minister David Anderson explained that the cap on fishing is necessary for conservation purposes. The fishers of eastern Quebec are furious and have organized protests, even occupying a federal fisheries ship.

14 September 1998 *Quebec*	The Bloc Québécois (BQ) wins the federal by-election in Sherbrooke. The by-election was called after Jean Charest, MP for Sherbrooke and leader of the federal Progressive Conservative Party gave up his seat to lead the provincial Liberal Party in Quebec. Gilles Duceppe, the leader of the Bloc Québécois, says that the BQ's win shows that the sovereignist movement is very strong. Prime Minister Jean Chrétien suggests otherwise and points out that the number of federalist votes far outnumbered the votes for the BQ.

17 September 1998 *Social Union*	Prime Minister Chrétien is criticized by the Ontario and Quebec premiers for comments he made in a news interview. In the interview, Chrétien said that the provinces are demanding too much control over financial resources and programs in their quest for a social union. Ontario Premier Mike Harris says that the provinces are not seeking more power, but are trying to come up with a better formula for sharing federal and provincial powers. Quebec Premier Lucien Bouchard accuses the prime minister of being arrogant.

17 September 1998 *Senate*	Douglas Roche is appointed to the Senate to fill the vacant Alberta seat. Premier Ralph Klein angrily states that Prime Minister Chrétien has ignored the wishes of Albertans in making the appointment without waiting for the election of senators-in-waiting next month. Earlier this month the Federal Court of Canada ruled that the prime minister has the authority under the constitution to appoint senators. The case was launched by the Reform Party to prevent Prime Minister Chrétien from appointing a senator without an election.

17 September 1998 *Health*	The provincial and territorial health ministers release a statement pledging to maintain a financially viable publicly funded health-care system. To this end they are calling on the federal government to reinstate previously cut funds to the Canada health and social transfer. The ministers agree to work together to develop a comprehensive anti-smoking strategy; as well, they plan to focus on improving Aboriginal health care.

18 September 1998 *Health*	Federal Health Minister Allan Rock presents an offer to the provinces in an effort to resolve outstanding issues concerning hepatitis C victims. Last spring the federal and provincial governments committed to spending $1.1 billion in compensation to people who contracted the virus between 1986 and 1990 (the period wherein the governments may be legally liable for the spread of the virus). This new offer arises in response to calls from Ontario and Quebec to compensate pre-1986 victims. The proposed deal would spend money on increased health services to all people infected with hepatitis C but does not include financial compensation to the victims. Ontario has committed to spending $200 million in compensation to pre-1986 victims.
24 September 1998 *Transportation*	The provincial and territorial transport ministers meet in Regina to discuss highway construction and rail-line abandonment. Despite a report that says Canada urgently needs to upgrade its highways, the federal government will not commit to financing such a project. The report calls for $17 billion in construction, but says that the improved roads would result in a net return of $13 billion, much of that from increased trade. The other topic, rail abandonment, is a problem in the prairies as rail lines that are not profitable have been shut down, thus increasing shipping costs for farmers. David Collenette, the federal transport minister, says that he will work with the provinces to address these two issues.
29 September 1998 *Gun Control*	The Alberta Court of Appeal decides that the federal government does have the jurisdiction to make gun control legislation, including the requirement that firearms be registered. The governments of Alberta, Saskatchewan, Yukon, the Northwest Territories, and Ontario launched the suit complaining that Ottawa is overstepping its constitutional powers in making laws dealing with private property.
8 October 1998 *Aboriginal Peoples*	Cree leaders in Quebec and that province's government will recommence negotiations over logging rights. On the agenda are forest allotments for Cree communities, a shared land-use strategy, an end to new logging areas, and an audit of current forestry laws and policies. The Cree

are still pursuing a $700 million claim against the Quebec government for allegedly unlawful logging practices.

12 October 1998 *Aboriginal Peoples*	A federal study concerning the quality of life of Aboriginal peoples in Canada is released. The findings demonstrate that the standard of living for native Canadians, especially those living on reserves, falls far below the national average. Life expectancy is 7.5-10 years lower for Aboriginal peoples and wages for Aboriginal peoples are more than 50 percent below that of non-Aboriginal Canadians.
14 October 1998 *Budget*	Federal Finance Minister Paul Martin delivers his annual fall budget update. His message to Canadians is that while the Canadian economy is in fairly good shape, it is necessary to be cautious in economic forecasting and in the planning of future spending, given the rough shape of the world economy. Martin says that there may not be the money expected earlier this year to cut taxes and increase spending in next year's budget due to lower than predicted growth rates.
14 October 1998 *Fisheries*	Federal Fisheries Minister David Anderson reveals a plan to cut down the size of British Columbia's fishing fleet. The government will buy back licences and will develop even stricter quotas; the goal is to have a smaller, more profitable fishing fleet. The current quotas have already been sharply criticized by the BC government and fishers.
19 October 1998 *Senate*	Alberta finally elects its senators-in-waiting, Ted Morton and Bert Brown. The two are Reform Party members; Reform was the only party to nominate candidates for the election, although two independents also ran. The Chief Returning Officer says that many voters did not fill out ballots for the Senate vote which was held in conjunction with municipal elections.
19 October 1998 *Aboriginal Peoples/ Nisga'a*	Gordon Campbell, leader of the British Columbia Liberal Party, launches a bid to have the Nisga'a treaty deemed unconstitutional in the BC Supreme Court. He is asking the court to rule that a provincial referendum is necessary to ratify the agreement. He argues that it creates another level of government by granting the Nisga'a law-making

powers and contravenes the *Charter of Rights and Freedoms* by allowing only Nisga'a band members to participate in the Nisga'a government. Campbell deems this to be racial discrimination.

24 October 1998 *Political Parties*	The Progressive Conservative Party holds its leadership vote. Joe Clark comes out ahead but fails to garner 50 percent of the vote, necessitating a second ballot. Hugh Segal, Brian Pallister, and Michael Fortier will not be competing in the second round. This leaves David Orchard, a Saskatchewan farmer, as Mr. Clark's only challenger for the second ballot. The second vote will be held 14 November.
27 October 1998 *Media*	The *National Post*, the newest of the Southam Inc. papers, makes its debut. The Toronto-based paper is being billed as providing "truly" national news coverage.
28 October 1998 *Quebec*	A general election is called in Quebec for 30 November 1998. Lucien Bouchard states in his election announcement that the Parti Québécois will hold a referendum on the question of secession if it is elected. Liberal leader Jean Charest explains that his party will focus on improved federalism, tax cuts, and restricting government's role in the economy.
10 November 1998 *Agriculture*	Saskatchewan asks Ottawa to develop an emergency farm aid strategy. Farming incomes have fallen drastically due to low commodity prices and a subsidy war on agricultural products between the United States and the European Union.
12 November 1998 *Aboriginal Peoples/* *Nisga'a*	The Nisga'a First Nation holds a referendum on the approval of their treaty with the BC and federal governments. The accord is ratified as 61 percent of eligible voters voted in favour. Despite attempts by the BC Liberal Party and the BC Fisheries Survival Coalition to thwart the provincial legislature's ratification of the deal, both the premier and the prime minister say they will speed up the process in their respective legislative assemblies.
14 November 1998 *Political Parties*	Joe Clark wins the Progressive Conservative party leadership with 77 percent of the second-round ballots. Clark

says that his agenda as the new leader includes eliminating the party's debt, readying an election platform, and attracting more support from Canadians. He has dismissed the United Alternative movement as being ineffective and refuses to become involved in discussions with the Reform Party about a possible union between the parties.

26 November 1998
Northwest Territories

Don Morin steps down as premier of the Northwest Territories amid accusations that he broke conflict-of-interest rules. He is resigning as premier, but will maintain his seat in the government. Morin denies any wrongdoing and will fight the allegations made against him.

30 November 1998
Quebec

The Parti Québécois (PQ) wins a majority in the Quebec provincial election, renewing Lucien Bouchard's term as premier. While the Liberal Party had a higher percentage of the popular vote, 44 percent compared to 43 percent for the PQ, the distribution of voters meant that the PQ won 75 seats and Liberals took 48. The PQ's modest win means it is unlikely that the new government will call a referendum in the near future.

30 November 1998
Aboriginal Peoples/
Nisga'a

The BC government opens a special session of the legislature to introduce the bill to ratify the Nisga'a treaty.

1 December 1998
Gun Control

Canada's gun registry law comes into effect. The law requires that every gun owner be licensed by 2001 and that all firearms be registered by 2003. Some of the provinces are appealing the law in a case before the Supreme Court of Canada.

4 December 1998
Fisheries

Brian Peckford submits his final report on the west-coast fishery and Ottawa's management thereof to the Government of British Columbia. The report slams the current system and suggests that a new agency is needed to replace both the federal Department of Fisheries and Oceans and the BC Fisheries Ministry. The new agency would be located on the west coast and would be a shared project between British Columbia and the federal government.

7 December 1998
Social Services

Prime Minister Chrétien announces that a youth-employment program will be extended for a second three-year period. It is a shared-cost program between federal and provincial governments and helps young people gain work experience through subsidies to employers. The announcement is attacked by the premiers who were not consulted in the decision to extend the program and yet are expected to continue funding it. The provinces are demanding that they be consulted on new social spending; federal-provincial consultation is a key part of the social union talks.

10 December 1998
Agriculture

Federal Agriculture Minister Lyle Vanclief announces that the federal government will commit $900 million to a farm aid plan. The problem in getting the money to farmers is how to structure the program so as not to incite US anger at what might be perceived as an agricultural subsidy.

10 December 1998
Northwest Territories

Jim Antoine is elected premier in the Northwest Territories to replace Don Morin who stepped down last month. Antoine was a leader in the Dene community and a long-time member of the NWT legislature. His term will last until 1 April 1999 when the territory will split in order to create the new eastern Arctic territory of Nunavut.

14 December 1998
Financial Services

In a much anticipated announcement, Finance Minister Paul Martin rejects the merger plans of four of Canada's most prominent banks. The decision came after almost a year of deliberation and reports from different groups on the likely outcome for consumers of the proposed bank unions. Two reports in particular influenced the government's decision: one from the Bureau of Competition Policy and the other from the Superintendent of Financial Institutions, which stated that services to customers would likely be compromised and prices would increase. The banks argue that they would be better equipped to compete internationally with the larger pool of resources which would result from the mergers. The government will continue to implement changes to its financial services policy which are intended to increase competition.

17 December 1998
Western Canada

The prairie provinces and the two territories announce plans to work together to promote economic development and attract international business and tourism. The group says that it is the fastest growing region in Canada and criticizes the federal government for doing little to improve transportation.

18 December 1998 *Health*	The federal government finally reaches a compromise with hepatitis C victims on a compensation package. Hepatitis C sufferers were angered several days ago when health ministers across the country offered financial payments to Canadians who contracted the AIDS virus through a partner or parent infected by the tainted blood supply when the same ministers have been slow in addressing the claims of hepatitis C patients.
21 December 1998 *Aboriginal Peoples/* *Metis*	The Metis gain recognition as a distinct Aboriginal People by the Ontario Court. The official recognition is part of a ruling that absolves two Metis of any wrongdoing in hunting a bull moose. The Metis have long faced difficulties in gaining the recognition, not only in Ontario but across the country. The difficulties arise in that it is difficult to define Metis, and because the different levels of government argue over who has jurisdiction over off-reserve Aboriginal people. Approximately 210,000 Canadians are identified as Metis.
30 December 1998 *Transportation/* *Agriculture*	Willard Estey's report on Canada's grain transportation system is made public by the Ministry of Transport Canada. Estey, a former Supreme Court Justice, was called upon to investigate the issue last year when farmers suffered huge financial losses due to delayed grain shipments. The report recommends that the Canadian Wheat Board should give up control of grain transportation to private companies.
10 January 1999 *Newfoundland*	Newfoundland plans celebrations in honour of its fiftieth year as a Canadian province. Newfoundland joined confederation in 1949. The celebrations are also expected to boost tourism, which has been growing since the 1997 festivities marking the 500th anniversary of explorer John Cabot's arrival in Newfoundland.
12 January 1999 *Social Union*	Ottawa agrees to limit its ability to introduce new shared-cost programs at a federal-provincial meeting in Halifax. The ministers met to discuss the social union, and while no deal has yet been agreed to, all parties have been compromising and are optimistic that a deal will soon be reached.

14 January 1999
Unity

Saskatchewan Premier Roy Romanow declares that the federal government's choice not to ratify the Calgary Declaration is insignificant. The Calgary Declaration is a statement made by the nine federalist premiers recognizing Quebec's unique character. The Declaration was seen as a provincial initiative and not one that requires Ottawa's approval. The Declaration has been rejected by Quebec as insubstantial.

14 January 1999
Homelessness

Toronto's task force on the homeless concludes its study by saying that the stereotype of homeless people is not accurate; in fact there are many families and children who are homeless and the fastest growing segment is youth under 18 years of age. The report suggests that shelter allowances should be higher in Toronto and that the working poor should be given rent payment assistance. Costs of the report's suggested programs are approximately $26 million for the city, $262 million for the Ontario government, and $84 million for the federal government.

18 January 1999
Newfoundland

Newfoundland Premier Brian Tobin calls a provincial election for 9 February. He explains that he needs to renew his government's mandate in the face of two important agreements for natural resource development. Others speculate that he has called the election so as to have another term in office before moving on to compete for the federal Liberal Party leadership when Chrétien decides to step down.

19 January 1999
Bilingualism

A report released by the federal Task Force on Government Transformations and Official Languages states that bilingualism has deteriorated as a result of federal government downsizing to provincial governments and due to increased privatization of services.

21 January 1999
Revenue

Revenue Canada begins collecting outstanding debts for the provinces. Revenue Canada will deduct monies owed to the provinces, such as student loans, sales tax, etc. from federal income tax refunds. It already does so for debts owed to the federal government. So far only Ontario, Nova Scotia, and British Columbia have asked that this measure be implemented on their behalf.

26 January 1999 *Aboriginal Peoples*	The British Columbia and federal governments reach an agreement with the Sechelt First Nation. If signed, it will be the first such agreement under the BC Treaty Commission; the agreement with the Nisga'a band did not fall under this commission because negotiations began before the commission's inception in 1991. The deal with the Sechelt First Nation includes 933 hectares of land and $42 million.
26 January 1999 *Justice*	The federal Justice and Attorney General of Canada announces that it will join the British Columbia government in an appeal in the BC Supreme Court in a child pornography case. A lower court in BC overturned a law prohibiting possession of child pornography saying that it violates the right to freedom of thought, belief, opinion, and expression.
29-30 January 1999 *Social Union*	Federal and provincial ministers meet in Victoria for social union talks. The provinces and the federal government have yet to reach a compromise on the most crucial issues. The provinces are demanding that they have more input into the design of social programs and want to have the power to opt out of Ottawa's programs and yet still receive federal funds if they run similar programs. Ottawa will not agree to these demands, and moreover is asking the provinces to remove barriers to social services to out-of-province Canadians. The provinces also want to prevent the federal government from being able to decrease transfer payments without consulting the provinces; the provincial ministers are calling on Ottawa to increase social transfers to their pre-1995 levels.
4 February 1999 *Quebec*	A new poll suggests that nationalist sentiment in Quebec is weakening. The poll indicates that over 65 percent of Québécois do not want a referendum in Premier Lucien Bouchard's current term in office, and almost half said they do not want another referendum at any time.
4 February 1999 *Social Union*	The federal government and the provinces, minus Quebec, sign a social union deal. The signing provinces are finally convinced to sign when Prime Minister Jean Chrétien promises to make a large increase to health-care funding. Ottawa will maintain its *de jure* control over the

interpretation and enforcement of the *Canada Health Act*, but a conflict-resolution process will be adopted as a concession to the provinces' demands. The federal government agrees to give the provinces three months warning about new policies and a greater say in the development of new policies. New shared programs will require the agreement of a minimum of six provinces and again provincial input will be sought in determining shared program costs and goals. The social union deal also relaxes the provinces' obligations to spend federal money on specific programs. The signing provinces agreed to remove provincial barriers to employment, postsecondary education, health care, and social assistance within three years. Quebec chose not to sign the deal because the federal government did not agree to allow provinces that choose not to participate in shared programs to use the federal money for a different but related service. Despite Quebec's refusal to sign the deal, Ottawa says it will allow the province to participate in any new initiatives. Quebec Premier Lucien Bouchard criticized the other provinces for agreeing to the social union and said that the deal signed without Quebec is evidence that there are growing differences between Quebec and the rest of the country.

9 February 1999
Newfoundland

The Liberal Party wins a majority of seats in the Newfoundland provincial election, giving Brian Tobin another term as the province's premier. The total number of seats won by the Liberals was down to 32 from the 36 held when the election was called. The Conservatives won 14 seats and the New Democratic Party, 2.

10 February 1999
Water

The federal government makes a proposal to the provinces to institute a nationwide suspension of large volume water diversions or sales. The government would like to use the suspension period to achieve an agreement with the provinces for an environmentally sound strategy to manage the country's water resources.

15 February 1999
Nunavut

The first election is held in Nunavut to choose the 19 new legislature members. As there are no political parties in the territory, the 19 members will choose a premier and Cabinet from among themselves. The legislature will operate like that of the Northwest Territories in that decisions will be made by consensus. Most of the administration for the new territory is already in place in anticipation of the establishment of Nunavut as an independent territory on 1 April.

16 February 1999
Budget

The federal government delivers its budget, focusing on health care and modest tax cuts. It is the second balanced budget in a row and Finance Minister Paul Martin promises balanced budgets over the next two years. To keep Ottawa's promise during social union negotiations the federal government pledges to increase health transfers by $11.5 billion over the next five years and to spend more money on research and innovation in health care. As for tax relief, the basic personal exemption will increase by $675 and a surtax on income above $50,000 instituted in 1985, said to be temporary at the time, will be repealed. Other areas being targeted for increased spending include youth employment, information technology, improved salaries and benefits to the military, Aboriginal Canadians and the Department of Indian Affairs, and an emergency contingency fund. In addition, $3 billion will be spent on paying down the $579.9 billion debt.

In response to the budget, anti-poverty activists point out that the budget makes a very weak attempt to address the growing poverty rate. Health groups were also critical. While they applaud the infusion of money to health care, they say it will not be enough to maintain an effective system. In contrast with the demands for greater spending, the Reform Party chides the government for not making greater tax cuts. Quebec Premier Lucien Bouchard complains that the change in CHST transfer payment calculations, now made on a per capita basis, will short-change Quebec. The prime minister responds that the federal equalization payment will make up for the change in transfers, emphasizing that the money is a benefit of federalism in that it comes primarily from Ontario's growing economy.

22 February 1999
Media

The Canadian Radio-Television and Telecommunications Communications Commission grants approval to Canada's first Aboriginal television network. The Aboriginal People Television Network will be carried as part of basic cable.

24 February 1999 *Agriculture*	Agricultural ministers from across the country meet in Victoria to sign an agreement on farm aid. All of the provinces, except Nova Scotia, grudgingly sign onto the federal government farm aid program. The program is designed to compensate farmers who have suffered economic hardship due to low commodity prices. The program will cost $1.5 billion, 60 percent to be paid by Ottawa and 40 percent by the provinces. Despite signing the accord, Manitoba and Saskatchewan say that it is too expensive for their agriculture-based economies. Nova Scotia withdrew from the agreement at the last moment because it says the program does not address the needs of its farmers which differ from the needs of prairie farmers.
5 March 1999 *Nunavut*	Paul Okalik is chosen as Nunavut's first premier. He will lead the territory once the official transfer of power takes place on 1 April.
8 March 1999 *Aboriginal Peoples*	Parliament approves legislation to transfer control of reserve lands to band councils away from the federal government. This means that leases, licences, and property management regulations will come under the jurisdiction of the local band. Critics say it gives the reserve councils too much power to expropriate land. Native women's groups say that the bill does not entrench women's equal right to property, especially in divorce.
10 March 1999 *Agriculture*	The Saskatchewan and federal governments pledge a further $85 million in relief for Saskatchewan farmers. This money supplements the money from the national farm aid program introduced this year.
11 March 1999 *Aboriginal Peoples*	Natives of the Treaty 7 bands in Alberta try to exercise their rights over natural resources. They have launched a suit against the federal government saying that they have maintained their rights to natural resources even with the Treaty 7 agreement, signed in 1877. The federal government says those rights belong to the Alberta government; the rights were transferred from the federal government to Alberta in 1930.
15 March 1999 *Quebec*	Premier Lucien Bouchard says that Quebec needs to have an independent voice from the federal government in

international relations concerning culture. Bouchard's comments follow Prime Minister Chrétien's statement in the House of Commons reinforcing the concept that diplomatic relations be conducted between countries and not provinces and countries. Earlier this month the culture minister from France invited representatives from both the Canadian and Quebec governments to a conference. Federal Heritage Minister Sheila Copps boycotted the affair because Quebec was invited independently.

22 March 1999 *Aboriginal Peoples/* *Premiers*	Aboriginal leaders meet with six of the premiers and territorial leaders to discuss the role of natives in implementing the social union. Native leaders criticized the social union process because they were not included. The premiers and territorial leaders support their demand to be consulted in future planning, but did not approve a proposal by First Nations' Assembly Chief Phil Fontaine that Aboriginals play a formal role. The conference did not determine what the role of Aboriginal leaders is to be, and native participation in the social union process must still be endorsed by Ottawa. Included in the Aboriginal leader delegation are the Assembly of First Nations, the Congress of Aboriginal Peoples, the Metis National Council, the Native Women's Association, and the Inuit Tapirisat. The premiers of Newfoundland, New Brunswick, Prince Edward Island, and Quebec do not attend the meeting.
25 March 1999 *Quebec*	Ottawa rejects a Quebec proposal that would allow it to have a formal role in international cultural and trade organizations such as UNESCO and the World Trade Organization. The federal government did say that it would work with Quebec to develop better federal representation for Quebec abroad. The Quebec Cabinet passed a resolution on 24 March saying that Quebec must "speak with its own voice in the name of the Quebec people."
25 March 1999 *Homelessness*	Toronto hosts a summit on homelessness. Accusations fly between the city, provincial, and federal governments as to which government is to blame for the enormous problem. Two days before the conference, Ontario Social Services Minister Janet Ecker pledged to spend $45 million on affordable housing and housing for people suffering

from mental illness. As well, the federal government has appointed its first minister on homelessness.

30 March 1999
Aboriginal Peoples

In an historic accord, Mohawk natives on Quebec's Kahnawake reserve will now be able to tax non-natives on the reserve. The deal allows the same natives the benefit of being exempt from sales tax when making purchases off the reserve in Quebec. The federal government will not participate in the deal and still demands that Kahnawake reserve natives pay GST on off-reserve purchases. Critics of the deal, including the federal government, say that it is unfair to tax some people and not others on reserves.

30 March 1999
Justice

The Alberta Court of Queen's Bench upholds a law banning the possession of child pornography. The decision states that possession of child pornography endangers the right to privacy and protection of children. The decision is the reverse of a recent ruling in British Columbia which struck down the law as a violation of the right to freedom of thought, belief, opinion, and expression. The British Columbia and federal governments are appealing the BC court decision in the BC Supreme Court.

1 April 1999
Nunavut

Nunavut, Canada's newest territory, is born. Nunavut is created from the eastern portion of the Northwest Territories and covers two million square kilometres with a population of 25,000. Per capita annual income is $11,000 and the unemployment rate is 22 percent. Nunavut's budget will be approximately $600 million, most of which will come from the federal government.

7 April 1999
Quebec

The federal government grants another $175.2 million to Quebec in disaster aid. The money will pay for further repairs needed as a result of the 1998 ice storm and the 1996 Saguenay floods.

12-15 April 1999
Atlantic Canada

The Atlantic premiers and business leaders travel through four northern states on a trade mission to expand cross-border trade. The trip is sponsored by the federal Atlantic Canada Opportunities Agency and is deemed to be a success by both the Canadian and American participants.

22 April 1999
Aboriginal Peoples

Brian Craik, spokesperson for the Cree, says that the Cree of northern Quebec have started a law suit in the Federal Court of Canada claiming that some 100 islands in the Hudson Bay and James Bay are part of their traditional lands. The islands are now part of Nunavut and were previously part of the Northwest Territories. The Cree say that they were not consulted when the boundaries of Nunavut were determined.

27 April 1999
Aboriginal Peoples/
Nisga'a

The Nisga'a treaty is signed by the British Columbia government and the Nisga'a band during an opening ceremony for the annual Nisga'a convention. The BC legislature ratified the accord on 22 April after the NDP government closed the debate in order to be able to sign the accord at the Nisga'a annual convention. The opposition Liberals were incensed by the close of debate and highlighted the fact that one-third of the document remains to be debated. The federal government is not expected to introduce the accord for ratification in the House of Commons until next fall when there will be more time available for debate.

29 April 1999
Newfoundland

Newfoundland changes its name to Newfoundland and Labrador. The legislation concerning the name change receives unanimous approval in the provincial legislature on 29 April. The House of Commons and the Senate must approve the change before it can come into effect.

29 April 1999
Revenue

The federal government creates the new Canada Customs and Revenue Agency. This single body would save about $60 million in tax-collection costs if used by all governments: federal, provincial, and municipal. Federal Revenue Minister Herb Dhaliwal expects that it will take a great effort to convince the other governments to use the centralized tax-collection system, although Revenue Canada currently collects personal income taxes for the nine provinces, and some other taxes for certain provinces.

5 May 1999
Ontario

Premier Mike Harris calls an election in Ontario for 3 June. The Progressive Conservative Party platform includes more tax cuts, health-care spending, and strong leadership. The Liberal Party campaign focuses on the health-care issue, which has been a hot topic in Ontario and across the country this past year. The NDP platform also promises increased health spending, but includes spending on education, increased shelter allowances for people on social assistance, the re-implementation of labour laws repealed by the Tory government, and improved environmental protection.

7 May 1999
Provinces

Federal and provincial leaders introduce a National Children's Agenda at a conference in Saskatoon. While the agenda lacks detail and does not address the issue of funding, it does target certain areas for future policy development. The four areas covered by the agenda are physical and emotional health, safety, success in learning, and becoming responsible and socially engaged citizens. All of the provinces with the exception of Quebec will participate in this endeavor.

8 May 1999
New Brunswick

A general election is announced by New Brunswick Premier Camille Theriault. Theriault says that his Liberal Party will address jobs, health care, and leadership. The leadership question is important as it is the first election after long-time premier and Liberal leader Frank McKenna's retirement. Important issues in the campaign will include tax cuts, which are favoured by the Liberal and Progressive Conservative Parties, and the question of tolls on a new highway running between Fredericton and Moncton.

12 May 1999
British Columbia

Federal Fisheries Minister David Anderson responds to a confidential report by the BC Forests Ministry, which was leaked a day earlier. He announces that the federal government will not provide relief funds for forestry industry restructuring. The report states that over 18, 000 jobs will be lost in the industry over the next two years and calls for federal aid to alleviate the economic impact. Anderson says the federal government will not provide help both because forestry falls under provincial jurisdiction and because the industry's problems are the result of mismanagement by the BC government.

12 May 1999
Nunavut

Nunavut's legislature opens for the first time. It is reported in the Throne Speech that the government will make itself as accessible as possible, and it introduces Inuktitut as the territory's official government language. Nunavut plans to join the other two territories to negotiate a greater share of resource revenues from Ottawa.

14 May 1999
Transportation

Federal and provincial transport ministers meet to discuss highway improvements. The provinces are asking Ottawa to share half the costs of proposed roadwork. Currently, all parties involved are finding it difficult to raise the money needed to improve the country's highways. They are necessary to maintain and increase trade.

15 May 1999
British Columbia

British Columbia Premier Glen Clark announces that his province will resume discussions with the federal government concerning Ottawa's lease of the area at Nanoose Bay. The federal government has leased the area since 1965, and it allows the United States military to use the area as a torpedo testing range. At issue is British Columbia's demand that the federal government pledge to ban vessels carrying nuclear weapons in the leased area. The federal government says that it cannot make such a commitment because, for security purposes, the US will not divulge whether or not a ship is carrying nuclear warheads. Ottawa had said a day earlier that it would move to expropriate the land given the suspension of negotiations with BC. BC has used the Nanoose Bay lease as a bargaining chip in a dispute over fishing with the federal government.

19 May 1999
Quebec

Quebec Premier Lucien Bouchard returns home from a trade mission to Mexico with millions of dollars of business contracts. Bouchard says his government will quadruple spending to promote Quebec internationally and plans to conduct similar trips to Argentina and Chile. Quebec's attempt to make itself known internationally and to conduct relations with other states without the federal government has angered federalist politicians in Ottawa. Chrétien's government refused to help Bouchard arrange a meeting with Mexican President Ernesto Zedillo.

20 May 1999
Aboriginal Peoples

The Supreme Court of Canada hands down a decision allowing off-reserve natives to vote in band elections. The requirement that natives be ordinarily resident on their reserves was found to be discriminatory. Many natives have been forced to move off-reserve in order to find work and better housing. The ruling will be particularly beneficial to native women who were forced off the reserves and lost their band membership when they wed non-natives prior to a 1985 ruling which ended that practice and reinstated band membership. However, often women were not permitted by their communities to return. This latest decision will now allow these women to participate in the election of their band leaders.

20 May 1999
Justice

The Supreme Court of Canada ruled that the definition of "spouse" in the *Ontario Family Law Act*, which applies only to heterosexual couples, is unconstitutional because it discriminates on the basis of sexual orientation. The ruling grants Ontario six months to update the Act and implies that other provincial laws ought to be changed as well to eliminate discrimination against gays and lesbians in the law. This means that other provinces will likely be forced to re-examine their own statutes. However, Premier Ralph Klein has suggested that his government may invoke the notwithstanding clause to avoid changing the definition of spouse in Alberta statutes.

20-21 May 1999
Western Canada

Postsecondary education tops the agenda at a meeting of western premiers and territorial leaders. They are asking the federal government to budget more money for postsecondary education transfers. The leaders say that postsecondary programs need ongoing support. The programs have not received support because of the social transfer cuts over the past several years. Also on the agenda is the development of a process to resolve cross-border disputes with the United States. To this end they met with North Dakota Governor Ed Schafer. The leaders of western Canada have been invited to attend the semi-annual meeting of western governors in Wyoming in June.

3 June 1999
Ontario

Ontario elects the Tories to a second term in government. It is the first election in the province in over 30 years where a party wins back-to-back majority governments. The Conservatives win 59 seats, the Liberals 32, and the NDP are down to just 9, which does not meet the required 12 needed for official party status.

3 June 1999 *Fisheries*	Federal Fisheries Minister David Anderson endorsed changes to the Pacific Salmon Treaty signed with Alaska, Washington, Oregon, and US native groups. The changes include fishing caps based on the fish available, not quotas, and a focus on conservation. However, BC fishers, environmentalists, the BC government, and natives are furious about a deal they see as selling out their interests.
7 June 1999 *New Brunswick*	In a surprise election landslide the Progressive Conservative Party comes to power in New Brunswick. The party wins 44 seats compared to the 9 held when the election was called. The Liberal Party went from a majority government to holding just 10. High unemployment on the Acadian peninsula, road tolls, and cuts to the numbers of health-care workers and police were among the reasons cited for voter dissatisfaction with the previous Liberal government. Bernard Lord will be the new premier of the province.
10 June 1999 *Supreme Court of Canada*	Louise Arbour is appointed to the Supreme Court of Canada. She will resign as chief United Nations' war-crimes prosecutor in order to fulfill the appointment. The vacancy comes after Justice Peter Cory's recent retirement.
17 June 1999 *Nova Scotia*	Premier Russell MacLellan's Liberal government is defeated in Nova Scotia. The Conservative Party joined the NDP in voting down the government's budget, thus toppling the government. At the dissolution of the legislature, the Liberals and NDP each held 19 seats and the Tories held the balance at 13. The Tories had agreed to support a Liberal minority government on the condition that the budget would be balanced. They withdrew their support when it was not. The Liberals have defended themselves by saying that the extra money would be spent on a much needed infusion into the health-care system. The election is called for 27 July.
21 June 1999 *Aboriginal Peoples*	An agreement in principle is reached between the Dogrib First Nation and the federal government. If ratified, the deal would grant the Dogrib $90 million, 39,000 square kilometres of the Northwest Territories, a share of resource revenue, and mineral rights to the land covered by the treaty

with the exception of current mining claims being honoured by the federal government. The agreement also sets the stage for self-government.

21 June 1999
New Brunswick

The Conservative government led by Bernard Lord is sworn in in New Brunswick. Lord has reduced the size of the Cabinet and says that the government will be much leaner than the Liberal government it replaces. Lord promises to raise the minimum wage, fight the federal gun control law, resolve outstanding issues with health-care workers, remove highway tolls, and create 300 new nursing positions.

30 June 1999
Justice

The British Columbia Court of Appeal upholds a lower court ruling, which found a law criminalizing the possession of child pornography to be unconstitutional. The appeal was initiated by the BC government and the federal government; federal Justice Minister Anne McLellan says that the governments are disappointed with the decision and that they will institute an appeal in the Supreme Court of Canada.

30 June 1999
Agriculture

Agriculture ministers from Manitoba and Saskatchewan meet with their federal counterpart in Ottawa to ask for more farm aid from the federal government. Lyle Vanclief, the federal minister, says that no more money will be spent on agricultural aid at this time, but he did commit to helping the provinces find money in other departments for disaster compensation.

5 July 1999
Political Parties

The Liberal task force on the west wraps up its meetings with a trip to Saskatchewan this week, after some discouraging news that Alberta tends to mistrust the central government. The task force was established by the prime minister in January in order to build a Liberal presence in the traditionally hostile region.

26 July 1999
Alberta

Albertan municipalities lash out at the Progressive Conservative provincial government for downloading its spending onto municipal governments. The municipalities have their hands tied when it comes to spending by a law that prevents them from running a deficit. This means that municipal governments can either raise taxes or delay infrastructure improvements.

27 July 1999
Nova Scotia

Led by John Hamm, the Progressive Conservative Party won the provincial election in Nova Scotia, capturing 29 of the legislature's 52 seats.

27 July 1999
Political Parties

The United Alternative holds a press conference in Toronto to kick off the next step in its unite-the-right crusade. As co-chair of the United Alternative steering committee, Ontario Tory minister Tony Clement announced the co-chairs of eight action committees and revealed changes to the United Alternative's executive council.

1 August 1999
Northwest Territories

A Supreme Court decision is forcing the government of the Northwest Territories to alter the number of seats in its Legislative Assembly after concerns were raised that non-Aboriginals represent the majority of people in the Northwest Territories after its split with Nunavut. The new system was also giving preference to urban rather than rural areas, which was an issue of great concern to many Aboriginals. The Legislative Assembly has until 1 September 2000 to make the necessary changes.

13 August 1999
Political Parties

Former Tory MP Bill Matthews of Burin-St. George, Newfoundland announced his resignation from caucus and joined the Liberals. As the Tory fisheries critic and deputy House leader, Matthews departure has humbled Progressive Conservative Party members and bolstered Liberal confidence.

16 August 1999
Premiers' Meeting

At their annual conference, premiers and territorial leaders unanimously called for full restoration of the CHST to fund social programs, with a specific focus on postsecondary education. The premiers attacked the rise in federal budgetary surpluses claiming that provincial expenditure responsibilities are outstripping provincial tax revenue. However, there were differences between the premiers over the need for increased transfers versus substantial tax cuts. Premiers Harris and Klein were particularly strident in their demands for tax cuts, but the other premiers were less enthusiastic in their support. The federal government has already announced that it will divide future revenue surpluses between debt reduction, tax cuts, and new spending.

16 August 1999 *Party Politics*	Jean Chrétien makes a mid-summer Cabinet shuffle that gets political circles buzzing. Among the shuffle, all-but-unknown Liberal backbencher, Toronto MP Maria Minna, was put in charge of international cooperation. The move shows a definite shift to the left and is also likely meant to cool the leadership aspirations of right-leaning Liberal Finance Minister Paul Martin.
16 August 1999 *Alberta*	The Alberta Urban Municipalities Association (AUMA) meets with provincial Treasurer Stockwell Day to ask that the school portion of property taxes be given to local government. The cash-strapped municipalities are suffering from a downloading of responsibilities from the provincial to the local level coupled with a decrease in provincial grants to municipalities from $75 in 1993 to $25 in 1994. In addition to the changes to taxation, the AUMA is also lobbying the Alberta government to draw up a charter delineating provincial and municipal responsibilities.
21 August 1999 *British Columbia*	Premier Glen Clark met with Lieutenant-Governor Garde Gardom and tendered his resignation. Clark continues to maintain his innocence in regard to the police allegations against him, but admits that he should have recognized that his actions had tarnished his public reputation. The NDP caucus announces that Deputy Premier Dan Miller will replace Clark as acting premier of the province.
23 August 1999 *Ontario*	At a Toronto meeting of the Association of Municipalities of Ontario, municipal leaders highlight the implications of province-wide restructuring of services. Changes to public services, in particular the health system and the education system, were discussed.
30 August 1999 *Supreme Court of Canada*	The appointment of Beverley McLachlin as the new Chief Justice of the Supreme Court of Canada, replacing Antonio Lamer, has generated criticism about the system of judicial appointments. There are concerns that the current procedures for appointing Supreme Court Justices are too vague and may reflect partisan interests. McLachlin is the first woman to be named as the Chief Justice of the Supreme Court of Canada.

9 September 1999
Trade

Prime Minister Jean Chrétien cancelled a Team Canada trade mission to Australia after several provincial premiers dropped out for various reasons.

12 September 1999
Political Parties

Reform Party leader Preston Manning and Progressive Conservative leader Joe Clark share the stage in Edmonton for a press conference updating the press on their pursuit of common ground between the two right-wing parties.

13 September 1999
Political Strategy

The narrow win in the Reform Party referendum to create the United Alternative raises concerns. Many of the *yes* voters were recruited after the beginning of the referendum campaign, which suggests that an aggressive pro-United Alternative campaign took place after it became obvious that the referendum would not be supported by the old rank and file Reformers.

13 September 1999
Governor General

Adrienne Clarkson is appointed to succeed Romeo LeBlanc in the Governor General's office.

17 September 1999
Supreme Court of Canada

The Supreme Court of Canada upholds an Aboriginal treaty signed in 1760 that allows Aboriginal People in Atlantic Canada to fish year-round for commercial purposes. The case was initiated by Mi'kmaq native Donald Marshall, who was initially made famous when he was wrongly convicted for murder and spent 11 years in jail.

21 September 1999
Manitoba

The New Democratic Party wins the provincial election with 32 out of 57 legislative seats. The new premier is Gary Doer.

26 September 1999
Homelessness

Federal Labour Minister Claudette Bradshaw wraps up a cross-Canada tour of shelters and programs related to homelessness with a commitment to seek short-term federal aid for homelessness while at the same time seeking a long-term solution.

27 September 1999
Political Parties

New Brunswick MP Angela Vautour, who represents the Beausejour-Petitcodiac constituency, announces her move from the New Democratic Party to the Progressive Conservative Party. The move means that both the NDP and the Progressive Conservatives occupy 19 seats in the House of Commons.

27 September 1999
Political Parties

The Reform Party has had to drop the idea of merging with Progressive Conservatives and instead is pursuing the creation of an entirely new party, the United Alternative. Although the third option of sharing candidates in some constituencies has not been dismissed by the Reform Party, the Tories are trying to ensure the presence of a Tory candidate in every riding.

28 September 1999
Atlantic Canada

Atlantic members of the Liberal caucus draft a report on the economic renewal of the region. The report targets government investment in high-tech industries and tax incentives as ways to improve the economic prospects of the region.

28 September 1999
Political Leaders

Finance Minister Paul Martin declares that he will run for re-election even if Jean Chrétien opts to retain the Liberal Party leadership. The finance minister has hinted at aspiring to the office of prime minister in the past, but continues to declare his support for Prime Minister Jean Chrétien.

29 September 1999
Education

Political wheeling and dealing may prevent students in Quebec from getting their share of the Millennium Scholarship Fund. Federal Human Resources Minister Jane Stewart and Quebec Education Minister François Legault cannot seem to agree on anything — from the colour of the cheques to the language in which they're printed. Both sides accuse the other of holding up the process, but neither seems willing to yield.

30 September 1999
Aboriginal Peoples

A Nova Scotia fishing group, the Scotian Fundy Mobile Gear Fishermen's Association, demands that the federal government compensate non-native fishers if Atlantic Aboriginal people are allowed to fish without restrictions. At the same time, Aboriginal chiefs from the Atlantic region are encouraging natives to continue fishing despite the rising tension.

30 September 1999
Health

Federal Health Minister Allan Rock requests that the Alberta College of Physicians and Surgeons wait until the Alberta Legislature reintroduces Bill 37 before making decisions on accrediting private hospitals. Bill 37 was dropped earlier this year by the government after critics charged that it would open the door to private health care.

30 September 1999
Social Services

NDP leader Alexa McDonough calls on the Liberal government to live up to its 1993 promise to create 150,000 new child-care spaces. The federal government has not created any new child-care spaces and McDonough argues that only 9 percent of children who need daycare receive it.

1 October 1999
Aboriginal Peoples

Federal Fisheries Minister Herb Dhaliwal announces his intentions to step into the east-coast fishing fray in order to negotiate an interim agreement with Aboriginal fishers so that a long-term solution — satisfying both native and non-native fishers — can be found. Unrest in east-coast fishing communities has been on the rise since a 17 September Supreme Court ruling allows east-coast Maliseet and Mi'kmaq Aboriginals to hunt and fish year-round without a licence.

2 October 1999
Alberta

On the last day of the Alberta Urban Municipalities Association convention in Edmonton it appears that the provincial government is prepared to meet some municipal demands for financial support.

3 October 1999
Aboriginal Peoples

Tensions run high in Burnt Church, New Brunswick where non-native fishers carry out threats to destroy any lobster traps put in the water after the official season closed. Over 3,000 traps were destroyed. Non-native fishers also stormed fish-processing plants accused of accepting off-season lobster from native fishers. The conflict stems from the 17 September Supreme Court decision confirming Aboriginal treaty rights to commercial fishing.

4 October 1999
Aboriginal Peoples

Leaders of five Innu communities in Quebec issue an ultimatum to the federal government saying that if Ottawa does not get involved in ensuring that Innu concerns over the impact on the environment and their territorial rights of the Churchill Falls hydroelectric project are addressed they will go to court. The provincial governments of Quebec and Newfoundland are jointly working on the Labrador-based project, but neither government has satisfied Aboriginal concerns for the integrity of their land. Talks between the Innu and the provincial governments currently appear to be at a standstill.

5 October 1999
Forum of Federations

The Liberal government tries to downplay a scheduled meeting between US President Bill Clinton and Quebec Premier Lucien Bouchard as a mere courtesy call. Quebec sovereignists, on the other hand, argue that the meeting is symbolic recognition of Quebec sovereignty. The private meeting is scheduled as part of the International Conference on Federalism beginning in Mont-Tremblant, Quebec, 6 October 1999.

6 October 1999
Forum of Federations

The International Conference on Federalism opens in Mont-Tremblant, Quebec. Prime Minister Jean Chrétien and Quebec Premier Lucien Bouchard face off over issues of Canadian federalism before the international crowd. Organizers attempt not to let the conference be overridden by Canada-specific issues.

Former Prime Minister Brian Mulroney defends Canadian federalism. Speaking at the conference, Mulroney claims that given the vast geography and diversity of Canada, specific provincial interests are served well, and that federalism is here to stay.

8 October 1999
Forum of Federations

President Bill Clinton spoke on the issue of unity in Mont-Tremblant, Quebec. The 45-minute impromptu speech was applauded by federalists, but has Premier Lucien Bouchard fuming as it lays out tough criteria for any group seeking independence. The US president is said to have taken a special interest in Canadian unity and has done extensive research on the topic.

11 October 1999
Aboriginal Peoples

Department of Fisheries and Oceans officers crack down on native fishers who are not covered by the 17 September Supreme Court decision to allow Mi'kmaq and Maliseet east-coast Aboriginals to hunt and fish year-round without a licence. Metis fishers are arrested for fishing illegally on a Mi'kmaq boat.

12 October 1999
Aboriginal Peoples

Eighteen charges are laid in connection with the destruction of thousands of Aboriginal lobster traps in New Brunswick. The RCMP announce that 25 people have been charged with 49 Criminal Code offences and a spokesperson for the Department of Fisheries and Oceans announces that an undisclosed number of non-native fishers will be charged with having lobster traps on the boats during the closed season. The charges all arise from the tension surrounding the 17 September Supreme Court decision.

12 October 1999
Throne Speech

In the Speech from the Throne the Liberal government restates its promise to use half the federal surplus on debt and tax reduction and the other half on increased social spending. Emphasis is placed on children and the role of the family. Using investment in areas that support the knowledge-based economy is also touted as a way to keep highly trained and skilled professionals in Canada. Critics of the speech say it lacks vision and merely represents more of the status quo.

12 October 1999
Quebec

In anticipation of today's Speech from the Throne, Quebec Premier Lucien Bouchard attacks the Liberal government's centralist approach to politics and intervention in provincial jurisdictions such as health and education.

13 October 1999
Gay and Lesbian Rights

Attorney General Jim Flaherty claims that Ontario needs more time to comply with the Supreme Court of Canada ruling that struck down its definition of a common-law spouse. Flaherty has just one month to allow same-sex, common-law spouses to claim alimony payments in the event of a separation. Critics claim that the Ontario government is dragging its heels for political reasons and argue that the province should be forced to obey the start date of 20 November.

17 October 1999
Aboriginal Peoples

James MacKenzie, lead negotiator for federal Fisheries Minister Herb Dhaliwal, visits Yarmouth, Nova Scotia to address the demands of commercial fishers who want to have native fishing restricted. Tensions in Yarmouth have been rising since the Supreme Court of Canada decision allowing year-round fishing without a licence, and there are fears that the dispute may get out of hand.

18 October 1999
Aboriginal Peoples

Mi'kmaq Chiefs meet with federal Fisheries Minister Herb Dhaliwal in an attempt to bring peace to the growing east-coast lobster dispute. The minister calls for a self-imposed moratorium on lobster fishing, but only 25 of the 35 Chiefs agree and many band members refuse to heed the moratorium.

A group representing the non-Aboriginal Nova Scotia lobster fishing industry requests that the Supreme Court of Canada review its controversial ruling which allows Mi'kmaq and east-coast Maliseet Aboriginals to earn a livelihood from hunting and fishing year-round without a licence. There is no deadline for the court's response.

19 October 1999
Quebec

A letter from federal Intergovernmental Affairs Minister Stéphane Dion to his Quebec counterpart Joseph Facal is released to the public. The letter suggests that Quebec is subject to the Supreme Court of Canada ruling made last year in which Quebec was denied the right to secede unilaterally. Meanwhile, some members of the Liberal caucus urge Prime Minister Jean Chrétien to put on the backburner a plan to establish federal ground rules for a future referendum on Quebec sovereignty. These caucus members worry that laying down the law to separatists will fuel their dissent.

20 October 1999
Quebec

Judge Danielle Cote rules that the provincial government failed to prove that the French language is still in jeopardy in Quebec. This means that section 58 of the French language charter is invalid and that the French language no longer has to be predominant on signs. The case was initiated by Gwen Simpson and Wally Hoffmann, who were fined $75 under the Language Charter for not making the French letters on the signs in their gift shop larger than the English letters.

21 October 1999
Quebec

Quebec Premier Lucien Bouchard lashes out against the ruling made by Judge Danielle Cote in which the Judge stated that the French language is not endangered. Bouchard argues that the French language is very much in danger and that the Québécois people have the right to take action to preserve it. The Quebec government is appealing Cote's ruling. However, lawyers for the government chose not to present arguments demonstrating that French is still at risk in the province. Liberal Leader Jean Charest described the case as "either provocation or incompetence at the highest level." He suggested that the government was deliberately trying to instigate a language debate in the province in order to generate support for sovereignty.

21 October 1999 *Aboriginal Peoples*	Indian Affairs Minister Robert Nault promises to pass the Nisga'a treaty in Parliament before the new year, even if it means quashing debate. The treaty was signed by the Nisga'a of British Columbia, the province, and the federal government earlier in the year but in order to be implemented it must be passed by Parliament. Only the Reform Party has threatened to delay its passing.
22 October 1999 *Aboriginal Peoples*	Nova Scotia Fisheries Minister Ernie Fage gives his support to a seven-point plan developed by non-native fishing groups in the region. The plan calls for one fishery with one set of rules that would apply equally to everyone and would bring an end to out-of-season Aboriginal fishing for commercial purposes.
22 October 1999 *Aboriginal Peoples*	Tenants on Musqueam land, in southwest Vancouver, have seen their rent soar and have become embroiled in a bitter fight that is taking them to the Supreme Court of Canada. The rent, which was typically about $400/year previous to 1997, was raised without dispute to $10,000/year in 1997 to reflect changing land values. However, the Musqueam band appealed that decision and last December the Federal Court of Appeal awarded rents in the $28,000 range. Leaseholders are refusing to pay that much, while the band is demanding more. Both sides have requested leave to appeal to the Supreme Court of Canada and in the meantime the land rent will average $10,000 a year and those refusing to pay will receive eviction notices.
25 October 1999 *Atlantic Canada*	The Atlantic Institute for Market Studies publishes research that examines Ottawa's mismanagement in transferring wealth to the Atlantic provinces. The research shows both inefficiency and negative economic impacts of the transfer payments on the Canadian economy.
1 November 1999 *Political Parties*	A growing number of grassroots Reform Party members are organizing in opposition to the new approach the Reform Party is taking to politics. Members of GUARD (Grassroots United Against Reform's Demise) are critical of Preston Manning's proposed United Alternative as well as his pandering to Ontario audiences in order to gain a stronger electoral backing.

3 November 1999 *Finance/Health*	Finance Minister Paul Martin threatens to act unilaterally to raise tobacco taxes if the provinces cannot agree to work together. In 1994 the federal government and five provincial governments cut tobacco taxes in order to counter smuggling. Martin is also working with the RCMP to ensure that incidences of smuggling do not go up as a result of a tobacco tax increase.
3 November 1999 *Aboriginal Peoples*	The all-party Commons committee responsible for reviewing the proposed Nisga'a treaty begins reviewing the controversial treaty. The meeting quickly becomes hostile.
8 November 1999 *Agriculture*	Saskatchewan Premier Roy Romanow decries federal Agriculture Minister Lyle Vanclief's decision not to implement a massive farm aid package. Vanclief commented that a bailout package was not worthwhile when it seemed that many farmers were going out of business anyway and such a package would only delay the inevitable. Vanclief lost his personal farming operation in 1998. However, this has not softened his stance to the plight of Canadian farmers.
14 November 1999 *Children*	Campaign 2000's Report Card reports that child poverty has increased 60 percent in the last decade. This statistic undermines the commitment made by the House of Commons in 1989 to eliminate child poverty.
22 November 1999 *Justice*	A former prominent Liberal organizer, John Richard, is appointed to the Federal Court of Canada as the new Chief Justice. The court has a large backlog of cases and it is expected that the new Chief Justice will be able to help with the crisis.
25 November 1999 *Political Parties*	Irwin Cotler, a McGill Law professor, wins a landslide victory in the Mount Royal by-election. A member of the Liberal Party, Colter wins 92.3 percent of the vote, a possible Canadian record. Cotler is firmly positioned on the left-wing of the Liberal Party and has already spoken to increased social spending.
29 November 1999 *Aboriginal Peoples*	Reform House Leader Randy White announces that the Reform Party will work hard to delay passing the Nisga'a treaty. He argues that Reform opposition to the treaty is a

response to the Canadians who are against the treaty and threatens to join forces with the Bloc Québécois in order to gain more support for the delay.

1 December 1999
Social Services

Alberta Treasurer Stockwell Day announces that he is exploring Alberta's options for opting-out of the Canada Pension Plan. Day says that he has brought up concerns about the plan with the federal government. Finance Minister Paul Martin argues that Day's questions are currently being addressed.

3 December 1999
Quebec/Clarity Bill

Quebec Premier Lucien Bouchard weighs in on the Quebec separation debate, arguing that Jean Chrétien is only playing tough with Quebec sovereignists in order to prepare for the next federal election. Bouchard assures the media that Quebec will determine the next referendum question, not Ottawa.

13 December 1999
Political Strategy

Government House Leader Don Boudria and other Members of Parliament discuss how to prevent legislation from being delayed by filibusters. The previous week saw the Reform Party stage a three-day voting marathon to delay the passing of the controversial Nisga'a treaty.

17 December 1999
Quebec/Clarity Bill

Prime Minister Jean Chrétien and Minister of Intergovernmental Affairs Stéphane Dion table a bill in the House of Commons which stipulates the conditions under which Ottawa would negotiate the separation of Quebec from Canada following a *yes* referendum vote. The bill indicates that after the Government of Quebec announces a referendum question on sovereignty, the House of Commons will meet to determine if the question is "clear." The bill also indicates that after a *yes* vote in the referendum, the House of Commons will determine if the majority is sufficiently "clear" to warrant negotiating separation with the province. As with the Supreme Court reference decision on secession, the federal legislation does not indicate what would comprise a "clear" question or a "clear" majority.

Chronology: Index

Aboriginal Peoples 15 July 1998, 8 October 1998, 12 October 1998, 26 January 1999, 8 March 1999, 11 March 1999, 30 March 1999, 22 April 1999, 20 May 1999, 21 June 1999, 30 September 1999, 1 October 1999, 3 October 1999, 4 October 1999, 11 October 1999, 12 October 1999, 17 October 1999, 18 October 1999, 21 October 1999, 22 October 1999, 3 November 1999, 29 November 1999

Aboriginal Peoples/Metis 21 December 1998

Aboriginal Peoples/Nisga'a 15 July 1998, 19 October 1998, 12 November 1998, 30 November 1998, 27 April 1999

Aboriginal Peoples/Premiers 22 March 1999

Agriculture 10 November 1998, 10 December 1998, 24 February 1999, 10 March 1999, 30 June 1999, 8 November 1999

Alberta 26 July 1999, 16 August 1999, 2 October 1999

Atlantic Canada 12-15 April 1999, 28 September 1999, 25 October 1999

Bilingualism 19 January 1999

British Columbia 12 May 1999, 15 May 1999, 21 August 1999

Budget 14 October 1998, 16 February 1999

Children 14 November 1999

Education 29 September 1999

Environment 13 July 1998, 17 August 1998

Finance/Health 3 November 1999

Financial Services 14 December 1998

Forum of Federations 5 October 1999, 6 October 1999, 8 October 1999

Fisheries 9 July 1998, 4 September 1998, 14 October 1998, 4 December 1998, 3 June 1999

Gay and Lesbian Rights 13 October 1999

Governor General 13 September 1999

Gun Control 29 September 1998, 1 December 1998

Health 15 July 1998, 17 September 1998, 18 September 1998, 18 December 1998, 30 September 1999

Homelessness 14 January 1999, 25 March 1999, 26 September 1999

Justice 26 January 1999, 30 March 1999, 20 May 1999, 30 June 1999, 22 November 1999

Manitoba 21 September 1999

Media 27 October 1998, 22 February 1999

New Brunswick 8 May 1999, 7 June 1999, 21 June 1999

Newfoundland 10 January 1999, 18 January 1999, 9 February 1999, 29 April 1999

Northwest Territories 26 November 1998, 10 December 1998, 1 August 1999

Nova Scotia/Newfoundland 6 August 1998

Nova Scotia 17 June 1999, 27 July 1999

Nunavut 15 February 1999, 5 March 1999, 1 April 1999, 12 May 1999

Ontario 5 May 1999, 3 June 1999, 23 August 1999

Party Politics 16 August 1999

Political Leaders 28 September 1999

Political Parties 31 July 1998, 24 October 1998, 14 November 1998, 5 July 1999, 27 July 1999, 13 August 1999, 12 September 1999, 27 September 1999, 1 November 1999, 25 November 1999

Political Strategy 13 September 1999, 13 December 1999

Premiers' Meeting 6-7 August 1998, 16 August 1999

Provinces 7 May 1999

Quebec 14 September 1998, 28 October 1998, 30 November 1998, 4 February 1999, 15 March 1999, 25 March 1999, 7 April 1999, 19 May 1999, 12 October 1999, 19 October 1999, 20 October 1999, 21 October 1999

Quebec/Clarity Bill 3 December 1999, 17 December 1999

Revenue 21 January 1999, 29 April 1999

Saskatchewan 27 July 1998

Senate 15 July 1998, 28 August 1998, 17 September 1998, 19 October 1998

Separation 20 August 1998

Social Services 7 December 1998, 30 September 1999, 1 December 1999

Social Union 17 September 1998, 12 January 1999, 29-30 January 1999, 4 February 1999

Supreme Court of Canada 10 June 1999, 30 August 1999, 17 September 1999

Throne Speech 12 October 1999

Trade 9 September 1999

Transportation 24 September 1998, 14 May 1999

Transportation/Agriculture 30 December 1998

Unity 14 January 1999

Water 10 February 1999

Western Canada 4 July 1998, 17 December 1998, 20-21 May 1999

Queen's Policy Studies
Recent Publications

The Queen's Policy Studies Series is dedicated to the exploration of major policy issues that confront governments in Canada and other western nations. McGill-Queen's University Press is the exclusive world representative and distributor of books in the series.

School of Policy Studies

Backbone of the Army: Non-Commissioned Officers in the Future Army, Douglas L. Bland (ed.), 2000 ISBN 0-88911-889-2

Precarious Values: Organizations, Politics and Labour Market Policy in Ontario, Thomas R. Klassen, 2000 Paper ISBN 0-88911-883-3 Cloth ISBN 0-88911-885-X

The Nonprofit Sector in Canada: Roles and Relationships, Keith G. Banting (ed.), 2000 Paper ISBN 0-88911-813-2 Cloth ISBN 0-88911-815-9

Security, Strategy and the Global Economics of Defence Production, David G. Haglund and S. Neil MacFarlane (eds.), 1999 Paper ISBN 0-88911-875-2 Cloth ISBN 0-88911-877-9

The Communications Revolution at Work: The Social, Economic and Political Impacts of Technological Change, Robert Boyce (ed.), 1999 Paper ISBN 0-88911-805-1 Cloth ISBN 0-88911-807-8

Diplomatic Missions: The Ambassador in Canadian Foreign Policy, Robert Wolfe (ed.), 1998 Paper ISBN 0-88911-801-9 Cloth ISBN 0-88911-803-5

Institute of Intergovernmental Relations

Managing the Environmental Union: Intergovernmental Relations and Environmental Policy in Canada, Patrick C. Fafard and Kathryn Harrison (eds.), 2000 ISBN 0-88911-837-X

Comparing Federal Systems, 2d ed., Ronald L. Watts, 1999 ISBN 0-88911-835-3

Canada: The State of the Federation 1999/2000, vol. 14, *Rebalancing and Decentralizing Fiscal Federalism,* Harvey Lazar (ed.), 2000 Paper ISBN 0-88911-843-4 Cloth ISBN 0-88911-839-6

Canada: The State of the Federation 1998/99, vol. 13, *How Canadians Connect,* Harvey Lazar and Tom McIntosh (eds.), 1999 Paper ISBN 0-88911-781-0 Cloth ISBN 0-88911-779-9

Canada: The State of the Federation 1997, vol. 12, *Non-Constitutional Renewal,* Harvey Lazar (ed.), 1998 Paper ISBN 0-88911-765-9 Cloth ISBN 0-88911-767-5

John Deutsch Institute for the Study of Economic Policy

Room to Manoeuvre? Globalization and Policy Convergence, Thomas J. Courchene (ed.), Bell Canada Papers no. 6, 1999 Paper ISBN 0-88911-812-4 Cloth ISBN 0-88911-812-4

Women and Work, Richard P. Chaykowski and Lisa M. Powell (eds.), 1999 Paper ISBN 0-88911-808-6 Cloth ISBN 0-88911-806-X

Equalization: Its Contribution to Canada's Economic and Fiscal Progress, Robin W. Boadway and Paul A.R. Hobson (eds.), Policy Forum Series no. 36, 1998 Paper ISBN 0-88911-780-2 Cloth IBSN 0-88911-804-3

Fiscal Targets and Economic Growth, Thomas J. Courchene and Thomas A. Wilson (eds.), Roundtable Series no. 12, 1998 Paper ISBN 0-88911-778-0 Cloth ISBN 0-88911-776-4

Available from:
McGill-Queen's University Press
Tel: 1-800-387-0141 (ON and QC excluding Northwestern ON)
1-800-387-0172 (all other provinces and Northwestern ON)

E-mail: customer.service@ccmailgw.genpub.com

Institute of Intergovernmental Relations
Recent Publications

The Spending Power in Federal Systems: A Comparative Study, Ronald L. Watts, 1999
ISBN 0-88911-829-9

Étude comparative du pouvoir de dépenser dans d'autres régimes fédéraux, par Ronald L. Watts, 1999
ISBN 0-88911-831-0

*Constitutional Patriation: The Lougheed-Lévesque Correspondence/Le rapatriement de la
Constitution: La correspondance de Lougheed et Lévesque,* with an Introduction by
J. Peter Meekison/avec une introduction de J. Peter Meekison, 1999   ISBN 0-88911-833-7

Securing the Social Union: A Commentary on the Decentralized Approach, Steven A. Kennett, 1998
ISBN 0-88911-767-5

Comparaison des régimes fédéraux des années 1990, Ronald Watts, 1997   ISBN 0-88911-771-3

Working Paper Series

1999

1. *Processes of Constitutional Restructuring: The Canadian Experience in Comparative Context*
by Ronald L. Watts, Queen's University

2. *Parliament, Intergovernmental Relations and National Unity* by C.E.S. Franks, Queen's University

3. *The United Kingdom as a Quasi-Federal State* by Gerard Hogan, Queen's University

4. *The Federal Spending Power in Canada: Nation-Building or Nation-Destroying?* by Hamish
Telford, Queen's University

1998

1. *The Meaning of Provincial Equality in Canadian Federalism* by Jennifer Smith, Dalhousie
University

2. *Considerations on the Design of Federations: The South African Constitution in Comparative
Context* by Richard Simeon, University of Toronto

3. *Federal Systems and Accommodation of Distinct Groups: A Comparative Survey of Institutional
Arrangements* by Ronald L. Watts, Queen's University

4. *De Jacques Parizeau à Lucien Bouchard: une nouvelle vision? Oui mais . . .* by Réjean Pelletier,
Université Laval

5. *Canadian Federalism and International Environmental Policy Making: The Case of Climate
Change* by Heather A. Smith, University of Northern British Columbia

6. *Through the Looking Glass: Federal-Provincial Decision-Making for Health Policy* by Candace
Redden, Dalhousie University

7. *Drift, Strategy and Happenstance: Towards Political Reconciliation in Canada?* Extraits des actes
du symposium tenu à l'Université Queen's les 28 et 29 mai 1998, avec annotations de Stéphane Dion,
David R. Cameron, Richard Dicerni, Daniel Soberman et John Courtney, sous la direction et avec une
introduction de Tom McIntosh

These publications are available from:
Institute of Intergovernmental Relations
Queen's University, Kingston, Ontario K7L 3N6
Tel: (613) 533-2080 / Fax: (613) 533-6868
E-mail: iigr@qsilver.queensu.ca

The publications of the Institute of
Intergovernmental Relations benefit from the
ongoing financial support of the J.A. Corry
Endowment Fund, the Government of Canada,
the Government of Ontario, the Royal Bank of
Canada, and Power Corporation.